DEDICATION

To my wife, Jan, whose "investment"
has been her confidence in me.

v

Acknowledgments

To Glenn Hoffer, Real Estate Editor of the Fort Lauderdale News, for printing the series of twenty-four investment real estate articles I have written. It was the response to that series that prompted the writing of this book. And to L.C. Judd & Company for their cooperation in the preparation of the original manuscript.

About the Author

MILT TANZER, C.C.I.M., has given many real estate investment seminars to the general public to introduce them to real estate investing and has taught numerous courses for professionals in the real estate field. A resident of Fort Lauderdale, Florida, Tanzer entered the real estate profession in 1967. Specializing in commercial real estate, he was sales manager and owner of his own firm prior to joining L.C. Judd & Company, Inc. of Fort Lauderdale as commercial sales training manager in 1978. His advanced professional standing in commercial real estate was recognized in 1977 when he was awarded the designation of Certified Commercial Investment Member of the Realtor's National Marketing Institute.

Tanzer is a member of the Greater Fort Lauderdale Board of Realtors, the Florida Association of Realtors, the National Association of Realtors, and the Realtors National Marketing Institute. While a member of the Pompano Beach, Florida Board of Realtors, he served on the board of directors and as chairman of professional standards for one year.

His previous publications include a series of articles on real estate investing which appeared weekly in the *Fort Lauderdale News* and prompted his writing REAL ESTATE INVESTMENTS AND HOW TO MAKE THEM.

Tanzer was graduated from Knox College, Galesburg, Illinois, in 1953 with a Bachelor of Arts degree in business administration. He is married and has three children.

What This Book Will Do For You

Have you ever wondered why the rich seem to get richer, without really trying, while you struggle to save enough money for retirement some day? Have you heard investors talk about real estate and come away convinced that real estate investing is a high risk, mysterious rich man's game that only the experts can play?

Thanks to REAL ESTATE INVESTMENTS AND HOW TO MAKE THEM, you can at last get into the real estate game and take advantage of the finest opportunity available for building your wealth. This comprehensive guide shows you why real estate is the best investment in today's economic climate and how to build a sound, solid investment program that makes inflation work *for* you instead of against you.

In plain, everyday English, REAL ESTATE INVESTMENTS AND HOW TO MAKE THEM takes you step-by-step through every phase of real estate investing. You'll see how to establish your investment objectives and analyze, purchase, and manage your investment property. You'll know when and how to sell, the tax consequences and tax benefits, and how to pyramid your investment into a larger one. If you are a first time investor, this book will show you how to get started. If you are already a real estate investor, you'll discover a wealth of ideas and techniques to make your investment program even more profitable.

REAL ESTATE INVESTMENTS AND HOW TO MAKE THEM is not just another "get rich quick" book on real estate. Instead, it helps you steer clear of dubious promises and unusual, high risk investments, while showing you how to make sound investment decisions. Here is just a sample of the practical help you can expect to find:

- How real estate investments can help you avoid the "inflation trap" when you are planning your retirement program.
- Where to locate sources of investment capital—including some sources you probably didn't know you had.
- How to buy property with little or no cash down.
- How to find the investment property that's right for you.
- How to use a sound, systematic method for analyzing your prospective investment to verify income and expenses and determine the maximum price you can afford to pay.
- How creative financing techniques can give you countless ways to buy real estate.
- How to take advantage of the unique tax benefits of real estate investments—benefits unequalled in any other type of investment of comparable risk.
- How to negotiate the purchase and close the deal.
- How to sell your property and how to time the sale to your advantage.
- How a professional can gain tremendous tax benefits by owning his own professional building and leasing it to his professional corporation.
- How to pyramid your investments so that building a substantial estate may be not only possible but inevitable.

REAL ESTATE INVESTMENTS AND HOW TO MAKE THEM is complete with checklists, charts, forms, and everyday examples that streamline the process of acquiring, managing, and selling your investment property. As your real estate investment program grows, you'll refer to this book again and again for workable ideas and sound advice. You will realize that you too can become a part of that elite group of real estate investors—and you don't have to be wealthy or an expert to do it.

Contents

APPENDIXES

GLOSSARY OF REAL ESTATE TERMS

1

Why Should You
Invest in Real Estate

Perhaps the best way to begin any book on investing is to discuss why we invest our money in the first place. Why not keep it in our mattress (and some people do) or bury it in a tin can in the back yard?

A textbook answer to the reason for investing goes something like this: "To curtail a standard of living by investing current income for use in the future." Putting it in everyday terms, you save your money so that when you are no longer capable of working, or no longer want to work, your savings will take over the task of supporting you. Hopefully, when that time arrives, you have saved enough to maintain your present standard of living. No one wants to end up broke when he reaches retirement age. None of us want to reduce our standard of living, in fact, you will probably want to travel around the world, or own a boat, or tour the country in a motor home. In any event, if you're like most people, you will work for forty years or more to reach that point in your life.

Before I continue this story, there is something that needs to be explained. You purchased this book to get a practical, understandable knowledge on how to invest in real estate, and that is exactly what you are going to receive.

By following the principles in this book, you *will* be successful in real estate investing, probably beyond what you can imagine.

What you are about to read is the only "negative" section in the entire book. It has been put here, in the beginning, to emphasize how vitally important it is for you to invest the bulk of your retirement savings in "non-fixed" investments. Those of you who do not believe that fact, keep reading.

THE PERILS OF "FIXED" INVESTMENTS

If you are average, you will earn in excess of a half million dollars in your lifetime. And, if you are average, you will be able to keep very little of it. While you still have beautiful visions of retirement in your mind, let me tell you a frightening story.

In 1960 the Kennedy administration made a study of social security for the Medicare program. Researchers tried to find out how much money people over the age of 65 had to live on. The results were shocking! Of the 19 million people in this country over the age of 65 (in the 1960s), 95 percent were non-wealthy. It sounds unbelievable but 22 percent of the people in this country over 65 years of age (at the time of the survey) were on charity, 28 percent were still working in order to survive, and 45 percent were dependent on relatives for survival.

Only five percent of our retired age population in the 1960s were financially independent. It's doubtful that those percentages have improved over the last couple of decades. What did the 95 percent do wrong? Why were they financially in trouble when they reached 65 years of age?

They did exactly what you and I have always been taught to do—THEY SAVED THEIR MONEY! They put their savings in banks, savings and loans, credit unions, mortgages, cash value life insurance and bonds. Why? To get a *Guaranteed* return on their investment. A fixed return of three, five or eight percent, regardless of how much money the savings institution was making on their investment. This is why they failed. This is the reason they ended up practically broke when they retired.

The *Wall Street Journal* recently ran an article about a middle income couple living in San Diego who dreamed of an early retirement to a Caribbean Island. They were saving on a regular basis in "fixed" investments which were earning only three to six percent per year. Suddenly, they realized their retirement dream was being shattered by taxes and inflation.

Through professional financial advice, they learned how to build an in-flation proof future. They cashed in their bonds, took some of their excess cash savings and used the cash value in their life insurance policies, replacing them with cheaper term policies. With these funds they invested in real estate. Today they estimate that they will be able to retire in ten years, with a monthly income of $2000—a much better return than their original "fixed income" figure. Until they revised their investment program, taxes and inflation would have destroyed their retirement.

Let's talk briefly about each, because you must understand the effects that each of these factors have on your retirement funds:

THE TAX BITE UNCLE SAM TAKES

Not much needs to be said about taxes. Every April 15th, after Uncle Sam gets his hand out of your pocket, you realize the size of the tax bite he has taken. Have you ever figured out how many months a year you work for the Federal Government. Don't . . . it's depressing!

I recently heard a comment that just about sums it up. The IRS has a new simplified tax form. It looks like this:

1. How much did you make last year?
2. How much do you have left?
3. Send Number 2.

Of course, there are some fixed investments such as tax exempt bonds that avoid taxation. We should, however, examine what is happening to the billions of dollars that are sitting in savings accounts and banks around the country.

Suppose you have $30,000 in a savings account paying an annual interest of six percent. At the end of the year you would expect to have earned $1800 in interest ($30,000 × .06). You may receive a check from the savings and loan association for that amount, but unfortunately, they also send the Internal Revenue Service a notice telling them that you received $1800 in "taxable" interest income. What does that do to you come tax time?

If You File the Long Form

Assuming you are one of the millions of taxpayers who either files the short form or has your taxes figured by an accountant or a tax specialist, you should at least be aware of how your "taxable" income figure is determined using the long form where deductions are itemized.

Your gross income is first established. This includes income from all sources—occupational income, interest received, dividends, etc. This "gross" income amount can be reduced by various factors to bring it down to a "taxable" income.

The first item is your exemptions. You are allowed to reduce your taxable income for each dependent you have. This includes you, your spouse, minor children, and others that qualify. You also receive an extra exemption for being over 65 or blind. Figure 1-1 illustrates the 1979 tax table that is used if you itemize deductions. You'll see that there is a separate column to use depending on the number of exemptions you are declaring. This table, for a married couple filing a joint return, is usable for two to nine exemptions where the "taxable" income is between $11,200 and $18,400.

The other item to be calculated, when using the long form, is your deductions. This includes such items as taxes paid (both sales and real estate), interest paid, allowable business expenses, a portion of medical expenses, etc. The process is lengthy and if you have never used the long form, you will still want to consult a tax specialist.

If You File the Short Form

Many taxpayers find that the short form is sufficient. Basically, if your itemized deductions for a couple filing a joint return were less than $3400 in 1979, you are better off filing the short form. This still allows you to figure business expenses, profits and losses from real estate and so on as separate items.

For our discussions, we will use the short form tax table for 1979 (Figure 1-2). We will use the "Married Filing Joint Returns and Qualifying Widows and Widowers" column under schedule "Y". This allows for deductions automatically.

If you had a taxable income of $16,000, the chart says you owe IRS $2265 in taxes. (This line has been underlined for easy reference.) The chart also adds that for every taxable dollar you earn over $16,000 up to $20,200, IRS will get 24 percent. As a taxpayer, you are in a 24 percent bracket. This is also referred to as your *Marginal Tax Rate*. The $1800 interest income that

1979 Tax Table B—MARRIED FILING JOINT RETURN (Filing Status Box 2) and QUALIFYING WIDOW(ER)S (Filing Status Box 5)

(Continued)

(If your income or exemptions are not covered, use Schedule TC (Form 1040), Part I to figure your tax)

If Form 1040, line 34, is— Over	But not over	And the total number of exemptions claimed on line 7 is— 2	3	4	5	6	7	8	9
		Your tax is—							
11,200	11,250	923	743	570	410	256	116	0	0
11,250	11,300	932	752	578	418	263	123	0	0
11,300	11,350	941	761	586	426	270	130	0	0
11,350	11,400	950	770	594	434	277	137	0	0
11,400	11,450	959	779	602	442	284	144	4	0
11,450	11,500	968	788	610	450	291	151	11	0
11,500	11,550	977	797	618	458	298	158	18	0
11,550	11,600	986	806	626	466	306	165	25	0
11,600	11,650	995	815	635	474	314	172	32	0
11,650	11,700	1,004	824	644	482	322	179	39	0
11,700	11,750	1,013	833	653	490	330	186	46	0
11,750	11,800	1,022	842	662	498	338	193	53	0
11,800	11,850	1,031	851	671	506	346	200	60	0
11,850	11,900	1,040	860	680	514	354	207	67	0
11,900	11,950	1,049	869	689	522	362	214	74	0
11,950	12,000	1,058	878	698	530	370	221	81	0
12,000	12,050	1,067	887	707	538	378	228	88	0
12,050	12,100	1,076	896	716	546	386	235	95	0
12,100	12,150	1,085	905	725	554	394	242	102	0
12,150	12,200	1,094	914	734	562	402	249	109	0
12,200	12,250	1,103	923	743	570	410	256	116	0
12,250	12,300	1,112	932	752	578	418	263	123	0
12,300	12,350	1,121	941	761	586	426	270	130	0
12,350	12,400	1,130	950	770	594	434	277	137	0
12,400	12,450	1,139	959	779	602	442	284	144	4
12,450	12,500	1,148	968	788	610	450	291	151	11
12,500	12,550	1,157	977	797	618	458	298	158	18
12,550	12,600	1,166	986	806	626	466	306	165	25
12,600	12,650	1,175	995	815	635	474	314	172	32
12,650	12,700	1,184	1,004	824	644	482	322	179	39
12,700	12,750	1,193	1,013	833	653	490	330	186	46
12,750	12,800	1,202	1,022	842	662	498	338	193	53
12,800	12,850	1,211	1,031	851	671	506	346	200	60
12,850	12,900	1,220	1,040	860	680	514	354	207	67
12,900	12,950	1,229	1,049	869	689	522	362	214	74
12,950	13,000	1,238	1,058	878	698	530	370	221	81
13,000	13,050	1,247	1,067	887	707	538	378	228	88
13,050	13,100	1,256	1,076	896	716	546	386	235	95
13,100	13,150	1,265	1,085	905	725	554	394	242	102
13,150	13,200	1,274	1,094	914	734	562	402	249	109
13,200	13,250	1,283	1,103	923	743	570	410	256	116
13,250	13,300	1,292	1,112	932	752	578	418	263	123
13,300	13,350	1,301	1,121	941	761	586	426	270	130
13,350	13,400	1,310	1,130	950	770	594	434	277	137
13,400	13,450	1,319	1,139	959	779	602	442	284	144
13,450	13,500	1,328	1,148	968	788	610	450	291	151
13,500	13,550	1,337	1,157	977	797	618	458	298	158
13,550	13,600	1,346	1,166	986	806	626	466	306	165
13,600	13,650	1,355	1,175	995	815	635	474	314	172
13,650	13,700	1,364	1,184	1,004	824	644	482	322	179
13,700	13,750	1,373	1,193	1,013	833	653	490	330	186
13,750	13,800	1,382	1,202	1,022	842	662	498	338	193
13,800	13,850	1,391	1,211	1,031	851	671	506	346	200
13,850	13,900	1,400	1,220	1,040	860	680	514	354	207
13,900	13,950	1,409	1,229	1,049	869	689	522	362	214
13,950	14,000	1,420	1,238	1,058	878	698	530	370	221
14,000	14,050	1,430	1,247	1,067	887	707	538	378	228
14,050	14,100	1,441	1,256	1,076	896	716	546	386	235
14,100	14,150	1,451	1,265	1,085	905	725	554	394	242
14,150	14,200	1,462	1,274	1,094	914	734	562	402	249
14,200	14,250	1,472	1,283	1,103	923	743	570	410	256
14,250	14,300	1,483	1,292	1,112	932	752	578	418	263
14,300	14,350	1,493	1,301	1,121	941	761	586	426	270
14,350	14,400	1,504	1,310	1,130	950	770	594	434	277
14,400	14,450	1,514	1,319	1,139	959	779	602	442	284
14,450	14,500	1,525	1,328	1,148	968	788	610	450	291
14,500	14,550	1,535	1,337	1,157	977	797	618	458	298
14,550	14,600	1,546	1,346	1,166	986	806	626	466	306
14,600	14,650	1,556	1,355	1,175	995	815	635	474	314
14,650	14,700	1,567	1,364	1,184	1,004	824	644	482	322
14,700	14,750	1,577	1,373	1,193	1,013	833	653	490	330
14,750	14,800	1,588	1,382	1,202	1,022	842	662	498	338

Continued next column

If Form 1040, line 34, is— Over	But not over	And the total number of exemptions claimed on line 7 is— 2	3	4	5	6	7	8	9
		Your tax is—							
14,800	14,850	1,598	1,391	1,211	1,031	851	671	506	346
14,850	14,900	1,609	1,400	1,220	1,040	860	680	514	354
14,900	14,950	1,619	1,409	1,229	1,049	869	689	522	362
14,950	15,000	1,630	1,420	1,238	1,058	878	698	530	370
15,000	15,050	1,640	1,430	1,247	1,067	887	707	538	378
15,050	15,100	1,651	1,441	1,256	1,076	896	716	546	386
15,100	15,150	1,661	1,451	1,265	1,085	905	725	554	394
15,150	15,200	1,672	1,462	1,274	1,094	914	734	562	402
15,200	15,250	1,682	1,472	1,283	1,103	923	743	570	410
15,250	15,300	1,693	1,483	1,292	1,112	932	752	578	418
15,300	15,350	1,703	1,493	1,301	1,121	941	761	586	426
15,350	15,400	1,714	1,504	1,310	1,130	950	770	594	434
15,400	15,450	1,724	1,514	1,319	1,139	959	779	602	442
15,450	15,500	1,735	1,525	1,328	1,148	968	788	610	450
15,500	15,550	1,745	1,535	1,337	1,157	977	797	618	458
15,550	15,600	1,756	1,546	1,346	1,166	986	806	626	466
15,600	15,650	1,766	1,556	1,355	1,175	995	815	635	474
15,650	15,700	1,777	1,567	1,364	1,184	1,004	824	644	482
15,700	15,750	1,787	1,577	1,373	1,193	1,013	833	653	490
15,750	15,800	1,798	1,588	1,382	1,202	1,022	842	662	498
15,800	15,850	1,808	1,598	1,391	1,211	1,031	851	671	506
15,850	15,900	1,819	1,609	1,400	1,220	1,040	860	680	514
15,900	15,950	1,829	1,619	1,409	1,229	1,049	869	689	522
15,950	16,000	1,840	1,630	1,420	1,238	1,058	878	698	530
16,000	16,050	1,850	1,640	1,430	1,247	1,067	887	707	538
16,050	16,100	1,861	1,651	1,441	1,256	1,076	896	716	546
16,100	16,150	1,871	1,661	1,451	1,265	1,085	905	725	554
16,150	16,200	1,882	1,672	1,462	1,274	1,094	914	734	562
16,200	16,250	1,892	1,682	1,472	1,283	1,103	923	743	570
16,250	16,300	1,903	1,693	1,483	1,292	1,112	932	752	578
16,300	16,350	1,913	1,703	1,493	1,301	1,121	941	761	586
16,350	16,400	1,924	1,714	1,504	1,310	1,130	950	770	594
16,400	16,450	1,934	1,724	1,514	1,319	1,139	959	779	602
16,450	16,500	1,945	1,735	1,525	1,328	1,148	968	788	610
16,500	16,550	1,955	1,745	1,535	1,337	1,157	977	797	618
16,550	16,600	1,966	1,756	1,546	1,346	1,166	986	806	626
16,600	16,650	1,976	1,766	1,556	1,355	1,175	995	815	635
16,650	16,700	1,987	1,777	1,567	1,364	1,184	1,004	824	644
16,700	16,750	1,997	1,787	1,577	1,373	1,193	1,013	833	653
16,750	16,800	2,008	1,798	1,588	1,382	1,202	1,022	842	662
16,800	16,850	2,018	1,808	1,598	1,391	1,211	1,031	851	671
16,850	16,900	2,029	1,819	1,609	1,400	1,220	1,040	860	680
16,900	16,950	2,039	1,829	1,619	1,409	1,229	1,049	869	689
16,950	17,000	2,050	1,840	1,630	1,420	1,238	1,058	878	698
17,000	17,050	2,060	1,850	1,640	1,430	1,247	1,067	887	707
17,050	17,100	2,071	1,861	1,651	1,441	1,256	1,076	896	716
17,100	17,150	2,081	1,871	1,661	1,451	1,265	1,085	905	725
17,150	17,200	2,092	1,882	1,672	1,462	1,274	1,094	914	734
17,200	17,250	2,102	1,892	1,682	1,472	1,283	1,103	923	743
17,250	17,300	2,113	1,903	1,693	1,483	1,292	1,112	932	752
17,300	17,350	2,123	1,913	1,703	1,493	1,301	1,121	941	761
17,350	17,400	2,134	1,924	1,714	1,504	1,310	1,130	950	770
17,400	17,450	2,144	1,934	1,724	1,514	1,319	1,139	959	779
17,450	17,500	2,155	1,945	1,735	1,525	1,328	1,148	968	788
17,500	17,550	2,165	1,955	1,745	1,535	1,337	1,157	977	797
17,550	17,600	2,176	1,966	1,756	1,546	1,346	1,166	986	806
17,600	17,650	2,186	1,976	1,766	1,556	1,355	1,175	995	815
17,650	17,700	2,197	1,987	1,777	1,567	1,364	1,184	1,004	824
17,700	17,750	2,207	1,997	1,787	1,577	1,373	1,193	1,013	833
17,750	17,800	2,218	2,008	1,798	1,588	1,382	1,202	1,022	842
17,800	17,850	2,228	2,018	1,808	1,598	1,391	1,211	1,031	851
17,850	17,900	2,239	2,029	1,819	1,609	1,400	1,220	1,040	860
17,900	17,950	2,249	2,039	1,829	1,619	1,409	1,229	1,049	869
17,950	18,000	2,260	2,050	1,840	1,630	1,420	1,238	1,058	878
18,000	18,050	2,271	2,060	1,850	1,640	1,430	1,247	1,067	887
18,050	18,100	2,283	2,071	1,861	1,651	1,441	1,256	1,076	896
18,100	18,150	2,295	2,081	1,871	1,661	1,451	1,265	1,085	905
18,150	18,200	2,307	2,092	1,882	1,672	1,462	1,274	1,094	914
18,200	18,250	2,319	2,102	1,892	1,682	1,472	1,283	1,103	923
18,250	18,300	2,331	2,113	1,903	1,693	1,483	1,292	1,112	932
18,300	18,350	2,343	2,123	1,913	1,703	1,493	1,301	1,121	941
18,350	18,400	2,355	2,134	1,924	1,714	1,504	1,310	1,130	950

Continued on next page

Figure 1-1

5

1979 Tax Rate Schedules

If you cannot use one of the Tax Tables, figure your tax on the amount on Schedule TC, Part I, line 3, by using the appropriate Tax Rate Schedule on this page. Enter the tax on Schedule TC, Part I, line 4.

Note: Your new zero bracket amount has been built into these Tax Rate Schedules.

SCHEDULE X—Single Taxpayers

Use this schedule if you checked Filing Status Box 1 on Form 1040—

If the amount on Schedule TC, Part I, line 3, is: / Enter on Schedule TC, Part I, line 4:

Not over $2,300........ -0-

Over—	But not over—		of the amount over—
$2,300	$3,400	14%	$2,300
$3,400	$4,400	$154+16%	$3,400
$4,400	$6,500	$314+18%	$4,400
$6,500	$8,500	$692+19%	$6,500
$8,500	$10,800	$1,072+21%	$8,500
$10,800	$12,900	$1,555+24%	$10,800
$12,900	$15,000	$2,059+26%	$12,900
$15,000	$18,200	$2,605+30%	$15,000
$18,200	$23,500	$3,565+34%	$18,200
$23,500	$28,800	$5,367+39%	$23,500
$28,800	$34,100	$7,434+44%	$28,800
$34,100	$41,500	$9,766+49%	$34,100
$41,500	$55,300	$13,392+55%	$41,500
$55,300	$81,800	$20,982+63%	$55,300
$81,800	$108,300	$37,677+68%	$81,800
$108,300	....	$55,697+70%	$108,300

SCHEDULE Y—Married Taxpayers and Qualifying Widows and Widowers

Married Filing Joint Returns and Qualifying Widows and Widowers

Use this schedule if you checked Filing Status Box 2 or 5 on Form 1040—

If the amount on Schedule TC, Part I, line 3, is: / Enter on Schedule TC, Part I, line 4:

Not over $3,400........ -0-

Over—	But not over—		of the amount over—
$3,400	$5,500	14%	$3,400
$5,500	$7,600	$294+16%	$5,500
$7,600	$11,900	$630+18%	$7,600
$11,900	$16,000	$1,404+21%	$11,900
$16,000	$20,200	$2,265+24%	$16,000
$20,200	$24,600	$3,273+28%	$20,200
$24,600	$29,900	$4,505+32%	$24,600
$29,900	$35,200	$6,201+37%	$29,900
$35,200	$45,800	$8,162+43%	$35,200
$45,800	$60,000	$12,720+49%	$45,800
$60,000	$85,600	$19,678+54%	$60,000
$85,600	$109,400	$33,502+59%	$85,600
$109,400	$162,400	$47,544+64%	$109,400
$162,400	$215,400	$81,464+68%	$162,400
$215,400	....	$117,504+70%	$215,400

Married Filing Separate Returns

Use this schedule if you checked Filing Status Box 3 on Form 1040—

If the amount on Schedule TC, Part I, line 3, is: / Enter on Schedule TC, Part I, line 4:

Not over $1,700........ -0-

Over—	But not over—		of the amount over—
$1,700	$2,750	14%	$1,700
$2,750	$3,800	$147+16%	$2,750
$3,800	$5,950	$315+18%	$3,800
$5,950	$8,000	$702+21%	$5,950
$8,000	$10,100	$1,132.50+24%	$8,000
$10,100	$12,300	$1,636.50+28%	$10,100
$12,300	$14,950	$2,252.50+32%	$12,300
$14,950	$17,600	$3,100.50+37%	$14,950
$17,600	$22,900	$4,081.00+43%	$17,600
$22,900	$30,000	$6,360.00+49%	$22,900
$30,000	$42,800	$9,839.00+54%	$30,000
$42,800	$54,700	$16,751.00+59%	$42,800
$54,700	$81,200	$23,772.00+64%	$54,700
$81,200	$107,700	$40,732.00+68%	$81,200
$107,700	....	$58,752.00+70%	$107,700

SCHEDULE Z—Heads of Household (including certain married persons who live apart (and abandoned spouses)—see page 7 of the Instructions)

Use this schedule if you checked Filing Status Box 4 on Form 1040—

If the amount on Schedule TC, Part I, line 3, is: / Enter on Schedule TC, Part I, line 4:

Not over $2,300........ -0-

Over—	But not over—		of the amount over—
$2,300	$4,400	14%	$2,300
$4,400	$6,500	$294+16%	$4,400
$6,500	$8,700	$630+18%	$6,500
$8,700	$11,800	$1,026+22%	$8,700
$11,800	$15,000	$1,708+24%	$11,800
$15,000	$18,200	$2,476+26%	$15,000
$18,200	$23,500	$3,308+31%	$18,200
$23,500	$28,800	$4,951+35%	$23,500
$28,800	$34,100	$6,859+42%	$28,800
$34,100	$44,700	$9,085+45%	$34,100
$44,700	$60,600	$13,961+54%	$44,700
$60,600	$81,800	$22,547+59%	$60,600
$81,800	$108,300	$35,055+63%	$81,800
$108,300	$161,300	$51,750+68%	$108,300
$161,300	....	$87,790+70%	$161,300

Figure 1-2

you received from the savings and loan will be subject to a 24 percent income tax, assuming it was earned in excess of the $16,000 base amount. Twenty-four percent of $1800 is $432. You will pay Uncle Sam $432 of the $1800 interest your savings earned. Subtract that from the $1800 and you are left with $1368 after taxes.

Throughout this book, we are going to talk in terms of "after-tax" income. It does not matter how much you earn, but how much you get to keep after paying income tax that is important. You want to know what you have left to spend.

In order to determine how much you really earned, after taxes, on your savings account, you divide the $1368 after tax income by your $30,000 investment. You actually earned 4.6 percent not six percent. If you were to put this money into a tax exempt bond at six percent, your interest income would, of course, not be subject to taxation so you would realize an actual six percent return on your investment. But that is just part of the story.

HOW INFLATION EATS AWAY AT YOUR RETIREMENT DOLLARS

There is another factor that affects your retirement funds more ominously and tragically than Income Tax. You at least understand taxes and even though you do not like them, you must accept them. What about inflation? The Social Security Administration has predicted that by the year 2050 a loaf of bread at the supermarket will cost $37.50. You and I may not be around then, but the figure illustrates where continued inflation may well be heading.

If long-range projections do not concern you, let's look at what has happened just in the past ten years. Coffee prices have increased from 69 cents a pound to $2.79 a pound—a whopping 404 percent increase. Average rents for apartments have risen from $155 per month to $315—five dollars more than doubling. The average home now costs $58,000, compared to $25,000 ten years ago—an increase of 232 percent. Housing costs, in other words, real estate values, have more than doubled in the last 10 years.

We read about inflation continually. But too few of us realize what it is really doing to us, and more importantly, to our retirement savings. Perhaps it can best be explained by some examples.

Each year, inflation is eating into the spending power of your dollars at the rate of four to ten percent a year, and it has been doing so since the end of World War II. In the past few years, the inflation rate has approached ten percent. I'm sure you've heard of "double digit inflation." Here are a couple of examples of how inflation is really affecting you.

On January 2nd last year, you decided to buy enough bars of soap to last your family the entire year. Don't ask why, you just decided to do it. You figured your family used two bars a week so you bought 100 bars. The price stamped on each bar was 25¢ so you paid $25.00 for the 100 bars. The idea was such a good one that on January 2nd of this year, you went back to the same supermarket to purchase 100 bars of the same soap with your $25.00. You were probably shocked to discover that you could purchase only 91 bars this year for your $25.00. The soap was the same, or probably a little smaller—it was the dollar that was different. It now took $1.10 to buy what $1.00 bought last year.

This loss in purchasing power affects all purchases—food, clothing, automobiles, homes, etc. By the way, in ten years if inflation continues at the same pace, you will need $50.00 to buy the same 100 bars of soap. So much for your day-to-day living. What about those dollars that you have been putting away for future use? The same thing is happening to each of them.

Here is a typical example of a couple (we'll call them Mr. & Mrs. Long) who had been saving all of their working life. When they decided to retire and enjoy life, they had $192,000 in a savings account. They reasoned that the $192,000 together with the interest it was drawing, would allow them to spend $15,000 a year for 25 years. Their home was paid for and they were able to live on $15,000 a year. They expected that another 25 years was the most they would be alive. Their analysis was as follows:

The $192,000 at six percent interest would give them $11,250 in interest. Although the interest income is taxable, for simplicity, it is not figured in this example. Their tax base is quite low now anyway. Since they need $15,000 to live on for the year, they would also draw $3480 from their $192,000 savings leaving them with a balance of $188,520. The next year, the $188,520 will draw $11,311 interest. This means that they will have to draw $3689 from savings to make up the $15,000. Each year they will reduce their savings account balance by a little more until, in 25 years, it will be gone. So far so good. The plan should work. But what the Longs failed to take into consideration was the effect that inflation would have on the dollars they had saved. They discovered that in the second year of retirement, they needed $15,900 to do what they did the first year for $15,000. By the tenth year it cost them $25,342 instead of the planned $15,000. The end result was that they ran out of money in ten to fifteen years and this is using only a six percent inflation factor.

No one goes through life intending to be broke when they retire. For most of us, it can easily be avoided. But, like the Longs, 95 percent of our population is in financial trouble when they retire because they chose to ignore the effects that taxes and inflation have on their investments. They saved today's dollars for use in tomorrow's economy.

THE ONES WHO MADE IT AND HOW THEY DID IT

Now let's look on the "positive" side of your retirement program. What about the five percent who made it? What did they do differently? They invested the bulk of their savings in the two "non-fixed" investments—stocks and real estate. Remember, it was said earlier that savings accounts, insurance, bonds, etc. were "fixed" investments because they pay the investor a fixed or guaranteed return on his investment.

Stocks and real estate, on the other hand, are not locked into a fixed return. As the economy grows these investments should grow proportionately. Anyone familiar with the stock market, however, also recognizes that, on a day-to-day basis, stocks are as likely to drop in value as they are to appreciate. There are a lot of investors in the stock market who would be happy to get out what they invested.

STOCKS AS INVESTMENTS

As an example, we'll compare a stock investment with your previous investment in a savings account. We'll invest your $30,000 in a solid, blue chip stock and assume that during the next year it will pay you a six percent dividend and increase in value or appreciate by ten percent. Most investors in the stock market would be elated with a return like that.

Remember, after taxes, our savings account produced a 4.5 percent return on our investment. If you invest $30,000 in the stock market and receive a six percent dividend at the end of the year, the dividend amounts to $1800. But like your savings account interest, it is taxable income. The IRS will still get 25 percent or $450, leaving you with $1350 after taxes.

Your stock, however, is not a "fixed" investment. As the economy grows, you expect the value of your stock to grow along with it. In our example, your stock is going to appreciate 10 percent. This means that your $30,000 investment has a market value of $33,000 next year. Adding that $3000 increased value to your after tax dividend of $1350, you find that the total return on your $30,000 was $4350 or 14.5 percent. *Now* you are staying ahead of inflation and remember, the reduced purchasing power of your dollars because of inflation is what caused the financial downfall of 95 percent of our population. We can do even better than the stock investment, however.

WHY IS REAL ESTATE A GOOD INVESTMENT

This brings us to why this book was written. Of all possible investments that are within the reach of the average investor, none offer the combination of outstanding benefits that are available to real estate investors. And, do you want to know something, banks and life insurance companies recognize this fact! So, they invest your money in real estate. While they pay you three to six percent for the use of your money, they are making 10 to 20 percent on it. The purpose of this book is to show you how to own a *real* "piece of the rock" and cut out the middleman.

Why is real estate such a good investment? It offers the investor four different returns or ways of making money, on his investment. We'll explore each first and then look at a typical example of a real estate investment.

Gross Spendable Income

Investors also refer to this as "cash flow" or how much money do you have to spend at the end of the year after all the operating expenses and mortgage payments have been made. We are referring to this as "gross" spendable because we have not taken income tax consequences into consideration at this point. Remember, we are going to be talking about "after tax" return. As in the example of the savings account, the investor is actually earning only 4.5 percent after taxes, not the six percent he thought he had. It is important to know how much you have left after taxes, not before.

Equity Income

This is also referred to as equity buildup or principal reduction. Anyone who has had a mortgage on a home or car recognizes that each time a payment is made, a certain portion of that payment is for the interest charged by the lender and the balance goes toward reducing the balance on the loan. In a real estate investment, this equity income can be a sizable amount. Although you cannot spend it each year, when the time comes to sell your property, you owe less on the mortgage, so you will receive more money at closing. It's like putting money in the bank each month.

Tax Shelter

In Chapter 10 you will see, in detail, how real estate offers this advantage that is not offered by any other common investment vehicle. You will see how some real estate investments will not only produce an excellent spendable income, all of which will be tax free, but owning the investment will produce a "paper loss" which IRS will allow you to write off against your other income. Owning a property structured real estate investment will not only give you a tax-free income, but will actually reduce your other taxes.

APPRECIATION: MAKING INFLATION WORK FOR YOU INSTEAD OF AGAINST YOU

The fourth and best is yet to come—Appreciation. Like inflation, you do not see it but it's there. Only now, it's working *for* you instead of against you. How does it work? Each year, because of inflation, your real estate is appreciating in value. Those of you who own a home, for example, would you sell it today at the same price you paid for it five or ten years ago?

Why does well located real estate continue to appreciate? Perhaps some statistics will help:

— An estimated 50 percent of the land in the United States is owned by the government, Federal, State or local. It's not available for the general public's use;
— 38 percent is considered "non-usable";
— three percent is currently being used for urban living; and
— nine percent is still available for use.

What does this availability of land mean in the context of a growing population? In 1769, there were about 4 million people in the original 13 colonies. By 1900, 131 years later, the population was 7½ million, not quite double the 1769 figure. By the year 2000, our expected population will be 380 million—a staggering 50 times the 1900 total.

What does this mean in terms of existing land values? It means that existing land is becoming more and more valuable each year. It explains why investment real estate, whether in single family homes, apartment buildings, office buildings, shopping centers, warehouses and even vacant land, has become the most secure and profitable way to beat inflation. We keep on having babies but God quit making land a long time ago. So, existing land in most parts of the country, is appreciating at a rate greater than that of inflation. The supply is limited. (In Chapter 17, we will also discuss appraisal methods and explore other reasons that real estate is appreciating each year.)

HOW REAL ESTATE STACKS UP
AGAINST OTHER INVESTMENTS

Now, let's invest your $30,000 in a typical real estate investment, say a small apartment building. As we progress, Chapter by Chapter through this book, you will be guided through each step that is used to substantiate the income, expense, depreciating and tax shelter figures used in this example. For now, however, please accept the facts as presented as reasonable. All that is intended here is an illustration of how real estate compares with savings accounts, bonds, or the stock market as an investment vehicle.

You invest your $30,000 in a building costing $125,000. You assume a $95,000 mortgage (the difference between the $125,000 and your $30,000 cash investment). Which brings up another outstanding feature you have available to you in real estate investing—the use of leverage or financing. You'll see in Chapter 9 a variety of ways to structure a real estate purchase by using creative financing. No other form of investing allows an investor the opportunity to control so much with a small amount of his own cash.

Your real estate investment looks like this:

Purchase Price	$125,000
Less: Mortgage(s)	95,000
Cash Investment	$ 30,000

and performs like this:

Gross Income (total rents collected per year)	$16,800.00
Less operating expenses and allowance for vacancies	4,830.00
Net operating Income, before mortgage payments	$11,970.00
Less Mortgage interest payments	8,550.00
Total Equity Income (Cash flow & Mortgage Principal reduction)	$ 3,420.00

$1800 is "cash flow" and $1620 is mortgage principal reduction, totaling $3420.00

Next, look at your income tax liability:

Equity Income from Above	$3,420.00
Less: Depreciation allowance	7,188.00
Taxable Income (Loss)	($3,768.00)

Here you will discover one of the advantages in real estate ownership. This building is producing $3420 a year in total income, but as far as the IRS is concerned, the property shows a $3,768 paper loss. This means that come income tax time, you file a schedule "E" a "Profit or Loss from Real Estate Ownership" form, which allows you to reduce your other income by the $3678 loss you were able to show on your apartment building ownership.

What does this mean to a taxpayer in a 25 percent tax bracket. He will pay $942 less taxes this year. (25 percent of $3768).

Adding the $942 tax savings to the $3420 profit actually produced by the property, you'll see that your total after tax profit is $4362 or a 14.5 percent return on your $30,000 investment. And there's more. We said that the stock investment would realize a 10 percent appreciation or growth rate. We also discussed how real estate is appreciating each year, at least equal to the inflation rate, which is now in excess of 10 percent a year. The 1979 inflation rates was 13.3 percent.

Let's be ultraconservative and assume your apartment building will appreciate less than the inflation rate or five percent. This means that your $125,000 property will be worth five percent more next year, or an additional $6250.

Adding this $6250 increase in value to the $4362 already produced by the building, you'll see that, conservatively, your real estate investment gave you a total return of $10,612 or a 35.4 percent return on your initial cash investment of $30,000. Figure 1-3 shows the comparison of the four different investments that were discussed and the final, after tax results of each.

	Savings Acct. at 6%	Tax Exempt Bond at 6%	Stock	Real Estate
Gross Proceeds	$1,800	$1,800	$1,800	$ 1,800
Less: 25% Tax	450	-0-	450	-0-
(or +25% Tax Savings)	-0-	-0-	-0-	942
Net Proceeds	$1,350	$1,800	$1,350	$ 2,742
% Return on $30,000	4.5%	6.0%	4.5%	9.1%
Plus: Mortgage Reduction	-0-	-0-	-0-	1,620
Total After Tax Return	$1,350	$1,800	$1,350	$ 4,362
Plus: 5% Appreciation	-0-	-0-	3,000	6,250
Total Return	$1,350	$1,800	$4,350	$10,612
% Return on $30,000	4.5%	6.0%	14.5%	35.4%

Figure 1-3

Now, you can see why real estate investing offers an investor the finest potential for building an estate. You are convinced, aren't you? Then keep on reading. Starting with Chapter 2, you will be guided through a step-by-step program, giving you everything you need to know to become an investor in real estate. If you are already a real estate investor, you will probably learn some new ideas and techniques to help you make your estate building program even more profitable.

2

How to Establish
Your Investment Objectives

You have already established the importance of properly investing excess funds for use in your retirement years. Since your future security hinges on making the correct investment decisions, I cannot overemphasize the need for estimating your future cash requirements. The way you invest and the type of real estate investments you acquire, must be correlated with your long-term (sometimes short-term) investment goals.

A SIX-STEP METHOD FOR TAKING STOCK OF YOUR PRESENT CIRCUMSTANCES AND FUTURE GOALS

As a starting point, you need to analyze your present financial and investment situation. To do so follow this simple six-step analysis outline:

1. What is your present financial situation;
2. What are your financial goals, or obligations, to be resolved prior to retirement;
3. How much investment capital do you have available;
4. Number of years until you intend to live off your investment;
5. Annual income you'll need after retirement; and
6. Number of years you expect this income to last.

Step 1: Analyze Your Present Financial Situation

Step 1 requires analyzing your present financial situation. Prepare a balance sheet (like a budget) showing where your present income is going—rent or mortgage payments, utilities, food, clothing, automobile, medical, insurance premiums, etc. If you are not in the habit of budgeting your income, you may be shocked to discover just how much you are spending for some items, especially the non-fixed ones like food and entertainment.

Your purpose here is to determine where you can accumulate investment capital. Don't worry about where you are going to find this investment capital at this point. (Sources of funds are discussed in Chapter 3.) If you are older, you probably already have funds set aside or invested for future use.

Next, make a list of where your investment funds are already placed. Be sure to include the following: Your home—including the equity in your home based on current market value, not what you paid for it—savings, stocks, bonds, securities, life insurance (and whether it is whole life or term) and other real estate should be included.

In effect, you are preparing a personal financial statement. Whether you end up investing in real estate or not, you should review your financial situation on a regular basis, especially after any major change in your position, such as the purchase or sale of any of the preceding investments. If you do not have a form to use for this statement, any bank or savings and loan association can provide one. Your outstanding debts are also taken into consideration on this statement. The ''bottom line'' will give you your total net worth.

Step 2: Establish Your Financial Goals and Obligations

Financial goals or obligations to be resolved prior to retirement are your next consideration. Both this step and step 5 are the most difficult to accurately estimate. A crystal ball would be helpful, but you can make some reasonable sound judgments without it.

Make another list, as best you can, outlining the *major* expenses you expect to incur prior to retirement. It is, of course, not possible to predict everything that may happen, but you probably already know of most of your expenses. At first, this list may look frightening, but keep in mind that you can probably expect at least cost of living increases in your salary during your remaining working years. An eight percent annual salary increase (about equal to the annual cost of living) will double your present income in nine years and triple it in 15. Your living expenses will also be increasing proportionately, of course.

Any funds that you can accumulate above your living expenses, will also grow accordingly. This is where you get ahead of the game and can accumulate extra cash for those future major expenses. As an example, if you are able to save $2000 above and beyond your living expenses this year, and your salary increases eight percent next year, you should have $2160 extra cash next year (eight percent above this year's $2000).

How One Investor Determined His Financial Future: May I introduce you to Bob and Joan Andrews and their two children—Suzie, Age 12 and Bob, Jr., age 10. We're going to use the Andrews' to illustrate how your six-step analysis program works. Later on, you'll see how the Andrews used their analysis to build a real estate investment program.

Bob is 35-years old and is employed as a junior executive with a local company. His present take home pay (after withholding tax and social security have been taken out) is $22,000 a year. His first step in determining his financial future was to prepare a current income and expense statement for his family situation. The statement looks like Figure 2-1 and can be quite simple.

You will notice that after budgeting all of his normal living expenses, including a sizable amount for unexpected items, he is able to save $2500 for future investments. (The general rule of thumb is that you should try to save at least 10 percent of your income.)

Bob also knows that he can expect to receive an annual salary increase at least equal to the increase in cost of living. He estimates it will average eight percent a year. This means that next year he will have a take home pay of $23,760 or eight percent more than this year. He also assumes that his $19,500 in living expenses will cost eight percent more or $21,060. The difference between the two (the amount he can put away for savings or investments) is $2700—a $200 increase over last year.

This may not sound like much, but in 10 years, his take home pay will be $43,978. His living expenses will be up to $38,980, giving him a cash

Step 1:   Annual Income and Expense Statement

Net Income (Take home pay after taxes and social security)			$22,000
Present Expenses:	Mortgage Payment and Taxes	$5,400	
	Utilities	2,500	
	Food—Including "take-out" meals	4,900	
	Entertainment	900	
	Medical	600	
	Clothing	1,100	
	Automobile Expense—Including car payments	3,100	
	Other	1,000	
	TOTAL EXPENSES		$19,500
	Balance Available for Investments		$ 2,500

Figure 2-1

reserve of $4998. As you can see, each year he should be able to save more to offset some of the expected major expenses he will incur.

What are these financial obligations he is expecting? He made a list as suggested in Step 2. This is shown in Figure 2-2. Bob has spread these major items out over the 25 year period he expects to continue working. Some items, such as college educations, are pretty much locked in, time schedule-wise, some are flexible, depending on his financial situation in any given year, such as a new car or redecorating the house; his daughter's wedding! Who knows? He planned it for just after her college graduation.

Bob's figures should also allow for the expected effects of inflation. For example, he estimates that if Suzie were to get married this year, it would cost him about $4000. But, he scheduled it for 10 years from now. With inflation at 10 percent per year, it will cost twice as much, or $8000 for her wedding in 10 years. It is obvious he cannot be exact. What he can do, at least, is recognize those expenses that he is certain will occur and plan for them.

Where is the $90,000 coming from? From the savings he is putting away each year. Since his initial $2500 savings amount is expected to increase eight percent each year due to salary increases, let's see how much he will be able to save each year for his 25 remaining years of working. This chart does not take into consideration any interest paid by the institution or

Step 2.   Financial Obligation – Next 25 Years

Bob and Joan Andrews—Suzie, Age 12; Bob, Jr., Age 10

Expected Expense	When	Cash Required
Major Medical Expense	Covered by Insurance	
College Education—Suzie	6 Yrs	$20,000 over 4 Yrs
College Education—Bob, Jr.	8 Yrs	$25,000 over 4 Yrs
Suzie's Wedding	10 Yrs	$ 8,000
New Cars	Yrs 4, 8, 12, 16, 20	$15,000
New Furniture	6 Yrs	$ 7,000
Redecorating Home	10 Yrs	$10,000
Redecorating Home	10 Yrs	$ 5,000
		$90,000

Figure 2-2

tax consequences on that interest. This is strictly the principal buildup he is able to accumulate. He will not leave all this cash in a savings account. The bulk of it will be invested in real estate as soon as it accumulates into a large enough sum.

Year	Current Amount	Total Savings to Date	Year	Current Amount	Total Savings to Date
1	$2,500	$ 2,500	14	$ 6,799	$ 60,536
2	2,700	5,200	15	7,343	67,879
3	2,916	8,116	16	7,930	75,809
4	3,149	11,265	17	8,565	84,374
5	3,401	14,666	18	9,250	93,624
6	3,673	18,339	19	9,990	103,614
7	3,967	22,306	20	10,789	114,403
8	4,285	26,591	21	11,652	126,055
9	4,627	31,218	22	12,585	138,640
10	4,998	36,216	23	13,591	152,231
11	5,397	41,613	24	14,679	166,910
12	5,829	47,442	25	15,853	182,763
13	6,295	53,737			

As you can see, his total accumulated savings at the end of 25 years is $182,763. He will have no trouble meeting his anticipated $90,000 in major expenses. But this takes him down the road 25 years to his retirement years. After his $90,000 in major expenses during that period, he is left with $92,763 —hardly enough to live on for the rest of his life.

This analysis assumes that the Andrews have $2500 in excess income that they can put into a savings account at the end of the year. Do not let that amount concern you. If you can save more, so much the better. You will be ahead of the game. But what if you need every dollar you earn at the present time just to make ends meet and stay ahead of the bills? This is the reason you started by preparing a budget. You can determine exactly how you are spending your money. Never lose sight of the fact that no matter how much or how little you earn, your future financial security depends on your saving a portion of that income. One advantage of cash value life insurance is that it is a "forced" savings program. Somehow, since it is one of your regular monthly bills, you find a way to pay it.

Even a small amount saved on a regular basis can become a sizable sum. The important thing is to do it, and do it every month. Once you get a reasonable sum built up, don't blow it on a trip to the islands, invest it in real estate.

Step 3:   Determine How Much Investment Capital You Have Available

As a third step, you should determine how much cash you have available for investment purposes. You may want to read Chapter 3 before attempting to determine this. Bob Andrews will be with us to show where he found his investment funds. For now, let's assume he has made that determination and figured he has $50,000 to invest in real estate.

Step 4:   Calculate Number of Years Until Retirement

In step 4, Bob Andrews decides he wants to be able to retire when he is 60-years old, or in 25 years. This means that he has 25 years to save and properly invest his excess income for use the remainder of his life.

Step 5:   Estimate Retirement Income Needed

Which brings us to step 5. How much money will you need for your retirement? Now, we're back to the crystal ball again. A number of factors enter into this decision, the *most important* of which is the effect inflation will have on future investments. In Bob Andrews case, the first thing he does is determine which of his present expenses will be eliminated when he retires. He prepares a revised expense statement, still based on today's costs, and is able to eliminate the following from his first list:

a) Mortgage Payments—in 25 years the house will be paid for; and
b) Reduced food and clothing costs—The children are gone and, being retired, his clothing costs are less.

His revised list looks like this:

Real Estate Taxes and Insurance	$ 1,000
Utilities	2,500
Food	3,000
Entertainment	500
Medical	1,000
Clothing	600
Automobile—Repairs and Gas	600
Other	1,000
Travel	2,000
	$12,700

He expects it to cost him $12,700 a year for expenses. This also includes $2000 a year for travel expenses, now that he and Joan are free to come and go as they please. This $12,700 is based on today's dollars, however, if inflation averages eight percent a year for the next 25 years, they will need an unbelievable $80,000 to do what they can do this year for $12,700. So, Bob must determine how to build his present investment into one that will pay him $80,000 income 25 years from now.

Assuming he can expect his real estate investment to give him a 10 percent return on his cash investment, he finds that his cash investment must be 10 times $80,000 or $800,000 by the end of the 25th year of his working years. Bob has to pyramid his $50,000 original cash investment into $800,000 equity over a 25-year period. He wants to figure just how many times he must double his investment to reach $800,000. The formula is easy:

Start with		$ 50,000		
doubled	=	100,000	–	(one time)
doubled	=	200,000	–	(two times)
doubled	=	400,000	–	(three times)
doubled	=	800,000	–	(four times)

He has to double his initial investment four times over the next 25 years or once every 6¼ years. In Chapter 19 on Pyramiding, you will see that not only is this possible, but you should expect it from your real estate investment.

Step 6:   Estimate Number of Years Funds Must Last

This brings Bob to the final step, estimating how many years he expects himself and/or his wife to need these funds. He assumes they will live another 25 years or to the age of 85. This step is important *only* if you intend to use up a portion of your principal or savings each year. In Bob's case, his real estate will continue to appreciate and he may *never* have to touch his principal or equity. From all indications, Bob should have no problem reaching his financial goals and remaining financially secure for his entire life.

TAILOR YOUR ANALYSIS
TO YOUR PERSONAL CIRCUMSTANCES

Not everyone is in the same financial or age bracket as Bob Andrews, and each individual must analyze his own situation. Here's how three prospective investors—one newlywed, another approaching retirement and another already retired—sized up their financial circumstances.

Tom and Betty Johnson are newlyweds—they just celebrated their first anniversary. Tom is 24 and they live in a rental apartment. Tom is working as a clerk in a department store and bringing home $1000 a month or $12,000 a year. There is no point in trying to kid anyone, they are currently spending everything he earns and in order to save for investing in real estate, they may find some useful ideas in the next Chapter. Chances are their first investment will be a home. Perhaps, they can buy on a contract for deed where they move in and pay rent, part of which applies toward their down payment. Once sufficient funds have been paid in to make up the required down payment, title to the house is transferred over to them. They have then reached that first plateau—the hardest one for a potential investor with no funds to invest. They now own a piece of real estate. From this point on, there should be no way but up for the Johnsons. Appreciation can now assist them in continuing their estate building program.

What about Roy Allison. He's already 50-years old and can still come up with only $50,000 to invest. He wants to retire in 10 years on $20,000 a year income. How are his chances of succeeding? He must build up an equity equal to $200,000, or 10 times his desired cash flow. Unlike Bob Andrews, he only has 10 years to do it, but he only has to double his initial investment twice ($50,000 to $100,000 and $100,000 to $200,000) or once every five years. The main reason he has a chance is that inflation will take a smaller toll on him because the time period is shorter.

Now, we'll take a brief look at Herb Olson. He is 65-years old and has been retired for three years. Suddenly he realized that the $200,000 he has saved during his working lifetime, will not last if he lives another 15 or 20 years (or the rest of his life). His situation is the most frightening of all because he is no longer bringing home an occupational income. He is totally dependent upon his savings. He decides to invest in real estate, but feels he'd better keep $50,000 of his $200,000 in savings for emergency purposes. This is a right decision.

Herb cannot afford to make a mistake for if he makes a wrong decision and loses all or part of his savings, he's had it. So, he invests in a sound, well located real estate investment producing an eight percent return on his $150,000 or $12,000. This investment has three benefits that Herb would not receive in any other type of investment. First of all, through depreciation benefits produced by the property, he is able to keep all of the $12,000 tax free. The second advantage is that this money is in an investment that is appreciating. As inflation eats into the value of the dollar and living costs increase, he is able to increase the rents he charges and thereby increase his income each year, thus keeping his income up with inflation. The third benefit is that he never has to use up his principal. In fact, the opposite is true—his principal is actually increasing each year that he owns his property.

YOU DON'T HAVE TO START OUT BIG

As you review your own investment requirements, don't forget that even though your initial investment may be a small one, you can add to that initial investment as your cash earnings increase. Perhaps, in five or ten years you will have accumulated enough added capital (if combined with your original investment that has also been appreciating), you can end up owning a much larger property.

The average investor who has sufficient occupational income to cover his living expenses, should also consider allowing all cash flows produced by his real estate investment to accumulate in an interest bearing savings account. This cash will accumulate rapidly, thus offering additional investment funds.

If Bob Andrews places the $4000 cash flow he receives the first year he owns his real estate investment into a five percent savings account, he will have accumulated $4200 at the end of the year, less income tax on the $200. Assume he keeps $140 of the $200 after taxes. In his second year the income produced by the property is up to $4320. That added to the amount already in the bank ($4140) gives him a savings account total of $8460 drawing interest, or $423 interest of which he will be able to keep $296. In just two years, Bob has been able to accumulate an additional $8756 toward a future investment. You can see what his possibilities are if he does this for the next 25 years. He will take these funds out of savings every few years and use them to increase his real estate holdings.

Remember, you do not have to start out big. If you use the techniques that are outlined here, you will be able to build an estate in real estate. You are using the principle that inflation is now working *for you* instead of against you—as prices go up, so do rents; as rents increase, the value of your real estate increases. You are merely working on the principle that every so many years you can expect your invested capital to double in value, and it does not matter how small you start—that principle remains the same.

I'm sure you've heard about the wealthy man who hired a young boy to do some work for him over a 30-day period. He offered the boy $25.00 a day. The boy said, "I'll tell you what. I'll work the first day for one penny. The second day, my pay is double, two cents. The third day it's double again or four cents. You pay me on the same basis for thirty days, doubling my previous day's pay each day." The wealthy man thought this sounded like a bargain and hired the young boy. I won't tell you how much the boy made—you can figure that out yourself.

That same basic principle of pyramiding or doubling your investment every few years in real estate is the principle that will help you reach your investment goals.

3

Where to Find Sources
of Start-Up Capital

If you are like most people, you have been working for several years (maybe more than you care to count) trying to save money for retirement. Then, someone writes a book that convinces you that the bulk of your estate building funds should be placed in real estate.

"That's great," you think, "but just where are my 'estate building' funds now?" The first thing you need to do is to refer to the financial statement you prepared in Chapter 2. (You did prepare one didn't you?) Without it, you really don't know how much money you have or where it's located.

Next, you need to determine how much of the funds in some of the investments, such as savings accounts, can be considered "excess funds." To clarify that, in Chapter 1 it was discussed that funds located in any "fixed" investment were working for the institution paying you interest and not for you. While they pay you four to eight percent interest, they earn 10 to 20 percent on *your* money. You also know that banks and insurance companies are earning 10 to 20 percent by investing your money in real estate. You are discovering how to eliminate that middleman and invest in real estate yourself. Then, *you'll* be making those high profits.

25

This discussion will start by looking into the usual places that people keep money and then, consider some possible sources you may not have thought of.

FOUR LIKELY SOURCES OF INVESTMENT CAPITAL

Savings Accounts

Banks and savings and loan associations are the "holders" of billions of dollars of investors' excess capital. People invest in these institutions because it's easy, safe and the interest the institutions pay is guaranteed. But, you already know what is happening to your estate building program if you are using one or more of these institutions as your primary source of investment. You already realize that the four to eight percent taxable interest you are receiving does not come close to keeping up with inflation. Each year, you are losing ground.

So, begin by making a list of how much cash you have tied up in banks, savings and loans, certificates of deposit, savings bonds and any other similar type of investment. Also, make note of any maturity date that affects the interest you will earn if you take your money out ahead of time. You may not want to touch those funds early if it means suffering a sizable interest penalty.

Next, determine what you consider to be a "reasonable" amount of money to have on hand in one of these "liquid" investments, funds for emergencies that may arise, medical bills, college tuitions, and even next year's vacaiton. Don't get too generous with this account. If you are still working, chances are you will be adding to it on a regular basis, but, do allow enough to feel secure. You'll recall that 100 percent of your investment capital should never be placed in any one investment vehicle, and that includes real estate.

Cash Value Life Insurance: Ideal If You've Built Up a Substantial Cash Reserve

Your insurance policies that have a cash value are an excellent source of capital. Review your policies and determine how much loan value you have built up. Perhaps, you have an Endowment Policy for yourself, your family or your child's college education that you have been paying into for years.

By the way, in Chapter 5, we will compare an insurance company's Endowment Policy being used for a child's college fund, with a small real estate investment. The results will amaze you!

Once you have determined how much cash or loan value you have in these policies, find out how much interest you will have to pay to borrow that money. Depending upon the age of the policy, it may be only four to six percent. Whatever it is, it will be at a much lower rate than current mortgage money because you're borrowing your own money. I might add that insurance companies are not overjoyed when you want to borrow against your policy. They realize that it is an inexpensive source of funds for policyholders.

A Word of Caution! You probably already know that if you do borrow against your insurance policy it reduces the lump-sum payment that would be paid the beneficiary in the event of the death of the insured.

This source of investment capital is ideal for the investor who, over the years, has built up a sizable cash reserve in his policies. It is the least expensive source of investment capital you can borrow.

Stocks: You Don't Necessarily Have to Sell

Do you own stocks? They are a source of capital. You have two choices. You can sell the stock outright and invest the after-tax proceeds. You may be a typical investor in the stock market and will have trouble selling for as much as you paid. If you are fortunate enough to sell at a profit, that profit is taxable.

There is another alternative. You do not have to sell and give up the fun and excitement of owning a piece of the New York Stock Exchange. You can use your stock as collateral and borrow against it. Your local banker will tell you how much he will loan, usually up to 75 percent of the current market value of the stock, provided the funds are going into a real estate investment and are not being used to buy more stock. That's a pretty good margin compared with the low margin that is available to buy additional stock. Even though you must pay interest for the use of this money, you will probably be able to earn at least double what it is costing you to borrow it.

There is another advantage in borrowing against your stock instead of selling. You retain ownership of the stock, even though the certificate is being held by the lender as collateral. This means that if your stock is paying a dividend and/or appreciating, you are still gaining those benefits.

On the other side of the coin, however, your banker checks the current market value on your collateralized stock on a regular basis. If your stock is decreasing in value, and drops below the bank's acceptable margin, you will be asked to either pay down the loan or add additional stock in order to bring your loan back up to the required margin. It becomes obvious that you do not want to pledge all of your stock for loan purposes. Save some for just such a situation.

Refinancing Real Estate: A Secure Source of Tax-Free Money in Today's Economic Climate

First, we'll discuss your home. A home mortgage is a touchy subject with many people, especially those who lived through the depression of the early thirties. They saw lenders foreclosing on real estate all around them, perhaps, they lost their own home. They learned, and then instilled in their children, the need to pay off the mortgage as soon as possible. Mortgage burning parties were a common and happy occasion.

But we are more secure now, through reduced stock margins, government insured savings and many other changes in our economic system. The chances for another all out depression is remote. You still don't believe it? Let's look at a couple of facts.

Fact Number One . . . What actually happened to property owners during that depression in the thirties? Here is a typical example of two investors—Jack and Al. They both purchased rental apartment buildings just before the depression hit. Both paid $100,000 for their properties. Jack had quite a lot of cash so he put $75,000 down on his building and obtained a $25,000 mortgage. Al, on the other hand, only had $25,000 in cash to invest, so he ended up with a $75,000 mortgage on his property. Then the depression hit, people lost their jobs. Both Jack and Al ended up with almost empty apartment buildings. Neither could pay their mortgage payments. The market value of each building dropped to $50,000—one half what they had paid for them.

The savings and loan association was also in trouble, there was no Federal Deposit Insurance to cover all of the withdrawals that were being made—they needed money, too. They looked at both Jack's and Al's apartment buildings. Both men were in default on their mortgage payments. Jack only owed them $25,000 but his building could be sold for $50,000. So they foreclosed. But what about Al's building? He owed them $75,000 but his building was also only worth $50,000. If they took it back, they knew they'd lose money. So, they let him keep it. He had to worry about renting it, maintaining it and, eventually, bringing the mortgage current.

When the depression ended, all of the "Al's" in the country were setting pretty. They still owned their properties and were ready for the economic boom that was about to take place. Investors who still had money in spite of the depression did even better. They were buying the properties that were taken back by the lender at distressed prices. When everything got back to normal, they were wealthy.

This brings us to Fact Number Two . . . Lenders are in the business of lending money at a rate higher than what they pay the investors in their institution. They are not, and have no desire to be, in the real estate business—the business of owning and managing real property. Most lenders will bend over backwards to help a borrower over the rough spots rather than foreclose on him.

This does not mean that you should drop this book and rush right down to your savings and loan and find out how much more money you can borrow on your home. If you do have a lot of equity in your home, you may want to consider this source of investment capital. The same opportunity is available for any other real estate you may own. You can refinance a property that has considerably equity in order to obtain additional investment funds. And that is tax-free money!

An Easy-to-Apply Refinancing Formula

Let's examine a formula that will help you determine how much capital you may be able to obtain by refinancing and then decide if it is practical to do so.

Step 1. Determine the current fair market value of the property. (Not what you paid for it, but what you could sell it for today).

Step 2. Subtract your current mortgage balance to determine how much equity you have in the property.

Step 3. Assume you can obtain a 75 percent mortgage on your property. What is 75 percent of the current market value?

Step 4. Determine how much it will cost to refinance and how much cash you will actually end up with after mortgage closing costs are paid.

Step 5. Determine how much more you will be paying in mortgage payments than you are now.

Step 6. Divide that amount (Number 5) by the amount of net cash you expect (Number 4). This percentage figure is the amount you will have to earn on your new investment to stay even, cash-flow-wise.

Example: Remember Bob Andrews in the last Chapter. I promised you I'd explain where Bob obtained his $50,000 of investment capital. Well, $20,000 came from refinancing his house. Following the above six steps, the following computation illustrates the results:

STEP 1 — Current Market Value of Bob's Home $90,000
STEP 2 — Current Mortgage Balance   45,000
                                                   Equity   45,000
STEP 3 — 75% Mortgage (75% of $90,000)   67,000 (rounded)
STEP 4 — Cost of Refinancing (estimated)
               5% of difference between existing and proposed mortgage:
                  Proposed Mortgage $67,000
                  Existing Mortgage   45,000

                  Gross Proceeds $22,000
                  Less 5% of $22,000   1,100

                  Balance for Refinancing $20,900
STEP 5 — Proposed Mortgage ($67,000 @ 9½% for 25 years)
                                    Annual Payment   = $ 7,025
               Less Existing Mortgage
               ($45,000 @ 9% – 17 Years Remaining)
                                    Annual Payment   = $ 5,178
               Added Annual Principal and Interest Payment
STEP 6 — $ 1,847   (Step 5)   =   8.8%
               $20,900   (Step 4)

Figure 3-1

Bob has to earn 8.8 percent on this $20,900 to offset his added increased house payment. He should have no problem doing at least this well!

As you can see, the formula is easy to apply. In a few minutes you can determine just how much cash you can generate from your present real estate holdings. You'll have to contact your local savings and loans to see what current interest rates are running. Shop around. Mortgage availability depends on who has money that must be loaned out. This varies from day to day and from lender to lender. You will usually find that increasing your mortgage through the lender who already has it is the least expensive way to borrow. This is especially true where the lender has a chance to upgrade your lower interest rate to the current rate.

Still not convinced that refinancing is an excellent source of investment capital? Here are a couple more arguments in favor of it. First, all of the cash you receive is "tax-free" income. Secondly, if you decide to sell your property in the future, the larger mortgage will make it easier to sell.

A couple of don'ts: Don't borrow the money from any of the suggested sources, until you need it. It will cost you to let it sit idle while you decide on an investment. Don't use half your proceeds to take a trip to Hawaii and then expect the remaining half to earn enough for the whole amount. Whatever you borrow, must be reinvested in its entirety. Don't forget, you're probably paying 9½ to 15 percent interest for the use of that money.

SOURCES YOU MAY HAVE OVERLOOKED

Here are a couple more sources of investment capital.

Friends and Relations

Don't overlook the opportunity of borrowing funds, on a secured basis, from people you know that have money. Talk to your rich aunt who has a bundle in a savings account. Show her how you will pay her two or three percent higher interest than she is currently earning. Her investment will be secured by a mortgage on your property.

The Husband and Wife Team

When both a husband and wife are working and the salary of just one is sufficient to cover living expenses, deposit the other spouse's check in an interest bearing account each week or month and let it build up. Don't touch it, except in an emergency. Everyone knows that if a check is cashed instead of just depositing it, all or most of it mysteriously seems to disappear. Before continuing, here are the remaining places that Bob Andrews found his $50,000 investment capital.

Bob had accumulated almost $25,000 in savings accounts and certificates of deposit. He took $15,000 from these sources, leaving a safe balance for emergency purposes. He next checked his stock investments and found he owned the following:

Stock	No. of Shares	Value Per Share	Total Value
IBM	35	$ 310	$10,850
Xerox	55	86	4,730
Walt Disney	60	36	2,160
Eastman Kodak	40	62	2,480
	Total Current Market Value	=	$20,220

Loan value at 75 percent would be about $15,000, but Bob wisely decided to borrow only $10,000. This left him with a safe margin. In the event his stock went down in value, he could always add a little more stock to his collateral with the bank and avoid paying down the loan.

Bob then looked at the cash value he had accumulated in his life insurance policies. He found he could borrow almost $6000. He chose to borrow only $5000 on which he only has to pay six percent interest. He recognizes that the value of his policy is also now reduced by $5000.

Totaling up all the sources of investment that Bob Andrews found, it looks something like this:

From Savings and Certificate of Deposits	$15,000
Borrowing Against Stocks	10,000
Borrowing on Insurance Policies	5,000
Refinancing of Home	20,000
Available for Real Estate Investing	$50,000

In Chapter 9 on Financing Techniques, we will discuss interest averaging and find out the overall average interest rate that it is costing Bob for the use of this money. In other words, how much is Bob paying for the use of the $50,000 he accumulated for his real estate investment. So, Bob is on his way toward a real estate investment. What about you?

HOW TO BUY REAL ESTATE
WITH LITTLE OR NO MONEY DOWN

What do you do if, after taking inventory of your assets, you realize that you have only a small amount of cash to invest in real estate or, perhaps, no cash. There are several books on the market explaining ways of buying real estate with little or no cash down payment. Most of them suggest investments that can be considered fairly high-risk situations.

Consider this. Any time you buy real estate that is 100 percent leveraged or financed, you can reasonably expect to have to "feed" it to make it break even. These carrying costs must be figured in your investment analysis.

How 100-Percent-Leveraged Property Can Offer a Good Return

Don't let this fact stop you. One-hundred-percent leveraged property can still offer a good return to the investor. Later in this book, you'll see how I purchased a 12-unit apartment building with none of my own money. Here is an example of how it can work for you.

Assume you are able to purchase a small duplex for $35,000. The seller wants out and will sell you the building with no money down. He will carry a second mortgage so that the duplex will have $35,000 in total mortgages. The income produced by the property is $3000 a year after all operating expenses, but the mortgage payments are $3500 a year, including principal and interest. This means that you will have to take $500 a year out of your pocket in order to keep the property on a break-even basis.

But, that is just part of the overall picture. As you progress through this book, you will learn the complete process of analyzing an investment property. You'll see that the gross spendable income, the income after all mortgage and operating expenses are paid, is not as important as your after-tax return.

As a preview of the coming Chapters and as a way of explaining your actual results if you were to purchase the duplex with no money down, refer to Figure 3-1. This chart illustrates the steps you will follow in a complete property analysis. When you reach Chapter 8, you will use an actual property analysis form to estimate the return you can expect to realize on your invested capital. This property analysis form will serve as an easy to follow procedure for examining any investment property that you may be considering. Get use to the terms and analysis sequence in Figure 3-1. You will be using them throughout this book.

Basic Format for Analyzing Any Real Estate Investment

Scheduled Gross Income
    Less: Vacancies
Gross Operating Income
    Less: Operating Expenses

		Duplex
Net Operating Income (N.O.I.)	=	$3,000
Less: Mortgage Payments	–	$3,500
Gross Spendable Income	=	$ (500)
Plus: Mortgage Principal Payments	+	$ 450
Gross Equity Income	=	$ (50)
Less: Depreciation	–	$2,950
Real Estate Taxable Income	=	($3,000) Tax Loss

Figure 3-2

By the way, the terms referred to in Figure 3-2 are universal. Any knowledgeable investor will know what you mean if you talk about "net operating income." The sequence of steps taken to analyze an investment are quite logical and easy to understand. Referring to Figure 3-2, you start with the total income the building should produce if 100 percent occupied. An allowance for vacancies is then taken out, giving you the "actual" Gross Operating Income you reasonably expect. Next, operating expenses, such as taxes, insurance, utilities, repairs, etc. are removed, leaving you with a net operating income *before* mortgage payments are made.

Now you want to determine how much money you will be able to put in your pocket, before taxes, so you reduce the Net Operating Income by the total mortgage payments that must be made. This gives you a Gross (pretax) Spendable Income. Since you want to know the *total* amount your property produced, add back the amount you paid down the mortgage during the year. The result is a combination of spendable income and principal payment, or Gross Equity Income.

But, you need to know how much income tax you must pay on your investment profit, so you reduce the Gross Equity Income by the amount of depreciation you will take for the year. The final result is your Real Estate Taxable Income.

As you progress through this book, each of these steps will be explained using the property you want to purchase as an example. Right now, you are interested in the sequence that you need to follow to determine if it makes financial sense to purchase the 100-percent-leveraged duplex.

The Net Operating Income (N.O.I.) of the duplex was $3000. You'll see by Figure 3-2 that N.O.I. is the income produced by the property after vacancy allowances and operating expenses have been removed. The duplex is figured off to the side of the Exhibit. Since mortgage payments were $3500, your gross operating income was a negative $500. It cost you $500 to keep it going. That number is in brackets to indicate it is a negative amount.

Now add in the amount you paid down on the mortgage during the year—$450. Tax-wise, the property still loses $50 a year. Even though the $450 principal reduction is not cash in your pocket, as far as covering your expenses, it must be figured here in order to determine your tax consequences.

Now for the good news. The IRS allows you a depreciation allowance of $2950 your first year. In other words, even though your property is actually appreciating, the IRS will allow you to reduce your total income by $2950. This will be covered in detail in Chapter 10. For now, let's see what this tax break will amount to if you owned this duplex.

The property produced a total income of *minus* $50. Therefore, instead of subtracting the $2950 you actually add it to the $50 loss shown by the property, giving you a $3000 tax loss for the year. The IRS is telling you that, as far as they are concerned, your property lost $3000. They will allow you to reduce your *other* taxable income by $3000. When your income tax return is prepared, it will show $3000 *less* taxable income. Assuming you are in a 40 percent tax bracket, you will pay $1200 *less* income tax as a result of owning the duplex (40 percent × $3000). That is $1200 more spendable money in your pocket after taxes that you keep from your other income, such as your job. So your building really didn't lose $500 for the year. Take that $500 from the $1200 tax savings you had and you'll see that the property gave you a $700 after-tax profit.

Even 100-percent-leveraged properties can give a positive cash return after taxes. With this thought in mind, you may want to search for this type of investment if your capital is limited. Do not expect to find a large selection of properties that can be purchased with little or no cash investment on your part. You'll have to search the market and negotiate with sellers to accomplish your goal. Here are some other ways of purchasing investment real estate with little or no cash.

The Option Contract

An option contract is nothing more than an executed contract between a buyer and a seller which allows the prospective purchaser the ''option'' to purchase a property within a given period of time. For this option, he puts up a sum of money which is non-refundable if he chooses not to exercise his option and purchase the property. This sum of money is generally much less than he would need to purchase the property outright. If he decides not to purchase the property, the option money reverts to the seller. When the buyer exercises the option, the deposit becomes part of the down payment.

Why would a buyer want an option? Suppose Mr. Allen sees an investment property that he really wants, but at the present time his available cash is limited. He knows that in three months he will have enough cash available to make an outright purchase. Perhaps he is waiting for another property, which he already owns, to sell or close. His money may be tied up in time certificates and withdrawing the funds prior to maturity would result in heavy interest penalties. Meanwhile, he does not want to lose this investment, so he options it, thereby tying it up.

An option contract is a ''unilateral'' contract, with all rights to buy or not to buy going to the purchaser. The seller has absolutely no control over what happens. This is why he will request a sizable option deposit. He is, in effect, taking his property off the market for a period of days, or months, and it still may not be sold at the end of the option period, if the purchaser decides not to exercise his purchase option.

Lease With an Option To Buy

A seller who is motivated to sell, may consider leasing his investment property to a would be purchaser and giving him an option to buy at a future date. This vehicle is ideal where a seller needs to ''get out'' of the ownership or management of his property. Perhaps he is ill or moving from the area. The purchaser agrees to lease the property for a period of time, until he can afford to purchase it. Depending upon the terms agreed to by both parties, part of the lease payments may be applied to the down payment.

Either of the options discussed may have extension clauses. What if the original option is for 90 days for example, and the purchaser is still not ready to purchase at the end of the option period? The two parties can agree to an extension. Usually, however, the seller will want two concessions:

1. Additional option money to be given by the purchaser; and
2. A price increase. It will now cost more to purchase the property because it has appreciated.

Contract for Deed

The contract for deed works basically the same as the lease option, except there is *no* option involved. The purchaser agrees to purchase the property, not option it, but does not have sufficient cash to do so. Likewise, the seller agrees to the purchaser's price. He and the seller reach an agreement in which the purchaser will give a small cash down payment. The balance of the down payment will come from the lease payments he makes to the seller. Perhaps one half of his lease payments will apply toward the down payment. When he has accumulated the agreed amount making up the full down payment, title to the property is transferred to his name. The seller retains title until that time arrives.

The buyer, in this type of transaction, may have to "feed" his investment during the period that he is making lease payments to the seller. At best, he may expect to break even. But, remember, he has the opportunity of building toward ownership of a small investment property . . . of taking that first step.

It is really a savings play in which he is adding to his real estate investment. In the meantime, he is realizing the appreciation and principal reduction benefits produced by the property. Let's say it takes him three years to build the necessary down payment in a $50,000 property that he has purchased on a contract for deed basis. Assuming the property will appreciate five percent per year, in three years the property will have a fair market value of $57,881 (That is five percent per year on $50,000, compounded over three years.) He has picked up $7,881 in property value increase during the period. In effect, he was able to buy a real estate investment three years from now at today's prices. Without this technique, he may not have been able to buy anything.

Distressed Properties

Occasionally, you may run across a distressed property—one in which the present owner has gotten into trouble and wants out. If, after careful analysis, you see that it has potential, you can try to convince him to sell you the property with no money down. He will carry a mortgage for the difference between the existing financing and the agreed upon price.

But remember, he wants out! A property in a substandard condition should be purchased at a price well below current market value. Your property analysis should allow for excessive vacancies, higher than normal operating expenses and, of course, 100 percent financing. Do not get yourself into the same position as the current owner. You can expect to incur above normal expenses in order to "turn" the investment around into a profit making investment. Extensive renovation and advertising expenses to attract tenants are just two that may be facing you. Many fortunes have been made by investors who do nothing but acquire distressed properties at "below market" prices, fix them up and sell at a profit. Financial success in this type investment requires the willingness to "work" toward the success of the project. If you are willing, start looking. If you expect a temporary negative cash flow, be sure to plan for it in your budget.

Ask the Broker for Help

It is not uncommon for a broker to take all or part of his fee in the form of a second or third mortgage on the property in lieu of cash. A sale that may not go together because the buyer lacks enough cash, may be the only incentive the broker needs. Having his fee spread out over the term of a mortgage is better than no fee at all. A broker who has had a good year may prefer spreading his income out over more than one year.

Asking the broker to cut his commission is also a very common practice. Unfortunately, many brokers are more than willing to do so in order to make a sale. As someone once said, "They know what they are worth." Asking a broker to cut commissions, in my opinion, is no more justified than asking your physician to give you a cut-rate operation. A good physician or broker, is well worth what he is paid. Real estate professional fees *are* frequently negotiated on large property sales.

Paying More for the Property

One method of getting a seller to agree to a no-down-payment sale is to offer him more for the property than he is expecting to receive from a buyer who can put up a cash down payment. You must carefully analyze the investment first, to determine what price you can afford to pay.

Profit Sharing

You can offer the seller a share in the profits produced by the property as added incentive to sell you the investment with no money down. Not only will he receive a share in the income produced by the building, but will still be carrying a second mortgage as well. The method of determining this profit and the length of time it is to be paid, are negotiable between you and the seller.

Mortgage Hypothecation

Suppose you own a home or other real estate that has a substantial equity. It is possible to offer the seller of an investment property a second mortage on your other real estate. Here is an example of how it would work.

Your home has a market value of $75,000. Your present mortgage balance is $40,000, giving you an equity of $35,000 in your home. You want to purchase an investment property requiring $25,000 in cash, which you do not have. You offer the seller of the investment property, a second mortgage on your home in the amount of $25,000 in lieu of cash.

This is another situation in which you want to weigh the consequences carefully. Many people do not want to "risk" the equity they have in their homestead. There are investors, however, who realize that the equity in their home is the best source of investment capital they have, perhaps, the only one! Rather than refinance and pay the closing costs plus higher interest rates, this is a quick inexpensive method of generating investment capital.

It is one more way of buying investment real estate when you have no available cash. But, it is another alternative that needs to be carefully analyzed.

HOW MUCH RISK ARE YOU WILLING TO TAKE?

It all boils down to how much risk you are willing to take, when your investment capital is small or non-existent. Each potential investment must be considered on an individual basis, based on these questions:

1. What is the potential of the investment?
2. How long will you have to carry or feed the investment before it reaches that potential?

3. If you are taking a risk by purchasing it, what are your chances of losing and what do you stand to lose?

4. Can you purchase this property at a price that makes some risk worth taking?

5. Have you thoroughly considered potential gain, carrying costs on the investment (if you have over-leveraged it) and risk, compared with staying in your present investment position, and not buying until you have more cash.

After you consider all the risks, all the costs, and all the possible benefits, you should be able to make a sound investment decision. When you feel you should invest in the property, by all means, do it! By the time you finish this book, you will be able to distinguish a good investment from a bad one. And you also know that the majority of investors who never take a risk who leave all of their investment funds in "secure" savings accounts or other fixed investments, end up practically broke when they retire.

Waiting to build a substantial amount of investment capital may prevent you from ever getting a start in real estate investing, and the sooner you start, the more time you'll have to secure your future.

4

To Manage or Not to Manage: The Question of Operating Your Investment Property

---

Recently, an ex-investor (we'll call him Henry Watson) in real estate had a long talk with me. He is an ex-investor because he has sold his 16-unit apartment complex and invested the proceeds in Certificates of Deposit.

During our discussion, he pointed out that he was sick of tenants calling him at 2 a.m. because they had locked themselves out of their apartments or because their water faucet would not stop dripping. He was also upset with prospective tenants who would make an appointment to see a vacant apartment and would never show up, leaving him sitting at the building for an hour waiting. He also disliked the monthly chore of collecting rents and paying bills. So, he sold his property and put his money in a carefree investment—Certificates of Deposit.

Henry probably made a big mistake just because he was never told how to avoid these headaches. No doubt there are other investors who have had, or are having, similar experiences, only because no one has explained ways of eliminating these annoyances.

Before you start looking for a real estate investment, one of the more important decisions you need to make is "just how involved do you want to become in the operation of your investment." The only decision you've had to make if you are primarily in the stock market, is when to buy or sell. Owning a few shares of General Motors stock did not entitle you to make any decisions regarding the operation of the company. Likewise, if you invest in savings associations or insurance companies, they reinvest your funds without consulting you first, and they take care of all the management decisions.

Now you have a different decision to make. If this is your first venture into real estate, you'll realize that you are now in control. You can make the decision that will affect the operation of your investment. It's not as frightening as it may sound. Managing an apartment building is not as complex as running General Motors. In fact, it's probably easier than managing your own household—at least your tenants know who's boss.

THREE FACTORS TO CONSIDER WHEN DECIDING
WHETHER TO MANAGE YOUR PROPERTY

You have to decide just how involved you wish to become. There are three basic factors that enter into this decision. First, how much free time do you have to manage your property? You may be working full time, so you have none. If you are retired, you may have nothing but time and ownership of a real estate investment is just what you need to keep yourself active, both mentally and physically.

Secondly, what is your mental attitude toward your investment? Perhaps you have the time but cannot stand the thought of talking with your tenants or helping them with the problems they may have in the apartment, store, or office that they are leasing from you.

Thirdly, how much, if anything, are you willing to sacrifice to maximize your profits? Obviously, we all would like to get rich without doing anything, but unless you have a wealthy relative who dies and leaves everything to you, that is not likely to happen. It may be *easier* to leave all the management responsibilities to someone else, but this will cost money and thereby reduce your profits.

Don't get the wrong idea about real estate investing at this point. We'll discuss how you can do as much or as little as you wish in the management of your real estate investment and still realize more profit than you are receiving from any of your present investments.

TYPES OF MANAGEMENT AVAILABLE TO YOU

To help you decide how much you want to get involved with your investment, here are the two phases of management that are available to you—Resident Management and Property Management.

Resident Management: How to Select and What to Expect

A resident manager is someone who is hired to take care of the day-to-day problems that may arise in the ownership of a property that is rented to tenants. What does this mean to the owner of an apartment building?

There are always minor problems that may come up. Many of you, at one time or another, have rented an apartment or house. Since the landlord is expected to maintain the property, it is only natural for a tenant to expect the maximum attention to his minor complaints, such as a dripping water faucet or broken wall socket. Then there are the more urgent needs, such as a tenant who locks himself out of his apartment at 2:00 a.m. and calls you to come and let him in.

So far, you're probably thinking, "who wants all those problems." Perhaps I should explain that the vast majority of tenants in a well maintained building are reasonable and trouble free. Like you and me, they need a place to live—a place to call home and they want to enjoy all the comforts that we all do.

If you are convinced that you do not have time or the patience to manage your investment, you will need a "resident manager." He lives in the building and can take care of all the day-to-day problems that arise.

Where do you find him? Pick someone in the building who has the basic qualifications you need. They are:

1. He or she has the time to watch after your property. Pick someone that you know spends a lot of time at home.
2. He is, or you feel he will be, conscientious.
3. He must be something of a handyman. This is an important point. He should be able to repair that leaking faucet or replace that broken electrical socket. He will be worth more than what you have to pay him (It would probably cost you $25.10 to have a plumber fix that faucet—ten cents for the washer and $25.00 for labor).
4. He should get along with the other tenants in the building.

How do you select this Resident Manager? Once you have owned your building for some time, you should know your tenants. As a new owner, you may have to rely on the judgment of the previous owner. Perhaps he has a dependable resident manager already. Your best bet is a retired age individual or couple who is usually there. He probably has had years of experience in handling people and doing minor repair work. Your next best bet may be a young married couple who will be happy to get a break on their rent in return for looking after your building.

If you are unable to find a manager within your building, you can run an ad in the help wanted section of the local newspaper. Spell out what you expect from him and the compensation he can expect to receive, such as a free apartment, salary, or both.

Make a list of what is expected of your resident manager and give him a copy—this may include additional duties such as showing a vacant apartment to a potential tenant.

A Word of Caution: Real Estate laws in many states require someone who negotiates a lease to be either the property owner himself, or a registered real estate sales person. Your safest approach is to have your manager show the apartment only. Any discussion about rent, lease terms, etc., should come from you. The advantage to you in operating this way, is to eliminate the need for you to run down to your building with every "suspect" that may want to rent the vacant apartment.

Your manager will also make sure that the lawn is maintained (even if you hire a yardman to do it), the garbage cans are being emptied and kept clean, the lawn is being watered regularly, etc.

How much should you pay him? That depends on the size of your building and how much he is expected to do.

A small complex, say eight or ten units, perhaps $25 to $50 a month in rent reduction is enough. But don't be "cheap." A good manager will be worth everything you pay him and more. In a large apartment complex, he may be given a free apartment plus a salary. Your local real estate investment counselor will be able to advise you as to what is customary for your area.

You have now made someone in your building, at a reasonable cost to you, a resident manager. You are now left with the only remaining task involved in the management of your property—the money end. This includes negotiating leases, collecting rents, paying bills and keeping an accounting of the operation.

In Chapter 14, we'll cover many of the details you need to understand in negotiating a lease. Regarding collecting of rents, most tenants in quality apartment buildings automatically send a rent check to you each month. This makes the rent collecting job an automatic operation. To protect yourself against those tenants who are habitually late in paying their rent, consider writing a "late penalty" clause in your lease as explained in Chapter 14.

The next task is to pay the monthly bills and make the mortgage payment. This task for a small apartment complex will only take an hour or two once a month.

The final item is to keep an accurate accounting of all income and expenses. The IRS will expect it, and you will want to keep an accounting of how your investment is doing. In Chapter 13 we will cover recordkeeping. Your system does not have to be a complicated one.

How Professional Property Management Additional Benefits Not Otherwise Available

After reviewing what is involved in this remaining management phase, if you decide you want no part of it, consider employing a professional property management company to do it for you. Basically, their job would consist of:

1. Finding tenants, showing apartments and negotiating leases;
2. Collecting rents;
3. Paying bills and mortgage payments;
4. Keeping bookkeeping records;
5. Sending you a monthly statement on the operation of your building;
6. Overseeing the resident manager;
7. Making certain the building and grounds are properly maintained; and
8. Contracting for any major repairs or replacements that may be needed. (Any major expenditure would be only with your authorization.)

You should give the management company some guidelines as to what expenditures they are allowed to make without your prior approval. If, for example, a hot water heater springs a lead on a Saturday morning, it's obvious the unit needs to be repaired or replaced. If you happen to be out of town that weekend, your tenants cannot wait until the following Monday to have it repaired or replaced. The management company may recommend, however, that the building needs painting. This is a major expense that needs your business judgment. In making this judgment, count more than the immediate dollars in your pocket. A well-maintained property draws a better quality tenant, produces higher rents and is more salable at a top price when the time comes to move into a larger investment.

A professional property management company offers additional benefits not available to you as an individual property owner:

— They manage a number of properties, so they may have their own contract handymen, lawn man, electrician, etc. Your costs of repairs and maintenance will be less.

— When it comes to replacement of major appliances, chances are they buy in volume and can pass additional savings on to you.

— Being in the business, they will probably have a ready source of potential tenants. Your only way of reaching a potential tenant is through ads in the newspaper or a "for rent" sign on the property.

A good management company also keeps abreast of the current rental market and can keep your income at a maximum. They are also experts in pre-screening of tenants to be sure those who lease space in your building are reliable.

Finally, there is something to be said for the fact that the management company is not *emotionally* involved with your building or tenants. They can look at the property objectively, as a business whereas you may not. They do not become personally involved with tenants, which you may do and in doing so, cause all types of problems as well as loss of income. We'll discuss that more in detail in a later chapter.

What does a management company charge for all of this service? It depends upon the size of your property and the neighborhood in which it is located. You can probably plan on spending five percent of the gross rents collected for management, more if the property is smaller. Some management companies will not consider smaller properties. Call a couple in your area and ask them.

You'll notice that I said a management company will charge five percent of "gross rents collected." This means that they will be paid five percent of the actual total income the building produces, before any expenses are taken out. There is a sound reason for this method of paying the management company. You do not want to pay them a fee based on what the building *should* produce in income or it would not matter to them if they rented the units or not. Basing their income on the rents that they actually collect also gives them the incentive to keep the units leased at the highest possible rent.

Likewise, you do not want to base their fee on the income *after* operating expenses have been taken out. The management company may then be unwilling to properly maintain the property because any reduction in net operating income (the income left after all operating expenses but before mortgage payments) would also reduce their fee. They may also charge a separate fee for negotiating leases. A typical fee would be 10 percent of the first year's rent and five percent for each additional year of the lease. This leasing fee is above and beyond their normal management fee.

How to Locate a Qualified Property Management Company: Your best approach in finding a qualified property management company is to check the yellow pages of your telephone book under Real Estate Management. Check with several and ask the following questions:

1. Are you a CPM? This stands for the professional designation of Certified Property Manager. A property manager having this designation is a pro. If your area has no CPM's, continue the questioning anyway and pick the best one available.
2. Are you licensed, bonded, and insured? This protects you and your property.
3. Is property management your full time business? Many real estate brokers "dabble" in property management because it is a source of listings.
4. What properties do you presently manage? May I contact the owners to see if they are satisfied?
5. How much do you charge? They will need to know full details about your property to answer this question. Size of the complex, type of property, and closeness to others they currently manage will enter

into their pricing. For example, a large office building with tenants on long term leases, is easier to manage than a small apartment building with month to month or yearly leases. Although the management function is the same for most types of investment properties, the cost may vary depending on the amount of time the management company must spend.

HOW MUCH MANAGEMENT DO YOU WANT?

You now know the two types of management available to you. As you can see, you can become as active or inactive in the operation of your investment real estate as you wish. May I suggest that you at least start out trying it all on your own, if you have or can find the time. You may quickly employ a tenant as resident manager, but keep the second management function yourself. This will be an invaluable education for you as your real estate investments start growing.

If you are working with a knowledgeable realtor who specializes in investment real estate, he can give you the guidance you will need to become familiar with the operation and management of your building. Maybe this is not your first venture into real estate investing, or you simply cannot find the time to manage it yourself, then consider a management company.

THE MOM AND POP OPERATION

Many smaller real estate investments are referred to as "mom and pop" operations, because that is just what they are. A husband and wife team who do everything themselves. And you want to know something? They would not trade the excitement and experience for anything!

Whether you are a "mom and pop" team or an experienced real estate investor, the rewards you receive will be outstanding. How much you want to do yourself is up to you. Which brings us back to Henry Watson. He was the investor who would not put up with the minor annoyances he had while he owned his sixteen unit apartment building, which prompted him to sell. What did he get out of his real estate investment?

On his $50,000 investment, back in 1968, he received about $5000 a year spendable income, or 10 percent return on his investment. Through depreciation benefits, he was able to keep *all* of his income, tax free, and even had a tax write-off against his other income. He sold the complex a little over two years later and made a $35,000 profit. This was back in 1970. He was left with $75,000 after capital gains tax, including his initial $50,000 investment.

Due to rent increases and property appreciation, the same property was recently offered for sale at a price over 50 percent higher than what he paid for it in 1968.

Let's take a look at what he has actually sacrificed by selling his property and putting his cash into Certificates of Deposit. Over the next eight years, his $75,000 produced eight percent per year taxable income, or $48,000. After taxes, he was left with about $30,000. His principal amount of $75,000 is still $75,000—eight years later. It has not appreciated.

What if he had kept his real estate investment and employed a management company to manage it for him. His spendable income, with rent increases, over the eight year period would have totalled about $36,000—all or most of which would have been tax-free income. At the same time, his property has increased in value by about 56 percent from $225,000 to $350,000. during this period, he has paid down his mortgages by about 30 percent so his equity is now $225,000 based on the current market value of $350,000. And remember, he only invested $50,000 in 1968.

Don't allow the thought of possible management problems cause you to make the same mistake. Management and the problems of management can be avoided. The decision is yours.

5

Guidelines for Choosing
Real Estate Investments

Another decision you need to make before you start looking for your real estate investment is: what type of property do you want? A number of factors enter into making this decision. In order to help you decide, you should have a basic background knowledge of some of the various types of real estate investments that are available and how each of them differs from the others. We will examine the ten most common types and look at each in terms of:

1. General locations;
2. Site improvements;
3. The lease form used;
4. Type of income produced;
5. Type of expenses;
6. Management requirements;
7. Financing methods;

8. Depreciation benefits available; and

9. Unique features that distinguish that particular investment from the others.

To keep from boring you with details, each type of property will be discussed in general terms only. Each of the above items will be mentioned only where they are of unique importance to a particular type of real estate. Entire books have been written on each of the ten forms of real estate investments that will be reviewed. Since rental apartment buildings are the most common and easiest form of real estate to understand, most of this book is devoted to using apartment buildings as examples. Rental apartment buildings are also the most flexible in terms of availability. There are size ranges to fit all investments, from a duplex to a thousand unit complex. While most new investors start with apartment buildings, many large, experienced investors still invest only in apartment complexes.

This Chapter will be your basic introduction to other types of investments. Throughout the book, however, other types of investments will be compared with apartment buildings when discussing certain subjects.

APARTMENT COMPLEXES: POPULAR, EASY-TO-UNDERSTAND INVESTMENTS THAT OFFER UNIQUE DEPRECIATION BENEFITS

Since apartment buildings can probably be considered as the most popular form of real estate investing, we'll start with them. Apartment buildings are usually used as a "buffer" between residential and commercial real estate. They can include anything from a duplex to a high-rise building. Local zoning laws limit the density number of dwelling units that can be placed on a given site. This density can be controlled by a number of various limiting factors other than number of apartments. These include such things as:

1. set back requirements;

2. height limitations;

3. parking requirements per each unit;

4. minimum acceptable square footage per apartment; and

5. "green area" of landscaping required around the property.

Size and mix of the individual apartments will usually be keyed to local market demands and may include hotel rooms, efficiency or studio apartments, one-, two- or three-bedroom units, or perhaps larger. In most areas, each apartment is individually metered for electric so each tenants pays his own electric bill. Depending on the area and the size of the complex, amenities such as swimming pool, tennis courts and recreation buildings may be included. Apartments are generally rented on an annual lease basis which offers the investor a reasonable guarantee of income. Such items as coin laundries on the premises also offer tenants convenience while producing a small additional income for the owner. If you intend to live in one of the units, you should still figure the value of that apartment as part of the annual income because you would be paying rent somewhere else if you were not living in your own building. Likewise, if you intend to manage the property, figure value of your time and add it in to the operating expenses of the building. The philosophy being that if you were working somewhere else, you would be paid for your time.

Apartment buildings offer the investor the highest possible depreciation benefits of all the various types of real estate investments. This will be covered in a later chapter.

HOTELS AND MOTELS: HARD TO MANAGE BUT POTENTIALLY PROFITABLE

Hotels and motels are generally considered the most difficult of all investments to manage. As a practical matter, tenants are generally overnighters. At best, in resort areas, they may stay for two to three weeks. In seasonal areas, such as South Florida, they may stay the entire four month winter season. Most motel owners accept the fact that whenever they have a vacancy, they must keep the "front desk" open. This could result in a 24 hour a day job, seven days a week. A large motel will also have a restaurant and lounge operation which, again, increases the management requirements.

Why do investors own motels? A successful motel operation can be very profitable. In our area, the so-called Gold Coast on the southeast coast of Florida, a well-run motel can generate as much income during the four month winter season as a yearly apartment building owner will earn all year long. But, an unseasonably cold winter in Florida, or a gas shortage, can also be very costly to a motel owner when tourists fail to come down. To protect himself, the motel operator usually requires a sizable deposit, non-refundable, well in advance of the season. A cancellation notice must be received well prior to the reserved date to entitle the guest to a deposit refund. When the guest arrives, the manager may then collect the balance of the rent, in advance. Then, if the weather turns bad, the guest will think twice before leaving.

Management is a major concern in a motel operation, if the owner does not choose to manage it himself. A dishonest manager or desk clerk can conceivably make more than the motel owner himself by pocketing sums of cash that are paid by overnight guests, especially when they arrive late at night without reservations. Various checks can be made by the owner to keep his manager honest, but few, if any, are foolproof.

When the motel has a restaurant and lounge operation, his management problems and control over profits are even more difficult.

When attempting to finance a motel, the owner may find it more difficult than a rental apartment building because of the fluctuating of income. A motel that can produce a successful track record over a several year period is most desirable not only to a lender but to a prospective purchaser as well.

If you feel that a motel type of investment is suited to your needs, verification of income and expenses are very important. A rental apartment building income can usually be verified by examination of leases, although it is recommended that each tenant be asked to verify the rent he is paying, the security deposit he has put up and the expiration date of his lease.

A motel's income is not that easy. The seller will usually tell you that he takes in "x" number of dollars a year plus another "x" number of dollars that does not show up on his books. First, request an examination by you, or your CPA, of his tax returns and sales tax records, if your state charges sales tax on motel rentals.

Secondly, purchase the property based on what these records show and *not* what the seller tells you he is doing. Just as in an apartment building, if you intend to manage it yourself, you should determine how much your time is worth and consider that as part of your operating expenses. A well-managed motel, for the right investor, can be an extremely profitable and rewarding experience.

WHY OFFICE BUILDINGS ARE SOUND, RELATIVELY EASY TO MANAGE INVESTMENTS

You will find that in the discussion of office buildings and shopping centers, the rules are different and, perhaps, somewhat more complicated. For this reason, if you are a first time investor in real estate, I would recommend a rental apartment building as a starter, unless you have someone with experience to help you.

Office buildings are generally leased on a square footage basis rather than a flat price per unit. As an example, an office suite having 2500 square feet of floor space and renting for $8.00 per square foot (and the $8.00 per square foot is a yearly rent, not monthly), would produce 2500 × $8.00 a year rent or $20,000. Sounds simple so far, but there is more that a knowledgeable investor needs to understand in order to maximize his base rent.

The first thing a possible tenant may do is pull out his tape measure and measure the distance from wall to wall, let's say he comes up with a room 50 × 50 or 2500 square feet. That is "inside" room dimensions. The walls between his suite and the one next door have 2 × 4 studding with ¾ inch drywall on each side. The actual wall thickness is 3⅛ inches. Who pays for that space? It may not sound like much, but if you add ½ of that 3⅛ inches (we'll split it between the two adjoining tenants) you'll find that you'll add a total of 3⅛ inches to both the length and width of the room for rent purposes (½ of 3⅛ inches on each of the 4 walls). Your tenant will be charged, therefore, for a room 50 feet 3⅛ inches × 50 feet 3⅛ inches or approximately 2528 square feet at $8.00 a foot, the rent will be $20,208 rather than $20,000 a year. That added $208 a year may not sound like much but if you have 10 such tenants, all having a five year lease, this amounts to $10,400 in rent you have lost over the lease term. The same treatment is generally used in charging a tenant for a hallway leading to his suite if he is the only tenant using it, or if there are more than one, the value may be divided equally among them.

Many office building owners prefer to quote a flat monthly rent rather than to explain these charges, but they still had to start with a base rent per square foot of floor space to determine the monthly rent.

Now, consider the next variable in office building rental. What is included in that base rent? Unlike rental apartments, most office buildings are not individually metered for electricity. The landlord pays the bill. This cost must be included when he is determining how much rent to charge. It is not uncommon to charge a doctor who makes extensive use of x-ray equipment, extra rent because of the large amounts of electricity this type of equipment uses.

Some office buildings offer daily cleaning service for all tenants. It is usually the accepted practice that the tenant maintains everything within his own suite except for major building repairs that may be needed, such as a leaking roof. There are leases drawn, however, where the landlord pays for everything including minor repairs such as the replacement of burned out light bulbs in the tenant's suite. The landlord also must maintain the common areas, including hallways, elevators and common rest rooms.

Now let's look at the brighter side, just in case your first thought is that office building ownership is a one-way street with the tenant receiving all the benefits.

As a general rule, the tenant will pay all or part of the cost of finishing the interior of his suite. The landlord may pay for the basic improvements including painted interior partitioning or walls. If the tenant desires more expensive treatment of walls, such as paneling, mirrors, etc., this will probably be at his own expense. When the suite is to be carpeted, the landlord will probably furnish a commercial grade of carpeting, or offer the tenant a carpet allowance if more expensive carpeting is desired. This is true of the entire interior finishing of the suite. This is where the landlord comes out ahead. Next time you visit your physician's or attorney's office, take a look at the finishing and decorations. Chances are he paid for most of it, to the tune of thousands of dollars. And, here's the nice part . . . when he decides to move out, the improvements stay—they belong to the landlord, not the tenant.

This brings us to the second advantage of office building ownership. Because your tenant is making a sizable investment in his suite, he'd want a longer lease than an apartment renter, perhaps five years or longer with renewal options. This means that you can usually expect less tenant turnover in an office building.

In order to protect yourself from increased operating costs and inflation, leases should contain such items as tax and utility stops (tenant is expected to pay any increases in real estate taxes and utilities over the base year or the year he moved in). The lease should also contain an automatic rent adjustment tied into a common measure of the economy. The consumer price index published by the Federal Government is frequently used for this "cost of living" increase. Unless you are familiar with the drawing up of a commercial lease, you should seek professional assistance until the terms and conditions become familiar to you.

Office buildings offer an investor a sound, relatively easy to manage real estate investment.

SHOPPING CENTERS: FROM SMALL TO MALL

Investments in shopping centers in most parts of the country are very popular. There are, as with office buildings, some unique features and cautions of which an investor should be aware.

Guidelines for Shopping Center Sizes

The term "shopping center" can mean anything from a couple of stores to a super regional shopping mall. Let's begin by establishing "size" as determined by one major shopping center developer. Just as with office buildings, the size of a shopping center is normally measured by the net leasable square footage of space it contains. We distinguished net leasable, or the number of square feet in which you can collect rent from gross square feet, which is the total building enclosure, including mall enclosures, public rest rooms, etc.

The smallest of shopping centers may contain 25,000 to 50,000 square feet of leasable space. It may contain such tenants as a small convenience store, laundromat, barber shop, dry cleaner, etc.

The next step will be in the area of 60,000 to 200,000 square feet and will contain a major food chain store, possibly a drug store and several small stores. The center, instead of a food store, may have a discount store such as a K-Mart. In a center of the 60,000 square foot size, you will not find two major tenants but you will in the larger ones (200,000 square feet).

Quite logically, the chain stores are referred to as "majors" or major tenants and the small, specialty stores are considered "locals" or local tenants.

The next size center will be 400,000 square feet or larger and contain at least two major department stores and many local tenants. When located in a community with a relatively small population, the 400,000 square foot size may be reduced.

The final step is the "super regional mall" which will be in excess of one million square feet in size and contain several major tenants. You may feel that a discussion of anything larger than a small neighborhood center with a convenience store is beyond anything you could ever conceive of owning. You may be surprised! There are many real estate investors who started out small but may have been able to pyramid their investments into a regional size shopping center.

Shopping Center Management Techniques to Keep in Mind

Anyone venturing into a shopping center investment should be aware of some of the problems and techniques involved in managing and owning one. There are several factors found in the operation of a shopping center, especially the larger ones, that are unique to this type of real estate investment.

The stability of the tenants determines the success or failure of the center. Therefore, it is of utmost importance that the owner take the necessary steps to insure stability of the center.

Think Twice Before Leasing to Competitors: A mistake frequently made by a novice shopping center owner is to rent space to tenants who are in the identical businesses. For example, two pizza parlors will have trouble making a go of it in the same center, or two coin laundries or two barber shops. A large mall type center, on the other hand, frequently thrives on competitive stores, such as shoe stores. Next time you visit your regional shopping mall, count the number of shoe stores it contains. Don't forget the shoe departments in the major tenants' stores. When the center is large enough, this type of competitor thrives, because the volume of traffic generated by the center supplies each competitor with many customers.

Your primary concern for now, however, is in the smaller size centers which may include a supermarket or discount store; think twice before you lease space to someone in the same business as a present tenant, because it could force both of them out of business. You're better off having your vacant store a little longer.

Prohibit "Going Out of Business" Signs: Speaking of going out of business, no matter how hard you try, you will always have a tenant who just cannot make it. You have probably been in centers displaying huge "going out of business" signs. A wise shopping center owner will have a clause written into the lease that forbids these signs. The reason is simple, the average shopper driving into a center and seeing one or more going out of business signs, may have second thoughts about shopping in the center at all.

Majors and Minors: A shopping center's goal, whether it is a large one or a small one, is to attract traffic (shoppers) into the center. In many large shopping malls, the major tenants actually own their own stores. They pay the landlord rent for use of the ground under the store and pay their share of common area maintenance. Where the owner of the center does own the "major" stores, chances are the major's rent is very low. In larger centers, the major tenants are the drawing card for the minor ones—it's actually the minor tenants who financially support the center and make it profitable.

While the base rent for a major may be $2.00 to $3.00 a square foot per year, the local tenant may be paying $7.00 or $8.00 or more. It is not uncommon, however, for a percentage clause to be written in a major's lease. This means that once his gross sales reach a certain dollar volume, he will pay, as additional rent, a percentage of his gross over the base amount.

Promotions and Special Attractions: You have probably also noticed that larger centers are always having promotions and special attractions to draw potential shoppers into the center. These promotions can be anything from "sidewalk sales" to great attractions such as fashion shows or musical concerts.

Who pays for these promotions? Usually a center above the size of the small neighborhood type, sets up a "merchants association." The association is sponsored by and contributed to by the merchants in cooperation with the landlord. Generally, lease clauses make membership in the association mandatory on the part of all tenants. The center's owner frequently contributes the lion's share because it is also in his best interest to create buying activity within his center. This association can also have other functions in the operation of the center, such as hiring security guards to watch the center, especially at night.

Lease Provisions and Restrictions: Shopping center leases, as with office building leases, usually contain common area maintenance (CAM) clauses. The tenants are expected to share in the cost of maintaining the common parking lots, landscaping, daily cleaning of the grounds, etc.

Both shopping centers and office buildings must pay strict attention to parking requirements. Usually, local zoning authorities control parking very closely. It is possible to run into a situation where you cannot lease to a tenant you may want in the center, such as a restaurant, because the zoning authority tells you that you do not have sufficient parking for a restaurant. Tenants like doctors, beauty shops and eating establishments deserve more parking than the normal retail type store.

Most shopping center owners also have sign restrictions written into leases. This will require that any sign advertising a store must conform with the overall decor or uniformity of the center. The wise owner will also forbid a tenant from parking his vehicle, containing signs advertising his store, in the front of the center. Restrictions in tenant parking areas and unloading areas for trucks are common, in order to insure that prime parking spaces are reserved for customers.

When figuring a vacancy allowance on a center you are considering, you will usually use a percentage of the local tenants only since the majors are secure on long-term leases.

Before you scratch shopping centers as a source of investing because they are too complicated or too expensive, keep these thoughts in mind. Small neighborhood centers offer an excellent investment with a moderate cash requirement. For a beginner, they do not require the expertise that is needed in a larger center. Don't be afraid to get involved in this type of investment if you are able to locate one that makes financial sense. You may find less tenant problems than in an apartment building. You may also be surprised how quickly your equity will grow in your neighborhood center and you will be ready to move up into the next size shopping center containing a major tenant such as a K-Mart or chain food store.

INVESTMENT OPPORTUNITES IN WAREHOUSES AND INDUSTRIAL BUILDINGS

These two types of real estate investments are discussed together because they are usually both found in industrial zone locations or industrial parks. That is where the similarity ends.

Rental warehouses are usually divided into "bays" or rooms that can range in size from 50 square feet to several thousand. The small storage bays are frequently used for personal belongings, etc. Larger bays may accommodate small workshops, manufacturing facilities or wholesale sales outlets. Tenant stability in the small spaces is probably the worst of all real estate investments. They may rent on a month to month basis and move out at any time. But, if you're in an area where demand for this type of facility is in demand, do not pass a good opportunity by. In Chapter 14, we will discuss how a landlord can protect himself through advance rents and security deposits.

The larger spaces are generally leased on longer terms to more stable tenants, such as manufacturing plants who need additional warehouse or manufacturing space. This brings us to industrial buildings. A building leased to a major industrial or manufacturing company makes an excellent, carefree investment. The tenant usually pays for everything, including maintenance, taxes, insurance and utilities.

The ultimate investment along these lines is a "sale/leaseback" situation wherein a major company offers to sell you their building and lease it back from you for several years on a "net" basis. In other words, they pay everything except mortgage payments. A few cautions, however. The tenant must be a stable one, preferably a top rated major corporation. Remember, if he goes out of business, your building will be 100 percent vacant.

Leases are critical and should be prepared by an attorney. Periodic cost of living increases, written into the lease, are a must to protect the building owner from the effects of inflation. Because Triple A Sale/Leasebacks are excellent investments, they are also difficult to find.

MOBILE HOME PARKS: PROFITABLE AND EASY TO MANAGE

In recent years, mobile home parks have become a sought after form of real estate investment. Consider this: with the cost of home construction skyrocketing and, therefore, the prices of homes climbing out of reach for many retired age people or young couples, there is a drastic demand for a more reasonably priced home. Enter the mobile home.

Before you jog your memory to the days of "trailers," go out and take a look at today's mobile homes. They will surprise you! In fact, most of them are no longer "mobile." Once placed in a mobile home park, they are tied down, skirted (frequently with decorative concrete block), landscaped and have patios installed. They become almost as permanent on the site as a conventionally built home. Mobile homes are available in both single and double widths. (Double widths, as the name indicates, are actually the equivalent of two homes side by side.)

Mobile homes are built with all the conveniences of a conventionally built home with two or more bedrooms, one or more baths, full kitchens and both living and family rooms. Double width mobile homes may contain 1000 square feet of living space, or more. When the owner decides to move, the days of attaching his mobile home behind his car and driving off, are gone. He will sell his home to a buyer the same as if he owned a conventional house. Convinced? Then let's see how mobile home park ownership differs from other forms of real estate investments.

Compared with most other real estate investments, the improvements in a mobile home park are minimal. They usually consist of the mobile home pads, or sites, which have water, sewer and electricity. A concrete slab for the patio area and tie down rings (or whatever local zoning requires) to anchor the home to the ground. Other improvements include the streets (which may be deeded to the local municipality, thereby eliminating maintenance requirements on the part of the park owner), recreation facilities, possibly a recreation building, and laundry facilities.

Density, or the number of homes you can have in the park, is usually controlled by zoning boards in terms of a maximum number of homes allowed per acre.

Income potential for a mobile home park owner comes from several sources. The primary source, of course, is from pad or space rental. But, there are some very profitable secondary sources. When a park has vacant spaces, the park owner can realize a handsome profit by selling new mobile homes. When tenants decide to sell their home and move, the park owner will generally be the selling agent for the home owner, and charge a fee for the service.

Mobile homes also require many accessories, such as skirting around the bottom of the home, fire extinguishers, smoke alarms, etc., which the park owner sells. Coin laundry facilities also bring in additional profit.

Operating expenses, on the other hand, are minimal. Maintenance requirements are probably limited to the common areas, such as swimming pool and clubhouse. Some park owners, for the sake of appearance, maintain the lawns for the entire park to insure they are all done uniformally. Although the landlord generally pays for water, sewer and trash removal, there are parks where each space has individual water as well as electric meters, and tenants pay for these services.

Because the physical improvements are minimal in a mobile home park, depreciation benefits are also minimal. Some park owners, however, actually own the mobile homes themselves and offer them as rental houses. They can depreciate these park-owned homes and gain some tax shelter benefits.

Travel trailer parks are a completely different type of real estate investment. They cater to travelers with motor homes, house trailers and campers. They compare, management wise, with a motel type of investment where renters are coming and going continuously.

Many knowledgeable investors are turning to mobile home parks (not travel trailer parks) as an investment. They are profitable and easy to manage.

VACANT LAND AND ACREAGE: AN INVESTMENT FOR THE SPECULATOR

Vacant land, as an investment, is for a different type of individual than those previously discussed. Vacant land does not produce income, in fact, it costs the investor money each year in real estate taxes and mortgage payments. A vacant land investment is frequently referred to as "an alligator" because all it does is eat, and since land does not depreciate, it does not even offer tax write-offs other than the actual outlay of taxes and mortgage interest payments being paid by the owner.

So why buy vacant land? Vacant land is for the speculator, the investor who is not looking for an immediate return on his invested capital. A land speculator usually uses excess investment funds, where cash flow is not important. His goal is to buy a parcel of land that will greatly appreciate during the holding period. Properly located, his land investment will double or triple in value (or more) in a few years. To obtain this goal, the land should be located in the path of progress, but outside the currently developed or populated areas. Prices will be less than on a similar parcel in the center or edge of a developed area.

The speculator does have ways of offsetting some of his expenses. When the land can be farmed or used to graze cattle, he may be able to lease it to a user. A developer will subdivide the property, put in streets, utilities and other facilities and sell lots at a considerably higher price per square foot than he paid for the land originally.

Your interest here, however, is for the investor who chooses vacant land for speculation. His investment is completely management free and his profit potential is far greater than in the ownership of improved, income producing property. Likewise, the risk is also greater.

Before leaving the review of various types of real estate investments, there are two others that you should know about.

HOW CONDO CONVERSIONS CAN BRING POTENTIALLY HIGH RETURNS IN A SHORT PERIOD OF TIME

Condominimum apartments have become the housing answer to millions of Americans, mostly the retired age citizens. These people are frequently referred to as "empty nesters" because their "nest" is now empty. Their children are all grown and gone. Suddenly, they find themselves living in a large, virtually empty home, requiring a lot of upkeep and expenses. The condo apartment becomes a rational answer to their problems. Their only maintenance requirements are within the four walls of their apartment. All major exterior maintenance is paid for out of the monthly maintenance fee paid by each apartment owner.

The condo owner soon discovers other benefits from trading his home for a condominium. His monthly living expense is usually reduced. He is free to come and go as he pleases. If he wants to spend the winter in Florida, all he has to do is lock his door and leave.

There is another, possibly unexpected, benefit he discovers. He has undoubtedly moved into a building with other owners who are in the same boat he is, retired, no children around, leisure time, etc. New friendships are readily found and he may feel less alone than he did in his home. All of this brings us to one conclusion. Condos have become a much needed form of housing.

One source of condominiums is through converting existing apartment buildings to condos. A properly converted building can give an investor a 50 to 100 percent profit on his invested capital in a short period of time.

What You Should Know Before Converting

Before you run out and buy an apartment building to convert, or try converting the one you already own, there are some things you need to know.

Assess the Market: The first requirement is to make a comprehensive market study of the area in which your potential project is located. You need to know what your competition will be in terms of location, price, amenities and square footage. You must compare apples with apples. Suppose your building has one-bedroom apartments of 800 square feet each. You cannot compare them with a new 1200 square foot apartment project down the street.

Once you know what your competition will be, you should be prepared to sell your apartments at a *lower* price than the competition, when his building is new and yours is not new. You must create an incentive for a potential purchaser to want your apartments.

Determine Conversion Costs: Next, you must determine how much it will cost for the conversion. Keep in mind that this discussion is for familiarization purposes only. You will not be a qualified conversion specialist after you finish reading it.

Conversion costs will vary from area to area and include at least these items:

1. Cost of purchasing the existing apartment complex.
2. Closing costs in the acquisition.
3. Professional fees including attorneys, accountants, engineering studies and real estate professional fees on the sellout or selling of the individual apartments.
4. Interim financing costs. (The mortgage you will place on the project while it is being converted, unless you can pay all cash for the proj-

ect.) Any existing mortgage will have to be paid off, unless a "release clause" can be negotiated into it. The lender will not allow you to sell parts of the building that is the collateral for the mortgage he holds. A release clause allows you to pay down the mortgage balance by lump-sum payments as units are sold. This reduces the lender's investment in the property, offsetting the reduced security he has as units are sold.

5. Renovation costs, including inside and out. The apartment probably need redecorating, carpet, and repairs prior to sale. Do appliances need to be replaced? An accurate estimate of renovation must be included in your cost of each apartment.

6. Promotional Expense. It has been proven that cutting corners through minimal advertising of a condo project, turns out to be quite costly. When the market is flooded with advertising on your project, sellout is much quicker and cost of carrying the project during sellout is reduced. Don't overlook the tenants already renting in your building. As additional incentive, they can be sold their apartment at a discount price, especially if they buy in an "as is" condition. You can expect half of your existing renters to become buyers of their apartments.

After computing all the potential costs of conversion, if you find that the project has the profit potential to make it worth pursuing, your work is just beginning. You need to know what building and zoning restrictions may apply to your building as a condominium that did not apply as a rental apartment. Such restrictions as number of parking spaces per apartment, maximum acceptable square footage or zoning in general may stop what had the potential of a profitable venture.

If your complex is a small one, costs may be prohibitive. As an example, an attorney will be needed to prepare your sales contracts and declaration of condominium documents. The work involved in preparing these documents is the same regardless of the size of the complex or the number of units it contains. This expense will be divided among the apartment units. General operating expenses of the building during conversion will usually be covered by the rent paid by tenants still on a lease basis in the building.

You should have a source of additional financing available besides your interim mortgage. This financing is referred to as "take out" mortgages, individual apartment mortgages that are available to qualified purchasers who cannot afford to pay all cash for their apartment. The lender furnishing the interim mortgage will frequently also offer the take out mortgages. Forget about retaining land or recreation leases on your project. They are becoming a thing of the past and most buyers will not accept them.

It is common practice to offer a tenant a discount of say 10 percent if he wants to purchase his, or any other, unit in the complex. Ideally, if you could convert all of your tenants to buyers, the conversion would be an immediate financial success. Interim mortgage money is currently in the 15 percent range. This means that an apartment selling for $35,000 may be costing you as much as $5250 in interest charges if it is 100 percent leveraged and it takes you one year to sell it. As you can see, giving a tenant a $3500 or 10 percent discount, releases that portion of the interim mortgage immediately upon closing and can save you up to $5250 in interest costs.

Since you figured a certain amount for renovation, you can afford to give your tenants an even larger discount if they buy their unit in an "as is" condition. Most converters expect 25 to 50 percent of their existing tenants to become buyers.

Office Condos

Not only apartment buildings can be converted into condos. There is a trend toward converting office buildings into condos. Each tenant purchases his own office suite. The formula and method works much the same as in a rental building. The professional who buys his own office space has all of the advantages any other type of real estate ownership offers: appreciation, tax shelter, and mortgage principal reduction. Chapter 18 discusses how a professional can greatly benefit from owning his own office building. This same benefit applies to the professional who purchases his own office condo.

Two Cautions About Converting

First, because of the tremendous trend toward converting rental apartment buildings to condos, many local governments and even entire states have, or are considering, legislation to restrict conversions. They are requiring a lengthy notice be given to tenants on an intent to convert. Some areas are stopping conversions altogether. There are laws that require a certain percentage of the tenants agree to allow a conversion before the owner can convert his building. If you are considering converting your apartment building to condo, check local and state laws first. You can do this prior to hiring an attorney to start the paperwork for conversion.

Secondly, if you choose to sell your units as individual condos instead of an outright sale of the entire complex, you will lose the capital gains treatment of your profit. Instead of paying a maximum of 28 percent capital gains tax on your profit, you will be taxed at ordinary income rates. This could take 50 percent or more of your profit. IRS in this case considers you a dealer, just as if you had subdivided acreage and sold off individual lots.

There is a way of avoiding this pitfall, through the use of a separate corporate structure. A knowledgeable tax specialist can offer you suggestions.

One final comment on condo conversions. If you own an apartment complex that is in a good condo market area and you want to do some speculating, look into the possibility of converting, but seek professional assistance. Your building could be worth considerably more than if it is sold as a rental apartment building.

HOW THE ENDOWMENT POLICY CAN BE A LUCRATIVE WAY TO START YOUR INVESTMENT PROGRAM

This may not sound like a real estate investment, but it is. What you are about to read could be worth 10 times what you paid for this book. We talked earlier about life insurance policies and the money that is tied up in "cash value" in some of these policies. Some insurance companies have gotten away from promoting an endowment type policy, but they are still popular.

Let's assume you are trying to build a fund or endowment for use in the future. We'll assume that in 15 years you want to have available to you, a lump-sum cash payment. It may be a retirement fund for yourself or a college fund for your child. Suppose, when your child is one year old, you take out a typical life insurance endowment policy on him with the idea that when he turns 16 years of age, the policy will be paid up and will have a cash value of $19,000 that can be used for college expenses.

You are buying a $15,000 life insurance policy on your child that is also building up a cash value for use 15 years from now. This policy will cost you $80.63 per month for the next 15 years (180 months).

In sixteen years, if you surrender the life insurance policy, the insurance company will pay you $19,035. But, don't forget, you made 180 payments of $80.63 or a total of $14,513.00 during the fifteen year period. Subtracting your contribution, you'll see that the insurance company has only paid you $4522 profit or somewhere between a 3 and 4 percent return on your investment. It does have two advantages, however. It is a forced savings program for those with very little excess cash and it does provide life insurance coverage for the child until it is cashed in. Low cost term insurance, however, also offers the latter benefit at a much lower rate. These figures, incidentally, were furnished by a senior agent of one of the country's largest life insurance companies.

Now, let's look at an alternate endowment policy. You find a small house that you can purchase for say $28,000. You arrange for 90 percent financing through a conventional lender and perhaps, partially by means of the seller of the home carrying a second mortgage (most lenders will not consider a 90 percent mortgage unless you intend to make the home your primary residence).

Your cash investment then is $2800 on the remaining 10 percent of the purchase price not covered by the mortgages. To this investment, we'll add on an additional $1200 to cover the closing costs on the purchase. Your total investment is $4000 and that is *all* you will ever invest in this "endowment policy."

Your mortgages are on a 15 year amortization schedule so that in 15 years you own the house free and clear. How do you pay the expenses? You find someone who wants to rent the house. Your expenses are estimated at $295 a month, including mortgage principal and interest payments. All you need is a tenant who will be willing to pay $300 a month and the house carries itself, expense-wise.

You already know that in 15 years you will have paid off the mortgage on your $28,000 house. But, you have something else going for you, property appreciation. Market value of houses has been increasing 8 to 10 percent a year. Let's be ultraconservative and assume your house will only appreciate three percent each year. In 15 years, the house will have a market value in excess of $43,000 and your total investment was only $4000. The mortgage is also paid off. At this point, you can sell the house or refinance it to get "tax-free" cash for your college fund and keep the house.

I told you that this bit of information could be worth 10 times what you paid for this book! You may want to start your investment program just this way. It's easy to understand and manage, and offers the least initial cash investment requirements.

6

What Forms of Real Estate Ownership Are Available to You

Until now, all of our discussion concerning the purchase of a real estate investment has been based on individual ownership. This is probably the most common form of investing. Most people are familiar with individual ownership because they already own a home. When they decide to get involved in investment real estate, individual ownership is the first approach that comes to mind. There are, however, various other methods of taking title to a real estate investment. We will briefly cover some of the more common types and examine what each has to offer.

Before venturing into any of these forms of ownership, you should seek professional advice to determine which method may be best for you. Tax and legal complications are not covered in this chapter.

PARTNERSHIP: ONE WAY TO OWN A LARGER PROPERTY THAN YOU ALONE COULD AFFORD

Many times, two or more investors will join together and form a partnership to buy property. They will each invest a sum of money and share proportionately in the returns produced by the investment. This allows the average investor the opportunity to be part owner in a larger property than he could have purchased by himself.

There are drawbacks to a partnership arrangement. Partners tend to have disagreements as to the operation of the property. For example, one partner feels he is doing all the work in maintaining or managing the building. Perhaps one feels the building needs painting and the other does not feel they should spend the money.

One way to avoid these unpleasant situations is to find a partner who will allow you to buy controlling interest (over 50 percent) of the investment. Your agreement should allow him to sell his partnership interest at a current market value if he wants out. You will also want the partnership agreement to give you first right of refusal to purchase his interest at whatever price he was able to obtain from an outside investor.

Some partnerships work well, but some of the best priced properties I have found for sale have been a result of partnership disagreements. Since it is not possible to itemize every possible area for disagreement and how it is to be resolved, any partnership agreement must carry with it the good faith of the partners themselves.

CORPORATE OWNERSHIP: TWO MAJOR DRAWBACKS FOR THE INVESTOR

A private corporation in most states is relatively easy to set up. A simple, private corporation is usable as an investment vehicle. There are two primary drawbacks to a corporate form of ownership. First, you are subject to double taxation. The profits of the corporation are subject to income tax and, if you take profits out of the corporation, you will also be taxed. The second drawback to a corporation is that you will not be able to realize the depreciation and tax shelter benefits offered by the investment.

Unless you obtain legal advice to the contrary, you probably will not want to consider the corporate form of investing.

SYNDICATION: THE REAL ESTATE SYNDICATE DOES THE WORK

Syndication generally takes the form of large investment groups who invest in a common pool. The syndicator, a Real Estate Investment Trust

(REIT) or similar group, invests these funds as they see fit, in various real estate investments.

Like buying stock, you have no control in the operation or selection of the investment property although some syndicates make a public offering of a specific investment property. You, at least, have the opportunity of examining the property in which your investment funds will be placed. But, you still have no control over the management or operation of the property.

Each year, a REIT is required to distribute 90 percent of its profits, or more, to the shareholders. By doing so, the trust will not be subject to taxation. Only the individuals who receive shareholder profits will be subject to individual taxation. Thus, the double taxation problem caused by the corporation is avoided as long as the trust continues to qualify for the tax exempt status.

Some REITS ran into financial difficulties in the early seventies recession. It was due in most part to inept management on the part of the trust. They ventured into real estate investments without adequate knowledge of selecting or operating the investments they acquired. Unfortunately, the REITS that were mismanaged, gave all REITS a bad name. There are some reputable REITS in the real estate market, but most of them have tied in with real estate professionals. This overcomes their initial management errors.

Pension trust funds and credit unions also place funds in real estate investments. A few of the larger stock brokerage firms are also venturing into real estate investments. They are beginning to realize the stability of real estate compared with the stock market. Most of these investment groups must be registered with the Securities and Exchange Commission (SEC) and their offerings have to be SEC approved.

LAND TRUSTS: HIGH APPRECIATION POTENTIAL BUT NO INCOME OR TAX BENEFITS

A common vehicle for the purchase of vacant land or acreage is the "land trust." A bank, or individual, is appointed trustee for the investment. Since no management is required for vacant land, the trusteeship is an ideal vehicle to use. Tax consequences are deferred until the property is sold. Land, as pointed out earlier, is for the speculator. It offers a high appreciation potential but no income or tax shelter benefits.

LIMITED PARTNERSHIPS:
THE BEST FORM OF GROUP OWNERSHIP

The limited partnership is probably the best method of group owner-ship of real estate investments. It offers all of the benefits of individual ownership without the management responsibilities, or large individual cash investment. The basic setup follows.

A group of investors is formed to purchase a specific property. Each contributes what he wishes toward the purchase, usually in easy-to-divide shares, such as 10 percent. One of the members of the group, or even an out-sider, becomes the "General Partner" for the group and the investment. He is given all of the decision-making powers for the investment. This includes management, although he may hire a professional management company rather than handle it himself. Everything that happens to the investment is at his sole discretion. He decides when major expenditures are needed, but will usually attempt to get a group opinion first. He determines the optimum time to sell or trade and establish the selling price. It is obvious that he must keep the goals of the group in mind at all times. The group is free to replace the general partner, if they are unhappy with him.

Now, the catch. As general partner, he also assumes total liability for the investment. Were a property to get into major financial difficulties, the cost (or loss) is his responsibility.

The remaining partners in the group are "limited" partners. Their financial obligation is limited only to their initial investment. If the whole in-vestment goes bad, the most they stand to lose is their initial investment.

This raises the question, why would anyone want to be the general partner? First of all, the likelihood of a properly selected and managed prop-erty going bad, is remote. The general partner is usually paid for his ser-vices. He also has a piece of the action, so, it is in his best interest to make the venture profitable.

Real estate brokers will frequently serve as the general partner. A knowledgeable investment Realtor knows the market and can locate the right investment for the group. He has no doubt been counseling each of the members and realized that none of them had sufficient capital to consider in-dividual ownership of an investment. When it is time to sell the investment, the Realtor will likely represent the group as exclusive agent. This is added incentive for him to serve as general partner.

Tax Consequences to the Investor

One of the best features of the limited partnership form of investing is that, properly structured, a limited partnership offers the advantages of a corporation without the drawbacks, such as double taxation. It is able to pass all tax benefits on to the limited partners.

A limited partner investing 10 percent of the capital that was raised to purchase the property, becomes a 10 percent owner of the investment. Each reporting period, as decided by the group, he receives his share of the profits, in this case 10 percent. At the end of each year, he receives a tax statement from the accountant for the group. He is able to take 10 percent of any tax shelter or depreciation benefits resulting from the ownership.

When the property is sold, he receives 10 percent of the total proceeds, after closing costs. In short, he has all of the advantages of individual ownership combined with the advantages of a management free investment.

Selling Your Share

When a partner decides he no longer wishes to retain his share in the partnership, he is free to seek a buyer for it. Selling of a portion of a limited partnership share in a real estate holding is not much different from selling the property itself.

The seller offers his portion to potential investors at what he considers to be a fair market value. This will no doubt be at a price higher than he originally paid. It is still a real estate investment that is appreciating each year. The only difference is that it may only represent a 10 percent interest in the entire project.

Once he has a ready, willing and able buyer to purchase his share at a certain price that is acceptable to him, the other partners will generally have a first right of refusal to buy that share on the same terms and conditions as the offer.

Some Cautions About Limited Partnerships

All members of the group should have the same basic investment goals. An investor who is looking for a high cash flow should not be put with an investor who wants a tax shelter with little or no cash flow produced by the property. Obviously, one property cannot offer both.

Select a knowledgeable individual to act as the general partner. He should also have a partnership interest in the venture so that his profit is tied to the success of the investment.

Determine the guidelines as to the operation of the property at the time the group is founded. This includes basic management policies, optimum holding period, etc.

Using this vehicle, investors with limited investment capital are able to join with others and share proportionately in the profits and tax benefits offered by real estate investments. Without the group, many would not have sufficient capital to become a real estate investor. At the same time, since control is in the hands of the general partner, partnership disagreements are eliminated.

WHY CONSIDER GROUP INVESTMENTS?

There are two primary reasons for considering any group form of investing that has been discussed. First of all, it offers an investor with limited investment capital the opportunity of getting involved in real estate investing. He is able to join forces with others and "pool" resources.

These "groups" as it was pointed out, can be anything from a single partner to a huge, national Real Estate Investment Trust. In the larger, the investor loses individual identity and probably does not even know where his funds are being invested.

The second reason for joining one of the larger groups is to completely divorce yourself from the task of locating, analyzing, purchasing and managing your real estate investment. The syndicate you join does all of that for you. But, then, if you did not want to become personally involved in real estate investing, why are you reading this book?

My recommendation, if you are asking for one, is to make every effort to "go it on your own." When your investment capital is limited, try some of the techniques that are outlined in Chapter 3. Whatever way you have to start, your financial rewards will be greater if you own and manage your own property. It also gives you a feeling of satisfaction to know that you are an investor in real estate and that you did it on your own. Those of you who already have real estate investments know what I mean.

So, use this brief Chapter as a basic background on the types of investment avenues that may be open to you. That's all it was intended to do. Before venturing into any of them, consult your legal advisor.

7

How to Locate
Your Investment Property

You have reached the point of seriously seeking the real estate investment that will best fit your investment goals. It is at this point, if not before, that you should consider whether or not you should employ the services of an investment Realtor.

HOW A REAL ESTATE INVESTMENT COUNSELOR CAN HELP YOU

Why should you consider employing an investment Realtor at all? What can he do for you that you may not be able to do yourself? First of all, if you select the right Realtor, he will be able to guide you from your initial goal setting phase through the selection, acquisition and management of your investment. He should already know everything you will read in this book and a lot more. His services may help make your venture an outstanding real estate investment, especially for the first time investor.

A knowledgeable real estate investment counselor not only understands and practices the many different facets of real estate investing, but he also knows the market. He can guide you into investments that you may never have found on your own. When it comes to negotiating the purchase, he is a middleman, able to get a contract agreement more easily than when a buyer and seller meet face to face.

Notice that I said "knowledgeable real estate investment counselor," not a licensed real estate associate who sells homes in his spare time. There may be many part-time real estate licensees who do not have the qualifications you are looking for in an investment counselor. There are also many full-time real estate sales people who have never been active or have never become knowledgeable in the field of investment real estate. A house salesperson is *not* what you want.

The Realtor you want has been schooled in real estate investing, taxation, depreciation, management, financing and exchanging. He is experienced in this field because it is his only business, not the house market. He knows he cannot do both and do them well. Just knowing the house markets or the investment markets are full-time jobs by themselves. If you need brain surgery, you don't go to a general practitioner, you find a specialist. Since you are about to invest the largest sum of money you have ever spent, it deserves the same special care.

How do you find this Realtor? Contact your local Board of Realtors and ask if they have members who have taken the National Association of Realtors' investment courses. They will probably be able to tell you who in their membership specializes in commercial and investment real estate, *full time*, and who has the background education in that field.

Although normal custom seems to dictate that a Realtor is employed by and paid by the seller, there is nothing wrong with you, as a buyer, employing him to find your investment and you paying him his professional fee. He then represents you and is obligated to purchase the property you want at the lowest price and best terms. As a practical matter, it's the buyer who pays the Realtor anyway, because the seller will not accept a purchase offer that is not high enough to net him what he wants, after the real estate professional fee has been paid.

The investment guidance you can receive from an investment Realtor is well worth what you pay him.

DOING IT ON YOUR OWN

Where do you begin if you choose *not* to employ a Realtor? Following "for sale by owner" ads is probably going to be your primary source of available investments. Although most ads do not tell you much, you can contact the owner and get enough questions answered over the phone to determine if it is worth pursuing.

You will rarely see "for sale" signs on investment properties, as you do with houses, because most owners do not want their tenants to know that their building is for sale.

A Word of Caution On This Point

You will have occasion to walk around a property that is for sale. *Don't* talk to the tenants, and especially, don't tell them the building is for sale and that you're considering buying it. You stand an excellent chance of having the owner take the property off the market and refusing to sell, just to prove to his tenants that it is not for sale.

Most owners seem to feel that if their tenants find out the building is for sale, they'll all move out. This, of course, is not true, but don't try to convince the owner of that. The odds are that every tenant in his building knew it was for sale within one hour after he offered it the first time, anyway.

How else can you find an investment property?

WAYS TO LOCATE PROBLEM PROPERTIES

You may have an interest in purchasing a "problem" property. There are several ways of locating one. Perhaps we should discuss the term "problem" property. They are not necessarily bad investments. They may be poorly maintained, poorly managed or have continual vacancies. Perhaps financial problems or owner problems are creating the situation.

Here are a few common reasons an investment property may be for sale:

1. Death of the owner or the settling of an estate. These properties are generally priced at fair market value or below so the estate can be settled quickly. There is no easy way to locate these properties.
2. Partnership disputes. Some of the most reasonably priced investments on the market are a result of two or more partners who are disagreeing and want to dissolve their partnership.
3. Financing problems with the property. Perhaps the present owner is facing a balloon mortgage in a few months and does not have the

money to pay it off. If he cannot refinance the property before the balloon is due, he may lose the property through foreclosure.

4. Run down properties. This usually indicates either financial or management problems and may be your clue to a well priced investment. What causes a property to be neglected?

5. Vacancies. An apartment building with continual vacancies is probably creating a financial burden on the owner. He, therefore, is letting the property deteriorate, which in turn, will create more vacancies. He may be willing to sell. When you did not see a property or are unsure of vacancy problems in any buildings, watch the "for rent" ads in the newspaper. When a building is continually running "for rent" ads, it may have vacancy problems. "For rent" signs always on the property may be another indication. But, don't be fooled. Some owners keep a sign up or run continual ads, especially on larger properties to be certain they have a tenant lined up when the next vacant apartment becomes available.

   When you find a building that always has vacancies, try to analyze the reason. Are rents too high, the building run down, poor management, etc. Perhaps a change in the type of tenants will keep the building occupied, like catering to elderly, or families with small children, or converting to all "swinging singles" etc. In Chapter 14 we will discuss the renting of apartments in more detail.

6. Management may be the second reason a building is run down. This usually occurs in one of the two ways. The owner is "milking" his investment. In other words, getting all he can out of it without putting anything back. He is failing to realize that eventually, it will catch up with him and he will have a difficult time turning his building and profit picture, around again.

   The other possible problem caused by management is where the owner has hired someone to manage his building for him. Perhaps he lives in another city or state. The manager is getting by doing as little as possible and the physical appearance of the property is beginning to suffer.

7. Length of Ownership. How long has the present owner had the building? When he has owned it for quite a few years, he has probably used up all of his tax shelter benefits and may have an interest in selling. You can find out how long the present owner has owned his property by checking the recorded deed at the courthouse.

8. Courthouse sales or sale of foreclosed properties by local lending in-

stitutions are additional sources of investments, but it is a foregone conclusion that you are buying problems. Even if the price is a bargain, this type of investment is not recommended for a beginning investor, contrary to the advice you'll find in some of the "Get Rich Quick" books you have read. You want your first few investments to be as trouble free as possible.

TRY THE DIRECT APPROACH TO LOCATING A PROPERTY

Suppose all these approaches fail to turn up an investment that looks interesting to you. Try a direct approach. Find a building that you would like to own, and appears to be in the size range you want. Find the owner and ask him if he'd consider selling it to you. Many properties are bought this way. If he says no, ask him if he knows of any other similar properties that may be for sale.

How to Locate the Owner

How do you find out who owns a specific property? Your county assessors office has complete records of all deed transfers. This information is a matter of public record and is available to anyone. To locate a specific property you will probably need the legal description. Your courthouse also has Plat Books available. Plat Books are area maps giving the legal description you need. Most tax rolls are indexed by the property legal description. The tax roll will tell you who owns the property and his mailing address. It may even tell when he purchased it.

While you are there, look up the recorded deed on the property. You will learn exactly when the property was purchased and usually the purchase price can be determined by the documentary stamps on the deed. Also recorded, are the complete details on any mortgages that may be on the property, including the possible balloon mortgage we discussed. A wealth of information is available at the courthouse. They have a staff to help familiarize you with locating information—don't be afraid to ask for help.

GIVE YOURSELF A CHOICE

As difficult as locating a good investment may be, do not limit yourself to just one choice. You should have at least two that, on the surface, seem to meet your investment requirements. You can then compare the two in complete detail to determine which is the best one for you.

You may also find that you are unable to purchase your first choice in a way that is acceptable to you. It is nice to have a second possibility to fall back on. Along these lines, once you have determined in your own mind, and on paper, the maximum you are willing to pay and the most restrictive terms you can accept, *do not* compromise your position. If you cannot purchase the property on terms that you can live with, drop it and find another property. This is on the assumption, however, that your purchase requirements are reasonable ones and in conformance with the current market situation.

Everyone would like to buy investment real estate at 25 percent less than current market values, but if you hold out for that non-existent bargain, you may never buy anything.

WHY NOT WAIT FOR LOWER INTEREST RATES?

This brings us to the investor who is waiting for mortgage interest rates to go down before he buys. In the first place, that probability is remote. Were interest rates to go down, the rate decrease will be a small one.

Let's assume that Pete Harris wanted to invest $30,000 in a small, $100,000 apartment building. In order to purchase the building, he had to obtain a new first mortgage, but since interest rates were 10 percent, he thought he'd wait until they went down. Sure enough, one year later, they had dropped to nine percent. How much did Pete save? Had he purchased the building a year sooner, he would have paid $100,000 for the property. His new $70,000, 10 percent mortgage would cost him approximately $7000 the first year in interest.

Now, one year later, that same building has appreciated five percent in value, so it will cost him $105,000 to purchase it. What did he save in interest payments? At nine percent interest, his annual interest payment his first year will be about $6300 or $700 less than on the ten percent mortgage. He will pay $5000 more for the building in order to save $700 in interest. And, as his rents increase, and his mortgage is paid down, that one percent difference in interest rates becomes less and less important.

Now that you have some ideas on where to find an investment you need to consider other factors.

HOW IMPORTANT IS LOCATION?

It has often been said that the three most important considerations in buying real estate are: Location, location and location. This is most certainly true in purchasing a home but may or may not always be true when purchasing investment real estate.

The most important fact to remember in purchasing a real estate investment is that you are buying a "money making machine." The property that may be of interest to you may not be in the best part of town, but it does offer the investment benefits you want . . . return on invested capital or cash flow, tax shelter, and appreciation. Don't let the location steer you away from an otherwise sound investment simply because you would not want to live there yourself. Your purpose for investing is to make money, to build your estate. Chances are, you'll sell or exchange that property within five to seven years anyway, and get into something larger.

I'm not suggesting that you pick the worst area in town for your acquisition. You want your investment to be located in an area that, from all indications, is appreciating. Examine the general trends of the area. Get a feel for which direction it is heading.

Check with local zoning authorities if you have questions about the area. They can tell you of any intended major changes, such as roadways, that may be planned. When you have logical reason to believe the area is a questionable one, do not invest there.

One advantage in investment real estate as opposed to your personal residence is that the door is virtually wide open when it comes to location and type of property you select. Your most important consideration is, does it meet your investment goals, such as spendable income, tax shelters and appreciation potential. If it meets these goals, physical location of the property may be secondary. Let's look at some examples.

Mr. Johnson is looking for a moderate investment in real estate. He saw a six unit apartment building that was run down. The price of the property, because of its condition and vacancies, was a good one. Mr. Johnson purchased the property with a low down payment, spent an additional few thousand dollars in repairs, redecorating and landscaping and was immediately able to lease the building. A year or two later, he sold the property and made a sizable profit. Mr. Johnson could have passed up that investment opportunity if his first thought would have been, "I sure wouldn't want to live there." But he did not pass it up and it turned out to be an excellent investment.

Now, consider Mr. Brown. His investment needs were quite different. He is not looking for income. He wanted something that, in ten or twenty years, would support him when he no longer had his present income coming in each month. Mr. Brown's investment Realtor recommended he purchase a fifty-acre tract of vacant land in an area that was completely underdeveloped. He visited the site with the Realtor and just shook his head. "This is great for an alligator farm," he said. But he could see the future potential. The land was certainly in the path of progress. So he purchased the land and within ten years, its value had tripled. Mr. Brown was not intimidated by the location.

An ex-merchant seaman once told me that on a stopover in South Florida some twenty-five or thirty years ago, a Realtor contacted him on a Saturday and tried to sell him some Florida land for $1000 an acre. After looking it over his comment was "are you crazy? Who would ever pay $1000 an acre for that pile of sand?" He passed up the offer. You may be interested in knowing that the property he passed up was oceanfront property in the middle of Fort Lauderdale.

Our final investor is Dr. Hendrix. His occupational income has him in an overall tax bracket of 50 percent. In other words, Uncle Sam is getting half of everything he earns. The last thing he needs is a real estate investment that increases his taxable income. Dr. Hendrix needs an investment property that carries itself without adding a large cash income to his present tax situation.

His search is for a sound investment that can be structured to give him a large tax shelter or write-off against his occupational income. Again, his primary research is for the property that meets his needs financially and not necessarily the physical location of the building. He finds a 16-unit apartment complex. Dr. Hendrix may have no desire to live in the building he found. He doesn't expect to. The investment is structured so that it only gives him a three percent pre-tax cash return on his investment, but keep in mind, he is not looking for additional income. This property gives him something else, tax shelter. He will be able to reduce his other taxable income by $20,000 next year. We said that Uncle Sam is getting one half of what he earns. By reducing his taxable income by $20,000, through the depreciation benefits of his real estate investment, he will be able to keep $10,000 of his income (half of $20,000) which he would have had to pay out in income taxes if he had not owned the building.

While location is still important in selecting investment real estate, it is not as critical as the location for your home. Your primary concern is in finding a real estate investment that meets your investment needs and goals. There are out of state investors who never see the property they purchase. They invest based on the financial performance of the investment. Needless to say, these investors are not intimidated by the location of the property. Which brings up the next question.

HOW FAR AWAY SHOULD YOUR INVESTMENT PROPERTY BE?

How far from your residence should your property be located? There are two parts to this answer? When you purchase a rental apartment building close to your home, you can be certain that some of your tenants will find it convenient to stop by on a regular basis and complain. I've known some investors who hire a resident manager and he is the only one who knows the owner's name and address. One such investor actually lives in his own apartment building but the only one who knows that he owns the building is his manager. There is another thing to be said about living too close to your investment. Your property will probably go on for years with few, if any, problems, but if you are in a position to see it regularly, you will undoubtedly see things going on that you don't like. I'm not talking about major problems that will affect the appearance of the building or the peace of the tenants, but unimportant things that have no effect on the security or operation of the property.

What about the other extreme? How far away can you live from your investment? This depends on three factors, the size of the investment, the type of investment and the amount of management you have. Since they are all intertwined, we'll look at all of them together.

A small property being managed by you, should be close enough to make it convenient for you to visit the building to show vacant apartments or attend to problems. You do not want to drive for an hour each time you have a prospective tenant who wants to see an apartment. Employing a resident manager to handle these problems will allow you to increase this distance.

If your investment is a large one, where resident management handles everything, you can live in a different city or state if you wish. The same holds true for easy to manage properties such as sale/leasebacks or even small investments with one or two tenants on long-term net leases. In case you have forgotten, if the lease is a "net" lease to the landlord, the tenant is responsible for all operating expenses and repairs.

Many investors, owning fully managed larger properties, never see them. They live out of state, even out of the country, and rely on the management team to handle their investments. Any why shouldn't they? Their property managers are probably more qualified to manage the property than the investor himself. You do not live in Detroit simply because you own General Motors stock and you need to look at their buildings on a regular basis.

PROPERTY DETAILS TO CHECK

You have now located the investment property that you feel has what you want and it's appropriately named *The Always Full Apartments*. Before you get involved with the analysis of income and expenses in the next Chapter, you need to find out more about it. Although the sample property analysis form in the next Chapter contains most of the items that are of interest to you, let's discuss them and some that are not on the analysis form, and see why they are important.

Age of the Property

When the property is older, repairs or appliance replacement expenses may be expected in the near future. This should be taken into consideration in the price you are willing to pay for the property. An older building, on the other hand, will offer a higher depreciation rate and, therefore, a larger tax write-off. If tax sheltering of other income is your primary goal, do not pass up an older building just because some repairs or replacements are needed. Those expenses can be written off to increase your tax shelter. Assuming you are in a 50 percent tax bracket, for example, you are only spending 50 cents for repairs—Uncle Sam is contributing the other 50 cents. This makes the cost of repairs quite inexpensive.

Rental History

Look at a property that is a few years old. Has it enjoyed a high occupancy level over the past few years? What happened to its occupancy or rent level during the period of economic slowdown?

Three Easy Tests to Determine Whether a Building is Fully Leased: There are three easy and inconspicuous ways of finding out whether or not the building is fully leased. I stress *inconspicuous* because you do not want to alert the tenants that something is going on.

1. The least accurate check is to look at names on the mailboxes. Blank slots may indicate vacant apartments. This is the least accurate check because many landlords will leave an old tenant's name on the mail slot until the apartment is re-rented.
2. A more accurate check is to look in the meter room. Where each apartment is individually metered for electric. See how many meters have been turned off by the power company, indicating those apartments are unoccupied.
3. The final check is designed for the night owl. Drive by the building at three or four o'clock in the morning and see if all the parking spaces are filled. This test won't work during the day because most of the tenants are usually gone.

This inspection also gives you an idea of the quality of tenants in the building. When the lot is filled with junkers, hot rods, and motorcycles, don't expect the building to be occupied by wealthy, retired people.

Neighborhood

What kind of properties surround the building you are considering acquiring? Is yours the only well kept building on the street? You may have trouble keeping it that way. Deteriorating areas are usually followed by difficulty in renting apartments and, therefore, vacancies climb.

Building Condition

What is the physical condition of the building? Your contract to purchase should give you, at your expense, the option of having at least a roof and termite inspection made by a licensed inspector. Are the apartments well maintained? This will not only tell you what repairs you may be facing, but will also give you an indication of the type of tenants that are renting the apartments.

Lot and Building Sizes

This information, along with the present zoning on the property, gives you an indication as to whether or not the property is being put to highest and best use. Perhaps, at a future date, you will be able to add additional rental units on the property.

Sewers

Is the property serviced by sewers and are all assessments paid for.

Amenities

It was pointed out earlier that amenities such as clubhouse, swimming pool, tennis courts, and coin laundries affect how your property can compete with other rentals in the area. Major amenities, such as tennis courts and swimming pools, however, cannot be justified on smaller complexes. Consider a swimming pool, for example. Suppose it costs $15,000 to install and you capitalize that cost over five years. Your building expenses just increased by $3,000 a year or $250.00 a month. Pool service costs another $100.00 a month. You are now increasing your operating expenses by $350.00 a month by offering your tenants a swimming pool.

A 100-unit apartment building can amortize that $350 over 100 units—$3.50 per month in increased rents per apartment will cover the cost of the pool. Now, consider a 10-unit apartment building. You would have to increase rents $35.00 a month on each apartment to cover the cost. This indicates that, unless you can only rent your apartments by having a swimming pool, you cannot justify the cost.

Parking

In today's society, parking has become a serious problem. Almost every family in America has at least one car. Unless the building you are considering has at least one parking space for each apartment, plus a proportionate number of "guest" parking spaces, you'd better think twice. One and one half to two parking spaces per unit are desirable, but not necessary. Check local zoning—does the building comply with parking regulations?

Where the complex is situated on a major street, do all or part of the parking spaces front on the street? If they do, what happens to your parking if the street is widened?

Furnished or Unfurnished

There is something to be said both for and against furnished apartments. First, the good news. Furnished apartments usually demand a higher rent. Since furniture has a relatively short life, it can be depreciated more quickly and offer the investor a greater tax shelter. This will be covered more in a later chapter.

Now for the bad news. Furnished apartments deteriorate more quickly. The furniture will not last too many years and tenants will not be as careful with your furniture as they are their own. Tenants in furnished apartments tend to be less stable. It's easy for them to pack up and move, so they do. A tenant who has to hire a moving company will probably think twice, unless circumstances other than finding a better place for less money are his motivating factors.

These basic details concerning the property you want to purchase will add to your evaluation of the investment.

The ''comment'' section on the sample analysis form, illustrated in the next Chapter, can be used to make any notes that will help you remember this particular property. When you have looked at several, they all begin to blend together unless you make notes of what first caught your eye on each. It has already been suggested that you should carry a Polaroid Camera with you. It still holds true that a picture is worth 10,000 words.

Your are now ready to gather the income, expense and financing information from the seller and make your own analysis of the property to determine how much you can afford to pay for the *Always Full Apartments*.

8

A Step-by-Step Guide
to Preparing a Financial Analysis
of Your Property

This chapter is the most important one in this entire book. It covers, step-by-step, the process by which you can analyze an investment property and determine just how good an investment it will be for you. Follow the procedures outlined here to make the complete analysis. *Do not* rely on short cuts. Once completed, this analysis is the best method of making your investment decision. It tells you what you need to know to make that decision. Learn *and use* the analysis formula. Your investment decisions will be more soundly made if you do.

As you proceed through the various phases of analyzing a property, do not be critical of the rental rates or breakdown of operating expenses that are used in the examples. The figures, although from hypothetical case studies, are based on typical "real world" applications.

Income and expenses will vary from area to area, but the basic formulas that are presented to analyze a property are universal. When analyzing properties, you will learn the rental rates and average operating expenses that are common in your particular area.

OBTAINING THE COMPLETE INFORMATION

So far, the property you like has met all of the qualifications that have been discussed to this point. Now comes the real test. How does the investment stack up financially? You meet with Mr. Seller, the owner of the *Always Full Apartments*. He gives you the following information on the property:

Purchase Price

The price he wants is $155,000. It is at this point that an interesting process takes place. The seller is no doubt convinced that he is practically "giving" his building away at the $155,000 offering price. The building has to be worth much more than he is asking and he'll probably have a long list of reasons to prove it. These may include such things as:

1. The 8-unit building down the street sold last year for $165,000 and the *Always Full Apartments* is a much more attractive building.
2. Due to inflation, his building has appreciated far more than the price he is asking.
3. His rents are the lowest on the street. Next year, when you own the building, you will be able to increase your gross income by at least 10 percent.
4. Mr. Seller can produce paid bills showing he spent over $15,000 in repairs last year.

The list is endless. What he really means is that he likes his building, he is not overly motivated to sell and he wants to make as much profit as possible.

As a practical matter, it is up to you to determine just how overpriced his property really is, if it is at all. Surprisingly, many sellers offer their property at a fair market value or below. You may want to remember this when you become the seller. Here is the reason he may price it too low:

Assume that Mr. Seller purchased the *Always Full Apartments* eight years ago for $85,000. The difference between $85,000 and his $155,000 asking price is $70,000. He will realize a $70,000 pre-tax profit on the sale. This is difficult for many investors to comprehend—$70,000 profit for just sitting eight years and waiting. His property may really be worth much more, but even this price seems unbelieveable to him. Because he is overwhelmed by the profit picture, he may be doing himself a disservice and not know it.

At a future date when you sell, you will not have that problem. You know how to establish a fair market value on your property, or you will know by the time you finish this book. But, for now, you are the buyer, not the seller. This brings us to the second part of the interesting process that is taking place.

No matter how low the price is set on an investment offering, if you are a typical buyer, your first impulse is that the property is overpriced. Most buyers automatically assume that a seller puts a higher price on his property than he ever expects to obtain. "It leaves him room to negotiate."

You should be a little different type of buyer. You can analyze the investment and determine how much it is worth, at least to you. It should be compared with the others that you are considering. Maybe it is not overpriced compared with everything else on the market. This means you that will have to be reasonable on your judgement. If you only buy at bargain prices, you may not be able to buy anything.

Present First Mortgage Balance

The present first mortgage balance is $73,500 at 7.5 percent with just under 20 years remaining. His monthly principal, interest and escrow payment is $840.00. Mr. Seller also indicates that he will consider carrying a second mortgage and accepting $45,000 down payment. In a later chapter, you'll see why it is to his benefit to do so.

Number of Units

The building has six 1 bedroom/1 bath apartments renting for $228.00 a month and two 2 bedroom/2 bath apartments renting for $256.00 a month, for a total of eight units.

What You Should Know About Apartment Types

We should briefly discuss various types of apartments at this point. We all understand one, two or three bedroom apartments, but there are a couple of others that often show up in a rental apartment building.

The first is the efficiency or studio apartment. It generally consists of one large room that serves as the living room, dining area, bedroom and kitchen. The kitchen is usually in a "closet" arrangement that can be closed up and hidden from sight when not in use. Of course, they have a separate bathroom. Efficiencies are usually rented furnished because they attract young couples or singles who have no furniture.

The other type of rental unit, "hotel rooms", bears careful consideration if the building you want to buy contains one or more. Contrary to what you may expect, hotel rooms do not show up only in hotels and motels. The owner of a rental apartment building often includes hotel rooms as part of the total number of apartment units he is selling. Hotel rooms are most often a second bedroom/bath combination that can be separated from what would normally be a two bedroom/two bath apartment. Double locking doors between the units, as in adjoining rooms in a motel, give each tenant security. So, if you think you are buying an 8-unit building, but two of the units are hotel rooms, do not give them as much value as you would a full-size apartment. Because they contain no cooking facilities and are rented furnished, tenant turnover can be frequent.

Rental Income

Total rental income is $22,560 a year, fully rented, and according to Mr. Seller, he never has a vacancy.

Taxes

His Real Estate taxes are $2,350 a year. You had better make certain that is the current tax bill and not one that is a year or two old. If he cannot produce his copy of the current tax bill, call the county tax collector's office and request the information. Like recorded deeds, it's a matter of public record.

Insurance

The insurance is $580.00. Again, request a copy of the policy and make certain his coverage is adequate for you. When he has owned the property for several years and has not updated his coverage, it may be well below the current value of the improvements. Notice that only the improvements (buildings) are covered by insurance. Even if the buildings burned to the ground, the land value is not affected. (Unless current zoning changes, and they will not allow the same structure to be replaced.) You may want your insurance agent to review the policy—insurance can be complicated.

Electric

Electric, for house lights only is $140.00 a year. The tenants pay their own apartment electric.

Water and Sewer

Water and sewer costs run $30.00 a month. (Don't forget to convert that to annual cost of $360.00 a year.)

Licenses

Licenses are $25.00 a year.

Mr. Seller says he does all his own repairs and maintenance so it only costs him about $150.00 a year. It is important for you to obtain itemized income and expenses. Only by seeing an item by item breakdown of each source of income and each expense can you first determine if they are in line with other properties you have examined and secondly, you are able to pick out which ones are too high or too low. Do not accept "blanket" figures from the owner.

HOW TO PREPARE THE PROPERTY ANALYSIS FORM

You are now ready to analyze the investment. Each item is filled in on the analysis sheet, Figure 8-1. This same analysis form can be used for any type of income producing real estate. The numbers will vary, expense wise, for office buildings, shopping centers, etc., but the same formula still applies.

Step 1:   Fill in the Data You Have Gathered About the Property

First, fill in all the information that you gathered (in the previous Chapter) including any comments you may have in observing the potential investment. Remember, the more details you write down, the easier it will be for you to remember what the property looked like. Take some polaroid pictures as well.

• PROPERTY ANALYSIS •

Name: _ALWAYS FULL APTS._

Location: _147 NE 8TH ST._

Type of Property: _8 UNIT APT. BLDG_   Area: _____

LIST PRICE ___155,000___

CASH REQ'D. ___81,500___

EXISTING ASSUMABLE FINANCING:

	Amount	Ann. Pmt.	Int.	Years To Go
1st $	73,500	7,150	7½%	19+
2nd	_____	_____	___%	
3rd	_____	_____	___%	

POTENTIAL FINANCING:

				Years
1st $	_____	_____	___%	
2nd	_____	_____	___%	
3rd	_____	_____	___%	

Folio:	Ex — S.O.O		File:
Date:	Units: 8		Lister:
Zoning R-3	Pool NO		Parking 12 CARS
Size 100X150	Rec. Rm NO		A-C YES
Sq. Ft. 6500	Util. Rm. YES		Heat YES
Age 7 YRS	Office NO		T V NO
Stories 2	Lobby NO		Furniture YES
Sewers YES	Elevators NO		Waterfront NO
Constr. CONCRETE & FRAME			

Description —	# Units	Rent Sch
1 BEDROOM, 1 BATH	6	$228/mo.
2 BEDROOM, 2 BATH	2	$256/mo.

		%			COMMENTS:	CODE _____
SCHEDULE GROSS INCOME						
Less. Vacancy & Credit Loss						
GROSS OPERATING INCOME						
Less. Operating Expenses						
Taxes						
Insurance						
Utilities						
Advertising						
Licenses & Permits						
Management						
Payroll & Payroll Taxes						
Supplies						
Services						
Maintenance						
Reserve for Replacement						
Ground Lease						
TOTAL EXPENSES		%				
OPERATING INCOME						
Plus Other Income						
NET OPERATING INCOME					INFORMATION HEREIN IS BELIEVED TO BE ACCURATE BUT IS NOT WARRANTED	

INCOME ADJUSTED TO FINANCING: Actual ☐   Potential ☐   Equity $ _____

NET OPERATING INCOME	Cap. Rate - List Price:			%		
Less. Loan Payment	3rd Loan	2nd Loan	1st Loan	TOTAL		
Interest						
Principal						
Total Loan Payment						
GROSS SPENDABLE INCOME	Rate:	%	(GSI ÷ EQUITY)			
Plus. Principal Payment						
GROSS EQUITY INCOME	Rate:	%	(GEI ÷ EQUITY)			
Less. Depreciation	Personal Property	Improvements				
REAL ESTATE TAXABLE INCOME						

* Based on Form "B," copyrighted by REALTORS NATIONAL MARKETING INSTITUTE OF NATIONAL ASSOCIATION OF REALTORS. Copyright 1974. All rights reserved. Used with permission of copyright owner.

** Reprinted with permission of L.C. Judd & Co., Inc.

Figure 8-1

Step 2:   Include Purchase Price and Financing

Next, proceed with the actual analysis, starting with purchase price and financing. Mr. Seller wants $155,000 for his property and he told you that his first mortgage payment was $840 a month, including his escrow payment for real estate taxes and insurance. You need to remove the escrow portion from the total mortgage payment. You'll see why in a few minutes. His mortgage payment is $840 a month:

$840	monthly payment
× 12	months
$10,080	a year including principal, interest, taxes and insurance
Less: $2,350	Taxes
580	Insurance
− $ 2,930	
$ 7,150	Principal and Interest Payment

This information is inserted in the upper left-hand corner of your analysis form. Although Mr. Seller indicated he would carry a second mortgage, do not consider that for a moment.

Step 3:   Calculate Scheduled Gross Income

Referring to Figure 8-2, you next fill in the income and expenses that were given to you by Mr. Seller. Property analysis forms are always figured using a full year's (12 months) income and expense operation. Since income and expenses may vary from month to month, this is the only accurate way to analyze a property. You will also want to make a couple of modifications in the figures he gave you.

Income:	6 Apartments @ $228/Mo.	=	$1,368.00
	2 Apartments @ $256/Mo.	=	$ 512.00
	Total Monthly Rent	=	$1,880.00
	$1,880/Mo. × 12 Months	=	$22,500/Year

This is your Scheduled Gross Income, the total potential rental income the building would produce if it were 100 percent leased at all times.

Name: *ALWAYS FULL APTS.*

Location: *147 NE 8TH ST*

Type of Property: *8 UNIT APT. BLDG* Area:

LIST PRICE __155,000__

CASH REQ'D. __81,500__

EXISTING ASSUMABLE FINANCING:

	Amount	Ann. Pmt.	Int.	Years To Go
1st $	73,500	7,150	7½ %	19+
2nd			%	
3rd			%	

POTENTIAL FINANCING:

				Years
1st $			%	
2nd			%	
3rd			%	

Folio:	Ex — S.O.O	File:
Date:	Units: 8	Lister:
Zoning R-3	Pool NO	Parking 12 CARS
Size 100×150	Rec. Rm. NO	A-C YES
Sq. Ft. 6500	Util. Rm. YES	Heat YES
Age 7 YRS	Office NO	TV NO
Stories 2	Lobby NO	Furniture YES
Sewers YES	Elevators NO	Waterfront NO
Constr. CONCRETE & FRAME		

Description —	# Units	Rent Sch
1 BEDROOM, 1 BATH	6	$223/mo.
2 BEDROOM, 2 BATH	2	$256/mo.

SCHEDULE GROSS INCOME		22	560
Less: Vacancy & Credit Loss 5%		1	128
GROSS OPERATING INCOME		21	432
Less: Operating Expenses			
Taxes	2 350		
Insurance	580		
Utilities ELECTRIC	140		
Advertising			
Licenses & Permits	25		
Management			
Payroll & Payroll Taxes	1 200		
Supplies			
Services WATER/SEWER	360		
Maintenance 5%	1 072		
Reserve for Replacement			
Ground Lease			
LAWN SERVICE	720		
TOTAL EXPENSES 30 %		6	447
OPERATING INCOME		14	985
Plus Other Income		-0-	
NET OPERATING INCOME		14	985

COMMENTS: CODE _____

INFORMATION HEREIN IS BELIEVED TO BE
ACCURATE BUT IS NOT WARRANTED

INCOME ADJUSTED TO FINANCING: Actual ☐ Potential ☐ Equity: $

NET OPERATING INCOME	Cap. Rate - List Price:		%			
Less: Loan Payment	3rd Loan	2nd Loan	1st Loan	TOTAL		
Interest						
Principal						
Total Loan Payment						
GROSS SPENDABLE INCOME	Rate: %		(GSI ÷ EQUITY)			
Plus: Principal Payment						
GROSS EQUITY INCOME	Rate: %		(GEI ÷ EQUITY)			
Less: Depreciation Personal Property		Improvements				
REAL ESTATE TAXABLE INCOME						

Figure 8-2

Step 4: Enter Vacancy Allowance

Although Mr. Seller insists he never has vacancies, you decide to be cautious and allow five percent of the scheduled gross income for vacancy allowance (5% of $22,560 is $1,128/Year). You will, in your neighborhood research, have a "feel" for the average vacancies that you can expect in the *Always Full Apartments*. If you run less than five percent vacant during the year, it's a bonus to you. This amount is entered in the vacancy and credit loss box. Subtracting the vacancy allowance from the $22,560 scheduled gross income gives you a Gross Operating Income of $21,432.00.

Step 5: Itemize Operating Expenses

Next, you itemize the operating expenses for the building. When you get to Maintenance, recall that Mr. Seller told you that his maintenance cost was only $150 a year. Even if he does everything himself, his time is worth something. Assuming you are willing to work for free, you will still have maintenance expenses from time to time. When an air conditioner or furnace fan motor needs replacing, you cannot create one no matter how handy you may be. You'll have to buy one. It is even a good idea to set aside a portion of each year's income as a reserve for eventual replacement of stoves, refrigerators, water heaters, carpeting, etc. There is a block, directly under "maintenance" for this entry.

Repairs Vesus Capital Improvements: You need to understand the difference between repairs and maintenance and reserve for capital improvements before proceeding. Repairs and maintenance are exactly what the term indicates. When a faucet is leaking and a plumber is needed, that is a repair. Painting the walls of a hallway is a maintenance expense. Repairing a refrigerator is a repair item, but, if the refrigerator cannot be repaired and you have to replace it with a new one, that is a capital expense.

Capital expenses can be anything of major cost, such as replacing instead of repairing a leaking roof, new appliances, new carpeting, adding a swimming pool, etc. Repair and maintenance items are expensed off in the year in which they are paid for, as a general operating expense. Capital improvements, on the other hand, are written off over the projected life of the improvement. Let's assume you re-carpet an apartment and the cost is $500. You expect the new carpeting to last five years, so you expense it off over a five-year period at $100 a year.

The property analysis pro-forma that you are preparing in order to analyze a specific property has an area to "project" any anticipated capital expense you wish. This is a projected estimate only. It *cannot* be written off as part of your building's operating expenses unless it is actually spent for a capital improvement.

It is, however, a good idea to actually set this reserve aside each year so that when one of these major capital improvement expenses comes up, you already have the money in your "building reserve" bank account to pay for it.

Caution—Don't Go Overboard: Be reasonable with your estimates when preparing your property analysis. It is possible to add so much in your pro-forma for repairs, maintenance, and capital improvements, that you will make any investment you analyze appear to be a bad investment. This error can completely defeat your ever getting into a real estate investment . . . and that is not your intention, or the intent of this book.

You decide to allow five percent of your gross operating income for a maintenance allowance, or $1072 a year.

Step 6: Total Anticipated Operating Expenses

Once all the expense items are entered, the column is totaled. The result is $6447 a year in anticipated operating expenses. This number is divided by the Gross Operating Income to determine what percentage of your gross you expect to spend on operating the building:

$$\frac{\$\ 6,447}{\$21,432} \ = \ 30\%$$

You expect your operating expenses to run 30 percent of your gross operating income. Note that this property is located in Fort Lauderdale, Florida. In northern cities, where taxes are higher and the landlord pays for heating, expenses may be 50 percent or more of the gross operating income.

Step 7: Calculate Net Operating Income or N.O.I.

Subtracting the $6447 expenses from your $21,432 gross operating income, gives you a Net Operating Income or N.O.I. of $14,985.00.

If you bought this building for $155,000 cash with no mortgages, this would be your pre-tax spendable income or cash flow. You will see a couple of lines which allow room for "other income." This can be from sources such as coin laundries, etc. I personally prefer to consider those miscellaneous incomes as a bonus and not figure them into the overall income of the building that you expect to receive.

Step 8: Adjust N.O.I. to Financing

You are now ready to adjust this N.O.I. to the financing on the property. At the present time there is an existing first mortgage on the property in the amount of $73,500 at 7.5 percent. The remaining term is not important at this point. The annual principal (or mortgage reduction) and interest payments are $7150. You'll recall you took the escrow (taxes and insurance) portions out of the payment earlier and put them where they belong, under operating expenses.

You next want to separate the principal portion of the payment from the interest portion. The principal portion actually reduces the remaining balance you owe on the mortgage. This increases your equity in the property each year. Even if you sell the building for what you paid for it, a few years down the road, your equity or what you get out of the sale has increased because you have been paying down the mortgage.

An Easy Way to Separate Principal and Interest Payments: Here is a simple way to separate the two. Multiply the remaining principal balance on the mortgage by the interest rate ($73,500 × .075 (or 7½%) = $5,512.00).

This is a close estimate of the amount of interest you will pay during the next year. It will be a little high because your monthly payment actually reduced the balance each month, therefore, reducing the amount of interest paid each month. We'll illustrate this in a minute. This method is accurate enough for your figuring in an analysis. Each year it needs to be refigured based on the new remaining balance on the mortgage. When you buy the property, you will have a mortgage amortization schedule that will give you an accurate month to month principal and interest breakdown.

Your total annual mortgage payment is	$7,150.00
The interest this year was determined to be:	$5,512.00
Subtracting the two, your mortgage balance was reduced during the year by:	$1,638.00

Using an electronic calculator and a lot of time, you can get an accurate principal and interest breakdown by figuring each month during the year, if the mortgage payments accrue monthly. The procedure is as follows:

STEP I

First Month Mortgage Balance	$73,500	
	× .075	(7½ % Interest Rate
	$ 5,512	Annual Interest
divided by	12	Months
	$ 459.33	Interest Paid the 1st Month

STEP II

Monthly Payments	$ 595.33	
Less:	$ 459.33	Interest Portion
	$ 136.50	Principal Paid the 1st Month

STEP III

Beginning Mortgage Balance:		$73,500.00
Less: Principal Paid		
1st Month	=	$ 136.50
Mortgage Balance beginning		
2nd Month	=	$73,363.50

Now, repeat the above steps for the Second Month.

STEP I

Second Month Mortgage Balance	$73,363.50	
	× .075	(7½ % Interest Rate)
	$ 5,502.26	Annual Interest
divided by	12	Months
	$ 458.52	Interest Paid the 2nd Month

STEP II

Monthly Payment	$ 595.83	
Less:	$ 458.52	Interest Portion
	$ 137.31	Principal Paid the 2nd Month

STEP III		
Beginning Mortgage Balance:		
2nd Month		$73,363.50
Less: Principal Paid		
2nd Month	=	$ 137.31
Mortgage Balance beginning		
2nd Month	=	$73,226.19

You must do this each month for the entire year in order to obtain the exact principal to interest breakdown for the year. You'll find an actual breakdown of: Interest paid of $5,455.02 and a total principal payment of $1,694.98. The simplified method we used earlier was off only $56.98 for the year, which is not enough to influence your decision to purchase the property, and, you must admit, it's a lot easier to figure.

Where there is more than one mortgage on the property, follow the same procedure for each. You'll see that you first indicate whether your analysis is based on existing or potential financing. Since this analysis is based on only the existing first mortgage, you mark the approximate box.

Equity and Mortgage Payments: Next, show the amount of equity or cash down payment that is required. You then bring your $14,985 N.O.I. down into the Income Adjusted to Financing section. You'll see the N.O.I. line on the analysis sheet. This is the income produced by the building from which you must deduct the mortgage payments.

The loan payment section allows for three different mortgages, and, each is broken down by interest, principal and total loan payment. All mortgages are then totaled together under the "Total" column so that you know how much interest, principal and total mortgage payments were made during the year.

The building has only the $73,500 mortgage. You determined that $5512 of the total $7150 payment was interest and the remaining $1638 was principal reduction. These are filled in under first loan and then totaled. In this example, since there is only one loan, the "total" column is the same as the "First Loan" column.

Calculating Gross Spendable Income (Cash Flow) and Principal Payment: Next, bring the total payments out in line with the previously entered N.O.I. figure ($14,985) and subtract the two. The resulting amount

• PROPERTY ANALYSIS •

Name *Always Full Apts*

Location *147 NE 8th St*

Type of Property *8 Unit Apt. Bldg.* Area

LIST PRICE *155,000*

CASH REQ'D *81,500*

EXISTING ASSUMABLE FINANCING:

	Amount	Ann Pmt	Int	Years To Go
1st $	73,500	7,150	7½ %	19+
2nd			%	
3rd			%	

POTENTIAL FINANCING

				Years
1st $			%	
2nd			%	
3rd			%	

Folio	Ex — SOO	File
Date	Units: *8*	Lister
Zoning *R-3*	Pool *NO*	Parking *12 cars*
Size *100 X 150*	Rec Rm *NO*	A-C *YES*
Sq Ft *6500*	Util Rm *YES*	Heat *YES*
Age *7 Yrs*	Office *NO*	TV *NO*
Stories *2*	Lobby *NO*	Furniture *YES*
Sewers *YES*	Elevators *NO*	Waterfront *NO*
Constr *Concrete & FRAME*		

Description —	# Units	Rent Sch
1 Bedroom, 1 Bath	6	$228/mo.
2 Bedroom, 2 Bath	2	$256/mo.

				COMMENTS	CODE
SCHEDULE GROSS INCOME		22	600		
Less: Vacancy & Credit Loss 5%		1	128		
GROSS OPERATING INCOME		21	432		
Less. Operating Expenses					
Taxes	2 350				
Insurance	580				
Utilities *ELECTRIC*	140				
Advertising					
Licenses & Permits	25				
Management					
Payroll & Payroll Taxes	1 200				
Supplies					
Services *WATER/SEWER*	360				
Maintenance 5%	1 072				
Reserve for Replacement					
Ground Lease					
LAWN SERVICE	720				
TOTAL EXPENSES 30 %		6	447		
OPERATING INCOME		14	985		
Plus Other Income			0		
NET OPERATING INCOME		14	985	INFORMATION HEREIN IS BELIEVED TO BE ACCURATE BUT IS NOT WARRANTED	

INCOME ADJUSTED TO FINANCING: Actual ☒ Potential ☐ Equity $ *81,500*

	3rd Loan	2nd Loan	1st Loan	TOTAL		
NET OPERATING INCOME Cap Rate - List Price ___ %					14	985
Less Loan Payment						
Interest			5 512	5 512		
Principal			1 638	1 638		
Total Loan Payment			7 150	7 150	7	150
GROSS SPENDABLE INCOME Rate *9.6* % (GSI ÷ EQUITY)					7	835
Plus Principal Payment					1	638
GROSS EQUITY INCOME Rate *11.6* % (GEI ÷ EQUITY)					9	473
Less Depreciation Personal Property ___ Improvements ___						
REAL ESTATE TAXABLE INCOME						

Figure 8-3

($7835) is the "Gross Spendable Income" produced by the building. This is commonly referred to as "cash flow." It is the amount of spendable income produced by the property prior to income tax consideration. Divide this amount by your $81,500 cash investment and you arrive at the percentage of spendable return you will earn on this investment:

$$\frac{\$\ 7,835}{\$81,500} = 9.6\% \text{ return on cash invested}$$

If you have difficulty in remembering which way to divide to obtain the percentage figure, an easy rule of thumb is: Always divide the "little" number by the "big" number. In this case, the "little" number is the gross spendable income ($7835) and the "big" number is your cash investment or equity ($81,500). The only time this rule would not hold true is if your income *exceeded* your cash investment. Don't worry about that happening!

You'll see that there is a space on the Gross Spendable Income line to enter this percentage figure. There is additional, non-cash flow, income also being produced by your building in the form of reduction of the mortgage through the principal portion of the mortgage payment.

To obtain a complete financial picture on the investment, you should also consider the $1,638 principal payment you made. This amount is entered on the proper line, under the gross spendable income or cash flow amount and added to it.

The final, pre-tax return shown is $9473. This is called "Gross Equity Income" because, first of all, no tax considerations have been taken into account, hence the term "Gross" income. Secondly, it is "equity" income because it not only includes "cash flow" but "equity buildup" or mortgage principal reduction as well.

Step 9: Calculate the Overall Return on Your Cash Investment

Following the same procedure that you did for "cash flow," if you divide your $9473 equity income by your $81,500 investment in the property, the little number by the big number, the investment is producing an 11.6 percent overall return on your cash investment:

$$\frac{\$\ 9,473}{\$81,500} = 11.6\%$$

The final two lines on the property analysis form are for income tax consequences. These will be discussed in a later chapter.

Don't be afraid to use several analysis sheets to try various approaches in determining how best to purchase a property. You may want to figure rent increases that are due and see if increasing the income on the building makes it even more attractive. You may want to adjust operating expenses and see if the property can justify the cost of a property manager, etc. The next Chapter on Financing Techniques will give you several ideas for adjusting the financing on a proposed investment. You may be surprised to see how simple changes in a potential mortgage can completely alter the return on an investment.

EXAMPLE OF PROPERTY ANALYSIS TAKING POTENTIAL FINANCING AND REDUCED CASH REQUIRED INTO ACCOUNT

Remember Bob Andrews—He's the fellow who has $50,000 to invest. You'll recall that Mr. Seller stated he would sell this building with $45,000 cash down. It will fit Bob's investment requirements and leave him $5,000 to cover his closing costs.

Let's prepare another property analysis reducing the "cash required" to $45,000 and under "Potential Financing" second mortgage, figure in the second mortgage to be carried by Mr. Seller. (See Figure 8-4, upper left hand corner):

Selling Price	$155,000
Less 1st Mortgage	$ 73,500
Cash required without 2nd Mortgage	$ 81,500
Less: Actual Cash to be Invested	$ 45,000
Second Mortgage to be carried by Seller	$ 36,500

Assume that Mr. Seller will carry this $36,500 second mortgage with nine percent interest for a 25 year term. This, of course, is subject to negotiation with Mr. Seller at the time you try to purchase the building. You should always try to negotiate the lowest interest rate possible. The seller,

● PROPERTY ANALYSIS ●

Name: ALWAYS FULL APTS
Location: 147 NE 8TH. ST.
Type of Property: 8 UNIT APT. BLDG.   Area

LIST PRICE 155,000

CASH REQ'D. 45,000

EXISTING ASSUMABLE FINANCING:

	Amount	Ann. Pmt.	Int.	Years To Go
1st $	73,500	7,150	7½ %	19+
2nd			%	
3rd			%	

POTENTIAL FINANCING:

				Years
1st $			%	
2nd	36,500	3,676	9 %	25
3rd			%	

Folio:	Ex — S.O. O	File
Date:	Units: 8	Lister
Zoning R-3	Pool NO	Parking 12 CARS
Size 100X150	Rec. Rm. NO	A-C YES
Sq. Ft. 6500	Util. Rm YES	Heat YES
Age 7 YRS	Office NO	TV NO
Stories 2	Lobby NO	Furniture YES
Sewers YES	Elevators NO	Waterfront NO
Constr. CONCRETE & FRAME		

Description —	# Units	Rent Sch
1 BEDROOM, 1 BATH	6	$228/MO.
2 BEDROOM, 2 BATH	2	$256/MO.

SCHEDULE GROSS INCOME			22 560	COMMENTS	CODE
Less: Vacancy & Credit Loss 5%			1 128		
GROSS OPERATING INCOME			21 432		
Less: Operating Expenses					
Taxes	2 350				
Insurance	580				
Utilities ELECTRIC	140				
Advertising					
Licenses & Permits	25				
Management					
Payroll & Payroll Taxes	1 200				
Supplies					
Services WATER/SEWER	360				
Maintenance 5%	1 072				
Reserve for Replacement					
Ground Lease					
LAWN SERVICE	720				
TOTAL EXPENSES	30 %		6 447		
OPERATING INCOME			14 985		
Plus Other Income			0		
NET OPERATING INCOME			14 985	INFORMATION HEREIN IS BELIEVED TO BE ACCURATE BUT IS NOT WARRANTED	

INCOME ADJUSTED TO FINANCING:	Actual ☐	Potential ☒	Equity $45,000				
NET OPERATING INCOME	Cap. Rate - List Price		%				14 985
Less: Loan Payment	3rd Loan	2nd Loan	1st Loan	TOTAL		
Interest		3 285	5 512	8 797		
Principal		391	1 638	2 029		
Total Loan Payment		3 676	7 150	10 826	10 826	
GROSS SPENDABLE INCOME	Rate 9.2 %	(GSI ÷ EQUITY)			4 159
Plus: Principal Payment					2 029
GROSS EQUITY INCOME	Rate 13.8 %	(GEI ÷ EQUITY)			6 188
Less: Depreciation	Personal Property	Improvements			
REAL ESTATE TAXABLE INCOME					

* Based on Form "B," copyrighted by REALTORS NATIONAL MARKETING INSTITUTE OF NATIONAL ASSOCIATION OF REALTORS. Copyright 1974. All rights reserved. Used with permission of copyright owner.
** Reprinted with permission of L.C. Judd & Co., Inc.

Figure 8-4
105

when motivated to sell, will usually accept a lower rate than the current prime rate. In this case, with current interest rates at 12 to 15 percent, you hope to get him to accept nine percent on the second mortgage. If, in his example, Mr. Seller were to insist on 15 percent interest, annual mortgage payments on his mortgage would increase by almost $2000 a year. The property would not make sense for you as an investor. In the next chapter, we will see the effects of varying interest rates. The payments for principal and interest on this second mortgage came out to $3676 a year.

You did not alter the income and expenses on the building, so they stay the same. Drop down to the ''Income Adjusted to Financing'' section at the bottom of the analysis sheet. The existing first loan entry stays the same. Under second loan, enter the interest portion, principal portion and total second mortgage payment. This breakdown is figured exactly the same way as you did the first mortgage.

The two mortgages are totaled giving a total interest payment for the year of $8797, principal payment of $2029 and total principal and interest payments of $10,826. This amount is subtracted from the same $14,985 N.O.I. you had before. The cash flow has now dropped to $4159 (it was $7835 with just the first loan). But, the down payment has also been reduced from $81,500 to $45,000.

Dividing the new cash flow by the down payment gives you the cash return on the invested capital:

$$\frac{\$\ 4,159}{\$45,000} \ = \ 9.2\%$$

Adding the new principal payment of $2029 to $4159 cash flow gives a total gross equity income of $6188:

$$\frac{\$\ 6,188}{\$45,000} \ = \ \begin{array}{l} 13.8\% \text{ equity return on a} \\ \$45,000 \text{ cash investment.} \end{array}$$

USING YOUR ANALYSIS TO MAKE SOUND INVESTMENT DECISIONS

The sequence you have just followed in analyzing a potential investment will, in a matter of minutes, tell you everything you need to know about a specific property and help you make a sound, knowledgeable investment decision.

Again I repeat, if you learn nothing else from this book, retain the information in this Chapter. Develop an analysis form to work with, and use it before making any purchase. Forget any rules of thumb you may have heard that makes property analysis something you can do in your head. Most of them are inaccurate, many meaningless. We'll discuss them in a later Chapter.

Most knowledgeable investors, large or small, experienced or beginners, rely on this type of system for determining if a property meets their investment requirements. It also serves as a convenient way to analyze various ways of purchasing the same property and choosing the best one for you. It gives you an easy way to compare several properties, using the same formula on each. You cannot make a sound business judgement without such an analysis.

9

Financing Techniques
That Offer You Countless Ways
to Buy Real Estate

Considerable space has been allocated for the subject of financing because of its importance. By the time you finish reading this Chapter, you will discover that creative financing offers an investor unlimited methods of purchasing real estate. No other phase of the real estate structure can alter your investment as much as financing.

Entire books have been written on real estate financing. The purpose of this Chapter is not to try to make you an expert in all, or even one type of real estate financing. It is, however, intended to give you a background knowledge of such areas as:

1. How a mortgage works;
2. How financing or leverage can alter your investment;
3. How to determine how much leverage you should have;

109

4. What are sources of mortgage funds;
5. Which mortgage clauses affect you;
6. What are financing techniques;
7. What are land leases; and
8. How to determine your overall interest rate.

By way of illustration, the various financing techniques will be applied to the *Always Full Apartments*. Since you are only interested in the effects created by each mortgage, you will use only the "Income Adjusted to Financing" or bottom portion of the property analysis form. With the exception of the "Land Lease" example, the N.O.I. (Remember, that's Net Operating Income or income after all expenses but before mortgage payments) will always be the same. All you will be doing is trying different types of financing and discovering how each affects the profits produced by the *Always Full Apartments*.

HOW DOES A MORTGAGE WORK?

A typical mortgage consists of two parts—a note and a mortgage deed.

The Note

The mortgage note is the document you execute stating that you owe the lender (mortgagee) "x" number of dollars and agree to pay it back over a certain number of years, paying a prescribed interest rate and making payments of a given amount on a monthly (or quarterly, yearly, etc.) basis. The note, then is your signed agreement of indebtedness and the manner in which you intend to pay it back.

The Mortgage Deed

The mortgage deed is the collateral that you are pledging to secure the note that you signed. It gives the lender the security of having your property pledged in the event you fail to make mortgage payments in accordance with the note. If you default, or fall behind on these payments, the lender, by law, has the right to force payment or, through the courts, start foreclosure proceedings. One thing to keep in mind. Most lenders do not want to foreclose on your property. If, for some reason, you have problems in meeting mortgage payments, talk it over with the lender. You will find him cooperative in most circumstances. I might add, in case you're wondering, the chances of serious financial problems occurring on a good investment property are remote.

Once you have executed a mortgage deed and note, these documents are recorded in the public records at the county courthouse in which the property is located, by the mortgagee or lender. Recording these documents protects their interest because they become a matter of public record and show recorded evidence that they, the lender, have a vested interest in your property.

When you, in selling real estate, have occasion to carry a mortgage, make sure you also record it. What happens if a mortgage is *not* recorded? In the event that the property owner has foreclosure proceedings against him, an unrecorded mortgage will probably have little chance of being recognized in a court of law. In the event of a forced sale, in order to pay debts, tax liens usually take first precedence, and recorded mortgages and liens follow in the order in which they were recorded. Anything that is left, after all recorded debts are taken care of, will cover such things as an unrecorded lien, but the funds rarely extend that far.

HOW FINANCING, OR LEVERAGE, CAN ALTER YOUR INVESTMENT

The intelligent use of "leverage" or "use of other people's money" gives real estate investing an advantage offered by no other investment vehicle. As a rule of thumb, anytime you can use someone else's money and make more on it than it cost you to borrow it, it probably makes sense to do so.

Assume you have $50,000 to invest and you have three choices. You can purchase a small rental house for cash at $50,000. You can purchase a $100,000, five-unit apartment complex with a $50,000 mortgage and $50,000 cash down, or a $500,000, 25-unit apartment building with $50,000 cash down and assume $450,000 in mortgage or mortgages. Without regard to which is best for you, let's analyze each possibility. All three properties will give you a 10 percent spendable return on your invested capital or $5000 a year. So far, there is no difference.

Next, consider the principal reduction on each of the mortgages.

Remember, this added to your gross spendable income of $5000 gives you the total equity return on your investment. The first situation, has *no* mortgage so you have zero principal reduction. On the second investment, you used 50 percent leverage. The principal reduction on the $50,000 mortgage will amount to about $500 the first year. Added to your $5000 spendable income, you now have $5500 in equity income.

The third alternative you are considering is 90 percent leveraged. In other words, you are putting up a 10 percent cash down payment and taking on a 90 percent or $450,000 mortgage. The principal reduction on this mortgage for the year will be about $4500. Added to your $5000 cash flow, your equity income has almost doubled to $9500. Now you are really making other people's money work for you. But, we're not finished yet.

You know that your real estate investment is appreciating in value each year. We'll be conservative and assume each of your three possible investments will appreciate four percent next year. In other words, if you were to sell each of the investments in twelve months, you could sell them for four percent more than you paid for them.

You paid $50,000 for your first investment. Four percent of $50,000 is $2000, which means you could sell the property for $52,000 and make a $2000 profit, before taxes. You paid $100,000 for the second property, even though your investment was still $50,000. Four percent of $100,000 is $4000 profit. The third property cost $500,000. Four percent of $500,000 is $20,000. You could sell this building for $520,000 and realize a $20,000 pretax profit. Figure 9-1 shows how the three choices compare.

	Small Rental House	5-Unit Apartment Complex	25-Unit Apartment Complex
Purchase Price	$50,000	$100,000	$500,000
Mortgage	-0-	50,000	450,000
	$50,000	$ 50,000	$ 50,000
Gross Spendable Income	$ 5,000	$ 5,000	$ 5,000
+ Principal Reduction	-0-	500	4,500
+ Appreciation @ 4%	2,000	4,000	20,000
TOTAL RETURN	$ 7,000	$ 9,500	$ 29,000

Figure 9-1

It's easy to see what properly used leverage can do for you. But, before you rush out and look for a property with a 90 percent mortgage, you have another decision to make.

DETERMINING HOW MUCH LEVERAGE YOU SHOULD HAVE

Use of leverage or other people's money can greatly increase your ability to buy a larger property than if you had to pay all cash for it. Before you take on one or more mortgages in order to purchase a property, sit down and analyze not only the property with the proposed mortgages, but your personal attitudes as well. Just how much financing can you comfortably live with? Some people are still frightened by the thought of mortgages on the real estate they own. Others, with the benefit of careful planning and careful selection of an investment property, will venture into a 100-percent-leveraged situation if they can find one. They will buy a real estate investment with *all* mortgages and *no* cash investment on their part.

A 100-Percent-Leveraged Investment That Paid Off

Let me tell you about a 12-unit apartment complex that I purchased a few years ago. The seller wanted $30,000 cash down payment. The property was priced at $200,000. A friend of mine had a sizable amount of money tied up in a "blue chip" stock paying him a low return. He pledged part of the stock as collateral at his bank and borrowed the $30,000. This cost him 7.5 percent interest. He then loaned the $30,000 to me. I purchased the property and created a land lease. In other words, I sold him the land under my buildings for $30,000. I paid him 10 percent rent ($3,000 a year) for the use of his land. Without any effort on his part, and little or no risk, he was able to earn 2.5 percent a year additional interest on his $30,000. And, as we pointed out before, he still owned his stock and obtained the dividends and any growth potential. Not only that, the land lease also had a cost of living index written into it. The longer he held the lease, the more it would cost me to buy the land back from him. Every way you look at it, he was coming out ahead.

What did I get out of the transaction? First of all, I was able to purchase a property that was beyond my reach at that time. The 100-percent-leveraged position obviously left little or no cash flow. Mortgage and land lease payments consumed it all. But, I was careful to analyze the situation before venturing into the project. I knew the property was an attractive one in a prime rental area. I allowed for "extra" operating expenses and still had some cash flow left over. I determined that I could have one vacant apartment on a year round basis and still break even.

Economic conditions were also favorable for the rental market. It was not until after all these variables were considered that I purchased the property. The point is, never rush out and buy something just because it looks like a good deal. If you end up in financial difficulties, it ceases to be the "good deal" you thought it was.

I owned that complex for about three years. The property carried itself and gave me a couple hundred dollars a month cash flow. Not much of a return on a $30,000 investment, but *my* investment was zero. The coin operated washer and dryer in the complex kept my three children in school lunch money for three years.

The best part is yet to come. The investment gave me the two things I wanted from it, tax shelter and appreciation. While I owned it, the complex gave me a $10,000 a year tax write-off against my other income. Remember, I did not own the land. I had sold it. This meant that 100 percent of what I did own was depreciable improvements. We'll discuss land leases a little later in this Chapter.

My second investment goal, appreciation, was also accomplished when I sold the property three years later. The sale gave me a $25,000 profit. All this with not one penny of my own money invested. You may want to reread the portion of Chapter 3 that suggests possible ways to purchase property with little or no money down.

What's Right for You

What about you? By now you realize how much you can profit from the proper use of financing, but what are you comfortable with, from an investment point of view? Some people could not sleep nights knowing they owned a parcel of real estate that was 90% leveraged. The thought of having to make large mortgage payments, even if the investment could easily justify them, would give the investor ulcers.

Rather than arbitrarily decide that you will not consider any property that has a 50, 75, or 90 percent mortgage on it, take the time to thoroughly analyze the potential investment and determine just how secure it will be with the mortgage you are considering. If it is reaching the "break even" point with the amount of leverage you need to purchase it, you'd better think twice. Consider what will happen if you have unexpected vacancies or operating expenses. Will you have to "feed it" to keep the payments current? Perhaps you'd better consider a smaller property with a higher ratio between your cash investment and the size of the mortgage. It may take a few years longer to build your estate, but you'll sleep nights.

SOURCES OF MORTGAGE FUNDS

Getting involved in investment real estate opens some financial doors not open for home financing. Savings and loan associations offer financing for investment real estate, but regulations usually limit the dollars they are allowed to invest in commercial real estate loans in proportion to residential real estate mortgages.

Bank loans are possible, but usually shorter in term. Insurance companies are a primary source for commercial mortgages, but they usually consider only larger properties requiring, for example, $500,000 mortgages or larger. Real Estate Investment Trusts and Pension Funds are another source of larger size mortgages.

Private lenders are many private investors who will carry mortgages, both first and second mortgages. They usually demand a high interest rate and relatively short term.

The seller of the property is generally one of the best sources of financing. It's fast, convenient, and inexpensive. Getting the seller to take back a first or second mortgage will also save you the closing costs (points) charged by a commercial lender.

Don't overlook a friend or relative who might benefit by loaning you money at an interest rate higher than he is presently earning. He will have a mortgage deed against your property, as security. It could be a good investment for both of you.

When looking for a new loan, shop around. Like any other business, commercial lenders are in a very competitive situation. You also have to find the lender who has excess funds that he has to loan out, and this can, and does vary from day to day and from lender to lender. Someone who had money to lend yesterday may be out of it today and vice-versa. Keep looking. Find the best "deal" for you.

MORTGAGE CLAUSES THAT AFFECT YOU

Points

Although it is not really a clause in the mortgage, closing charges made by a savings and loan when you place a new mortgage on your property have an effect on your investment. Depending on the lending institution, you can expect to be charged "points" or a percentage of the mortgage as an added cost. This charge actually increases the effective interest rate you are paying on that mortgage. How does it work?

Suppose you want to borrow $100,000 on a $150,000 apartment building. You intend to invest $50,000 so you require a $100,000 mortgage. The lender agrees and offers you the $100,000 mortgage at an annual interest rate of 10 percent. They will also charge you four points or four percent closing costs. Four percent of $100,000 is $4000, but you do not have to pay it—yet! Instead of loaning you $100,000, they will deduct the $4000 in points and loan you only $96,000. Although the mortgage you execute, the indebtedness you incur, is $100,000, you walk away from the mortgage closing with only $96,000. Since your mortgage repayment is based on $100,000, you really end up paying a higher interest rate. It looks something like this.

A one-hundred thousand dollar loan at 10 percent interest for 20 years equals $965.02 a month principal and interest. However, you are paying that $965.02 a month for 20 years and you only receive $96,000. The effective interest rate on a $96,000 loan over a 20 year period with payments of $965.02 a month is 10.6 percent.

Pre-payment Penalty

Another "kicker" that you will frequently find in commercial mortgages is a pre-payment penalty. Suppose you want to pay the mortgage off ahead of schedule. The lender will charge a pre-payment penalty. They do this to protect themselves. A sizable number of borrowers may all decide to pay off their mortgage at the same time. The lender would suddenly have an abundance of cash on hand that was not earning interest. And, as you know, they are paying depositor's interest for the use of the money. In order to remain in a profitable position, they must keep that money loaned out at an interest rate higher than they are paying their depositors. You may not consider a pre-payment penalty a problem, but it could prevent you from re-financing the property at a future date. That pre-payment penalty is usually reduced as the loan matures, until it may be eliminated after the loan has been paid for several years.

Assuming a Mortgage

Here is another caution when assuming a mortgage when you purchase an investment property, or even a home. Many mortgages are now being written allowing the lender to upgrade the interest rate to current market levels in the event that title to the property changes hands. You may find out that what you think is an eight percent interest mortgage will become a 10 percent interest mortgage as soon as you take title to the property.

You also want to be certain the mortgage is assumable. Many second mortgages are *not*. You do not want to go to a closing on the property you are buying and find out you are $25,000 short on cash because a second mortgage on the property could not be assumed.

Watch Out for "Balloons"

Watch out for "balloon" mortgages. These are mortgages written for a long-term amortization but the entire remaining balance becomes due and payable long before the normal amortization schedule would have liquidated it. Federal law requires a statement such as "This is a Balloon Mortgage" be prominently printed across the face of a balloon mortgage.

Look for "Catches" in Government Financing

One final caution before we discuss actual mortgages. When the property is Federal Government financed, such as an FHA or HUD project, read the mortgage carefully. You will no doubt find several "catches" such as:

You cannot pre-pay the mortgage. You are locked into a rent control situation. You will probably not be able to get a second mortgage on the property because the primary lender, the Federal Government, will not recognize it as a valid indebtedness against the property. FHA mortgages are only available for rental housing units, including some mobile home parks.

How to Check for Problems

So, how do you check all of these possible problems? Look at the mortgage documents, or have your attorney review them *prior* to purchasing the property. You may want to know that you have control of the property and can purchase it on acceptable terms to you prior to having your attorney research it. This can be done by entering into a purchase contract with the seller. The contract will have a contingency allowing you or your attorney a few days to examine the mortgage documents and determine that they are satisfactory. If they are not, the contract is null and void and your deposit is refunded.

Don't be alarmed. The majority of mortgages are straightforward, assumable mortgages. But, it is best to find out before the closing and not during it.

HOW CREATIVE FINANCING TECHNIQUES CAN MAKE A POOR INVESTMENT PROFITABLE

There are numerous ways of structuring the purchase of investment real estate through the use of creative financing ideas. By using creative financing, it is often possible to turn what seems like a poor investment into a highly profitable one. Consider the following.

Conventional Loans: How the Term of the Mortgage Affects Your Investment

The most common type of mortgage is the one received from the institutional lenders we have already discussed. There is no need to explain how they work, you already know that. You should, however, take a look at what happens to a mortgage and how it can affect your investment if you do nothing more than increase the term, or payout years of the loan.

Let's assume that you are borrowing $110,000 to buy the *Always Full Apartments*. Your Net Operating Income (or N.O.I.)—surely you know what that is by now—is $14,985 a year. You are purchasing the building for $155,000 and putting $45,000 down as you will recall. Assume a 10 percent interest rate and disregard closing "points" in this analysis.

What happens if the term of the loan varies from 10 years to 20 years and to 30 years. A typical mortgage amortization table is reproduced in the Chapter on Rules of Thumb. A complete amortization book is available at most savings and loan associations or banks at no cost. You will want one for future use.

The table below shows the results of doing nothing more than amortizing the same mortgage over a different number of years:

	10 Year Term	20 Year Term	30 Year Term
N.O.I.	$14,985	$14,985	$14,985
Less Annual			
Mortgage Payment	17,444	12,738	11,584
Gross Spendable Income	($2,459)	$ 2,247	$ 3,401
Plus Principal Payment	6,444	1,738	584
Gross Equity Income	$ 3,985	$ 3,985	$ 3,985

Figure 9-2

The first thing you will notice is that the N.O.I. being produced by the building cannot support a mortgage amortized for only ten years. The mortgage payment exceeds the income by $2459. Placing this mortgage on the property, you will have to take $2459 a year out of your pocket to keep the building on a break-even basis.

Extending the term to 20 years reduces the annual mortgage payments from $17,444 to $12,738. Now, the building is carrying itself and giving you a $2247 spendable income. That income increases to $3401 if you extend the loan term to 30 years.

Now, notice what has happened to your principal payment. On the short-term loan, you obviously have to pay off the mortgage more quickly. Your first-year principal payment on the 10-year loan is $6444. By the time you spread the loan out for 30 years, you are only paying down the principal balance $584 in the first year.

Look now at the bottom line, "Gross Equity Income." Surprised? All you have done by increasing the term of the mortgage and leaving everything else the same, is take part of the principal payment and put it back up into gross spendable income. The gross equity income remains the same regardless of the term of the mortgage. This is a method that can possibly be used to improve the "cash flow" on a property. Merely extend the term of the mortgage.

Interest Rate vs. Mortgage Constant: You have seen what happens to "cash flow" by merely extending the term of a mortgage and leaving everything else the same. Although the actual interest rate stays the same, the overall average rate *increases* as the mortgage term *decreases*.

Here is how it works. Assume a $10,000 mortgage with an annual interest rate of 10 percent. So far, so good. Now, let's use a comparison between a 10 year amortization and a 20 year amortization. Annual principal and interest payments on the ten year mortgage will be $1586 per year.

Annual payments on the 20 year mortgage will be $1158 a year. You already know that the difference in the two payments shows up in the *principal reduction* of the mortgage for the year. The interest rate on both is still 10 percent or about $1000 on a $10,000 mortgage.

This change in the overall payment, brought about by changing the term of the loan, is reflected in the actual overall interest rate on the mortgage. This overall interest rate is referred to as the "Mortgage Constant." The "Mortgage Constant" rate not only takes the interest rate into consideration, but the principal reduction portion as well. The result tells you what your overall interest rate is. It is figured like this:

10 Year Mortgage

$$\frac{\text{Annual Principal \& Interest Payment} \quad \$\ 1,586}{\text{Divided by Mortgage Balance} \quad \$10,000} = 15.86\%$$

The actual overall interest rate or "Mortgage Constant" on the 10 year loan is 15.86%.

20 Year Mortgage

$$\frac{\$\ 1,158}{\$10,000} = 11.58\%$$

The actual overall interest rate or "Mortgage Constant" on the 20 year loan is only 11.58 percent.

Use of the mortgage constant will help you determine the cash flow you can expect from your investment. When the mortgage constant percentage exceeds the percentage of cash return on cash invested, it is costing you more to borrow the money than you are earning on that money. This is known as "reverse leverage."

When a potential investment reaches a "reverse leverage" situation, take a close look at it. Are you sure you want to reduce your cash flow in order to increase your leverage. Assuming this is the only way you may be able to afford a highly desirable investment, you may be willing to sacrifice some of the cash flow in order to acquire the property.

Keep in mind that the reduction in cash flow is not lost. It turns up again in the form of principal payment on the mortgage, as illustrated in Figure 9-2.

Secondary Financing: Maximum Leverage for Buyers and Tax Advantages for Sellers

Unlike residential investments, secondary financing is quite common in commercial and investment real estate purchases. Most buyers want to obtain maximum leverage and the majority of sellers want the sale to qualify as an installment sale for tax purposes. (More on this subject later.) Therefore, second and even third and fourth mortgages are not uncommon.

One stumbling block that a first time investor must overcome is the fear or negative attitude that prevails when he sees a potential investment that is encumbered by two or more mortgages. He needs to review his original investment goals when he determined how much leverage he will be comfortable in carrying. If he wants to buy investment property with a maximum of 20 percent down payment, secondary financing will probably be a necessity. Eighty percent institutional first mortgages on investment real estate are rare, if not non-existent. As a practical matter, it is unimportant how many mortgages are on a property, as long as the total amount of financing falls within his acceptable leverage limit. Quite often, having secondary financing offers the investor more flexibility than if the entire amount was locked in on an institutional first mortgage. We will discuss some of the things you can do with creative financing—several of which would not be possible if the entire mortgaging consisted of only an institutional first mortgage.

In order to illustrate the next few concepts in mortgage financing techniques, we will concentrate on the bottom portion (Income Adjusted to

Financing section) of your property analysis form. You will use the *Always Full Apartments* and experiment with various ways of purchasing it through financing alternatives.

On each analysis, you will maintain the $155,000 purchase price, the existing $73,500 first mortgage at 7.5 percent interest and the N.O.I. at $14,985. You intend to invest $45,000 and will, therefore, need additional financing of $36,500. This conforms with your property analysis in Figure 8-4.

Deferred Payment Mortgage

Suppose you would like a year or two to improve the rental structure so it will better carry the secondary financing of $36,500. You talk the seller into a 12-month moratorium on second mortgage payments. Your analysis now looks like Figure 9-3. Notice how the return on your cash investment has improved. (17.4% spendable return on cash invested compared with the 9.2% in Figure 8-4.) It should, because in effect, you just reduced the price on a temporary basis at least, by $36,500—the size of the second mortgage. Don't expect to get a break like a "no payment mortgage" on a building that is already producing a reasonable return, such is the *Always Full Apartments*. This technique should be kept in mind when a seller refuses to consider a reduction in the selling price because within a few months, increased rents will justify the price. If you feel that this is still the investment for you, try to get a concession on the payments on the mortgage he is carrying.

Don't expect the seller to forgive interest payments on that mortgage for the first year. He will probably want to let the interest accrue and add it to the principal balance you owe him. Assume for example, that the interest rate on the $36,500 second mortgage is nine percent, at the end of 12 months, you will have accrued $3285 in interest. He will add that to the $36,500 second mortgage he is carrying, so you now owe him a second mortgage in the amount of $39,875. This could increase your annual mortgage payments by $331 a year. In this example, that doesn't look like much, but on a large mortgage, it can become a sizable sum and needs to be included in your financial analysis of the property. He can also agree to extend the term of the mortgage, adding a few months on the end to make up the $3285 additional amount he has coming to him. Doing this allows you to retain the same monthly payments that you already had projected in your property analysis.

In order to avoid this problem, you can take a different approach on the second mortgage.

INCOME ADJUSTED TO FINANCING: Actual ☐ Potential ☒ Equity: $ 45,000

NET OPERATING INCOME				14 985
Cap. Rate - List Price:			%	
Less: Loan Payment	3rd Loan	2nd Loan	1st Loan	TOTAL
Interest		0	5512	5512
Principal		0	1638	1638
Total Loan Payment		0	7150	7150
GROSS SPENDABLE INCOME	Rate: 17.4 %		(GSI + EQUITY)	7 835
Plus: Principal Payment				1 638
GROSS EQUITY INCOME	Rate: 21.1 %		(GEI + EQUITY)	9 473
Less: Depreciation Personal Property Improvements				
REAL ESTATE TAXABLE INCOME				

Figure 9-3

123

INCOME ADJUSTED TO FINANCING:	Actual ☐ Potential ☒			Equity: $ 45,000	
NET OPERATING INCOME					14,985
Cap. Rate - List Price: ____ %					
	3rd Loan	2nd Loan	1st Loan	TOTAL	
Less: Loan Payment					
Interest		3,285	5,512	8,797	
Principal		2,263	1,638	3,901	
Total Loan Payment		5,548	7,150	12,698	12,698
GROSS SPENDABLE INCOME	Rate: 5.1 % (GSI ÷ EQUITY)				2,287
Plus: Principal Payment					3,901
GROSS EQUITY INCOME	Rate: 13.8 % (GEI ÷ EQUITY)				6,188
Less: Depreciation	Personal Property	Improvements			
REAL ESTATE TAXABLE INCOME					

Figure 9-4

124

INCOME ADJUSTED TO FINANCING:	Actual ☐ Potential ☒	Equity: $45,000		
NET OPERATING INCOME				14 985
	Cap. Rate - List Price: ___ %			
Less: Loan Payment	3rd Loan	2nd Loan	1st Loan	TOTAL
Interest		3 285	5 512	8 797
Principal		0	1 638	1 638
Total Loan Payment		3 285	7 150	10 435
GROSS SPENDABLE INCOME	Rate: 10.1 % (GSI ÷ EQUITY)			4 550
Plus: Principal Payment				1 638
GROSS EQUITY INCOME	Rate: 13.8 % (GEI ÷ EQUITY)			6 188
Less: Depreciation Personal Property Improvements				
REAL ESTATE TAXABLE INCOME				

Figure 9-5

Interest Only Mortgage

Assume that Mr. Seller agreed to carry a second mortgage but he did not want to be locked into a 20 to 25-year term. He will accept a 10-year term. A $36,500, nine percent interest mortgage, amortized over a 10-year term will result in $5548 a year principal and interest payments.

Figure 9-4 shows what will happen to your spendable income if you accept it on that basis. Your spendable income drops to $2287 or 5.1 percent. You feel that this is not an acceptable return so you request an interest only mortgage for a year in order to reduce the payment by $2263 or the amount of principal payment. Before leaving Figure 9-4, you'll notice that your overall equity return remained the same, just as it did in the example in Figure 9-2.

The results of the interest only mortgage are shown in Figure 9-5. You'll notice that the gross spendable return on your $45,000 cash investment has actually increased to 10.1 percent from the 9.6 percent you had in Figure 9-3 where no second mortgage was involved. The reason is simple. You are borrowing $36,500 (the amount of the second mortgage) at nine percent interest but you are earning 9.6 percent (the original return without the second mortgage) on the money you borrowed. Remember, that is the advantage in using leverage. You are able to earn more on the borrowed money than it cost you to borrow it. This results in your overall return increasing.

At the end of the "interest only" period of this mortgage, normal principal and interest payments would commence. Keep in mind, however, that Mr. Seller was only willing to carry a 10-year mortgage. You used up one of those years without paying down the principal balance. Assuming Mr. Seller will not give you an extra year to pay off the mortgage, you have two options:

1. Reduce the amortization period from ten years to nine years. This will increase the annual payments from $5548 to $5932.

2. The second option is to leave the mortgage as is with $5548 a year principal and interest payments and have a balloon (or the remaining balance) due at the end of the original 10-year period.

This brings us to another useful financing technique.

The Balloon Mortgage

Some investors, at the sound of "Balloon Mortgage" have an immediate negative reaction. At least one best selling book on real estate investing advises readers to "stay away" from balloon mortgages. Properly used, however, they offer an excellent financing alternative. In case you do not know how a balloon mortgage works, let's take another look at the $36,500 mortgage that you want Mr. Seller to carry on the *Always Full Apartments*.

In Figure 9-4 you saw the cash return on your investment drop to 5.1 percent because Mr. Seller would not carry a mortgage longer than 10 years. Conversely, in Figure 8-4 you were able to realize a 9.2 percent cash return on your investment by merely extending the term of the second mortgage to 25 years. How about getting what you want, and giving him what he wants at the same time? You can do it with a balloon mortgage. He agrees to amortize the loan over a 25-year term, and you agree to pay off the remaining balance at the end of ten years. In ten years, you will have paid the $36,500 mortgage down to $30,202.

This is the point at which a potential investor gets worried. How do you come up with $30,202 in ten years to make that balloon payment? You have to look at the overall picture on your proposed investment over the next ten years.

How much is real estate appreciating in your area each year? In South Florida it is appreciating at a rate of about 10 to 15 percent. In other words a $100,000 building, with 10 percent appreciation, will be worth $110,000 next year. You'll have to make a judgment as to how much you expect your property to appreciate over the next ten years.

First, to keep with inflation, it will appreciate 8 to 10 percent a year minimum. Since rents usually increase with inflation, and the value of your building is determined by the rents it produces, you can logically expect your property to at least keep up with inflation.

But, be very conservative and assume your real estate will appreciate at only one-half the rate of inflation or four percent per year. At a four percent annual inflation rate, your $155,000 *Always Full Apartment* building 10 years from now, will have a fair market value of approximately $229,400. At the same time your property is appreciating you have also been paying down your mortgage. The $73,500 mortgage has been paid down to approximately $49,220 and you have already determined that the second mortgage balance will be paid down to $30,202. Deduct the two remaining mortgage balances from your projected market value, in 10 years, of $229,400, it looks something like this:

Market Value		$229,400
Less: First Mortgage	$49,220	
Second Mortgage	$30,202	
TOTAL		$ 79,422
Your Equity in 10 Years	=	$149,978

Ten years from now, your equity will be about 65 percent of the value of the property. When the balloon payment comes due, you can refinance the property for at least enough to pay off the balloon. To be on the safe side, you will probably start looking into the mortgage market several months before the balloon is due, and pick the best time to refinance.

In Chapter 3 it was pointed out that refinancing your present real estate is an excellent source of obtaining tax-free investment capital. Even if the *Always Full Apartments* did not have a balloon mortgage due, it might pay to refinance it and free up some of your equity for use in another real estate investment. We are looking at the situation in 10 years, however, chances are you will have sold that property and purchased another one within five to seven years because that is when your tax shelters start to run out. But, suppose you keep it. Assuming you could obtain a 75 percent loan on the $229,400 property, that would be about $172,000. Subtract the existing $79,422 mortgages and an estimated $6,880 in new mortgage closing costs, your financial picture will look something like this:

Market Value	—	$229,400
75% Loan	$172,000	
Less: Existing Loans	$ 79,422	
	$ 92,578	
Less: Estimated 4 Points closing costs	$ 6,880	
Net Proceeds	$ 85,698	

You will end up with about $85,000 tax-free money to reinvest.

Do not let a balloon mortgage frighten you, unless it is for an extremely short term, like one year. Then you'd better think twice, unless you expect a rich uncle to will you some money in 11 months.

Discounting a Mortgage: Sell the Mortgage to a Broker

There is another way to get the seller to take back a second mortgage when he does not really want to carry one. There are many mortgage brokers, both private and commercial, who buy second mortgages. Before considering this source, you must first understand how they operate.

Their primary criteria is that the owner of the property have sufficient equity (a large enough cash investment) to give the lender security. Secondly, they will buy the mortgage only at a discounted price, probably about 25 percent or perhaps more on a less stable investment. What does that do for the purchaser of the mortgage?

Assume he is considering purchasing the second mortgage of $36,500 that you want the seller of the *Always Full Apartments* to carry. You'll recall this was to be a nine percent interest mortgage. The mortgage broker agrees to purchase the mortgage but only at a 25 percent discount. He will pay $9125 less than the face amount of the mortgage, or $27,375. Since you still owe 25 years of mortgage payments at $3676 a year, based on the original $36,500 amount, his actual interest rate increases to 12.88 percent.

One additional restriction that would probably make this particular mortgage unsalable, or at least difficult to sell, is the 25-year term. Most buyers of mortgages will consider only short-term mortgage purchases. This is where combining the discounted mortgage with the balloon mortgage concept might work.

One tremendous advantage you have with the secondary financing of an investment property is the creative flexibility that is possible to make an investment a sound one for you. You can already see some of the various ways of using financing to structure an investment to make it attractive to both you and the seller.

Before leaving this discounted mortgage, you cannot overlook the seller's outcome in this transaction. He did not wish to carry the second mortgage, so he sold it to a mortgage broker. But, in the process, it cost him $9125 to do it, because he was paid only $27,375 for his $36,500 mortgage. When the seller is motivated to sell and receive all cash from the transaction, he may accept this loss in order to get what he wants—cash.

It is also possible for him to increase the selling price of the property enough to cover all or most of the cost of selling the second mortgage at a discount. Or, as the buyer, you can negotiate some type of sharing or splitting of the cost.

The Wraparound Mortgage: High Interest for the Seller and a Bigger Investment for You

You have probably heard the term "wraparound mortgage" but what does it mean, and more important, how can you, as a buyer or seller of investment real estate benefit from it?

First of all, a wraparound mortgage is just what the name implies. It "wraps around" any existing mortgages that may already be on the property. It is also referred to as an "all Inclusive Deed of Trust" in some parts of the country. We can best explain how it works by using an example.

You'll recall that your original intent was to purchase the *Always Full Apartments* by investing $45,000 and having the owner carry a $36,500 second mortgage at nine percent for 25 years. Perhaps he does not like the idea of being in a second loan position with no control over whether the first mortgage payment is being kept current. More likely, he will be unwilling to be locked in on a long-term second mortgage at nine percent interest when current first mortgage interest rates are 10 to 12 percent.

You know, from the previous examples, that as you increase the interest rate or decrease the term to say 10 years, the size of the second mortgage payments will ruin your cash flow.

Try a wraparound mortgage. Here is how a wraparound mortgage can benefit both buyer and seller.

First, the buyer. You will ask Mr. Seller to carry a $110,000 wraparound mortgage at 8.5 percent for 25 years. (I'll explain how you'll get him to accept 8.5 percent interest in a minute.) Remember, this mortgage "wraps around" the existing first mortgage, plus covers the $36,500 that you wanted him to carry in the form of a second mortgage.

Annual mortgage payments on the wraparound will be $10,629. This is actually $197 less than if he would have carried the straight second mortgage and added that payment to the first mortgage payment. Your revised position is shown in Figure 9-6. Notice that the cash return on your cash investment (gross spendable income) has increased 0.5 percent from 9.2 percent to 9.7 percent. You will also see that your gross equity income has dropped 1.3 percent from 13.8 percent to 12.5 percent. This is because you are, in effect, paying 8.5 percent interest on the first mortgage rather than the actual 7.5 percent that is on it. Although your overall return has been slightly

INCOME ADJUSTED TO FINANCING:	Actual ☐	Potential ☒	Equity: $ 45,000		
NET OPERATING INCOME	Cap. Rate - List Price:		%		14 985
Less: Loan Payment	3rd Loan	2nd Loan	1st Loan	TOTAL	
Interest			9 350	9 350	
Principal			1 279	1 279	
Total Loan Payment			10 629	10 629	
GROSS SPENDABLE INCOME		Rate: 9.7 %	10 629 (GSI + EQUITY)		4 356
Plus: Principal Payment					1 279
GROSS EQUITY INCOME		Rate: 12.5 %	(GEI + EQUITY)		5 635
Less: Depreciation Personal Property		Improvements			
REAL ESTATE TAXABLE INCOME					

Figure 9-6

131

reduced, keep in mind that you are using this financing alternative because Mr. Seller would not give you a straight second mortgage. You now have a chance to acquire the property that you may not have had without the wraparound technique. Properly structured, it does not substantially reduce your returns on the investment.

Which brings us to Mr. Seller. How do you convince him to carry an 8.5 percent wraparound mortgage when he considered a nine percent interest rate on a second mortgage too low? The secret lies in the fact that he is collecting 8.5 percent on a $110,000 mortgage, but he only has $36,500 invested (the portion that would have been the second mortgage that you wanted him to carry). The remaining $73,500 balance is being carried by the first mortgage lender. The first mortgage lender is only collecting 7.5 percent interest on the $73,500 but Mr. Seller is collecting 8.5 percent on it, or a one percent profit.

In order to convince Mr. Seller what this means to him, you have to see just how much he can expect to make over the 25-year term of the wraparound. Start by totaling his entire proceeds on the wraparound, over 25 years of payments at $10,629 or $265,725. Out of this amount he must make the first mortgage payments. They amount to $7150 for the remaining 19.71 years or a total of $140,955. To determine his return, we follow the procedure shown in Figure 9-7.

STEP I   -   Total Wraparound Payments over 25 years $265,725
            Less: Existing 1st Mortgage Payments for
                  19.71 years $140,955
            Net Proceeds received by Mr. Seller $124,770

STEP II   -   Total Proceeds Received by Mr. Seller $124,770
            Less: *His* Investment on the Mortgage $ 36,500
            Total Interest Received by Mr. Seller $ 88,270

STEP III   - $\dfrac{\$88{,}270}{25 \text{ Years}}$ = $3,530.80 Average Interest Per Year

STEP IV   -   Average Interest Per Year $\dfrac{\$\ 3{,}530.80}{\$36{,}500.00}$ = 9.7%
             Mr. Seller's Investment

Figure 9-7

Mr. Seller will actually receive an average interest ratio equal to 9.7 percent, even though the overall rate of the wraparound is only 8.5 percent. This should help convince Mr. Seller to carry the wraparound.

If you were to offer Mr. Seller a nine percent wraparound mortgage instead of 8.5 percent, the actual interest return he makes is even more impressive and should really appeal to him.

The results, using the previous formula in Figure 9-3, looks like this:

STEP I	Total Wraparound Payments @ 9%	$276,935
	Less: 1st Mortgage Payments	$140,955
	Net Proceeds Received by Mr. Seller	$135,980
	Less: His 2nd Mortgage	$ 36,500
	Total Interest Received	$ 99,480

STEP II $$\frac{\$99,480}{25 \text{ Years}} = \$3,979 \text{ per Year}$$

STEP III $$\frac{\$ 3,979}{} = 11\%$$

You can show him how he is really earning 11 percent interest on his $36,500 portion of the wraparound mortgage. He'll have a difficult time turning that down. In the process, you have increased your annual mortgage payments by only $448 a year.

Using the 8.5 percent wraparound, in general practice, you would make the $10,629 annual mortgage payment on a monthly basis of $885.75 to the seller, or better yet, to a bank trust officer. Out of this payment, $595.83 (or $\frac{1}{12}$ of the $7150 annual first mortgage payment) would be paid to the first mortgage lender and the balance ($289.92) to the seller. When the first mortgage is paid off, the seller will receive the entire $885.75 monthly payment for the balance of the twenty-five year term of his wraparound mortgage. He also has the added security of knowing that the first mortgage payments are kept current because a bank trust department is making them.

Not all investment real estate purchases can be structured with a wraparound mortgage. Each transaction must be individually analyzed. In some cases, a wraparound just will not work. As a rule of thumb the larger the existing mortgage and the lower the interest rate it carries, the better the possibility of a wraparound mortgage being practical.

In any case, the wraparound mortgage bears consideration when mortgage money is tight. When used properly, both buyer and seller can benefit.

Land Leases: Another Way to Buy Property Otherwise Out of Your Reach

Although a land lease is not exactly the same as a mortgage, it is used to serve a similar purpose and is, therefore, discussed in this Chapter. The words "land lease" frighten many would-be investors away from a real estate investment that could be one of the best buys in town. The first thought that many investors have is the need (or security) of owning the land under their real estate.

Let's take a look at this "undesirable monster" and find out why a land lease does not frighten a knowledgeable investor. Many investors actually want them. First, we have to realize exactly what a land lease is. It is nothing more than a non-amortizing, or, an interest only, type of mortgage. The difference is that a mortgage encumbers your entire property, land and buildings. A land lease encumbers only the land under the buildings. This is what bothers many investors. They have grown up with mortgages and do not mind having a lien against their property, but they still have that feeling of ownership. Under a land lease they feel that the owner of the land, at any time he wishes, can request that the buildings be moved off his property. Of course, this cannot happen. Remember, he is carrying nothing more than a mortgage on your land, the same as a savings and loan does on your entire property, but it is an interest only mortgage. You are not reducing the principal balance.

How does it work in actual practice? Instead of placing a second mortgage on the *Always Full Apartments*, you'll propose, that Mr. Seller accepts a land lease in the amount of $36,500. One caution must be observed, however, the size of your land lease ($36,500) is approximately 24 percent of the total value of the property ($36,500 divided by $155,000—Remember, divide the little number by the big one in order to find the percentage). This land-to-improvement ratio should be kept in line with the county assessors estimate of the land-to-improvement ratio of the property. It may be hard to justify a land lease that only represents 10 percent of the total value of the property, when you get involved with depreciation and tax shelters in the next chapter.

How does the land lease affect your overall return on the *Always Full*

Apartments? You offer Mr. Seller 10 percent interest in return for the $36,500 land lease he will carry. You do not treat the land lease payment as a mortgage payment. It is carried on your property analysis form as an "operating expense." Ten percent of $36,500 is $3650, a year "rent" payment on the land.

Your Revised Property Analysis is shown in Figure 9-8. The first change that appears on your property analysis form is in the price you are paying for the building (upper left hand corner). You are only buying the improvements (buildings) and not the land. Your purchase price, therefore, is reduced $36,500 to a purchase price of $118,500 on the *Always Full Apartments*.

Only the first mortgage is being assumed on your purchase. Income and operating expense remain unchanged, except for the addition of your land lease payment of $3650. This increases your total operating expenses to $10,097 and leaves you with an N.O.I. of $11,335.

In the "Income Adjusted to Financing" section, you have only the $7150 first mortgage payments to deduct leaving you with a gross spendable income of $4185 or 9.3 percent return on your $45,000 investment. This return is almost the same as you had in Figure 8-4, with the second mortgage instead of the land lease. You'll notice that the Gross Equity Return drops from 13.8 percent to 12.9 percent because you are no longer adding a second mortgage principal payment to your total.

Based on a "pre-tax" return on your cash investment, your position remains about the same. I say "pre-tax" position because you also have another advantage when you start figuring your depreciation allowance for tax purposes. Since you cannot depreciate the value of the land, and since you do not own it anyway, 100 percent of what you *do* own can be depreciated. The philosophy here is, "why own the land and have your money tied up in it, when you cannot depreciate it?" The land itself produced *no* income and offers *no* depreciation benefits, so it is of no value to you.

As an investor, you accomplish three things by the creation of the land lease. First, and of primary importance, you are able to purchase a property that was beyond your reach, cash investment wise—normal financing would have been difficult and too costly. Secondly, your overall return on cash invested remained unchanged. Thirdly, 100 percent of what you own can be depreciated for tax purposes and your land lease payments are deductable as an operating expense.

What does Mr. Seller realize from this transaction? First of all, the thought of 10 percent interest is much more appealing than the nine percent you were willing to offer on the second mortgage. Secondly, he still owns the land as security for his loan. Most land leases will be written for a long term

Name: *ALWAYS FULL APTS*

Location: *147 NE 8TH ST.*

Type of Property: *8 UNIT APT. BLDG.*   Area

LIST PRICE *118,500 + LAND LEASE*

CASH REQ'D. *45,000*

EXISTING ASSUMABLE FINANCING:

	Amount	Ann. Pmt.	Int.	Years To Go
1st $	*73,500*	*7,150*	*7½* %	*19+*
2nd			%	
3rd			%	

POTENTIAL FINANCING:

				Years
1st $			%	
2nd			%	
3rd			%	

Folio:	Ex – S O O	File:
Date:	Units:	Lister:
Zoning	Pool	Parking
Size	Rec. Rm.	A-C
Sq. Ft.	Util. Rm.	Heat
Age	Office	T V
Stories	Lobby	Furniture
Sewers	Elevators	Waterfront
Constr.		

Description –	# Units	Rent Sch.

SCHEDULE GROSS INCOME		22	560
Less: Vacancy & Credit Loss 5%		1	128
GROSS OPERATING INCOME		21	432
Less: Operating Expenses			
Taxes	2 350		
Insurance	580		
Utilities *ELECTRIC*	140		
Advertising			
Licenses & Permits	25		
Management			
Payroll & Payroll Taxes	1 200		
Supplies			
Services *WATER/SEWER*	360		
Maintenance			
Reserve for Replacement			
Ground Lease	3 650	←	
LAWN SERVICE	720		
TOTAL EXPENSES %		10	097
OPERATING INCOME		11	335
Plus Other Income		0	
NET OPERATING INCOME		11	335

COMMENTS   CODE

INFORMATION HEREIN IS BELIEVED TO BE
ACCURATE BUT IS NOT WARRANTED

INCOME ADJUSTED TO FINANCING: Actual ☒   Potential ☐   Equity $ *45,000*

NET OPERATING INCOME	Cap Rate - List Price		%		11	335
Less: Loan Payment	3rd Loan	2nd Loan	1st Loan	TOTAL		
Interest			5 512	5 512		
Principal			1 638	1 638		
Total Loan Payment			7 150	7 150	7	150
GROSS SPENDABLE INCOME	Rate: 9.3 %		(GSI ÷ EQUITY)		4	185
Plus: Principal Payment					1	638
GROSS EQUITY INCOME	Rate 12.9 %		(GEI ÷ EQUITY)		5	823
Less: Depreciation Personal Property		Improvements				
REAL ESTATE TAXABLE INCOME						

Figure 9-8

with periodic cost of living increases written into them. This means that he is not "locked" in at 10 percent return. As inflation increases, his payments will increase.

Thirdly, the land lease usually contains a "re-capture" clause or clause that allows you, as the building owner, the right to buy back the land. This clause, like the lease payment clause, will also be tied to the cost of living index. Perhaps you decide to buy back the land, say one year later, and the cost of living for the year went up 10 percent, you would pay 10 percent more than the original $36,500 for the land or $40,150. As you can see, this method of purchasing can be very appealing to Mr. Seller. Not only does he start out with a higher rate of interest, but he has the opportunity of increasing both his lease payments and selling price of the land as time passes.

As the investor, you may want to consider this approach to purchasing the property only after the others you have learned have been tried. Although it is not the least expensive form of financing, it does offer an alternative when there is no other way you could purchase a highly desirable property.

Interest Averaging: A Quick Way to Compare Financing Alternatives

Before we leave our discussion of various financing techniques, we should cover a simple method of determining just how much interest you are really paying. This system can give you a quick way of comparing various financing alternatives.

Overall rate, or interest averaging, takes into account the various size or mortgage balances you have and the interest rate on each. You then determine what your overall average interest rate will be. The process is simple. You multiply each mortgage balance by each interest rate. These answers are totaled and divided by the total of the mortgage balances.

Figure 9-9 shows how it works. We'll determine the overall interest rate you would be paying on the *Always Full Apartments* if Mr. Seller had agreed to carry the $36,500 second mortgage at nine percent.

First Mortgage Balance	$73,500 × 7.5%	=	$5,512
Second Mortgage Balance	$36,500 × 9%	=	$3,285
totals	$110,000		$8,797
$ 8,797	8%		
$110,000			

Figure 9-9

Your overall interest rate for both mortgages is eight percent. If you had more than two mortgages, the same procedure would be followed for each.

Using this formula, you can quickly compare various alternatives to see which offers you the best overall rate.

To carry it one step further, suppose Mr. Seller was insisting on a 12 percent interest rate on his $36,500 mortgage. You had a friend you who offered you a new first mortgage in the amount of $110,000 (the total of the two mortgages) at only 10 percent interest. Which is the better alternative? Figure 9-10 compares the two choices:

Choice I — 1st Mortgage $ 73,500   ×7.5%   = $5,512

                2nd Mortgage $ 36,599   × 12%   = $4,380

                          $100,000 $9,892

$$\frac{\$\ 9,892}{\$110,000} \ =\ \text{9\% Overall Interest Rate}$$

Choice II — Is a $110,000, 10% Mortgage

Figure 9-10

Even at 12 percent interest on the second mortgage, the overall interest rate is still less than the new 10 percent mortgage on the entire amount.

You can see how this formula can be used to select the best financing alternate. This system can also be used in other places. Let's go back to Bob Andrews. He's the fellow who, in the Chapter on Sources of Investment Capital, came up with $50,000 to invest. He found it in the following places:

Source	Amount	Cost of Using the Capital
Savings and C.D.'s	$15,000	6% Average in Lost Interest
Borrowing Against Stocks	$10,000	9% Interest Charged by Bank
Borrow on Insurance	$ 5,000	6% Interest Charged by Insurance Co.
Refinancing Home	$20,000	9.2% Overall Increase in Mortgage Payment Interest
TOTAL	$50,000	

Applying the same formula that we used in Figure 9-9, you can find out exactly what overall interest rate he will be paying for the use of these various sources of funds. Figure 9-11 illustrates the results.

Savings	$15,000	×	6%	=	$ 900
Stocks	$10,000	×	9%	=	$ 900
Insurance	$ 5,000	×	6%	=	$ 300
Refinancing Real Estate	$20,000	×	9.2%	=	$1,840
TOTALS	$50,000				$3,940

$$\frac{\$\ 3,940}{\$50,000} = 7.9\%$$

Figure 9-11

Bob Andrews was able to obtain $50,000 to invest, and it only cost him 7.9 percent overall interest including the six percent interest he will lose by taking $15,000 out of his savings account. As you can see, the ways of structuring the purchase of investment real estate through the use of creative financing ideas, are numerous.

Don't be afraid to try various approaches on the property you are considering. "Play" with the numbers until you find a financial structure that will be most beneficial to you. Then try to purchase the property in that manner. It's also advisable to prepare an outline of "seller benefits" to help you prove to the seller that the way you want to purchase the property will also offer him some benefits as well.

Don't lose your objectivity, however. You seldom will be able to buy a property with everything going your way. You must be reasonable and flexible in your requests, and be willing to negotiate areas of differences, as long as your overall investment goals do not suffer in the process. Remember, one of these days, you'll be on the selling end of the fence. Use these financing ideas to determine which method of *selling* your property will benefit you the most and still offer the buyer a reasonable return on his investment.

10

How to Figure
Your Tax Consequences
and Tax Shelter Benefits

Up to this point, we have been talking in terms of "pre-tax" returns on your investment. All of the results on the *Always Full* Property Analysis forms you have prepared, are based on "gross" spendable income and "gross" equity income. The "gross" referring to "pre-tax" return.

You already know that it does not matter how much you earn. It is how much you get to keep after income taxes that's important. Income producing real estate offers an investor the finest tax benefits available in any type of investment, with the possible exception of high risk investments such as speculative oil well drilling.

The highest benefits, tax wise, are available to the investor in rental apartment buildings. The reason is understandable. In order to encourage investors to furnish much needed housing for the average citizen, the Federal Government allows a tax break, in the form of depreciation allowances, to the investor who furnishes rental apartments to tenants.

HOW TO TAKE THE MAXIMUM ALLOWABLE AMOUNT
OF DEPRECIATION

To understand tax shelters, you must begin with the basic depreciation concept that is offered to investors by the Federal Government. In simplified form, IRS allows you to write-off the cost of your property improvements over the anticipated useful life of the improvements, even though the real estate is actually appreciating (in most cases) in value each year. Assume you own a property on which the buildings (not including the land) were purchased for $100,000. Over a 25-year period (useful life), you can take four percent of the $100,000 or $4000 a year depreciation. Four percent per year times 25 years equals 100 percent. In 25 years, you will have depreciated your building down to zero value at the rate of four percent per year. We will not consider "salvage value" in our discussion because you will not be holding a property long enough to fully depreciate it.

Before you figure your depreciation, there are four separate steps that must be considered.

Step I.   Estimate the Land/Improvement/Personal Property Ratio

When talking about land leases in the last Chapter, it was noted that land cannot be depreciated. Land, as a practical matter, does not wear out nor need replacing, so IRS will not allow you to depreciate it. Your first step in determining the amount of depreciation you can take, therefore, must be to separate the estimated value of the land from the value of the improvements or buildings on the property. "Buildings," in this case, refer to any structures connected with the property. They may be support buildings to the operation of the real estate investment, such as a recreation building.

Since your aim is to legally declare as much depreciation as IRS will allow, it is in your best interest to place as low a value on the land as possible, because the land is the non-depreciable investment in the overall property. Care must be taken, as pointed out in the last chapter, to establish a "reasonable" ratio between the land and improvements. The IRS would probably question a depreciation schedule that estimates land value at only five percent of the total investment.

The "Safe" Way: As a general rule, one of the "safest" ways to estimate the land to improvement ratio of an investment property is with the help of county tax assessors in which the property is located. They generally give a breakdown between land and improvement values. This gives you a defendable position in the event that IRS questions how you established this value ratio. But first, look up the property on the county tax rolls. You usually need the "legal" description of the property to do this. The legal description on most properties consists of a lot number, block number and subdivision name. This can be located in the county "plat" books, also available without charge at the county courthouse. Their personnel will assist you in locating the informaiton you need. Spend a little time at your local county courthouse digging into property records. You'll find a wealth of information available to you at no charge, except for the tax dollars you are already spending. Plat Books, tax rolls, recorded deeds and mortgages, etc. are all a matter of public record and available to anyone for review. You find the legal description of the *Always Full Apartments* to be: Lot 3, Block 5, Fair Acres Subdivision 43-22. The 43-22 at the end of the legal description refers to the plat book (43) and the page number (22) in which this particular property is recorded.

Next, you check the tax rolls to find the assessed value of your property. The tax rolls show: Land: $14,000, Improvements: $80,500 Total: $94,500. In most areas, the total assessed valuation will be somewhat lower than the current market value of the property. That does not mean that the *Always Full Apartments* are only worth $94,500. Assessed value and fair market value are two different things.

Checking Local Tax Rolls: Before continuing, a few additional things should be pointed out about the tax rolls. Not all counties handle their tax rolls alike. Some areas have all of their records filed by a "Folio Number" rather than by legal description. If this is the case in your county, have a member of the recorder's office staff explain how to use the books, using folio numbers.

Not all county tax rolls have a land/improvement breakdown. There is other information you may find once you locate your property in the tax rolls:

1. Owner's name and address (this may not be the actual owner, but rather the person to whom the tax bill is mailed);
2. Previous date and selling price of the property;
3. Type of property; and
4. Size of property.

Not all county tax rolls have the same information, however—at this time your primary interest was in determining a land to improvement ratio on the *Always Full Apartments*. From this information, you determine the percentage each is to the entire valuation. The formula is an easy one—

Land	$14,000
Improvements	$80,500
TOTAL	$94,500

Now, divide the improvement portion by the total valuation:

$$\frac{\text{Improvements } \$80,500}{\text{TOTAL} \quad \$94,500} = 85\%$$

Eighty-five percent of the total value of the property is improvements and the remaining portion (15 percent) is land.

Separate Personal Property and Improvements: When you have the improvement value separated from the land value, you can break it down one step further and separate personal property from the improvements.

Personal property consists of: furniture in apartments, refrigerators, carpeting, dishwashers, and other items that have a shorter useful life than can be expected from the building itself. Remember, we are trying to obtain the maximum depreciation allowance possible in order to realize the maximum tax shelter benefits. We will see in step II that, in order to gain maximum depreciation, we want to use the shortest useful life possible or depreciate the property as quickly as possible. Since personal property will not last as long as the building itself, let's separate it from the total building value. We can then depreciate it over a much shorter useful life. Taking another look at the *Always Full Apartments*, notice that the apartments in the complex are furnished, which will allow you a higher personal property valuation for depreciation purposes than if the apartments were unfurnished.

Now, you want to separate the personal property value from that of 85 percent. You decided that 15 percent is a reasonable amount. In other words, 15 percent of the total value of the property consists of stoves, refrigerators, furniture, carpeting, and other items with an expected short useful life. This leaves 70 percent for the actual improvements after the personal property portion (15 percent) was removed; and the final 15 percent is land value.

To complete your first step, you established the actual dollar value of each of these three items based on your property market value of $155,000:

Land	15%	×	$155,000	=	$ 23,250
Improvements	70%	×	$155,000	=	$108,500
Personal Property	15%	×	$155,000	=	$ 23,250
TOTALS	100%				$155,000

STEP II. Determine the Shortest Possible Useful Life

The useful life you establish for your property determines how quickly you can depreciate the property. Your goal in most investment situations, to to "write-off" the property in the fewest number of years that you think IRS will allow, in order to gain the maximum appreciation or tax benefits.

If your accountant tells you that you *must* use a 40 year useful life, you'd better change accountants, unless you are retired and intend to keep this property for many years and live off the income it produces. You may not be concerned about tax shelters if this is your income situation.

Depending on the area, a new building can probably be depreciated over a 33⅓ year term. Unfortunately, or perhaps fortunately, the IRS does not specify an "acceptable" term for the depreciating of investment real estate. The secret is to have a tax consultant that can prepare your tax returns so that IRS will consider your property depreciation "reasonable and allowable."

If you accept 33⅓ year useful life as reasonable for a new building, you can easily continue from there. If the building is eight-years old, subtract eight from 33 years and a 25 year useful life would be reasonable. If the property is 13-years old or older, do not use less than a 20 year useful life. Both you and the IRS realize that your property is undoubtedly increasing in value not decreasing, so do not get greedy. Unless you have reasonable proof that the life of your building will be less than 20 years, it is doubtful that the IRS will agree.

Economic Life: This brings us to an alternative to "useful" life—the "economic" life of the property.

Perhaps you have proof that "economically" your property will have little or no value in 10 or 15 years. You can then use a shorter life. Maybe a major expressway is expected to cut your property in half in 10 years. The IRS, in this case, would probably allow a 10-year economic life as reasonable for depreciation purposes.

The Always Full Apartments are seven-years old. Since it will be eight-years old in a few months, we'll use a 25-year useful life. Keep in mind that we want the maximum depreciation benefits possible. Now, let's consider the 15 percent we attributed to personal property. You can expect furniture to last maybe five years or less. The appliances may last a little longer. We'll assume a five-year useful life on the 15 percent personal property.

The 15 percent land portion of your investment you disregard. It cannot be depreciated.

Here is where you stand so far:

Item	Value	Useful Life
Land	$ 23,250	-
Improvements	$108,500	25 Years
Personal Property	$ 23,250	5 Years

STEP III.   Select the Fastest Depreciation Possible

If you were to write-off or depreciate your improvements over a 25 year period, you could depreciate them four percent per year (4% × 25 years = 100%). This is known as "straight-line" depreciation.

Faster Write-Offs for Apartment Investors: But the IRS, as an incentive for investors to invest in rental apartment buildings, allows an accelerated depreciation allowance on certain types of property for any investors who choose to use it.

Under current laws, they will allow you to write-off your yearly rented apartment building on a 125 percent declining balance schedule. *This applies to rental apartment buildings only.* This amounts to 1¼ times the straight-line or 5 percent per year in our example. It is called a "declining balance" method because each year your depreciable assets are declining, so your depreciation allowance will be less.

Straight-Line Versus Declining Balance: Let's look at a comparison between straight-line and 125 percent declining balance depreciation:

Straight-line on your $108,500 improvements for the *Always Full Apartments* is four percent per year or $4340. Each year, for 25 years, you can declare a $4340 depreciation write-off against the income produced by the property.

Now, consider the 125 percent declining balance method. The first year, you can write-off five percent of the $108,500 improvement value, or $5425. The second year, however, we can only write-off five percent of the remaining (or declining) balance of the improvements or:

	$108,500	Improvement Value
Less:	5,425	Last Year's Depreciation
	$103,075	New Balance
	× 5%	
	$ 5,153.75	2nd Year's Write-Off

This process is continued for each year of the depreciation term. As you can see, the amount of write-off you receive diminishes each year. Using the 125 percent "accelerated" method gives you higher depreciation benefits than the straight-line method, but after about five to six years, it starts decreasing below the straight-line amount. When investing to gain maximum tax-free income and tax shelters, you should consider using the fastest depreciation allowed by law. If you are, in the process, building your estate, you will not want to hold on to any property more than five to seven years. By that time, your equity in the property should be sufficient to move up to a much larger property where you can start your depreciation all over again.

That is the best part about depreciation allowances on investment real estate. As soon as you get out of one property and into another, you can start depreciating the new one all over again. The buyer of your old property also starts the depreciation process over.

One Caution Should Be Observed: Once you start a depreciation program on your property, you cannot switch. If you start out using a straight line depreciation schedule and decide a year or two later that you should have used a 125 percent declining balance method, the IRS will not let you change. They may, however, allow you to change *to* straight line from an accelerated method. There are actually five depreciation methods that are available, depending upon the investment property. Only two have been covered to this point.

Other Types of Depreciation and Who Can Use Them: Before reviewing the other types of depreciation, we need to distinguish the difference between the "first owner" of an investment property and any subsequent owner.

The first owner of an investment property is the individual who rents to the first tenant and/or signs the first lease on a new building.

A builder who has tenants lined up for his buildings, prior to selling it, may be considered the first owner by the IRS. Suppose he sells you the building in a completely vacant state, with no signed leases, you will be the first owner. This fact becomes important when you discover the accelerated depreciation that is available to the first owner of a building. When you are purchasing a new building with the idea of qualifying for first owner depreciation, be certain that the builder or developer has not contracted for any tenants prior to closing. Here are the depreciation methods that are available under current tax laws:

Type One: is called the "Sum-of-the-Year's-Digits" method. It is fastest depreciation available, and can be used only if you are the first owner of a rental apartment building. Since it is complicated and used infrequently, it will not be discussed in this book.

Type Two: is the "double declining balance" method (200 percent). As the name indicates, it is double the straight-line method. If the straight-line method you intended to use was three percent per year, the double declining method would allow you six percent depreciation per year. Because the building is new, you will use a 33⅓ useful life or three percent per year. You could not get by using a 25-year life as you did on your seven-year old building.

The same "declining" schedule method is used, as with 125 percent declining balance, only now your remaining balance will be reduced six percent per year instead of five percent per year. Let's compare the three methods over a three-year period. See Figure 10-1.

This uses the *Always Full Apartments* with a 25-year useful life in the straight-line and 125 percent declining balance examples and a new, first owner building of comparable value on the 200 percent declining balance table, assuming a 33⅓ year useful life. The remaining balance for improvements, under the straight-line schedule, does not affect the depreciation allowance. It remains at $4340 each year you keep the property.

	Straight-Line	125% DB	200% DB
Year 1			
Improvements	$108,500	$108,500	$108,500
Depreciation for Year	4,340	5,425	6,510
Year 2			
Improvements (Balance)	$ -	$103,075	$101,990
Depreciation for Year	4,340	5,154	6,119
Year 3			
Improvements (Balance)	$ -	$ 97,921	$ 95,871

Figure 10-1

You can see how the accelerated depreciation methods offer a larger write-off, but they are declining each year. This 200 percent declining balance depreciation method, like the Sum-of-the-Year's-Digits method, can only be used by the first owner of a rental apartment building.

Type Three: is the "150 percent declining balance" method. The schedule works the same as the 200 percent and the 125 percent method, except that it allows one-and-one-half times the straight-line method. One-hundred and fifty percent declining balance depreciation can be used by the first owner of any type of income producing property, including office buildings, shopping centers, warehouse and industrial buildings, motels, and rental apartments.

Type Four: is the "125 percent declining balance" method. This is available for any of the new, first owner, investors listed above and to the owner of an apartment building, even if he is the second owner or later. The only "used" investment property owner that can use the 125 percent method is an apartment building owner, and this does *not* include motels. They are not considered apartments for depreciation purposes.

Type Five: The "straight-line" method is useable by all investment owners.

Figure 10-2 gives you a handy reference showing which type of depreciation is acceptable for various types of properties. Since tax laws change regularly, you will want to be certain no changes have been made that alter this chart, as you use it through the years.

Depreciation Type	Who Can Use It
Sum-of-the-Year's-Digits and 200% Double Declining Balance	First owner of a rental apartment building only (use 33⅓ year minimum useful life).
150% Declining Balance	First owner of any income producing real estate investment. (use 33⅓ year minimum useful life).
125% Declining Balance	Any of the above *plus* owner of a *used apartment building*.
Straight-Line (S/L)	Any of the above *plus* owner of *any* used income producing investment real estate.

Figure 10-2

STEP IV.   Determine Whether to Use the Composite or Component Depreciation

The final step in establishing a depreciation schedule for your property is to determine if you want to use composite or component depreciation. In the previous examples, you have been using *composite* depreciation. In other words, you have used a common depreciation allowance, in terms of its useful life for the entire $108,500 improvement value. Chances are, this is the only type of depreciation you will ever use.

You should at least be aware of *component* depreciation and how it works. Although there are defendable cases where component depreciation has been applied to a used investment property, it is generally a new building depreciation method.

We have already discussed that in order to gain the maximum depreciation benefits, you want to assign the shortest acceptable useful life to the improvements unless your investment goals dictate otherwise. Component depreciation does exactly this. Rather than lump the entire building into one value with a single useful life, it is broken down into its various "components" and each component is assigned a useful life. A typical component structure appears in Figure 10-3.

		Value	Useful Life		% Per Year	Amount
Shell	60%	$ 65,100	33⅓	Yrs	3	$1,953
Plumbing	10%	10,850	30	Yrs	3.33	361
Roof	5%	5,425	20	Yrs	4	217
Electrical	10%	10,850	30	Yrs	4	434
Carpeting, Etc.	5%	5,425	10	Yrs	20	1,085
Air Conditioning & Heating	10%	10,850	10	Yrs	20	2,170
*TOTAL		$108,500				$6,220

*Numbers are rounded to nearest dollar.

Figure 10-3

Using this depreciation method allows part of the building such as the roof, to be depreciated at a faster rate (over a shorter useful life) than the shell of the building. Component depreciation is generally used by the first owner of the property because it is easy, through the builder's construction costs, to establish values on each component.

Although component depreciation can be applied to a used building, proving the value of each component becomes more difficult. There have been cases in which the IRS has challenged the use of component depreciation on a used building and the building owner successfully defended his position.

As you can see, this method offers a high depreciation allowance, but must be prepared by a knowledgeable tax consultant who is ready, preferably with the builder's itemized construction costs, to justify the component percentage and value breakdown. Assuming you will probably never use the component method in establishing your depreciation schedule, all you have is three simple steps:

1. Separate land from improvements from personal property;
2. Establish a useful life for the improvements and the personal property; and
3. Determine what type of depreciation you can use, straight-line, 125 percent, 150 percent or 200 percent.

A SAMPLE DEPRECIATION SCHEDULE FOR THE
ALWAYS FULL APARTMENTS

The purpose the IRS had in allowing such things as accelerated depreciation, as we have already discussed, was to encourage real estate investors by giving them tax breaks.

Let's set up a depreciation schedule for the *Always Full Apartments*. You have already established the land/improvement/personal property ratio and the useful life of both the improvements and the personal property. To that, you need to add the third step—type of depreciation you intend to use. You decide to use the maximum allowable depreciation for your used apartment building or 125 percent declining balance. Since you are writing-off the value of the personal property over a short five-year term, use straight-line depreciation. The law, however, allows you to use the same depreciation method on personal property that you are using on the improvements. But again, since you are only using a five-year useful life to begin with, it would not pay to use accelerated depreciation on top of that.

Your first year's depreciation schedule on the *Always Full Apartments*, looks like Figure 10-4.

Item	Useful Life	Type of Depreciation	=	% of Value	×	Value	=	First Year Depreciation
Improvements	25 Yrs	125%		5%		$108,500		$ 5,425
Personal Property	5 Yrs	S/L		20%		23,250		4,650
	TOTAL FIRST YEAR DEPRECIATION							$10,075

Figure 10-4

Referring to Figure 10-5, you can now fill in this $10,075 depreciation on the "Less depreciation" line near the bottom of your property analysis form. You then subtract the $10,075 from the $6188 gross equity income figure above it, and you end up with a negative number of $3887. This has been bracketed on your form to indicate that the property will actually show a tax loss, according to the IRS, even though it gave you a $6188 equity return on your invested capital.

• PROPERTY ANALYSIS •

Name: *Always Full Apts.*
Location: *147 NE 8th St.*
Type of Property: *8 Unit Apt. Bldg.* **Area:**

LIST PRICE **155,000**

CASH REQ'D. **45,000**

EXISTING ASSUMABLE FINANCING:

	Amount	Ann. Pmt.	Int.	Years To Go
1st $	73,500	7,150	7½ %	19+
2nd			%	
3rd			%	

POTENTIAL FINANCING:

	Amount	Ann. Pmt.	Int.	Years
1st $			%	
2nd	36,500	3,676	9 %	25
3rd			%	

Folio:	Ex — S.O.O	File:
Date:	Units: 8	Lister:
Zoning R-3	Pool NO	Parking 12 CARS
Size 100 X 150	Rec. Rm. NO	A-C YES
Sq. Ft. 6500	Util. Rm. YES	Heat YES
Age 7 YRS	Office NO	T.V. NO
Stories 2	Lobby NO	Furniture YES
Sewers YES	Elevators NO	Waterfront NO
Constr CONCRETE & FRAME		

Description —	# Units	Rent Sch
1 Bedroom, 1 Bath	6	$228/mo.
2 Bedroom, 2 Bath	2	$256/mo.

SCHEDULE GROSS INCOME			22	560
Less: Vacancy & Credit Loss	5%		1	128
GROSS OPERATING INCOME			21	432
Less: Operating Expenses				
Taxes		2 350		
Insurance		580		
Utilities ELECTRIC		140		
Advertising				
Licenses & Permits		25		
Management				
Payroll & Payroll Taxes		1 200		
Supplies				
Services WATER/SEWER		360		
Maintenance 5%		1 072		
Reserve for Replacement				
Ground Lease				
LAWN SERVICE		720		
TOTAL EXPENSES	30 %	6 447		
OPERATING INCOME		14 985		
Plus Other Income				
NET OPERATING INCOME		14 985		

COMMENTS: CODE _____

DEPRECIATION SCHEDULE:

LAND VALUE = 15%

IMPROVEMENTS = 70%
@ 25 YR. USEFUL LIFE,
125% DECLINING BALANCE
DEPRECIATION = $5,425

PERSONAL PROPERTY = 15%
@ 5 YR. USEFUL LIFE,
S/L (STRAIGHT LINE) DEPRECIATION
= $4,650

INFORMATION HEREIN IS BELIEVED TO BE
ACCURATE BUT IS NOT WARRANTED

INCOME ADJUSTED TO FINANCING: Actual ☐   Potential ☒   Equity: $ 45,000

NET OPERATING INCOME	Cap. Rate - List Price:		%			14 985
Less: Loan Payment	3rd Loan	2nd Loan	1st Loan	TOTAL		
Interest		3 285	5 512	8 797		
Principal		391	1 638	2 029		
Total Loan Payment		3 676	7 150	10 826	10	826
GROSS SPENDABLE INCOME	Rate: 9.2 %	(GSI ÷ EQUITY)			4	159
Plus: Principal Payment					2	029
GROSS EQUITY INCOME	Rate: 13.8 %	(GEI ÷ EQUITY)			6	188
Less: Depreciation	Personal Property= $4,650	Improvements = $5,425			10	075
REAL ESTATE TAXABLE INCOME			TAX LOSS		(3	887)

---

* Based on Form "B," copyrighted by REALTORS NATIONAL MARKETING INSTITUTE
OF NATIONAL ASSOCIATION OF REALTORS. Copyright 1974. All rights reserved.
Used with permission of copyright owner.
** Reprinted with permission of L.C. Judd & Co., Inc.

Figure 10-5

153

This is what is referred to as a "tax shelter." Come income tax time, you can actually show a $3887 tax loss on your tax return, even though the building actually produced a $6188 profit. Owning this building reduced your other taxable income by $3887 or gave you a $3887 "tax shelter."

If you are a 33⅓% taxpayer, an individual who pays Uncle Sam 33⅓% of every taxable dollar you earn, the *Always Full Apartments* just saved you $1295 in income tax you would normally have paid from your other income (⅓ of $3887 = $1295). Even if the building had just broken even for the year, it put an additional $1295 in your pocket by saving you taxes on your other income. Now you know why you will usually want to take the maximum amount of depreciation allowed to you by law.

For your convenience, depreciation tables for a 20-, 25-, 30-, and 33⅓-useful life term are in the Appendix of this book. They show you the annual percentage you can use for each type of depreciation for the useful life you are using. They have been simplified to give you the amount of depreciation you can take from the original balance each year.

Figure 10-6 shows the 25-year useful life table you have been using. Notice that under the "Straight-Line" column, the annual percentage rate you can take from the original improvement amount is four percent each year for the entire 25 years.

Using a 125 percent declining balance method, the annual percentage that you can deduct from the original improvement amount decreases, or declines, each year. The second column under each type of depreciation, gives you a cumulative total for the number of years shown at the left. If, for example, you want to know the total amount of depreciation you will have taken in five years, using the 125 percent declining balance method, locate the cumulative depreciation percentage figure opposite five years and under 125 percent cumulative, and you'll see it is 22.62 percent. You have, therefore, used up 22.62 percent of the improvements value on depreciation after five years. Let's use the five year column and see how straight-line depreciation would compare with 125 percent declining balance on your $108,500 of depreciable improvements on the *Always Full Apartments*.

First, the straight-line method. In the fifth year you can take four percent or $4340. As you can see by the chart, you can take four percent or $4340 each year for the entire 25 years.

The cumulative total opposite five years for straight-line depreciation shows 20 percent. At the end of five years, you will have taken 20 percent of $108,500 or $21,700 in depreciation. The fifth year row under 125 percent method of depreciation shows that you can take 4.07 percent of your

25 Years Useful Life

Year Number	Straight-Line Rate: 4%		125% Declining Bal. Rate: 5%		150% Declining Bal. Rate: 6%		200% Declining Bal. Rate: 8%	
	Annual	Cum.	Annual	Cum.	Annual	Cum.	Annual	Cum.
1	4.00	4.00	5.00	5.00	6.00	6.00	8.00	8.00
2	4.00	8.00	4.75	9.75	5.64	11.64	7.36	15.36
3	4.00	12.00	4.51	14.26	5.30	16.94	6.77	22.13
4	4.00	16.00	4.29	18.55	4.98	21.92	6.23	28.36
5	4.00	20.00	4.07	22.62	4.68	26.60	5.73	34.09
6	4.00	24.00	3.87	26.49	4.40	31.00	5.27	39.36
7	4.00	28.00	3.68	30.17	4.14	35.14	4.86	44.22
8	4.00	32.00	3.49	33.66	3.89	39.03	4.46	48.68
9	4.00	36.00	3.32	36.98	3.66	42.69	4.10	52.78
10	4.00	40.00	3.15	40.13	3.43	46.12	3.78	56.56
11	4.00	44.00	2.99	43.12	3.23	49.35	3.48	60.04
12	4.00	48.00	2.84	45.96	3.03	52.38	3.19	63.23
13	4.00	52.00	2.70	48.66	2.86	55.24	2.94	66.17
14	4.00	56.00	2.57	51.23	2.68	57.92	2.71	68.88
15	4.00	60.00	2.44	53.67	2.52	60.44	2.49	71.37
16	4.00	64.00	2.32	55.99	2.37	62.81	2.29	73.66
17	4.00	68.00	2.20	58.19	2.23	65.04	2.11	75.77
18	4.00	72.00	2.09	60.28	2.10	67.14	1.94	77.71
19	4.00	76.00	1.99	62.27	1.97	69.11	1.78	79.49
20	4.00	80.00	1.89	64.16	1.85	70.96	1.64	81.13
21	4.00	84.00	1.80	65.96	1.74	72.70	1.51	82.64
22	4.00	88.00	1.70	67.66	1.64	74.34	1.39	84.03
23	4.00	92.00	1.62	69.28	1.54	75.88	1.28	85.31
24	4.00	96.00	1.54	70.82	1.45	77.33	1.17	86.48
25	4.00	100.00	1.46	72.28	1.36	78.69	1.08	87.56

Figure 10-6

155

$108,500 depreciable improvements or $4416. By the end of the fifth year, using this method of depreciation, the chart says you have taken a total of 22.62 percent or $24,543.

Notice that by using the 125 percent depreciation, you have been able to take $2843 additional depreciation over the straight-line method. Now, check the tenth year figures for both straight-line and 125 percent declining balance method. You'll see that in the tenth year you can still take four percent of the $108,500 under the straight-line method but only 3.15 percent under the 125 percent method.

Look at the cumulative depreciation you would have taken in ten years if you were using a *200 percent*, or double declining method of depreciation. You will see that the building in ten years, is already 56.56 percent depreciated or over half, even though you still have 15 years to go. Your goal, of course, is not to keep the property that long, but just until you have obtained the maximum tax benefits and are able to move into a much larger property because of the increase in your equity.

HOW YOU CAN SHELTER OTHER INCOME
BY OWNING INVESTMENT REAL ESTATE

It is important to realize the tremendous potential you have to "shelter" other income by owning investment real estate. No other form of investing offers you the high returns on your invested capital, outstanding chance for capital appreciation and a tax shelter against your other income all at one time.

Assume you are in a high tax bracket, say 50 percent. You pay the IRS 50 percent of everything you earn over your base income. You decide to purchase an apartment building that has appreciation potential but does not show much of a cash flow. The last thing you need is to add more taxable income to your present tax problems.

The *Never Full Apartments* are located in an excellent area, but because of poor management, they always have vacancies. You are able to purchase the property for $200,000 with $45,000 cash down. After operating expenses and mortgage payments, the property analysis looks like Figure 10-7. You probably do not want to bother managing your own property so you employ a professional property manage who charges five percent of the gross rents collected. That fee is figured into the operating expenses.

● PROPERTY ANALYSIS ●

Name: **NEVER FULL APTS.**

Location: _____

Type of Property: _____ Area _____

Folio:	Ex — S.O.O	File:
Date:	Units:	Lister:
Zoning	Pool	Parking
Size	Rec. Rm.	A-C
Sq. Ft.	Util. Rm.	Heat
Age *12 YRS*	Office	T V
Stories	Lobby	Furniture *YES*
Sewers	Elevators	Waterfront
Constr.		

Description —	# Units	Rent Sch

LIST PRICE *200,000*

CASH REQ'D. *45,000*

EXISTING ASSUMABLE FINANCING:

	Amount	Ann. Pmt.	Int.	Years To Go
1st $	*105,000*	*10,977*	*9* %	*22*
2nd			%	
3rd			%	

POTENTIAL FINANCING:

				Years
1st $			%	
2nd	*50,000*	*5,790*	*10* %	*20*
3rd			%	

SCHEDULE GROSS INCOME		27	9??
Less: Vacancy & Credit Loss *5%*		1	397
GROSS OPERATING INCOME		26	540
Less. Operating Expenses			
Taxes		3	200
Insurance			950
Utilities		1	020
Advertising			
Licenses & Permits			
Management		1	310
Payroll & Payroll Taxes			
Supplies			
Services			950
Maintenance		1	310
Reserve for Replacement			
Ground Lease			
TOTAL EXPENSES	%	8	740
OPERATING INCOME		17	800
Plus Other Income			ø
NET OPERATING INCOME		17	800

COMMENTS: _____ CODE: _____

DEPRECIATION SCHEDULE

LAND = 15%

IMPROVEMENTS = 70%, 20 YR.
USEFUL LIFE, 125% D.B.
= 6.25% 1ST YR = $8,750

PERSONAL PROPERTY = 15%, 5 YR.
USEFUL LIFE, S/L DEPRECIATION
= 20% YR. = $6,000

INFORMATION HEREIN IS BELIEVED TO BE
ACCURATE BUT IS NOT WARRANTED

INCOME ADJUSTED TO FINANCING:	Actual ☐	Potential ☒	Equity: $ *45,000*			
NET OPERATING INCOME	Cap. Rate - List Price:	%			17	800
Less: Loan Payment	3rd Loan	2nd Loan	1st Loan	TOTAL		
Interest		5 000	9 450	14 450		
Principal		790	1 527	2 317		
Total Loan Payment		5 790	10 977	16 767	16	767
GROSS SPENDABLE INCOME	Rate: %	(GSI + EQUITY)			1	033
Plus: Principal Payment					2	317
GROSS EQUITY INCOME	Rate: %	(GEI + EQUITY)			3	350
Less: Depreciation	Personal Property	Improvements			14	250
REAL ESTATE TAXABLE INCOME		*TAX LOSS*			(11	400)

---

* Based on Form "B," copyrighted by REALTORS NATIONAL MARKETING INSTITUTE OF NATIONAL ASSOCIATION OF REALTORS. Copyright 1974. All rights reserved. Used with permission of copyright owner.

** Reprinted with permission of L.C. Judd & Co., Inc.

Figure 10-7

157

After all operating expenses and debt service (mortgage payments) the property only produces a gross spendable income of $1033. Don't bother to divide that by your $45,000 cash investment to find out the cash return, it's pretty bad, but not for someone in a high tax bracket. You do want to be certain that the property will carry itself. As you see, the analysis allowed for five percent or $1397 in vacancies and it still shows a $1033 cash flow. Unless you know exactly what you are getting into, you do not want to reach the point where you have to "feed" the building to keep it running. Because of the age of the building, you'll use a 20-year useful life and 125 percent declining balance depreciation (see Figure 10-8). This gives you a first year write-off of 6.25 percent on the improvements.

This building will offer you an $11,400 tax loss or tax write-off against your other income. For a 50 percent taxpayer, you just saved $5700 that you would have paid Uncle Sam if you hadn't owned the *Never Full Apartments*. And all this time, you own $200,000 worth of real estate that is becoming more valuable each day that you own it. There is no other investment vehicle that offers this potential.

RECAPTURE

Before leaving the subject of depreciation, we should take a look at the long range effects of taking the depreciation benefits available to us in real estate. In one sentence, the end result is "the IRS makes you pay it all back."

Before you close this book and throw it away, keep reading. To put your mind at ease, I should add, you may have to pay it back, but not necessarily. In Chapter 16 we will discuss exchanging and you will learn how you may never have to pay it back.

For now, you should know that if you were to sell your investment property, all the depreciation you have taken will be deducted from what you paid for the property, thus increasing the amount of taxable profit you realize from the sale. The subject is actually more involved and will be covered in detail in Chapter 16.

THE TIME VALUE OF MONEY AND HOW IT WORKS
IN YOUR FAVOR

What is of interest here is the "time value of money." If you were given $10,000 today, to use for five years, how much is that worth knowing that in five years you'll have to pay it back with interest.

Comparisons of Depreciation Methods
Cost of Asset – $100/Salvage Value – Zero

Year Number	Straight-Line Rate: 5%		125% Declining Bal. Rate: 6.25%		20 Years Useful Life 150% Declining Bal. Rate: 7.5%		200% Declining Bal. Rate: 10%	
	Annual	Cum.	Annual	Cum.	Annual	Cum.	Annual	Cum.
1	5.00	5.00	6.25	6.25	7.50	7.50	10.00	10.00
2	5.00	10.00	5.86	12.11	6.94	14.44	9.00	19.00
3	5.00	15.00	5.49	17.60	6.42	20.86	8.10	27.10
4	5.00	20.00	5.15	22.75	5.94	26.80	7.29	34.39
5	5.00	25.00	4.83	27.58	5.49	32.29	6.56	40.95
6	5.00	30.00	4.53	32.11	5.08	37.37	5.91	46.86
7	5.00	35.00	4.24	36.35	4.70	42.07	5.31	52.17
8	5.00	40.00	3.98	40.33	4.35	46.42	4.78	56.95
9	5.00	45.00	3.73	44.06	4.02	50.44	4.31	61.26
10	5.00	50.00	3.50	47.56	3.71	54.15	3.87	65.13
11	5.00	55.00	3.28	50.84	3.44	57.59	3.49	68.62
12	5.00	60.00	3.07	53.91	3.18	60.77	3.14	71.76
13	5.00	65.00	2.88	56.79	2.94	63.71	2.82	74.58
14	5.00	70.00	2.70	59.49	2.72	66.43	2.54	77.12
15	5.00	75.00	2.53	62.02	2.52	68.95	2.29	79.41
16	5.00	80.00	2.37	64.39	2.33	71.28	2.06	81.47
17	5.00	85.00	2.23	66.62	2.15	73.43	1.85	83.32
18	5.00	90.00	2.09	68.71	1.99	75.42	1.67	84.99
19	5.00	95.00	1.96	70.67	1.84	77.26	1.50	86.49
20	5.00	100.00	1.83	72.50	1.70	78.96	1.35	87.84

Figure 10-8

159

This requires a closer look. The *Never Full Apartments* gave a $14,750 tax write-off which in turn produced an $11,400 tax loss or $5700 tax savings for a 50 percent taxpayer.

Figure 10-9 gives you a year-by-year review of your after tax benefits from the ownership of the *Never Full Apartments*. It is assumed that you do not increase rents during the five years and operating expenses also stay the same.

Year	Cash Flow +	Principal Payment +	Tax Savings From Other Income +	Yearly Total Return
1	$1,033	$2,317	$5,700	$ 9,050
2	1,033	2,533	5,427	8,993
3	1,033	2,772	5,168	8,973
4	1,033	3,030	4,930	8,993
5	1,033	3,313	4,706	9,052
TOTALS	$5,165	$13,965	$25,931	$45,061

	Depreciation Taken		
Year	Improvements	Personal Property	Total
1	$ 8,750	$ 6,000	$14,750
2	8,204	6,000	14,204
3	7,686	6,000	13,686
4	7,210	6,000	13,210
5	6,762	6,000	12,762
TOTALS	$38,612	$30,000	$68,612

Figure 10-9

During the five years that you owned the *Never Full Apartments*, you were able to put $5165 tax-free cash in your pocket from the cash flow produced by the building. You paid your mortgage down by $13,965 and were able to save $25,931 in tax savings from your other income. All total, you made, after taxes, $45,061.

Now, for the other side of the picture. You also took $68,612 in depreciation during that same five-year period. That will be recaptured by the IRS and taxed, when you sell your property. Although part of the depreciation you took was at an accelerated basis (the 25 percent over straight-line) we will, for simplicity here, consider it all as straight-line depreciation. The accelerated portion of depreciation that you take is actually taxed as ordinary income and not at capital gains rates. Your accountant is the one who can give you the exact effects to you, based on your tax situation.

Assume that you owe 28 percent of the depreciation you took as capital gains tax. So, if you were to sell, rather than exchange, you would have to pay Uncle Sam $19,211 in capital gains tax or 28 percent of the $68,612 depreciation you took. But, you had the use of this $19,211 for five years tax-free and were able to earn $45,061 on it.

Suppose you were given the chance of receiving $10,000 today, in cash, or $12,000 in cash five years from now. Which would you take? This is where the "time value of money" comes into effect. If you wait 5 years to collect and are given $12,000 each of those $12,000 dollars has a reduced purchasing power due to five years of inflation, and you already know what inflation is doing to you. Assuming inflation is 10 percent per year for the next five years, that $12,000 in 5 years is only worth what $7541 is today. Look at it another way.

Take the $10,000 today and put it in a "fixed" investment, one that does not even keep up with inflation, and see what happens. Ten thousand dollars in a six percent interest bearing C.D. for five years, compounded, will give us a cash value in five years of $13,382.26 or $1382.26 more than if we had waited five years to collect the $12,000.

Getting back to your capital gains tax on the sale of the *Never Full Apartments*, multiply the $45,061 you earned by 28 percent because your tax consequences were only 28 percent of the $68,612 depreciation you took—$45,061 multiplied by 28 percent equals $12,617. You earned $12,617 on the $19,211 that you must pay Uncle Sam when you sell five years from now. How much did it cost you to "borrow" that $19,211 for five years? Figure it like this:

Step 1	What you owe IRS	$19,211
	What you made on that money	$12,617
	What it cost to use that money	$ 6,594

Step 2 $\dfrac{\$6,594}{5 \text{ Yrs.}}$ = $1,319 per year

Step 3 $\dfrac{\text{What it cost per year}}{\text{What you owe IRS}}$ $\dfrac{\$ 1,319}{\$19,211}$ = 6.9%

In other words, you had the use of $19,211 at an annual average interest rate of 6.9 percent. Where else can you borrow money as inexpensively? What did you earn by using that money?

Referring again to Figure 10-9, your five year cumulative totals show that combining cash flow, principal payment and tax savings on your other income, you put $45,061 in your pocket *after taxes*, during the five year period, or $9012 per year:

$$\frac{\text{Annual Return}}{\text{Initial Investment}} \quad \frac{\$\ 9,012}{\$45,000} \ = \ 20\%$$

You were able to earn 20 percent after taxes, part of which was on money that you "borrowed" from the Federal Government at 6.9 percent interest.

The time value of money should always be considered when you have a choice of taking money today or a larger sum in the future. The prudent use of other people's money, even Uncle Sam's, can give you the maximum possible after-tax income and growth potential with the cash you have to invest.

When you are deciding on the investment you want to purchase, as you did with the possible financing avenues, look at your tax consequences and see which way will benefit you the most. A knowledgeable real estate oriented tax specialist or a Realtor specializing in this field, can assist you. Remember, it doesn't matter how much you earn, but how much you get to keep after taxes that is important. A properly structured real estate investment can not only give you tax-free income, but can shelter part of your other income as well.

11

How to Negotiate the Purchase

Before we discuss entering into a formal offer to purchase the property you have selected, you need to understand what will probably happen to your thinking at this point.

DON'T HIT THE PANIC BUTTON

Assuming you are a typical, first time real estate investor, you will probably have a tendency to reach for the "panic button." This is a normal reaction, the fear of venturing into a real estate investment without the prior experience of how financially rewarding it will be is very common. This fear may be comparable to flying a plane for the first time or making your first speech before a large group of people—it is a natural reaction. *Don't let it stop you from making the decision to purchase.*

Let me encourage you with three basic facts:

1. If you did your homework and understand what you have read in this book, you are really well qualified to make a decision to purchase;

2. Again, assuming you did your homework and properly evaluated your intended purchase, your chance of making a wrong business judgement is remote; and

3. It is virtually impossible to make a totally bad investment in real estate, unless you did exactly the opposite of what this book instructed you to do.

Let me tell you of a few would-be investors I have had over the years and what it cost them to NOT buy. Each of these people (the names have been changed) reach the point that you are right now. They located the property that met their investment goals, in a good location, and could be considered a sound real estate investment. But each investor hit the "panic button" and did not buy.

Mr. and Mrs. McCall wanted a small ocean front motel on the southeast Florida coast. Mrs. McCall had always wanted to live on the ocean and they had just retired to Florida. One of the properties we examined was priced at below market value. It contained almost five acres of land, had both ocean and intracoastal water frontage, and a small motel on the ocean. Mrs. McCall decided she did not like the property because there were three steps down to the beach. They felt $450,000 was too high a price to pay even though it contained five acres of prime property. So, they passed it up. The property was subsequently sold to another investor for $450,000. One year later, he turned down a $1,000,000 offer for the property. But the McCalls really lost because they were afraid to take that first step.

Mr. Raymond spent a couple of days with me looking for an industrial building that was leased to a stable company. We located a $300,000 building for sale that was leased to a computer manufacturer. It had everything he wanted. We drew up a contract and had verbal agreement from the seller; at the last minute, Mr. Raymond had second thoughts. "Let me call my attorney," he said. His attorney, in a 60 second conversation, without knowledge of the proposed investment, advised him against *any* real estate investment in our "unstable" economy. "That's it," Mr. Raymond said, closing up his briefcase. He did not buy. Within two years, the computer company had to expand into an additional building. Mr. Raymond had passed up a long-term, sound real estate investment.

Mr. and Mrs. Reed flew to south Florida from New York. They wanted to purchase a rental apartment building. They had been thinking about it for a couple of years. We looked at several properties over a three day period and reviewed all of the financial information on each. They made an offer on a 15-unit building in a prime rental area. The agreed to price was $190,000. They left for home that evening pleased with their purchase. Then fear set in. They called me the first thing the next morning and said they had changed their minds. They wanted out of the contract and had stopped payment on the deposit check they had given me. I talked the seller into releasing them from the contract. (He could have legally sued them, at least for liquidated damages.) The property was sold to another investor a week or so later. Within two years, he was able to re-sell at a price of $230,000. He made a $40,000 profit and only had $40,000 of his own cash invested.

Finally, Mr. and Mrs. Shaw wanted to purchase a 15 to 20-unit apartment building. Over a one month period, we met several times and in the process, examined some 20 possible properties, each of which would give them what they needed. They turned each one down, usually for an obviously meaningless reason. They never did buy. I prepared a letter to them, one year later, showing them what it cost them during that year to have passed up the first property that they had considered. The context of the letter read as follows:

> I was wondering where you would have been now, if 12 months ago you had purchased the _____ apartments, one of the first properties we looked at.
>
> First of all, I am making the assumption that your investment funds are still in six percent certificates. Your annual pre-tax interest on the $150,000 was $9000. Since you are in a 40 percent tax bracket, your after-tax return was $5400 or 3.6 percent.
>
> If, instead, you would have purchased the _____ apartments at a price of $525,000 with $150,000 cash down, your investment capital would have earned the following in the past 12 months:

Cash Flow	=	$12,353	(all tax free)
Mortgage Reduction	=	3,691	(all tax free)
Tax Savings on $24,405 @ 40%	=	5,762	
Minimum of 5% appreciation	=	26,250	
Total Return	=	$48,056	or 32% return on your $150,000 Cash Investment.

In other words, Mr. and Mrs. Shaw, it is costing you a minimum of $3555 for every month you leave your investment capital in the bank.

The moral behind these stories is to take that final step. Do not reach the point of making the offer and then freeze. Without exception, each of these investors have come back to me and said, "I made a big mistake. Why didn't you *force* me to buy that property?"

On the brighter side, here is a brief review of a few investors who *did* take that final step.

Mr. Hunt purchased a small motel and ran it himself for three years. His initial investment was $60,000. During the three years he owned it, the motel gave him a 12 to 15 percent tax-free return each year. Three years later, he sold it and made a $35,000 profit after taxes.

Mrs. Russell, a widow, had owned a parcel of vacant land for 15 or 20 years. She had paid about $40,000 for it when she purchased it many years ago. She decided to sell the land and invest the proceeds in rental apartment buildings. She was amazed to discover that her land was now worth $500,000 and a developer was ready to sign the contract. We convinced Mrs. Russell to exchange, rather than sell, because capital gains tax would have taken a large bite out of her profits. An exchange took place and Mrs. Russell now owns $1,500,000 worth of income producing real estate.

Mr. Cooper owned a meat market. He had been leasing space, for several years, in a small strip shopping center. He asked me to check into the feasibility of acquiring a closed gas station property and building his own store. Complete details were prepared including the cost of acquiring the lot and building a small four store building on the property. Mr. Cooper did just that. His total cost in the project was about $250,000, only $75,000 of which he had to put up. The remaining portion was financed. He ended up owning his own store and the other three tenants are paying his "rent" for him. He has now decided to retire and his building is on the market for $400,000, not too far from what it will sell for.

Finally, Mr. and Mrs. Clark moved to Florida. They planned on renting an apartment for a few years until they decided where they wanted to live. After counseling with them, they realized that they would be paying $300 a month for an apartment and have nothing to show for their expense. It cannot even be deducted from their income tax as an expense.

Instead, they invested $15,000 in a four-unit apartment building. They paid $60,000 for the property. The Clark's moved into one of the apartments and rented the other three. Not only did the three "paying" tenants' rent cover all mortgage payments and most of the expenses but the Clarks were able to write-off three-fourths of the mortgage interest payments and real estate taxes as expenses on their income tax return. They were, in effect, living rent free and reducing their other taxable income at the same time. Three years later, when they decided to move to a different area, they were pleased to find that their $60,000 building had a current market value of $73,000. At the same time, their mortgage had been paid down by $2500. Their original $15,000 investment had grown to over $30,000 or double what they had invested. They will never consider renting again.

All of these examples have been given for just one reason. When you find the property that you feel is right for you, BUY IT. The first one will be the most difficult. Once you see your investment capital grow in a real estate investment, you will be an avid investor from then on. So, now is the time to take that step.

You have now reached the point where you have decided that a real estate investment is right for you. You have found the property you want to purchase, analyzed it thoroughly and tried various forms of financing to see how you can benefit the most from the investment. You have a pretty good idea as to your tax consequences. And, if you have done everything you should to this point, you have established your investment goals and determined just how involved you want to become in the management of your investment. You know exactly how much capital you plan to invest, including a reserve for closing costs.

Now, you are ready to buy the property that fits your needs. Where do you go from here? Assuming this is your first investment purchase, consider using a knowledgeable investment Realtor to assist you. Purchase contracts can be tricky.

It is interesting to note how some investors feel it is wise to negotiate the purchase of investment real estate without professional help even though they are probably about to spend the largest sum of money in their entire life. And yet, they will call a mechanic friend to look at a used car before they buy it to be certain it's a good deal for the price they are paying.

This book is intended to explain how to "do it yourself." The first step in negotiating a purchase is to determine exactly how much you are willing to pay for the property and under what terms you want to buy. There are outside factors that enter into a possible modification of your purchase criteria.

KNOW THE MARKET

First of all, you must get a "feel" for the market. What are comparable properties in the area selling for. When you are in a "sellers" market, where prime investments are difficult to find and buyers, your competitors, are plentiful, you may have to revise your minimum standards for purchasing. Remember, while you are deciding what is best for you as a purchaser, the seller is deciding what is best for him as a seller.

Generally speaking, you hope to meet somewhere in the middle. You may go into a property negotiation hoping for a 10 percent cash return on a 15 percent down payment. The seller may want all cash to the mortgage which may require a 50 percent down payment and he has a price on the property that will only give you a five percent return on your investment.

You then try to reach a happy medium with him, one that you both find acceptable and you both can live with. Neither you nor the seller can expect to get everything you both want. This is the reason for determining your maximum acceptable price and minimum acceptable terms before you meet the seller face-to-face. If he does not get within reasonable range of these terms, don't give in and buy anyway. You may be sorry later. Again, I must emphasize that you must be realistic in your request. You may end up with a little less than you hoped for, but do not lose sight of two facts.

Fact One: You have chosen this as your first priority investment. it was better than any other you have been able to find.

Fact Two: Even at a higher price or terms somewhat less than you hoped for, how will it stack up compared with your present investments?

NEVER MAKE A VERBAL OFFER

Never, I repeat, *NEVER* make a verbal offer to a seller. Don't expect to walk up to the owner of the *Always Full Apartments* and say, "I want to purchase your building, but $155,000 is too high. I'll give you $145,000." Do you know what he'd say? I will not repeat it here. You cannot buy a new car without signing a contract and making a deposit, so do not expect to purchase a $155,000 apartment building without one. And yet, you would be surprised how many "knowledgeable" investors ask a Realtor to "call up the seller and see what he'll take."

How to Do It Right

The proper way to negotiate a purchase is to prepare a formal written offer to purchase, spelling out all of the terms and conditions under which you want to acquire his building. Equally important is that the executed offer to purchase will be accompanied by an earnest money deposit check, preferably in the amount of 10 percent of the offering price. When the purchase is a sizable one and you do not want to tie up 10 percent of the price with the contract, you can offer a smaller amount, say $1000, with the balance of the 10 percent deposit due within a few days after the contract is accepted by the seller on terms also agreeable to you.

What is the difference between the verbal and written offer? Suppose you were the seller of the *Always Full Apartments* and someone you did not know told you he would give you $145,000 for your property. What would your reaction be? He is asking you to reduce your price by $10,000. If you agree, he may or may not purchase the property. You do not know, and he has not obligated himself to anything at this point. Even if he agrees to purchase it, you have no idea as to the terms he wants. Maybe he is trying to buy your property with only a $5000 or $10,000 down payment. Assuming you do not come to contract with this buyer and your property is still on the market, you can be certain that every potential buyer will shortly know that the price is now $145,000 not $155,000. The next potential buyer will probably offer $135,000.

A formal contract protects both buyer and seller. You can probably locate a standard form contract in your area, often prepared by the local bar association. The standard contract in Fort Lauderdale, Florida has been prepared jointly by the county bar association and the Board of Realtors. Some states require that a purchase contract be prepared by an attorney. You will have to check local custom in your area.

HOW MUCH SHOULD YOU OFFER?

Purchasing real estate is a unique experience. Even the most experienced investors like to "haggle" or negotiate on the price. It is customary to assume that any seller has "padded" his asking price to allow for negotiating with a prospective buyer. It is also customary for a buyer to make an offer *below* the price he expects, and is willing to pay. With this basic unwritten law in mind, you need to determine how much you should offer.

Never offer full price, unless the property is such a "good deal" that it is well worth what the seller is asking and you have been told by him that he will not negotiate on the price.

Conversely, a "low ball" offer, one way less than the listed price, may not be taken seriously by the seller. Unless he is highly motivated to sell, he will probably be insulted by an obvious attempt to "steal" his property and you may not get a counter offer at all. I have seen sellers look at a "low ball" contract offer and tear it up in front of the buyer. When this happens, the buyer will have a difficult time getting the seller to consider another, more reasonable, offer. He might as well start looking for another property.

So, what should you offer? Assuming the property is priced fairly close to a fair market value, try five to ten percent less than the listed price. Your offer should be such that the final price you will accept is halfway between the listed price and your offer. Assume you are willing to pay $150,000 for the *Always Full Apartments*, which are being offered for $155,000. You offer will be $145,000 or about 6½ percent below the listed price.

Keep in mind that this is a rough rule of thumb. Circumstances may dictate an even lower offer. These could include:

1. A highly motivated seller—he *must* sell;
2. Distressed or problem properties; or
3. An offering price far above current, comparable prices in the area.

In any event, make an offer and be prepared to negotiate with the seller. That's half the fun of buying investment real estate. You may even end up paying less than you expected, but you won't know unless you try.

TIME LIMIT FOR ACCEPTANCE

If you are the one negotiating your purchase, do not be hasty. Some negotiations take hours, days, or even months! On the other hand, most purchase contracts can be negotiated in a matter of hours, or less, if there are only minor areas of disagreement. You want to avoid giving the seller too much time. It is advisable to have a time limit for acceptance by the seller written in your contract. Given too much time to accept, it is common for some sellers to "shop" your contract. In other words, they will use your offer to purchase to get a better one from another prospective buyer.

CONTRACT CLAUSES THAT PROTECT YOU

Several contract clauses can be written into a contract to protect yourself. Listed below are a few you may want to use, although proper wording will vary depending on your area and who is drawing up the contract. I would suggest that all of these clauses be inserted in your contract, unless they do not apply.

Inspection Clause

Where a property, such as a rental apartment building is being purchased, it may not be possible to see every apartment, inside, prior to buying. As a practical matter, the seller cannot be expected to disturb every tenant for a ''tour'' of their apartment by every stranger who comes by and may want to buy the building. Doing this is also a breach of the tenant's rights which are probably spelled out in his lease.

The seller, therefore, shows the prospective buyer one or two typical apartments. The contract then has a clause allowing the purchaser to examine the remaining apartments, once a contract is agreed to. The clause should allow him to verify that the remaining apartments are in the same basic condition as the one or ones he already inspected. For protection of the seller, this clause should not be worded in such a way that it becomes an ''escape'' clause for the buyer. In other words, the buyer should not be able to say, ''I don't like the other apartments'' for no reason whatsoever and back out of the contract. That is the reason for the wording, ''that the apartments are in the same basic condition as the ones already inspected.'' You can store this thought in your memory bank for use when *you* become the seller.

Income and Expense Verification

A clause, offering the buyer or his accountant, the right to examine the operational books of the building, should be included in the offer to purchase contract. Like the inspection clause, it should not serve as an out for the buyer, but rather as a verification that the actual, recorded, income and expenses are as represented in the property offering.

Leases

Not only should a contract clause allow for verification of lease term, rent being paid, and security deposit that was paid by the tenant and is being held by the owner, but it may also request ''estopple'' letters being sent to each tenant so that they can personally verify these three items. Leases can be falsified, but the tenant will certainly tell you what the status of his lease is.

Mortgage Assumptions

When you are assuming a mortgage or mortgages, estopple letters must be sent to the mortgagee(s) (lenders) in which they verify the mortgage balance, interest rate, term, monthly payment and escrow account balance. We have already discussed what can happen if the lender has a right to refuse new buyer assuming the mortgage. You also want to be certain the remaining balance is not considerably less than you were told and that the interest rate will remain the same for you as the new owner. Any change in the balance or interest rate requires your reworking your analysis form before you proceed to purchase.

Inspections

You may want to have any number of inspections performed, at your expense, to be certain there are no physical problems with the property. These may include, termite inspection, roof inspection, appliance inspection, etc.

That last one, "appliance inspection" can be troublesome. I've seen contracts written that read, "Seller guarantees that all appliances shall be in satisfactory working condition at the time of closing."

First of all, the seller cannot "guarantee" their working condition. What is "satisfactory" to the seller, may not be "satisfactory" to the buyer. Just leave that word out altogether. Contract clauses should be inserted where needed for the purpose of verifying or spelling out specific terms of the purchase. It is not possible to cover them all here. When you prepare a purchase contract, items you want included will become evident.

It is possible to fill a contract so full of clauses to protect both the buyer and seller, that the two will never agree, and neither of them really want that to happen or they would not be wasting time negotiating a purchase and sale in the first place.

"A NEW FIRST MORTAGE" CLAUSE

When you are purchasing a property in which you intend to apply for a new, institutional first mortgage, be sure to make that a contingency in your purchase contract with a clause similar to:

> This contract is contingent upon the purchaser securing a firm commitment for institutional first mortgage in the approximate amount of $100,000 at prevailing rates and terms, within 14 working days of the acceptance of this contract.

Several points about the way this clause is worded:

If you cannot obtain a mortgage commitment that is in the approximate amount you need, the contract will be void and liability on all parties shall cease. This is a critical point. I have actually seen a purchase contract written that did not allow the buyer to "get out" of it if he was unable to secure a large enough mortgage and at best, he stands to lose his deposit if he is unable to close due to lack of funds.

Since you can expect to obtain a commitment based on "prevailing rates and terms" at the present time, spell it out that way. What if you pin it down to 9½ percent interest for 25 years? The seller can be left a couple of weeks later with no contract, if you refuse to accept a ¼ percent additional interest. A knowledgeable seller will not want specific terms written into a mortgage contingency because the lender's terms vary too much from day to day to be reliable.

When the seller is carrying the financing, he will probably want certain clauses written into the mortgage, such as: "No pre-payment of the mortgage for the first year." The reason is understandable. When he sold you the property, he probably wanted it structured in a way that qualified him for an "installment sale", in order to pay minimum capital gains tax in the year of the sale.

Suppose you receive a large amount of cash all of a sudden, and decide to pay his mortgage down by, say $10,000, in the same calendar year that you purchased the property. He could be forced into an undesirable capital gains tax situation. There are other special clauses that your counsel will advise you are common in second mortgages. Always seek legal counsel when purchasing real estate.

WHAT TO DO WHEN ASSUMING EXISTING MORTGAGES

Whether an existing mortgage is being assumed, or a seller is carrying a mortgage, all the terms and conditions should be spelled out in detail. For example, "buyer will assume the existing first mortgage held by Federal Savings and Loan Association with the approximate remaining balance of $73,500 at 7½ percent annual interest, 19 + years remaining, monthly principal and interest payments of $595.83 per month."

Figure 11-1 is a completed, sample contract, using a standard form being used in the Fort Lauderdale area. You are offering to purchase the *Always Full Apartments* at a price of $145,000.

DEPOSIT RECEIPT AND CONTRACT FOR SALE AND PURCHASE

... .. John M. Seller and Jean B. Seller his wife. of 1267 NE 77th Street
. Suntown, Florida   (PH 702-4333)hereinafter called the Seller, and
       James Q. Buyer and Sally J. Buyer   his wife. of 101 Atlantic Avenue
       Suntown, Florida . . ..   (PH 703-4021)hereinafter called the Buyer, hereby

agree that the Seller shall sell and the Buyer shall buy the following described property UPON THE TERMS AND CONDITIONS HEREINAFTER SET
FORTH AND CONTINUED ON REVERSE SIDE OF THIS CONTRACT.

1. LEGAL DESCRIPTION of real estate located in .. Brown . . .   . Country. Florida

Lot 3, Block 5, Fair Acres Subdivision 43-22

a/k/a The Always Full Apartments

TAX FOLIO NUMBER: 4234-00-5407

PERSONAL PROPERTY INCLUDED: Inventory to be taken, attached to, and become a part
                            of this contract.

Street Address: 147 NE 8th Street, Suntown, Florida

Seller represents that the property can be used for the following purposes: Rental Apartments

2. PURCHASE PRICE IS .... $ 145,000.00

Method of Payment:

Deposit to be held in trust by A. Trust Officer (deposit with contract) $ 1,000.00
        Added deposit within 5 working days of acceptance   13,000.00
Approximate principal balance of existing first mortgage which Buyer shall

assume, if any. Mortgage holder Federal Savings and Loan Ass'n. $ 73,500.00

Interest 7.5 % per annum. Method of payment $595.83/month Incl. P. & I.

Other. Seller to take back a second purchase money mortgage
at nine (9) percent annual interest for 25 years, payable
monthly at $306.33 including principal and interest. First
payment due thirty (30) days after closing. This mortgage can
be paid in full, without penalty, after the first year.*
Cash attorney's trust account, certified or cashier's check on closing and
delivery of deed (or such greater or lesser amount as may be necessary to
complete payment of purchase price after credits, adjustments and prorations.) Said funds
to be held in escrow pursuant to provisions of Paragraph R on reverse side of this contract. $ 21,000.00

TOTAL $ 145,000.00

3. SPECIAL CLAUSES: (addendum attached, if any)

*Any difference between the actual balance of the first mortgage and the amount
shown above, shall be reflected in the second mortgage and not in cash.

4. CLOSING DATE: This contract shall be closed and the deed and possession shall be delivered on or before the 10th day of July 19 --.
unless extended by other provisions of this contract or separate agreement.

WITNESS: (Two, separate, are required)   Executed by Buyer on JUNE 3rd   19 --
A. Witness   James Q. Buyer   (SEAL)
B. Witness   Sally J. Buyer   (SEAL)
                                                                  Buyer

ACCEPTANCE OF CONTRACT & PROFESSIONAL SERVICE FEE: The Seller hereby approves and accepts the offer contained herein and recognizes

                                                                                         as Broker(s)

in this transaction, and agrees to pay, as a fee   % of the gross sales price, the sum of   Dollars
($) or one half of the deposit in case same is forfeited by the Buyer through failure to perform, as a compensation for service rendered.
provided same does not exceed the full amount of the agreed fee

WITNESS: (Two, separate, are required)   Executed by Seller on JUNE 4th   19 --
A. Witness   John M. Seller   (SEAL)
B. Witness   Jean B. Seller   (SEAL)
                                                                  Seller
Deposit received on   19   to be held subject to this contract, if check, subject to clearance.
By A. n. ATTORNEY   By
        Broker or Attorney

BE ADVISED: When this agreement has been completely executed, it becomes a legally binding instrument.
The form of this "Deposit Receipt and Contract for Sale and Purchase" has been approved by the
Broward County Bar Association and the Fort Lauderdale Area Board of Realtors, Inc.

                                                                            REV. 2/78

Figure 11-1

STANDARDS FOR REAL ESTATE TRANSACTIONS

A. EVIDENCE OF TITLE: The Seller shall within _____days (15 days if this blank is not filled in) furnish to Buyer a complete abstract of title prepared by a reputable abstract firm purporting to be an accurate synopsis of the instruments affecting the title to the real property recorded in the Public Records of that county to the date of this contract, showing in the Seller a marketable title in accordance with title standards adopted from time to time by the Florida Bar subject only to liens, encumbrances, exceptions or qualifications set forth in this contract and those which shall be discharged by Seller at or before closing. Buyer shall have fifteen (15) days from the date of receiving said abstract of title to examine same. If title is found to be defective, the Buyer shall, within said period, notify the Seller in writing, specifying the defects. If the said defects render the title unmarketable, the Seller shall have ninety (90) days from receipt of such notice to cure the defects, and if after said period Seller shall not have cured the defects, Buyer shall have the option of (1) accepting title as it then is, or (2) demanding a refund of all monies paid hereunder which shall forthwith be returned to the Buyer, and thereupon the Buyer and Seller shall be released of all further obligations to each other under this Contract.

B. CONVEYANCE: Seller shall convey title to the subject property to Buyer by Statutory Warranty Deed subject to: (1) zoning and/or restrictions and prohibitions imposed by governmental authority; (2) restrictions, easements and other matters appearing on the plat and/or common to the subdivision; (3) taxes for the year of closing; (4) other matter specified in this contract, if any.

C. EXISTING MORTGAGES: The Seller shall obtain and furnish a statement from the mortgagee setting forth the principal balance, method of payment, interest rate, and whether the mortgage is in good standing. If there is a charge for the change of ownership records by the mortgagee, it shall be borne equally by the parties to the transaction. In the event mortgagee does not permit the Buyer to assume the existing mortgage without a change in the interest rate, terms of payment or other material change, the Buyer at his option may cancel the contract and all monies paid on the purchase price shall be refunded to him and the parties shall be released from all further obligations. Any variance in the amount of a mortgage to be assumed from the amount stated in the Contract shall be added to or deducted from the cash payment or the purchase money mortgage, as the Buyer may elect. In the event such mortgage balance is more than three percent (3%) less than the amount indicated in the contract, the Seller shall be deemed to be in default under the Contract. Buyer shall execute all documents required by mortgagee for the assumption of said mortgage.

D. NEW MORTGAGES: Any purchase money note and mortgage shall follow the forms generally accepted and used in the county where the land is located. A purchase money mortgage shall provide for insurance against loss by fire with extended coverage in an amount not less than the full insurable value of the improvements. In a first mortgage, the note and mortgage shall provide for acceleration, at the option of the holder, after thirty (30) days default and in a second mortgage after ten (10) days default. Second mortgages shall require the owner of the property encumbered by said mortgage to keep all prior liens and encumbrances in good standing and forbid the owner of the property from accepting modifications, or furture advances, under a prior mortgage. Buyer shall have the right to prepay all or any part of the principal at any time or times with interest to date of payment without penalty and said payments shall apply against the principal amounts next maturing. In the event Buyer executes a mortgage to one other than the Seller, all costs and charges incidental thereto shall be paid by the Buyer. If this contract provides for Buyer to obtain a new mortgage, then Buyer's performance under this contract shall be contingent upon Buyer's obtaining said mortgage financing upon the terms stated, or if none are stated, then upon the terms generally prevailing at such time in the county where the property is located. Buyer agrees diligently to pursue said mortgage financing, but if a committment for said financing is not obtained within _____ days (15 days if this blank is not filled in) from the date of this Contract, and the Buyer does not waive this contingency, then either Buyer or Seller may terminate this Contract, in which event all deposits made by Buyer pursuant hereto shall be returned to him and all parties relieved of all obligations hereunder.

E. SURVEY: The Buyer, within the time allowed for delivery of evidence of title and examination thereof, may have said property surveyed at his expense. If the survey shows any encroachment on said property or that the improvements located on the subject property in fact encroach on the lands of others, or violate any of the covenants herein, the same shall be treated as a title defect.

F. INSPECTIONS: 1) Termite: Prior to closing, at Buyer's expense, the Buyer shall have the right to have the property inspected by a licensed exterminating company to determine whether there is any active termite or wood destroying organism present in any improvements on said property, or any damage from prior termite or wood destroying organism to said improvements. If there is any such infestation or damage, the seller shall pay all costs of treatment and repairing and/or replacing all portions of said improvements which are infested or have been damaged.

2) General: Prior to closing, the Buyer shall at his expense, have the right to have a roof, seawall, pool, electric and plumbing inspection made by persons or companies qualified and licensed to perform such services. If such inspection reveals functional defects (as differentiated from esthetic defects), Seller shall pay all costs of repairing said defects, and if repairs are not completed prior to closing, sufficient funds shall be escrowed at time of closing to effect said repairs.

3) Personal Property: The Seller represents and warrants that all appliances and machinery included in the sale shall be in working order and repair as of the date of closing. Buyer may, at his sole expense and on reasonable notice, inspect or cause an inspection to be made of the appliances and equipment involved prior to closing. Any necessary repairs shall be made at the cost of the Seller and, if appropriate, adequate funds shall be escrowed at time of closing to effect such repairs. Unless otherwise agreed by the parties, the buyer shall by proceeding to closing be deemed to have accepted the property as is.

4) Escrow for Repairs: If repairs called for in sub paragraphs 1,2 and 3 hereof are not completed prior to closing, sufficient funds shall be escrowed at time of closing to effect said repairs.

5) Limitation and Option Clause: Seller shall be responsible for all of the above repairs up to 4% of the purchase price. In the event the total of the repairs to be accomplished under this paragraph exceed 4% of the purchase price, then either party shall have the option of paying any amount above 4% of the purchase price and this contract shall then remain in full force and effect. However, if neither party agrees to pay the additional amount above the 4% of the purchase price, then at the Seller's or Buyer's option this Contract may be cancelled by giving written notice by U.S. Certified Mail, Return Receipt Requested, to the other party, and the deposit shall be returned to the Buyer.

Figure 11-1 (Continued)

G. INSURANCE: The premium on any hazard insurance policy in force covering improvements on the subject property, shall be prorated between the parties, or the policy may be cancelled as the Buyer may elect. If insurance is to be prorated the Seller shall, on or before closing date, furnish to the Buyer all insurance policies or copies thereof.

H. LEASES: The Seller shall, prior to closing, furnish to Buyer copies of all written leases and estoppel letters from each tenant specifying the nature and duration of said tenant's occupancy, rental rate, advance rents or security deposits paid by tenant. In the event Seller is unable to obtain said estoppel letters from tenants, the same information may be furnished by Seller to Buyer in the form of a Seller's affidavit.

I. MECHANICS LIENS: Seller shall furnish to the Buyer at time of closing an affidavit attesting to the absence of any claims of lien or potential lienors known to the Seller and further attesting that there have been no improvements to the subject property for 90 days immediately preceding the date of closing. If the property has been improved within said time, the Seller shall deliver releases or waiver of all mechanics liens, executed by general contractors, sub-contractors, suppliers or material men. In addition to Seller's mechanic lien affidavit setting forth the names of all such general contractors, sub-contractors, suppliers and material men and further reciting that in fact all bills for work to the subject property which could serve as the basis for a mechanic's lien have been paid.

J. PLACE OF CLOSING: Closing shall be held at the office of the Buyer's attorney if located within Broward County; if not, then at the office of Seller's attorney.

K. DOCUMENTS FOR CLOSING: Seller's attorney shall prepare deed, mortgage, mortgage note, bill of sale, affidavit regarding liens, and any corrective instruments that may be required in connection with perfecting the title. Buyer's attorney will prepare closing statement.

L. EXPENSES: State surtax and documentary stamps which are required to be affixed to the instrument of conveyance, the cost of recording any corrective instruments, intangible personal property taxes and the cost of recording the purchase money mortgage, if any, shall be paid by the Seller. Documentary stamps to be affixed to the note or notes secured by the purchase money mortgage, if any, and the cost of recording the deed shall be paid by the Buyer.

M. PRORATION OF TAXES (REAL AND PERSONAL): Taxes shall be prorated based on the current year's tax, if known. If the closing occurs at a date when the current year's taxes are not fixed, and the current year's assessment is available, taxes will be prorated based upon such assessment and the prior year's millage. If the current year's assessment is not available, then taxes will be prorated on the prior year's tax, provided, however, if there are completed improvements on the subject premises by January 1st of the year of closing, which improvements were not in existance on January 1st of the prior year, then the taxes shall be prorated to the date of closing based upon the prior year's millage and at an equitable assessment to be agreed upon between the parties, failing which, requests will be made to the county tax assessor for an informal assessment taking into consideration homestead exemption, if any. However, any tax proration based on an estimate may at the request of either party to the transaction, be subsequently readjusted upon receipt of tax bill and a statement to that effect is to be set forth in the closing statement. All such prorations whether based on actual tax or estimated tax will make appropriate allowance for the maximum allowable discount and for homestead or other exemptions if allowed for the current year.

N. PRORATIONS AND ESCROW BALANCE: Taxes, hazard insurance, mortgage guarantee insurance, interest, utilities, rents and other expenses and revenue of said property shall be prorated as of date of closing. Seller shall receive as credit at closing, an amount equal to the escrow funds held by the mortgagee, which funds shall thereupon be transferred to the Buyer.

O. SPECIAL ASSESSMENT LIENS: Certified, confirmed and ratified special assessment liens as of the date of closing (and not as of the date of this contract) are to be paid by the Seller. Pending liens as of the date of closing shall be assumed by the Buyer.

P. RISK OF LOSS: If the improvements are damaged by fire or other casualty before delivery of the deed and can be restored to substantially the same condition as now existing within a period of sixty (60) days thereafter, Seller may restore the improvements and the closing date and date of delivery of possession hereinbefore provided shall be extended accordingly. If Seller fails to do so, the Buyer shall have the option of (1) taking the property as is together with insurance proceeds, if any, or (2) cancelling the contract and all deposits will be forthwith returned to the Buyer and the parties released of any further liability hereunder.

Q. MAINTENANCE: Between the date of the contract and the date of closing, the property, including lawn, shrubbery and pool, if any, shall be maintained by the Seller in the condition as it existed as of the date of the contract, ordinary wear and tear excepted.

R. ESCROW OF PROCEEDS OF SALE AND CLOSING PROCEDURE: The deed shall be recorded and evidence of title continued at Buyer's expense, to show title in Buyer, without any encumbrances or changes which would render Seller's title unmarketable, from the date of the last evidence and the cash proceeds of sale shall be held in escrow by Seller's attorney or by such other escrow agent as may be mutually agreed upon for a period of not longer than ten (10) days. If Seller's title is rendered unmarketable, Buyer's attorney shall, within said ten (10) day period, notify Seller or Seller's attorney in writing of the defect, and Seller shall have thirty (30) days from date of receipt of such notice to cure said defect. In the event Seller fails to timely cure said defect, all monies paid hereunder by Buyer shall, upon written demand therefor, and within five (5) days thereafter, be returned to Buyer and, simultaneously with such repayment, Buyer shall vacate the premises and reconvey the property in question to the Seller by Special Warranty Deed. In the event Buyer fails to make timely demand for refund, he shall take title as is, waiving all rights against Seller as to such intervening defect except such rights as may be available to Buyer by virtue of warranties contained in deed. In the event the transaction is not consummated because of an uncorrected or unwaived defect in title, the Seller will be deemed to have defaulted under this contract. Possession and occupancy will be delivered to Buyer at time of closing. If Seller provided Escrow Disbursement insurance or if Buyer executes a Disclosure and Consent Statement, then disbursement of closing proceeds shall be made to Seller immediately upon closing. The broker's professional service fee shall be disbursed simultaneously with disbursement of Seller's closing proceeds. Payment shall be made in the form of cash, cashier's check, certified check or attorney's trust account check. In the event a portion of the purchase price is to be derived from institutional financing or refinancing, the requirements of the lending institution as to place, time and procedures for closing and for disbursement of mortgage proceeds shall control, anything in this contract to the contrary notwithstanding.

Figure 11-1 (Continued)

S. ESCROW: The party receiving the deposit agrees by the acceptance thereof to hold same in escrow and to disburse it in accordance with the terms and conditions of this contract. Provided, however, that in the event that a dispute shall arise between any of the parties to this contract as to the proper disbursement of the deposit, the party holding the deposit may at his option; (1) take no action and hold all funds (and documents, if any) until agreement is reached between the disputing parties, or until a judgment has been entered by a court of competent jurisdiction and the appeal period has expired thereon, or if appealed then until the matter has been finally concluded, and then to act in accordance with such final judgment; or (2) institute an action for declaratory judgment, interpleader or otherwise joining all affected parties and thereafter complying with the ultimate judgment of the court with regard to the disbursement of the deposit and disposition of documents, if any. If a licensed real estate broker, the escrowee will comply with provisions of Section 475.25 (1) (c), F.S. as amended. In the event of any suit between Buyer and Seller wherein the escrow agent is made a party by virtue of acting as such escrow agent hereunder, or in the event of any suit wherein escrow agent interpleads the subject matter of this escrow, the escrow agent shall be entitled to recover a reasonable attorney's fee and costs incurred, including costs and attorney's fees for appellate proceedings, if any, said fees and costs to be charged and assessed as court costs in favor of the prevailing party.

T. ATTORNEY FEES AND COSTS: In connection with any litigation arising out of this contract, the prevailing party whether Buyer, Seller or Broker, shall be entitled to recover all costs incurred including reasonable attorney's fees for services rendered in connection with such litigation including appellate proceedings and post judgment proceedings.

U. DEFAULT: In the event of default of either party, the rights of the non-defaulting party and the Broker shall be as provided herein and such rights shall be deemed to be the sole and exclusive rights in such event: (a) If Buyer fails to perform any of the covenants of this contract, all money paid or deposited pursuant to this contract by the Buyer shall be retained by or for the account of the Seller as consideration for the execution of this contract as agreed and liquidated damages and in full settlement of any claims for damages by the Seller against the Buyer. (b) If Seller fails to perform any of the covenants of this contract, all money paid or deposited pursuant to this contract by the Buyer shall be returned to the Buyer upon demand, or the Buyer shall have the right of specific performance. In addition, Seller shall pay forthwith to Broker the full professional service fee provided for on the reverse side of this contract.

V. PERSONS BOUND: The benefits and obligations of the covenants herein shall inure to and bind the respective heirs, executors, administrators, successors and assigns (where assignment is permitted) of the parties hereto. Whenever used, the singular number shall include the plural, the plural the singular, and the use of any gender shall include all genders.

W. SURVIVAL OF COVENANTS AND SPECIAL COVENANTS: Seller covenants and warrants that there is ingress and egress to subject property over public or private roads which covenants shall survive delivery of deed. No other provision, covenant or warranty of this contract shall survive the delivery of the deed except as expressly provided herein.

X. FINAL AGREEMENT: This contract represents the final agreement of the parties and no agreements or representations, unless incorporated into this contract, shall be binding on any of the parties. Typewritten provisions shall supersede printed provisions and handwritten provisions shall supersede typewritten and/or printed provisions. Such handwritten or typewritten provisions as are appropriate may be inserted on the face of this form or attached hereto as an addendum. The date of this Contract shall be the day upon which it becomes fully executed by all parties.

The form of this "Deposit Receipt and Contract for Sale and Purchase"
has been approved by the Broward County Bar Association and
the Fort Lauderdale Area Board of REALTORS®, Inc.

Y. Purchaser has the option to inspect the remaining apartments, within five (5) days of acceptance, to determine that they are in the same basic condition as the ones previously inspected.

Z. Purchaser or his accountant shall have the option of verifying the income and expenses from the seller's books to determine that they conform with the original offering. This shall be completed within five (5) working days of acceptance of this contract.

AA. If this contract is not accepted by midnight, June 4, 19--, it shall, at the purchaser's option, be declaired null and void, the deposit refunded to the purchaser, and liability on all parties shall cease.

Figure 11-1 (Continued)

a) Starting at the top, the seller's name, address and phone number appears.

b) Next, your name, address and phone number are inserted.

c) The county in which the property is located is next.

d) You need to insert the property's legal description that you have previously obtained. Care must be taken to insure that no mistakes are made in this description. A typographical error of say ''lot 4'' instead of ''lot 3'' could result in the wrong property being processed for transfer. Chances are the error would be caught, but you do not want to take chances. Whenever possible copy the legal description from the present owner's deed. That should be correct.

You'll notice the term: ''a/k/a *The Always Full Apartments*'' follows the legal description. The ''a/k/a'' stands for ''also known as.''

e) There is a line on this contract for the property's tax folio number, for counties that use these numbers.

f) The next item states that an inventory of any personal property, which is to be included in the sale, will be taken, attached to, and become a part of this contract.

g) The street address of the property is next shown. You are now down to the financial portion of the contract.

h) You are offering $145,000 for the *Always Full Apartments*.

i) A $1,000 earnest money deposit has been placed by you in your attorney's trust account.

j) Upon acceptance of the contract by all parties, you further agree to deposit an additional $13,000 in his trust account to make a full 10 percent deposit. You have given yourself a reasonable amount of time, five working days, to accomplish this.

How Deposits Are Handled

Notice that these two deposits are being held in the Trust Account of a ''neutral party'' such as a Realtor, Attorney, or Bank. It should not be turned over to the seller. As the terms indicate, this deposit is held ''in trust'' until the sale is consummated or something else happens. If the sale does not close, it is due to either the buyer or the seller.

When the buyer backs out, and refuses to close, the deposit is usually forfeited to the seller. When a Realtor is involved, the deposit is generally divided equally between the seller and the Realtor up to the maximum amount the Realtor would have received if the transaction had closed.

What if the sale does not close because of the seller? There are two possible reasons that this could happen. First, if the seller, for some reason, cannot give clear title to the property, the transaction will probably be declared null and void, the deposit refunded to the buyer, and liability on all parties shall cease.

Suppose the seller changes his mind and does not want to sell? The buyer has two options if he wants to pursue it. He can sue for "specific performance" and try to force the seller to close through court action, or he can merely sue for liquidated damages to recover what he feels it cost him in time and expense.

As a practical matter, a court of law will rarely force a property owner to sell his property. Liquidated damages may be the most the buyer can expect to receive.

k) Notice that the complete terms of each mortgage are spelled out. Because the exact balance of the first mortgage cannot be obtained until the estopple letter is received from the lender, the contract spells out "approximate" balance.

l) The footnote, under special clauses, protects the buyer in the event the actual first mortgage balance turns out to be smaller than specified in the contract. If, for example, the balance was only $72,500, rather than the $73,500 shown, the buyer could find himself at the closing spending an additional $1,000 in cash in order to close. This clause says that if the first mortgage is different from the amount shown on the contract, the second mortgage will be adjusted accordingly. In this example, the second mortgage would be increased to $37,500 from $36,500. The mortgage payments would likewise be revised to reflect the new balance unless both parties agree to leave them the same and extend the term to make up the extra $1,000.00.

The way this clause is written, the size of the second mortgage will be reduced by any amount that the first mortgage balance is actually larger than shown on the contract. Again, the payments would have to be altered.

m) Finally, the balance due from the buyer at closing is to be in cash, or a cashier's check. Personal checks are *not* acceptable, unless the closing takes place in escrow and title is not transferred until the buyer's check clears the bank.

n) The estimated closing date is inserted after the financial portion is completed.

o) "Buyer" signature lines appear next. Notice that there is room for two witnesses. You can check with your legal counsel but you'll probably find that two witnesses are necessary, even if you are purchasing the property alone.

p) The next section spells out any brokers in the transaction and their professional fee.

q) There are then, two "seller" signature lines with room, again, for two witnesses.

r) The final portion of the first page allows for the "trust" agent to execute the contract showing how much money he is holding in trust on your behalf.

The remaining three pages of the sample form contract contain items "A" through "X" which are the standard acceptable terms for a purchase contract in that particular area.

You should also note paragraphs "Y", "Z" and "AA". These are three additional clauses that you wanted added to the basic contract. Paragraph "AA" places a time limit for the seller's acceptance. You'll see that it can be extended at your (the purchaser) option only.

Keep in mind that this is a typical contract form for one particular area. Your attorney can advise you of contract forms that are acceptable for your area.

Your contract is now prepared and ready to submit to the seller. Since you are offering $10,000 less than the price he wants, you had better be prepared to defend your position. Any documentation you can take with you showing area comparables that are in line with your offer, a property analysis showing how at your price the property "makes sense" to you and at his, the return is too low, will be helpful to your case.

THE COUNTER OFFER

You can rarely expect to have the seller agree with everything you put in your offer to purchase contract, unless of course, you are offering him the full price and terms he said he wanted. You can expect him to make a counter offer, telling you what price, terms and conditions are acceptable to him. Hopefully, it will be a compromise between what you want and what he expected.

Unless the seller is in financial trouble, you will not be able to steal his property. If you can, take a close look at what you're buying. Maybe he knows something that you don't.

After you give him your contract and review the price, terms and conditions with him, sit quietly and give him time to think about it. There is a lot to be said for not saying anything at all. It is possible to talk yourself right out of a purchase by talking too much. According to the Bible, Sampson killed 10,000 Philistines with the jawbone of an ass. There have no doubt been that many real estate purchases killed the same way.

When the conversation begins again, get the various contingencies out of the way first—the verification of leases, expenses, inspections, etc. These are the easy items to get accepted by the seller. When you have his head nodding in agreement, talk about the offering price, if that is the primary area of disagreement.

Get the seller to agree to something, as close to what you wanted as possible—Let's say he agrees to $150,000 not $145,000. He also states that he will go along with a 25 year second mortgage but not at 9 percent. Since the going rate is 10 percent, he at least wants 9½ percent. At this point, alter the contract by striking out any changes that need to be made, get him to execute the contract and *initial all changes* that were made.

If you had done your homework, you probably prepared a property analysis form starting with the price and terms the seller wanted and other property analysis forms based on compromises you anticipated him to offer. Hopefully, you are prepared to agree, or disagree, with the seller's counter offer while you are with him.

Remember, you do not have a binding contract until you have both agreed to it by executing the contract and *initialing all changes* that were made. Unless you do not care whether or not you purchase the building, don't try to play a bluffing game with the seller and tell him, "I want to think about it and I'll call you tomorrow."

Since you still do not have a valid contract, he is free to sell the property to someone else while you are waiting for a call from him accepting a lower price, or whatever your reasoning may have been.

Do not just jump into the contract, however, if you really are not certain about it. Take the time you need to review all your figures based on the terms acceptable to the seller. If you lose the building because of your delay, don't worry about it. You found that one, you can find another. After re-evaluating the property, based on the final terms he will accept and you decide it is a right investment for you, initial all the changes. You now have a binding contract to purchase the *Always Full Apartments*. This should be a happy occasion for you. You've taken that first step in real estate investing!

Once you have a contract, agreed to by all parties, the next step is to get prepared for the closing. Figure 11-2 shows the first page of your contract after changes were made and all parties have initialed these changes.

REMOVING CONTINGENCIES: A CHECKLIST

There are several things you need to do prior to closing to insure that everything has been done and there will be no problems or surprises on the day of closing. Your first duty is to get any contingencies removed or satisfied that may have been written in the purchase contract.

- ☐ If you have a mortgage contingency in which your purchase depends on obtaining a new mortgage, start looking immediately. That may be the slowest contingency to satisfy.

  Visit various lenders in your area who are making commercial loans. Be prepared to furnish personal financial statements and copies of your contract to each. Some may also request an operating statement on the building. You should have prepared a property analysis form based on the final contract terms. That should be acceptable.

  You may be fortunate enough to obtain commitments from more than one lender. Review them all and pick the best one for you.
- ☐ Contingencies such as inspections for termites, roof, etc., should be completed as quickly as possible.
- ☐ Whenever a contingency has been removed, be certain to inform the seller, preferably in writing, so that he knows there should be no last minute problems on the day of closing.
- ☐ Inspection of apartments and any other item that will be disturbing to the building tenants, should be performed during reasonable hours with the least possible inconvenience to the tenants as possible.

DEPOSIT RECEIPT AND CONTRACT FOR SALE AND PURCHASE

John M. Seller and Jean B. Seller _____ his wife, of _ 1267 NE 77th Street
Suntown, Florida _____ (PH 702-4333)hereinafter called the Seller, and
James Q. Buyer and Sally J. Buyer _____ his wife, of _ 101 Atlantic Avenue
Suntown, Florida _____ (PH 703-4021)hereinafter called the Buyer, hereby
agree that the Seller shall sell and the Buyer shall buy the following described property UPON THE TERMS AND CONDITIONS HEREINAFTER SET
FORTH AND CONTINUED ON REVERSE SIDE OF THIS CONTRACT.

1. LEGAL DESCRIPTION of real estate located in __ Brown _____ County, Florida

   Lot 3, Block 5, Fair Acres Subdivision 43-22

   a/k/a The Always Full Apartments

TAX FOLIO NUMBER: _ 4234-00-5407

PERSONAL PROPERTY INCLUDED: Inventory to be taken, attached to, and become a part of this contract.

Street Address: 147 NE 8th Street, Suntown, Florida _____ JBJB

Seller represents that the property can be used for the following purposes: _ Rental Apartments

2. PURCHASE PRICE IS: .... $ ~~145,000.00~~ 150,000.00
                                                                         JB JS

Method of Payment:

Deposit to be held in trust by A. Trust Officer (deposit with contract) ... $ 1,000.00
   Added deposit within 5 working days of acceptance.   13,000.00
Approximate principal balance of existing first mortgage which Buyer shall

assume, if any, Mortgage holder Federal Savings and Loan Ass'n. .... $ 73,500.00
Interest 7.5 % per annum; Method of payment $595.83/month incl. P.& I.

Other: Seller to take back a second purchase money mortgage .... $ 36,500.00
9.5% at ~~nine (9)~~ percent annual interest for 25 years, payable
$318.90 monthly at ~~$306.33~~ including principal and interest. First
payment due thirty (30) days after closing. This mortgage can
be paid in full, without penalty, after the first year.*
Cash attorney's trust account, certified or cashier's check on closing and
delivery of deed (or such greater or lesser amount as may be necessary to   26,000.00 JBJS
complete payment of purchase price after credits, adjustments and prorations.) Said funds ~~21,000.00~~ JBJB
to be held in escrow pursuant to provisions of Paragraph R on reverse side of this contract. $

TOTAL $ ~~145,000.00~~ 150,000.00
3. SPECIAL CLAUSES: (addendum attached, if any)   JJ JS

   *Any difference between the actual balance of the first mortgage and the amount
   shown above, shall be reflected in the second mortgage and not in cash.

4. CLOSING DATE: This contract shall be closed and the deed and possession shall be delivered on or before the 10th day of July 19 --
unless extended by other provisions of this contract or separate agreement.

WITNESS: (Two, separate, are required)   Executed by Buyer on JUNE 3rd   19--
   A. Witness   _____ (SEAL)
   B. Witness   Sally J. Buyer (SEAL)
                                                                      Buyer
ACCEPTANCE OF CONTRACT & PROFESSIONAL SERVICE FEE: The Seller hereby approves and accepts the offer contained herein and recognizes

.... as Broker(s)

in this transaction, and agrees to pay, as a fee _____ % of the gross sales price, the sum of .... Dollars
($ ....) or one half of the deposit in case same is forfeited by the Buyer through failure to perform, as a compensation for service rendered,
provided same does not exceed the full amount of the agreed fee.

WITNESS: (Two, separate, are required)   Executed by Seller on JUNE 4TH   19--
   A. Witness   John M. Seller (SEAL)
   B. Witness   Jean B. Seller (SEAL)
                                                                      Seller
Deposit received on JUNE 3RD 19 -- to be held subject to this contract, if check, subject to clearance.
By: An. Attorney   By: _____
      Broker or Attorney

BE ADVISED: When this agreement has been completely executed, it becomes a legally binding instrument.
The form of this "Deposit Receipt and Contract for Sale and Purchase" has been approved by the
Broward County Bar Association and the Fort Lauderdale Area Board of Realtors, Inc.

REV. 2/78

Figure 11-2

S. ESCROW: The party receiving the deposit agrees by the acceptance thereof to hold same in escrow and to disburse it in accordance with the terms and conditions of this contract. Provided, however, that in the event that a dispute shall arise between any of the parties to this contract as to the proper disbursement of the deposit, the party holding the deposit may at his option; (1) take no action and hold all funds (and documents, if any) until agreement is reached between the disputing parties, or until a judgment has been entered by a court of competent jurisdiction and the appeal period has expired thereon, or if appealed then until the matter has been finally concluded, and then to act in accordance with such final judgment; or (2) institute an action for declaratory judgment, interpleader or otherwise joining all affected parties and thereafter complying with the ultimate judgment of the court with regard to the disbursement of the deposit and disposition of documents, if any. If a licensed real estate broker, the escrowee will comply with provisions of Section 475.25 (1) (c), F.S. as amended. In the event of any suit between Buyer and Seller wherein the escrow agent is made a party by virtue of acting as such escrow agent hereunder, or in the event of any suit wherein escrow agent interpleads the subject matter of this escrow, the escrow agent shall be entitled to recover a reasonable attorney's fee and costs incurred, including costs and attorney's fees for appellate proceedings, if any, said fees and costs to be charged and assessed as court costs in favor of the prevailing party.

T. ATTORNEY FEES AND COSTS: In connection with any litigation arising out of this contract, the prevailing party whether Buyer, Seller or Broker, shall be entitled to recover all costs incurred including reasonable attorney's fees for services rendered in connection with such litigation including appellate proceedings and post judgment proceedings.

U. DEFAULT: In the event of default of either party, the rights of the non-defaulting party and the Broker shall be as provided herein and such rights shall be deemed to be the sole and exclusive rights in such event: (a) If Buyer fails to perform any of the covenants of this contract, all money paid or deposited pursuant to this contract by the Buyer shall be retained by or for the account of the Seller as consideration for the execution of this contract as agreed and liquidated damages and in full settlement of any claims for damages by the Seller against the Buyer. (b) If Seller fails to perform any of the covenants of this contract, all money paid or deposited pursuant to this contract by the Buyer shall be returned to the Buyer upon demand, or the Buyer shall have the right of specific performance. In addition, Seller shall pay forthwith to Broker the full professional service fee provided for on the reverse side of this contract.

V. PERSONS BOUND: The benefits and obligations of the covenants herein shall inure to and bind the respective heirs, executors, administrators, successors and assigns (where assignment is permitted) of the parties hereto. Whenever used, the singular number shall include the plural, the plural the singular, and the use of any gender shall include all genders.

W. SURVIVAL OF COVENANTS AND SPECIAL COVENANTS: Seller covenants and warrants that there is ingress and egress to subject property over public or private roads which covenants shall survive delivery of deed. No other provision, covenant or warranty of this contract shall survive the delivery of the deed except as expressly provided herein.

X. FINAL AGREEMENT: This contract represents the final agreement of the parties and no agreements or representations, unless incorporated into this contract, shall be binding on any of the parties. Typewritten provisions shall supersede printed provisions and handwritten provisions shall supersede typewritten and/or printed provisions. Such handwritten or typewritten provisions as are appropriate may be inserted on the face of this form or attached hereto as an addendum. The date of this Contract shall be the day upon which it becomes fully executed by all parties.

The form of this "Deposit Receipt and Contract for Sale and Purchase"
has been approved by the Broward County Bar Association and
the Fort Lauderdale Area Board of REALTORS®, Inc.

Y. Purchaser has the option to inspect the remaining apartments, within five (5) days of acceptance, to determine that they are in the same basic condition as the ones previously inspected.

Z. Purchaser or his accountant shall have the option of varifying the income and expenses from the seller's books to determine that they conform with the original offering. This shall be completed within five (5) working days of acceptance of this contract.

AA. If this contract is not accepted by midnight, June 4, 19--, it shall, at the purchaser's option, be declaired null and void, and the deposit refunded to the purchaser. Liability on all parties shall cease.

Figure 11-2 (Continued)

☐ Estopple letters to current lenders and to the tenants should be handled by your attorney or closing agent, prior to closing.

Furnish your attorney with all the details of the purchase he requests, including copies of the contract, as soon as it is agreed to by all parties. He also has work to do on it prior to closing and will want all the time he can get.

☐ Your contract calls for an inventory of personal property, such as furniture included in the purchase. The complete inventory needs to be taken jointly between you and the seller. Copies of the inventory should be executed by both you and the seller and attached to and become a part of your purchase contract.

☐ When you inspect the apartments, as your contract allowed, you can expect to hear all kinds of complaints from the tenants as soon as they know you are the new owner. Take most of them with a grain of salt. Any complaint that is a legitimate one, should be checked out.

HOW MUCH CASH DO YOU NEED TO CLOSE?

There are several items that you must consider, beyond the down payment called for in the contract, when purchasing the property:

Mortgage Closing Costs

A new mortgage will cost several points in closing costs. You will recall, from our discussion of financing, that this charge is usually deducted from your mortgage proceeds. Assume this cost, for example, is four percent and you are obtaining a $100,000 mortgage. You will end up with only $96,000. You should have known prior to signing the contract where the added $4000 was coming from.

Normal Real Estate Closing Costs

These must also be paid at closing. If you are working through a Realtor, he can furnish you with a list of charges you can expect in order to close.

Checklist of Closing Costs: Although not all of the items shown in Figure 11-3 will apply, the list gives you some idea of what to expect:

☐   1. Attorney's Fee $ _____
☐   2. Escrow Account Balance   _____
☐   3. Hazard Insurance   _____
☐   4. Recertification of Abstract   _____
☐   5. Survey   _____
☐   6. Title Insurance   _____
☐   7. Transfer Fee on Existing Mortgage   _____
☐   8. Appraisal Fee   _____
☐   9. Credit Report   _____
☐ 10. Documentary Stamps on New Note   _____
☐ 11. Intangible Tax on New Mortgage   _____
☐ 12. Mortgage Co.'s Attorneys' Charges   _____
☐ 13. Prepayment of Taxes & Insurance
        for Escrow Account   _____
☐ 14. Service Fee (or Origination Fee)
        on Any New Mortgage   _____

Figure 11-3

Watch for Surprises

Check the balance in the escrow account if you are assuming a loan from an institutional lender. Your closing is scheduled for July, for example, and Real Estate taxes are due in January. You would expect the escrow balance for taxes to be about one half the annual tax amount. Taxes are $5000 so there should be $2500 in escrow for taxes. Likewise a $2000 insurance bill is due in January. You would expect the lender to be holding $1000, or one-half year's insurance premium in the bank. That total escrow account balance should be about $3500. You have to "buy" this account at closing, because it is being transferred over to you. (In the next Chapter, we'll cover closing costs and you'll see where the seller reimburses you for the portion he owes.)

The problem that frequently occurs is that the savings and loan association may have been charging more than necessary to cover taxes and insurance. What you thought should be a $3500 balance in escrow, that you must pay the seller for, turns out to be $4500. You suddenly need another $1000 in cash to close. By the way, if the escrow amount being held by the lender is excessive, beyond any expected tax or insurance increases for the coming year, you can request a refund of the excess they are holding. You cannot do this, however, until after the closing and you own the property.

Security Deposits and Advanced Rents

Now, on the brighter side, (kind of), at the closing you will receive credit for any security deposits and advanced rents being held by the owner for the tenants. This helps reduce your cash requirement at closing, but be careful. This is NOT your money. Sooner or later all or most of it, will be used by or returned to the tenants.

Security deposits, in practice, are returned to the tenant (all or part) when he moves out at the termination of his lease, assuming he has met the lease terms and left his dwelling unit in the same condition it was when he moved in, except for normal wear and tear. Normal wear and tear is *your* expense.

Advanced or pre-paid rents, sneak up on you from a different direction. Assume half of your leases expire in December, and these tenants have paid the December rent in advance when they executed their lease. Your rental income for December will be cut in half, and you may not collect enough rent to pay your expenses and mortgage payments.

So, what may have appeared to be a "windfall" at closing can come back to haunt you later. Your best bet is to put that money in a separate account right after the closing, so it is available when you need it. Do not use it to reduce your cash requirement at closing.

All of these expense items, and others that may be expected in your particular area, should be itemized and planned for long before the day of closing. You'll recall that Bob Andrews saved $5000 of his $50,000 investment capital just to cover closing costs.

There is nothing more disastrous than to attend the closing on the property you are buying and discover you do not have enough money to close. Your attorney will no doubt advise you a day or two prior to closing, just how much cash you need. This will give you time to obtain a "cashier's check" for the closing balance. As mentioned earlier, a personal check is not acceptable.

Don't Get Caught Short

No matter how much you may want a particular property, do not over extend your investment budget. Allow more than enough reserve capital to cover all of the unexpected costs that have been discussed, and don't forget, meter deposits and licenses that may be required in your area.

Your love affair with your new real estate investment may be short lived if you are in a financial strain from the beginning. And investment real estate ownership is, and should be, a financially and emotionally rewarding experience.

12

What to Do at the Closing and After

By the time you reach the day of the closing, you should know exactly where you will stand after taking title to the *Always Full Apartments*. As soon as you agreed on the final purchase contract, you should have prepared another property analysis based on the contract price and terms agreed to. When the closing takes place, the only variable in your property analysis might occur in the area of the balance between the first and second mortgage.

FACTS YOU SHOULD KNOW BEFORE CLOSING

Before you get to the closing, there are several facts you need to know.

Never Close Your Own Real Estate Transaction

Pay the cost of an attorney or title company. They know how to protect you, to make certain you receive a "good marketable title." There are many possible problems that can turn up in a title that you would not find. I have seen situations where an attorney has discovered a need to obtain a Quit

189

Claim deed from someone who could still have a title interest dating back several years. It is not worth what you may save to take that risk.

Abstracts

Some areas have "Abstracts." An abstract is a written recorded history of the property you are buying from the day it became part of the United States. The abstract is updated (a new page added) every time anything happens to affect the title to the property, such as a new owner taking title to it.

When an abstract is available, it is usually the seller's responsibility to furnish a current, updated abstract to the buyer's attorney prior to closing.

Title Insurance

When you are in an area where abstracts are not used, the seller is generally obligated to furnish a title insurance policy. Title insurance is a one time policy issued by a title company or attorney, to the purchaser at the time of closing. It insures his title to the property for as long as he owns the property. It also protects him, after he sells the property, from any future owner finding a defect in the chain of title during his ownership. If this happens, the title company stands the responsibility and expense, if any, of defending the title. Title insurance is considerably more expensive than furnishing an updated abstract.

When you are furnished an abstract, title insurance is still advisable, even if you have to pay for it yourself. Why? Suppose Mr. & Mrs. Seller attend the closing and execute the deed, transferring title to you. They were joint owners of the property. Six months after the closing, the real Mrs. Seller shows up and says she still has an ownership right to the property. It was not her that signed the deed. It was Mr. Seller's girlfriend. Mrs. Seller hasn't lived with him for five years. Sound far fetched? It's not. There are many such things that can create title problems. If she really is Mrs. Seller, you're in trouble unless you have title insurance protecting you. Even an abstract cannot catch that type of a problem.

WHAT THE SELLER TURNS OVER TO YOU: A CHECKLIST

Here is a checklist of the items you and/or your attorney should be prepared to obtain from the sellers at the closing:

☐ Executed deed to the property.

☐ Certificate of no liens showing that the seller has not created any debts against the property, other than those of record, such as mortgages.

☐ Bill of Sale for the personal property included with the property.

☐ The original leases, signed over to you.

☐ Property Insurance Policy.

☐ Keys.

☐ Any service contracts.

☐ Names and phone numbers of service people being used, such as lawn man, air conditioning or heating service people, plumber, etc.

☐ Any building plans and surveys the seller may have.

☐ Letters prepared by the seller, addressed to each tenant, informing them that the building has been sold and informing them that all rent payments should now be sent to you. He may have already sent them out.

BE PREPARED FOR MURPHY'S LAW

You are now ready to attend the closing, but before you go, be prepared for Murphy's Law to come into the act. For those of you who are unfamiliar with Murphy's Law, it simply states that "If anything can possibly go wrong, it will." When the closing goes smoothly, which a well prepared closing should, you will be pleasantly surprised. Assume it doesn't, well . . . you'll be prepared.

What Can Go Wrong at a Closing

That would require writing another book! Just to name a few more common problems:

1. There's a $500 mistake on the closing statement, and you owe an additional $500. I might add that it does not matter if you are the buyer or the seller, the mistake will rarely be in your favor.

2. Since the closing statement was incorrect, your cashier's check is also $500 too small. (Usually a personal check for this small difference will be acceptable, however).

3. The seller decides he wants to take the TV antenna with him for his new building. It does not appear on the personal property inventory and since it is not permanently connected to the building, he feels he can have it.

4. Where a new mortgage is being placed on the property by the buyer, the lender refuses to disburse the loan proceeds to the seller until the lender's mortgage is protected by recording it. But, the lender cannot record it until you, the buyer, take title and record the deed. So, the seller is expected to leave the closing without the bulk of his proceeds and, yet, give you title to his property! (This is becoming common practice in many areas and should have been pointed out to the seller long before the day of closing.) It is advisable to add a "new mortgage" clause in the contract that reads, "Seller acknowledges that there is a new institutional mortgage being placed on the property and mortgage proceeds to the seller may be delayed until title is transferred and the mortgage has been recorded."

5. The seller ends up at his mother's funeral, 2000 miles away, on the day of closing.

6. If you really want a fouled up closing, let one of the sellers die prior to closing.

7. You and the seller get into a big argument because he removed a hanging lamp from the lobby that you thought went with the building. It was not on the list of personal property because it was "permanently" installed.

At this point, you probably think this is some type of comedy routine, but I have seen closings fall apart and sales not close because of trivial items like ownership of a TV antenna.

In spite of the many possible problems, the majority of closings take place with very few delays. Even when minor problems do occur, a sincere buyer and seller with the assistance of the closing agent(s), can iron them out and the closing will take place as planned. You at least can be prepared for unexpected situations to arise. Don't let them shake your confidence in the purchase of the property. You have still made a sound investment decision.

THE CLOSING STATEMENT

The first thing that confronts you at the closing is your copy of the closing statement. Hopefully, your attorney furnished you with a copy before now so any questions you had have already been answered. Your closing statement looks like Figure 12-1. We'll review it step-by-step so you will understand where all the numbers come from:

Buyer's Closing Statement   Closing Date—July 10, 1980

	Debts	Credits
Purchase Price	$150,000.00	
Deposit in Escrow		$ 14,000.00
Mortgage Transfer Fee	42.50	
Mortgage Assumed		72,920.80
Purchase Money Mortgage by Seller		37,079.20
Escrow Account Balance	1,776.65	
Title Insurance Premium	620.00	
Proration of Taxes		1,229.73
Proration of Interest		135.50
Proration of Rents		1,273.55
Security Deposits		1,850.00
Proration of Insurance	276.66	
Recording Warranty Deed	6.00	
SUB-TOTAL		$128,488.78
DUE FROM PURCHASER		$ 24,223.03
TOTAL	$152,711.81	$152,711.81

Figure 12-1

We'll first consider the "debt" column. This is what you owe:

1. The first item is the price you agreed to pay for the property, after all your negotiations with Mr. Seller—$150,000.00

2. The next debit item is $42.50, the charge by the lender to transfer the first mortgage into your name.

3. Escrow Balance. Remember, we said earlier that this could be one of your surprises at the closing. The property is being transferred on July 10th or 6 months and 10 days into the year. Assuming both the real estate taxes and insurance premium are due January 1st. You would expect there to be six or probably seven months of tax and in-

surance payments built up in the escrow account on the day of closing. What does that amount to?

    a) Taxes $2,350.00
       Insurance   580.00
       TOTAL $2,930.00
    b) $2,930.00 divided by 12 months = $244.17 per month
    c) January 1 through July = 7 months
    d) 7 months times $244.17 = $1,709.19

The escrow balance you have to buy from the seller is $1,776.65. The difference here is not too far from what you should have expected.

4. Title Insurance Premium. The cost of your title insurance policy is $620. Remember, this is a one time purchase.

5. Proration of Insurance. On January 1st, Mr. Seller, from the escrow account, paid the entire year's insurance premium. Since he only used the first 191 days of the policy year, you have to pay him for the remainder, from which you will benefit. The premium is $580.
    a) $580.00 divided by 365 days = $1.59 per day
    b) 174 days remaining in the year × $1.59 = $276.66. You owe $276.66.

6. Recording of the Warranty Deed. This is the final expense to you on the closing statement. It is, however, one of the most important. In order to protect your interest in your property and establish public notice that you are the legal owner, your deed must be recorded in the county courthouse in which the property is located. Your attorney will take care of recording it for you.

7. Your total expenses amount to $152,711.81.
Now, let's see what credits you have coming to you.
    a) Your first credit is the $14,000 deposit you made back when the contract was executed. The money is being held in a trust account, as you recall.
    b) Your next credit is the first mortgage you are assuming. The actual balance on the day of closing is $72,920.80. This amount is less than the $73,500 you had planned on.
    c) The contract calls for "any difference between the balance of the first mortgage and the amount shown on the purchase contract, shall be reflected in the second mortgage and not in cash." The second mortgage, therefore, has to be increased by

$579.20, the difference between the $73,500 and the actual balance of $72,920.80 on the first mortgage.

The second mortgage credit to you is for $37,079.20

d) Proration of taxes. The annual taxes, based on the last year, were $2,350.00. The seller owes that portion of real estate taxes for January 1st to July 10th when he owned the building. Figure it the same way you did the insurance proration:

   i. $2,350 – Taxes divided by 365 days = $6.44 per day

   ii. $6.44 × 191 days = $1,229.73

Mr. Seller owes you $1,229.73 real estate taxes for the first 191 days of the year when he owned the property.

e) Proration of Interest. The estopple letter received from the lender also spells out how much the seller's share of that month's interest he will owe if closing takes place on a certain day in the month. Mr. Seller owes $135.50 interest, which is a credit to you. This brings up an interesting point. When the mortgage is held by a savings and loan association, they collect interest in advance. When you make the July payment, you pay interest for the month of July. Most banks, however, charge interest in arrears or after you use the money. Your July payment would, therefore, pay the June interest.

f) Rents are prorated the same way, with the rent for the day of the closing, going in most cases, to the seller. Since he collected the rents a month in advance, he owes you the portion he collected for the last 21 days in July when you will own the property.

It is figured as follows:

   i.   Rents collected in July   = $1,880.00

   ii. $1,880.00 divided by 31 days   = $60.65 per day

   iii. $60.65 × 21 days = $1,273.55

Mr. Seller credits you with 21 days of July rent totaling $1,273.55

g) The final credit you receive is the sum of the security deposits being held by Mr. Seller. These amount to $1,850.00. Don't forget, that is *not* your money.

h) Your total credits amount to $128,488.78. Subtracting that amount from your $152,711.81 debit column shows you still owe $24,223.03 to close. If all went according to plan, that should be the exact amount you brought with you to the closing.

Once all figures are explained and approved, you execute the second mortgage and note, copies of your closing statement, etc., and title is transferred to your name. Keys and documents pertaining to the building and your cashier's check in the amount of $24,223.03 change hands. Your attorney will take care of recording the deed at the courthouse. Congratulations! You are now the owner of the *Always Full Apartments*.

WHAT TO DO AFTER THE CLOSING

There are a few things you will want to do shortly after closing:

Pay Your Tenants a Visit

Visit the *Always Full Apartments* personally to meet each of the tenants and introduce yourself as the new owner, if you did not do it prior to closing with the seller along. The letter that Mr. Seller has sent to each tenant, prior to closing, informing them that you have bought the building, has already introduced you.

Since you intend to ask one of your tenants if he would act as a resident manager, this gives you an opportunity to see who might be a likely candidate. You do not have to make that decision now. Wait until you become more familiar with the operation of the building and better acquainted with the tenants. You'll do a better job of selecting and instructing a manager after you've had some practical experience yourself.

Mr. Seller may also have some suggestions to make because he owned the property long enough to know the tenants and the building operation. You could have discussed this with him during one of your meetings prior to closing.

Refigure Your Property Analysis

Re-work your property analysis form based on the actual, final figures taken from the closing. Figure 12-2 shows the final statement. Notice that, according to the purchase contract, the price you paid is $150,000 with $40,000 cash down payment.

The contract also called for 9½ percent rather than 9 percent interest on the second mortgage.

Name: _ALWAYS FULL APTS_

Location: _147 NE 8TH ST._

Type of Property _8 UNIT APT. BLDG_ Area. _____

LIST PRICE _150,000_		
CASH REQ'D. _40,000_		

EXISTING ASSUMABLE FINANCING:

	Amount	Ann. Pmt.	Int.	Years To Go
1st $	_72,920_	_7,150_	_7½_ %	_19+_
2nd			%	
3rd			%	

POTENTIAL FINANCING:

				Years
1st $			%	
2nd	_37,080_	_3,888_	_9½_ %	_25_
3rd			%	

Folio:	Ex – S O O	File
Date:	Units: _8_	Lister.
Zoning _R-3_	Pool _NO_	Parking _12 CARS_
Size _100 X 150_	Rec. Rm _NO_	A-C _YES_
Sq. Ft. _6500_	Util. Rm _YES_	Heat _YES_
Age _7 YRS_	Office _NO_	T.V. _NO_
Stories _2_	Lobby _NO_	Furniture _YES_
Sewers _YES_	Elevators _NO_	Waterfront _NO_
Constr _CONCRETE & FRAME_		

Description –	# Units	Rent Sch
1 BEDROOM, 1 BATH	_6_	_$228/mo._
2 BEDROOM, 2 BATH	_2_	_$256/mo._

SCHEDULE GROSS INCOME			22	560
Less: Vacancy & Credit Loss _5%_			1	128
GROSS OPERATING INCOME			21	432
Less: Operating Expenses				
Taxes	2	350		
Insurance		580		
Utilities _ELECTRIC_		140		
Advertising				
Licenses & Permits		25		
Management	1	200		
Payroll & Payroll Taxes				
Supplies				
Services _WATER/SEWER_		360		
Maintenance _5%_	1	072		
Reserve for Replacement				
Ground Lease				
LAWN SERVICE		720		
TOTAL EXPENSES _30_ %			6	447
OPERATING INCOME			14	985
Plus Other Income			6	
NET OPERATING INCOME			14	985

COMMENTS   CODE ....

FINANCIAL STATUS ON DAY OF CLOSING.

DEPRECIATION SCHEDULE:

LAND = 15%

IMPROVEMENTS = 70%, 25 YR. USEFUL LIFE, 125% D.B. = 5.0% - 1ST YR = $5,250

PERSONAL PROPERTY = 15%, 5 YR. USEFUL LIFE, S/L DEPR. = 20% YR = $4,500

INFORMATION HEREIN IS BELIEVED TO BE ACCURATE BUT IS NOT WARRANTED

INCOME ADJUSTED TO FINANCING:	Actual ☒	Potential ☐	Equity: $ _40,000_		
NET OPERATING INCOME	Cap. Rate - List Price	%			14	985

	3rd Loan	2nd Loan	1st Loan	TOTAL		
Less: Loan Payment						
Interest						
Principal						
Total Loan Payment					11	038
GROSS SPENDABLE INCOME	Rate: _9.9_ %	(GSI ÷ EQUITY)			3	947
Plus: Principal Payment					2	047
GROSS EQUITY INCOME	Rate: _15.0_ %	(GEI ÷ EQUITY)			5	994
Less: Depreciation	Personal Property = _$4,500_	Improvements = _$5,250_			9	750
REAL ESTATE TAXABLE INCOME			_TAX LOSS_		(3	756)

---

* Based on Form "B," copyrighted by REALTORS NATIONAL MARKETING INSTITUTE OF NATIONAL ASSOCIATION OF REALTORS. Copyright 1974. All rights reserved. Used with permission of copyright owner.

** Reprinted with permission of L.C. Judd & Co., Inc.

Figure 12-2

When you got to the closing, you discovered that the second mortgage starting balance would be $37,080 because of the decrease in balance of the first mortgage. The two mortgages still total $110,000.00.

Due to the change in interest rate and the slight increase in size of the second mortgage, the payments for principal and interest will now be $3,888 a year. Income and expenses remain unchanged.

When you get down to Income Adjusted to Financing on the analysis form, you'll see that your equity is now $40,000. After mortgage payments, you are left with a gross spendable income of $3947 or 9.9 percent return on your cash investment. Your total Gross Equity Income is now $5994 or 15 percent return on your cash investment.

Your overall pre-tax return has improved slightly due to the $5,000 reduction you negotiated in the purchase price. Part of the increase, however, was eaten up by the ½ percent interest rate increase in the second mortgage and the slight increase in size of that mortgage.

Your depreciation must be re-calculated based on the actual purchase price of $150,000. Subtracting your depreciation from your gross equity income indicates that you will be able to show a $3756 tax loss on tax write-off against other income the first year you own the building. It looks like you made an extremely good purchase.

Change Utility Meters to Your Name

Water, electric and gas meters need to be changed over to your name. You could have done this just prior to closing, by making your deposit and giving the utility company a July 10th changeover date. If you didn't you should do it right after you leave the closing. Most tenants pay their own electric bills, so the only meter you need to worry about with the power company is the one that controls the common area lighting, etc.

Change Services to Your Name

Contact all services—trash removal, lawn, air conditioning, etc. and have these services changed over to your name.

Get to Know Your Property

Get thoroughly familiar with your property. Spend some time walking around, checking everything out. You can be certain several tenants will volunteer the things that are wrong. Don't let them bother you—some of them may be very helpful.

If your purchase was a shopping center, office building, or an industrial building, you will still want to spend some time at the complex. Learn as much as you can about the investment. Talk with your tenants. Listen to what they have to say. Some may offer valid suggestions for improvements or point out minor problems that should be corrected.

The next step you need to take right away is to set up a bookkeeping system for your property. Record keeping is covered in the next chapter.

You are now on the road to your real estate investment program. At this point you will feel a joy, a pride of ownership that you probably have not had since you purchased your first home, especially if this is your first venture into investment real estate. It will be a good feeling to know that you are on the way to securing your financial future. You have taken that first step . . . the most difficult one to take.

13

How to Set Up a Simple and Efficient Record Keeping System

HOW TO SET UP YOUR BOOKS

One of your priorities, now that you own the *Always Full Apartments*, is to set up a bookkeeping or accounting system for the operation of the property. The system does not have to be a complicated accounting procedure that only a CPA can understand. The system shown here is adaptable to any type of investment property.

Keeping Ledgers

Any stationery store sells "ledger sheets" and binders to hold them. You will want a separate page for each tenant showing how much rent he pays, sales tax, if any, lease expiration, and security deposit held by you.

The sheet will have room to enter each month for the year in order to keep track of when he pays his rent.

TENANT: John Roberts
LEASE EXPIRES: March 31, 1981   SECURITY: $250.00

Month	Date Paid	Base Rent	Tax	Total
July	From Closing	$ 166.67	$ 6.67	$ 173.34
Aug.	August 5	256.00	10.24	266.24
Sept.	September 2	256.00	10.24	266.24
Oct.	October 2	256.00	10.24	266.24
Nov.	November 4	256.00	10.24	266.24
Dec.	December 3	256.00	10.24	266.24
Year End Totals:		$1,446.67	$57.87	$1,504.54

Figure 13-1

Figure 13-1 illustrates a simple ledger form for the tenant. This simple page not only tells you everything you need to know about the status of his lease, but also shows a record of rent payments. A separate ledger sheet will be needed for miscellaneous income, such as the coin laundry you have in the building.

The ledger will be closed out at the end of each calendar year, so each page should end on December 31st (unless you purchased the property as a Corporation and your corporation has a year ending other than December 31st).

Ledger sheets for each expense item are also prepared in the same manner. One for electric, water, lawn service, payroll and any other expense item that occurs monthly. Do not worry about the real estate taxes and insurance items. These are paid only once a year and can be incorporated on one page marked "miscellaneous" along with other nonrecurring expense items.

Another page will be set up for all repair and maintenance expenses. A typical ledger sheet for repair and maintenance expenses is shown in Figure 13-2. Notice that this ledger is not set up on a "one entry a month" basis because you do not know how many items you may have during the month. There is, however, a "cumulative" column at the right to simplify showing an end of the month total for that expense item.

Expenses—Repairs & Maintenance

Date	Check No.	To	Amount	Cumulative
Aug. 4	103	Ajax Plumbing	$32.50	
Aug. 18	109	Handy Hardware Co.	14.75	
Aug. 24	114	A.B.C. Enterprises	12.62	
Mo. Total				$59.87
Sept. 6	123	Handy Hardware Co.	22.45	

Figure 13-2

The accounting procedure on your first mortgage, will be a little different because it consists of three separate items: principal, interest and escrow payments. For accounting purposes, and for end of the year balance sheets and tax returns, this breakdown will be necessary.

Figure 13-3 illustrates the first mortgage payment ledger sheet for the entire remaining portion of the year.

First Mortgage Payment

Date	Check No.	Principal	Interest	Escrow	Total
Aug. 2	102	$140.08	$ 455.75	$ 254.00	$ 849.83
Sept. 3	121	140.96	454.87	254.00	849.83
Oct. 2	138	141.83	454.00	254.00	849.83
Nov. 5	151	142.72	453.11	254.00	849.83
Dec. 3	170	143.61	452.22	254.00	849.83
Year End Totals:		$709.20	$2,269.95	$1,270.00	$4,249.15

Figure 13-3

Once your books are set up, monthly posting of income and expenses becomes a simple matter. You also have an easy reference to make sure rents are being paid on time and that none of your operating expenses are out of line.

You may elect to prepare a monthly balance sheet to see how your investment is doing. It really isn't necessary on a small investment property, such as the *Always Full Apartments*. A quick look at your ledger book and bank book tells you if everything is going according to plan.

Preparing a Profit and Loss Statement

At the end of the year you will need to prepare a year-end profit and loss statement. On December 31st, your statement of the *Always Full Apartments* might look something like Figure 13-4.

ALWAYS FULL APARTMENTS   Year Ending_____

End of Year Profit and Loss Statement

Income:

Rental	$10,648.00	
Sales Tax	425.92	
Laundry	143.25	
Total Income:		$11,217.17

Expenses:

Real Estate Taxes	$2,420.00	
Sales Tax	425.92	
Insurance	Due in January	
Electric	67.50	
Licenses	25.00	
Payroll	567.00	
Water/Sewer	172.25	
Repairs & Maintenance	492.60	
Lawn Service	340.00	
LESS: Total Expenses		$ 4,510.27
NET OPERATING INCOME:		$ 6,706.90
LESS: 1st Mortgage Principal & Interest Payments—	$2,979.15	
2nd Mortgage Principal & Interest Payments—	$1.620.00	
Total Mortgage Payments:		$4,599.15
GROSS OPERATING PROFIT:		$2,107.75

Figure 13-4

The statement is in a very simple form. All income is totaled—rents, sales tax collected, and coin laundry income, for a total income of $11,217.17. Total expenses are then shown. You will notice that "sales tax" is shown since the $425.92 you collected from the tenants is immediately paid to the state and "washes out" that income amount by the "expense" entry. This assumes the *Always Full Apartments* is in a state that collects sales tax on rental apartments.

The tax bill for the current year was also paid in the amount of $2420. The insurance premium will be paid after the first of the year for the coming year. Total operating expenses for the *Always Full Apartments* ran $4510.27 for the five months and 21 days you've owned the property since closing. Subtracting the operating expenses from the total income leaves you with $6,706.90 out of which you made the first and second mortgage payments.

Only the principal and interest payments are shown on this statement, not the escrow payments. They are figured in above under taxes and insurance, where the actual paid bills are used not the amount held by the lender to pay these bills. The total first and second mortgage payments for the five months came to $4,599.15.

Mortgage payments for the last 21 days in July were not figured because that amount was prorated at the closing on the first mortgage, and no second mortgage payment was due until August 1st. Subtracting the $4,599.15 total mortgage payments from your net operating income left you with a "Gross Operating Profit" (pre-tax) of $2,107.75.

Your Revised Property Analysis Form (Figure 12-2) indicated your gross spendable income for 12 months should be $3,947.00.

You would expect to be able to divide that by 12 months and multiply by 5⅔ months and see how close you come to your expected income. It may look as if you did better than expected, but you cannot judge by this first, partial year's statement. Several items have given you a "false" report for checking the operational results:

1. You paid an entire year's tax bill but have only owned the building 5⅔ months. Also, notice that the taxes increased over what you had planned.

2. At the closing, you paid Mr. Seller $276.66 for the last 5⅔ months of insurance that he had already paid. This does not appear on your statement.

3. You had ⅔ of a month's "free" interest on the second mortgage because those payments did not start until August 1st.

4. So far, you have had 100% occupancy. The building is living up to it's name at the present time. Your analysis allows for a five percent vacancy factor, which you may be glad you planned for next year or the year after.

5. You picked up some coin laundry income that you had not previously considered in your analysis. This is like a small bonus of unplanned income.

In any case, your investment is off to an excellent start, with most income and expense items falling right in line with your projections.

HOW TO SET UP YOUR BANK ACCOUNTS

One of the first things you needed to do after closing was to set up two separate bank accounts. The $1,850.00 of tenant security deposits should be put into a separate, interest bearing savings account where it is not co-mingled with your personal or apartment account. Some states require you pay the tenant interest on the security deposits and advance rents that you hold.

Since the $1,850.00 showed up as a credit to you on the closing statements, you were able to pay $1,850.00 less cash at the closing. Now you have to write a personal check for that amount so that in effect, you are reimbursing the escrow account for the amount you used at closing.

The second, and separate, account you need to open is the building operating account (checking account). Do not try to cut corners and co-mingle the operation of the *Always Full Apartments* with your personal checking account. In the long run, it will be confusing to you to separate the two and frowned upon by any IRS auditor.

Posting to your ledger each month is a simple procedure when you have an account just for your building. Investors with several properties will usually have a separate operating account for each.

You may also want to consider establishing a capital improvement reserve account. As this account builds up, you will have sufficient funds available to cover the cost of a new refrigerator, etc., as needed, without digging into your pocket or trying to pull it out of the operating account.

Unless you plan on using the "cash flow" or profit produced by your investment, excess cash in your operating account should be taken out periodically and placed in another, interest bearing account. This is one place additional investment capital can be accumulated. Oh, there is nothing wrong with adding to this account from other excess funds that you may wish to accumulate for a future investment.

It may sound as if you are opening up an awful lot of checking and savings accounts just for one small building. Only the checking account is a special account exclusively for the *Always Full Apartments*. The others can be used to accumulate reserve funds for as many properties as you will eventually own. And, if you follow this book, you could end up owning several.

HOW TO COMPUTE YOUR END-OF-YEAR TAX RETURN

The following April, you will be including the *Always Full Apartments* in your income tax returns. You'll probably want a CPA to assist you, but let's take a look at what you can expect.

First, review your tax situation as if you had not purchased the real estate investment. Assume you were earning a six percent taxable income on the $50,000 you used to make the real estate purchase. Six percent of $50,000 is $3000.

Since you are in a 32 percent tax bracket, with a taxable income (after all deductions and exemptions) of $25,800.00, you owe Uncle Sam $4505 in taxes plus 32 percent of every taxable dollar you earn over the lower income in that particular bracket, $24,600. Figure 13-5 has your tax column underlined. Your taxable income, including the $3000 interest income you received on your $50,000 was $25,800 or $1200 *over* the lower limit on the tax table. This means that you owe an additional 32 percent of that $1200 or $384. Adding this to the base tax of $4505, you end up owing a total of $4889 in income tax. Your present tax situation looks like this:

Taxable Income (Including $3000 Interest)				$25,800
Tax Due: On base amount of $24,700	=		$4,505	
Total Taxable income	$25,800			
Less Base Amount	24,600			
Balance of taxable Income $ 1,200		@ 32%	=	384
Total Tax Liability				$ 4,889
Net Income After Taxes				$20,911

Now re-work your tax situation based on your ownership of the *Always Full Apartments*. Your taxable income was $25,800, but you have eliminated the $3000 interest income on your $50,000, so your taxable income is $22,800 *before* you consider the effects of the real estate investment.

1979 Tax Rate Schedules

If you cannot use one of the Tax Tables, figure your tax on the amount on Schedule TC, Part I, line 3, by using the appropriate Tax Rate Schedule on this page. Enter the tax on Schedule TC, Part I, line 4.

Note: Your new zero bracket amount has been built into these Tax Rate Schedules.

SCHEDULE X—Single Taxpayers

Use this schedule if you checked Filing Status Box 1 on Form 1040—

If the amount on Schedule TC, Part I, line 3, is:

Not over $2,300......0

Over—	But not over—	Enter on Schedule TC, Part I, line 4:	of the amount over—
$2,300	$3,400	14%	$2,300
$3,400	$4,400	$154+16%	$3,400
$4,400	$6,500	$314+18%	$4,400
$6,500	$8,500	$692+19%	$6,500
$8,500	$10,800	$1,072+21%	$8,500
$10,800	$12,900	$1,555+24%	$10,800
$12,900	$15,000	$2,059+26%	$12,900
$15,000	$18,200	$2,605+30%	$15,000
$18,200	$23,500	$3,565+34%	$18,200
$23,500	$28,800	$5,367+39%	$23,500
$28,800	$34,100	$7,434+44%	$28,800
$34,100	$41,500	$9,766+49%	$34,100
$41,500	$55,300	$13,392+55%	$41,500
$55,300	$81,800	$20,982+63%	$55,300
$81,800	$108,300	$37,677+68%	$81,800
$108,300	-----	$55,697+70%	$108,300

SCHEDULE Y—Married Taxpayers and Qualifying Widows and Widowers

Married Filing Joint Returns and Qualifying Widows and Widowers

Use this schedule if you checked Filing Status Box 2 or 5 on Form 1040—

If the amount on Schedule TC, Part I, line 3, is:

Not over $3,400......0

Over—	But not over—	Enter on Schedule TC, Part I, line 4:	of the amount over—
$3,400	$5,500	14%	$3,400
$5,500	$7,600	$294+16%	$5,500
$7,600	$11,900	$630+18%	$7,600
$11,900	$16,000	$1,404+21%	$11,900
$16,000	$20,200	$2,265+24%	$16,000
$20,200	$24,600	$3,273+28%	$20,200
$24,600	$29,900	$4,505+32%	$24,600
$29,900	$35,200	$6,201+37%	$29,900
$35,200	$45,800	$8,162+43%	$35,200
$45,800	$60,000	$12,720+49%	$45,800
$60,000	$85,600	$19,678+54%	$60,000
$85,600	$109,400	$33,502+59%	$85,600
$109,400	$162,400	$47,544+64%	$109,400
$162,400	$215,400	$81,464+68%	$162,400
$215,400	-----	$117,504+70%	$215,400

Married Filing Separate Returns

Use this schedule if you checked Filing Status Box 3 on Form 1040—

If the amount on Schedule TC, Part I, line 3, is:

Not over $1,700......0

Over—	But not over—	Enter on Schedule TC, Part I, line 4:	of the amount over—
$1,700	$2,750	14%	$1,700
$2,750	$3,800	$147+16%	$2,750
$3,800	$5,950	$315+18%	$3,800
$5,950	$8,000	$702+21%	$5,950
$8,000	$10,100	$1,132.50+24%	$8,000
$10,100	$12,300	$1,636.50+28%	$10,100
$12,300	$14,950	$2,252.50+32%	$12,300
$14,950	$17,600	$3,100.50+37%	$14,950
$17,600	$22,900	$4,081.00+43%	$17,600
$22,900	$30,000	$6,360.00+49%	$22,900
$30,000	$42,800	$9,839.00+54%	$30,000
$42,800	$54,700	$16,751.00+59%	$42,800
$54,700	$81,200	$23,772.00+64%	$54,700
$81,200	$107,700	$40,732.00+68%	$81,200
$107,700	-----	$56,752.00+70%	$107,700

SCHEDULE Z—Heads of Household

(including certain married persons who live apart (and abandoned spouses)—see page 7 of the Instructions)

Use this schedule if you checked Filing Status Box 4 on Form 1040—

If the amount on Schedule TC, Part I, line 3, is:

Not over $2,300......0

Over—	But not over—	Enter on Schedule TC, Part I, line 4:	of the amount over—
$2,300	$4,400	14%	$2,300
$4,400	$6,500	$294+16%	$4,400
$6,500	$8,700	$630+18%	$6,500
$8,700	$11,800	$1,026+22%	$8,700
$11,800	$15,000	$1,708+24%	$11,800
$15,000	$18,200	$2,476+26%	$15,000
$18,200	$23,500	$3,308+31%	$18,200
$23,500	$28,800	$4,951+36%	$23,500
$28,800	$34,100	$6,859+42%	$28,800
$34,100	$44,700	$9,085+46%	$34,100
$44,700	$60,600	$13,961+54%	$44,700
$60,600	$81,800	$22,547+59%	$60,600
$81,800	$108,300	$35,055+63%	$81,800
$108,300	$161,300	$51,750+68%	$108,300
$161,300	-----	$87,790+70%	$161,300

Figure 13-5

Looking at your end-of-the-year profit and loss statement (Figure 13-4), it shows a pre-tax profit on the bottom line of $2108 (rounded). To this amount, you must add the principal and interest using the same method you used in the chapter on financing. It will look like Figure 13-6. In actual filing of your tax return, you will have the exact breakdown between principal and interest on your mortgage amortization schedules.

1st Mortgage Balance—$72,920   ×   7.5% Interest   = $5469 per year
$5,469   divided by   12 months   ×   5⅔ months (that you have owned the property)   = $2584

Total 1st Mortgage Payments Made (Figure 13-4)	= $2979
LESS: Interest Portion Paid	2584
1st Mortgage Principal Payment	$ 395

2nd Mortgage Balance—$37,080   ×   9.5% Interest   = $3522 per year
$3522   divided by   12 months   = $293.50   ×   5 months payments   = $1467

Total 2nd Mortgage Payments Made (Figure 13-4)	= $1620
LESS: Interest Portion Paid	1467
2nd Mortgage Principal Payment	$ 153

Total Principal Payments:	1st Mortgage	$ 395
	2nd Mortgage	153
	TOTAL	$ 548

NOTE: Numbers were rounded to nearest dollar.

Figure 13-6

Your total pre-tax income on the *Always Full Apartments* consists of:

Gross Spendable	$2108
Principal Reduction	548
Total Pre-Tax Income	$2656

From the depreciation line on Figure 12-2 (next to the bottom line) you determined your first year's depreciation would be $9750. But, you only owned the complex 5⅔ months so you can only take that portion of the depreciation your first year:

$9750   divided by   12 months   = $812.50 per month
$812.50   ×   5⅔ months   = $4607

You can take $4607 depreciation your first year, but the complex only shows a $2656 profit. Deducting that from your depreciation, you have a tax loss or tax shelter against your other income of $1951. You can reduce your base taxable income of $22,800 by $1951. This gives you an actual taxable income of $20,849.00. Referring to the tax table (Figure 13-6) you will see that you have dropped to the next lower bracket. You owe IRS $3273 on the first $20,200 and 28 percent of everything over that amount. $20,849 (rounded) less $20,200   = $649   ×   28 percent   = $182. Total tax liability is: $3273   + $182 or $3455.

A comparison between your old position and your new one appears in Figure 13-7. This Figure also includes the six months interest income you received on your $50,000 prior to investing it in real estate.

HOW MUCH DID YOUR INVESTMENT EARN?

How much did your real estate investment earn altogether in your first 5⅔ months of ownership?

Tax Free Spendable Income	$2108
Principal Reduction	548
Tax Savings on other income (32% × $4607)	1474
Total After Tax Return	$4130

To that amount, you will add the amount you expect your real estate investment to appreciate. Let's use four percent as a conservative amount.

Property value—$150,000   ×   4%   = $6000
But, you only owned it for 5⅔ months:
$6000   divided by   12   ×   5⅔   = $2835

	Old Position With $3,000 Interest Income	New Position With Always Full Apartments
Base Taxable Income:	$22,800	$22,800
Plus Other Income:		
Interest	3,000	1,500 (6 mo.) Int.
Real Estate	-0-	Loss: (1,951)
Total Taxable Income:	$25,800	$22,349
Tax Liability (from table)	4,889	3,875

Total Taxable Income:	$25,800	(Includes Interest)	$24,300	(Includes Interest)
LESS: Tax Liability:	4,889		3,875	
NET INCOME:	$20,911		$20,425	
Plus Tax Free Real Estate Income (Spendable Portion Only	-0-		2,108	
TOTAL INCOME AFTER TAXES:	$20,911		$22,533	

NEW NET INCOME	$22,533
OLD NET INCOME	$20,911
ADDED AFTER TAX INCOME	$ 1,622

Figure 13-7

As you can see, you were able to put an additional $1622 in your pocket, after taxes, because you owned the *Always Full Apartments*. And, you owned them for less than six months.

Next year, your tax picture will look even better.

Your building should conservatively be worth an additional $2835 by the end of the year. Adding this to your total after tax income of $4130 gives you a total return of $6965.

In order to determine the return on your investment, you must use the same formula that was used before. You only used the $40,000 for 5⅔ months: $40,000 divided by 12 months = $3333.33 per month × 5⅔ months = $18,900.

In theory, you only had $18,900 invested in order to make the $6965 total return.

$$\frac{\$\ 6,956}{\$18,900} \quad = \quad 36.9\%$$

Your real estate investment gave you a 36.9 percent *after tax* return on your invested capital, including property appreciation. Now you realize what real estate investing can do for you. These figures are not just "pie in the sky" results. You can expect to do this well on any sound real estate investment. You probably wish you had started your real estate investment program long before now and the best is yet to come—pyramiding your investment. But first, there are some additional details that you must understand, starting with the leasing of your apartments.

14

What You Should Know About Leasing and Leases

It can be assumed that at some time you are going to have vacancies. You will want to be prepared for this event so that you will have a minimum period of time that a rental unit is not producing income. This Chapter is divided into three phases regarding this topic: (1) Establishing Your Rental Standards, (2) Preparing a Lease and (3) Finding and Qualifying a Tenant.

Assuming you intend to rent the *Always Full Apartments* on a lease basis, using a formal lease, perhaps the discussion should start with the question . . .

WHO DOES A LEASE PROTECT?

When it comes to a yearly rental apartment building, such as the *Always Full*, most experts agree that a lease protects the tenant but *not* the landlord (you). If that thought bothers or confuses you, keep reading and find out why.

When a lessor (you) and a lessee (the tenant) execute a lease, you both agree to several things, including the expiration date of the lease, the monthly rent to be paid, and the rights and privileges of both the tenant and landlord.

Legally speaking, a properly drawn lease is a binding contract for both parties. As a practical matter, it is more binding on the landlord than it is the tenant. As long as the tenant pays his rent on time, takes care of his apartment and does not create a nuisance within the building, the landlord is obligated to let him live out his lease term. Don't misunderstand—that is why you have a lease to begin with.

But, if the tenant fails to pay his rent, destroys his apartment or keeps the other tenants up all night with loud parties, your legal rights, spelled out in the lease, are difficult to enforce. The legal procedure to evict an undesirable tenant is time consuming. In the meantime, your income will suffer, especially if other tenants start moving out because of one undesirable tenant. The secret, of course, is not to rent to that type of tenant in the first place. We will cover that later.

When a tenant just moves out on you and disappears, collecting back rent is almost impossible. You may get a judgment from a small claims court that entitles you to recoup any lost rent, but as a practical matter, how much can you afford to spend trying to locate the "skipped" tenant. And if you do find him, you still cannot collect short of taking him to court. In most cases, it is not worth the time and expense involved. Looking at the brighter side of the lease, as far as the landlord is concerned, a properly qualified tenant will think twice before defaulting on the lease terms. It *is* a legally binding contract which permits you to take legal action in case of a default. He probably does not realize how difficult it may be to enforce.

Starting with this background knowledge of leases, your first task is:

HOW TO ESTABLISH YOUR RENTAL STANDARDS

Determining the "Fair Market Rent" Level

What determines the rent you should charge for your apartments? The obvious answer is "your competition." What are comparable apartments renting for in your area? You'll have to make a neighborhood survey to find out. Be sure you are comparing apples with apples. Your units are one and two bedroom, furnished apartments. Use the same rental units in other buildings for comparison.

Check the location, condition of the apartments, size, and amenities as well. A brand new building with new furniture may demand a higher rent than your seven-year-old property. Assuming your building is in first class condition or apartments in your area are scarce, this may not hold true. Where rent controls are in effect, you have an entirely different ball game. You are probably locked in at a maximum rent level. Although you want to be fair with your tenants, you also want to be fair to yourself as well by charging the maximum rent you can for the market you are in.

New rental apartment buildings will no doubt have a higher rent schedule because of the high building costs. The investor has to charge high rents to justify the cost of the building. The owners of older buildings, such as yourself, greatly benefit from these new properties. You have the opportunity to adjust your rents up to the rates charged by the new building's owner.

After a couple of years of owning your building, if you are able to brag that you still have never had a vacancy, the chances are your rents are too low.

Along those lines, never become too friendly with your tenants. Once you know all their problems, you will not want to raise their rent, and that's when *you'll* start having problems. Keep an "arms length" relationship with your tenants. When the market demands it (surely operating expenses will) get a rent increase when the lease comes up for renewal.

A reasonable increase is expected by most tenants. Unless the increase is unreasonably large, most tenants would rather pay the increase than face the thought of moving to something that may or may not end up less expensive.

This type of a rent increase is called a "nuisance" raise. The nuisance of trying to find another apartment at a comparable or lower rent and the nuisance and expense of moving, just is not worth it . . . so, they stay and pay the small increase in rent. It will probably be only five to ten percent.

The other type of increase you will seek is an "economic" increase. This increase may be larger than, and in lieu of, the nuisance raise. It is brought about by factors over which you have no control such as tax increases, higher utility bills, and, of course, inflation. A sizable jump in rents may be needed to keep you ahead of these factors.

Keep the Economy in Mind

When considering rental increases, you need to keep the overall economy in mind. It was pointed out earlier that, due to our continuing inflation, prices keep going up. This includes the cost of food, appliances, professional services, automobiles, *and housing*. This means that rents *must* go up to cover added building operating expenses created by inflation. If you fail to increase your rents to at least keep up with inflation, you will find that your real estate investment will cease to appreciate. Selling or trading your property at what should be the fair market price will be difficult. I'd like to have a dollar for every property that has come on the market at a price that greatly exceeds the fair market value based on the income currently being produced by the property. Without exception, everyone of these offerings includes a statement such as: "Rents are low for the area and can be increased."

Do not let yourself fall into this trap. Market conditions permitting, keep your rents up with the current comparable area rents. Your property will appreciate more rapidly and bring a higher price on the market when you sell.

The most important consideration here is the condition of your local rental market. An area experiencing a 10 percent average vacancy rate is not the market to request rent raises, at least not large ones. The tenant in that type of market has a wide selection of available apartments. You may want to sacrifice a few dollars added income in order to keep your building fully occupied.

When the rental market dries up and your area is experiencing a one to two percent vacancy rate, then you can safely increase rents.

FURNISHED VS. UNFURNISHED APARTMENTS

A furnished apartment complex such as the *Always Full Apartments*, makes "skipping" a lot easier. All a tenant has to do is pack his personal belongings. There is no furniture to move.

So why have furnished apartments? They demand more rent and offer you a larger depreciation amount. Depending on market conditions and what types of apartments are in demand, you may want to consider eliminating the furniture in your building as it wears out, and rent the units unfurnished. Do this instead of replacing it.

REPAIRS AND MAINTENANCE: KEEPING YOUR PROPERTY IN TOP CONDITION

You will want to be assured of higher occupancy and top rents. This requires keeping your property in first class condition. I've seen properties where the investor became greedy and took as much out of the building as he could without putting anything back into it. It wasn't long before his vacancy level started to increase and, as an indirect effect, he had to lower rents to obtain tenants. Once a building gets a bad reputation, it will be a long and costly process of bringing it back up to standard.

Keeping the exterior of your property painted and the landscaping well trimmed. This is the first impression a prospective tenant has of your property. If your property creates a low class appearance, you can expect low class tenants at a low rent level.

When a tenant moves out of an apartment, especially if he has lived in it for a couple of years or more, clean the carpet and give the walls a coat of paint before you show it to a prospective renter.

Your manager can probably rent a carpet cleaning machine and do it himself. He should also be able to do the painting and cleaning up that is necessary. You can offer to pay him extra for this added work which is beyond his normal management duties.

THE LEASE TERM

Decide what term you want on your lease, one year, two years, etc. One year is usually customary for a rental apartment, but, your local rental market conditions may dictate something different. When you do grant a lease for more than one year, make certain you are protected from the effects of inflation and increases in operating expenses. This will be covered more when we talk about preparing the lease.

Owners of stores or offices, where extensive costs can be involved in preparing the space for a specific tenant, will usually want a five year, or longer, base lease term.

When preparing a lease in excess of one year in length, you have three options:

First, you can prepare a base lease of, say, 6 years.

Secondly, you may prepare it for two years and give the tenant two, two-year renewal options.

Thirdly, you can combine the two. Give him an initial long term lease (4 years) with an additional two or four year option.

Seek legal assistance if you are not familiar with leases in excess of one year.

HOW TO HANDLE SECURITY DEPOSITS

A security deposit or damage deposit is collected at the time the lease is executed. It is usually in an amount equivalent to one month's rent. This deposit is held by the landlord as his "security" that the tenant will live out the terms of his lease. If the tenant defaults, the landlord is within his rights to keep as much of the deposit as it takes to offset his loss in rental income on the apartment until it is re-rented.

When the tenant moves out, assuming he has performed in accordance with the terms of the lease, the landlord is within his rights to inspect the vacated apartment and retain whatever portion of the security deposit is needed to repair any excessive damage that may have been done by the tenant. Notice that I said "excessive." You cannot charge him for "reasonable wear and tear," where the carpeting, for example, is soiled from use; cleaning it is your expense. When the tenant, on the other hand, burned holes in the carpet because of careless cigarette smoking, he pays for the carpet repairs out of his security deposit.

If you keep all or part of the deposit, furnish the tenant with an itemized list of the charges you are making, and make sure they are reasonable.

You do not want to get the reputation of a landlord who always keeps the tenant's security deposit even when there is no legitimate reason for it. Treat your tenants the same way you would want to be treated if you were in their position.

ADVANCE RENTS

Some landlords ask for the final month's rent in advance at the time the lease is executed. It gives the landlord an extra security, in the form of one month's rent, if the tenant moves out prior to the termination of his lease. Collecting the last month's rent in advance, along with the first month's rent and a security deposit is highly desirable from the landlord's point of view, but most young married couples cannot afford the equivalent of three months rent all at one time. They also face the expense of moving in, and utility deposits.

Depending on how well you are able to qualify a potential tenant, you will probably drop the request for the last month's rent and collect only the first month and security deposit at the time the lease is executed.

PROTECTING YOUR INVESTMENT

You have invested a sizable amount of capital in the *Always Full Apartments*. This investment was made based on your building producing the income you had projected prior to purchasing. You will never get an exact estimate, but you want to stay as close to it, as you possibly can. There is nothing wrong with the property producing *more* income or profit than you projected. It is in your best interest, therefore, to establish your rental standards to insure this income. Other than selecting stable tenants, which we will cover later, your primary concern should be to maintain a rent level on your apartments that is in line with current market rentals. This also requires keeping your building in such condition that you will attract the better tenants.

GUIDELINES FOR PREPARING A LEASE TO SUIT YOUR PROPERTY AND YOUR NEEDS

Unless you are leasing a commercial property, such as a store or office where leases are very involved and for longer terms, there are pre-printed lease forms available. Involved leases should be drawn by your attorney, in fact, most leasee's will require that their attorney get involved.

Normal, year to year apartment leases are not complicated. Check the leases that were signed over to you when you bought your property. Assuming they seem satisfactory, continue using the same form. If you are a first time real estate investor, you may still want to consult with your attorney, at the closing, and have him advise you on the lease form presently in use.

Most office supply stores carry standard lease forms that, in the majority of cases, will do the job quite satisfactorily.

LEASE EXPIRATION DATES

Some thought should be given to the time of the year that may be the best rental period in your area. Northern cities may have the best tenant market in the summer, when school is out and the weather is conducive to moving.

Resort areas, such as the Florida Gold Coast, has its highest apartment demand in the winter months. Even though you do not consider permanent, year round residents in Fort Lauderdale, Florida, living in a beach front motel, they do. When they are in the market for an apartment in the late spring through the fall months, they can probably live on the ocean at close to the same rent that an apartment further inland would cost. Come December, however, when higher winter seasonal rents take effect, they are all seeking the less expensive, non-beach front apartments.

It makes sense, therefore, to have leases on south Florida apartments come due during the season, preferably in December, the beginning of the winter tourist season. This is the highest demand period for rental apartments. There is another advantage for furnished apartment owners having their leases come up at the beginning of the tourist season. In Fort Lauderdale, for example, a furnished apartment rented for the four month tourist season should bring the same amount of rent that it will bring if rented on a yearly basis for the entire year. It is not uncommon for a yearly rented furnished apartment, bring in $250 a month rent, to rent for $750 a month for the four month season.

Take a survey of your area and determine what time of the year brings the highest demands for rental apartments. If it is July, try to write your leases to expire in July. This may mean writing a 16 or 18 month lease rather than one for 12 months, but the average lessee will be happy to get a few extra months with no rent increases.

When an area has no peak demand period for rentals, stagger your leases so that they come due throughout the year. This will prevent your having several vacant apartments all at once.

Who Pays What

Your leases will be written, of course, showing the exact monthly rent to be paid plus any state sales tax that your area may have. Most apartment buildings have individual electric meters. Your lease should spell out which utilities you, as the landlord, pay and which ones are paid by the lessee.

The lease should also specify which, if any, repairs are the responsibility of the lessee. If the toilet backs up, he is probably responsible and should pay the plumbing bill. Suppose, however, it backed up because the sewer line in the street was blocked. It was not his fault and he should not be expected to foot the repair bill.

The lease may be worded to require the tenant to pay for any repairs within his apartment that are a direct result of something he might have done. Normal wear and tear being the exception.

When the apartment has an "extra" or not normally included appliance, such as washing machine, the landlord may write a limited warranty into the lease. Since a washing machine is not a normal appliance in that rental apartment, he, the landlord, will not pay any repair bills if it quits working. Rather than repair an old machine, he may elect to just get rid of it whenever it quits working. The tenant, on the other hand, may want to have it repaired at his expense. He is welcome to do so.

Late Penalties

Some tenants will habitually be late paying their rent, but do eventually get it paid. Consider writing a "late penalty" clause in your lease. It works like this: Rent is due on the first of the month. It will be accepted through the fifth of the month, without penalty. Any rent payment made after the fifth of the month *must* include an additional $5.00 or $10.00 penalty charge. You'll be surprised how prompt your rent payments will arrive.

When you rent an apartment on the 15th of the month, prorate the first month's rent and collect for only 15 days for the remainder of the month, with the first full month's rent due the first of the following month or in 15 days.

Rental Increases: Protecting Yourself Against Inflation

Leases that exceed one year in length should be written to protect the landlord from the effects of inflation and increases in taxes, utilities, etc.

Tax and utility increases are easy to cover in a "tax stop" type clause in the lease. In effect, the clause states that the lessee agrees to pay any increases in taxes (or utilities) over the base year or first year of the lease. The taxes on the *Always Full Apartments* are $2350 a year. That breaks down to $293.75 for each of the eight units. Assume the taxes go up to $2460 next year or $307.50 per unit, each tenant would be expected to pay the added $13.75 difference attributable to his apartment. This only amounts to $1.15 a month rent increase to him, but saves you $110 in increased taxes.

Protection clauses covering the effects of inflation, on the other hand, are not as simple, but are a must if the investor intends to have his property appreciate with the economy.

The Consumer Price Index is the most common standard used for cost of living clauses in a lease. The Federal Government publishes an annual consumer price index showing how much prices have gone up (or down, if that ever happens) during the past year. A typical lease clause would state that on each renewal period, or any other length of time the landlord wants that is agreeable to the tenant, the rent would be adjusted according to the Consumer Price Index, using the year the lease commenced as the base year.

By way of example, we'll assume that you wrote a two year lease on an apartment in your building, but the rent was to be adjusted at the end of the first year based on the Consumer Price Index using the first year of the lease term as the base year. Monthly rent at the time the lease was executed was $250. The consumer price index, for simplicity, we'll say was "100."

On the first anniversary date of the lease, the new consumer price index is "110" or up 10 percent from the previous year. This means that the monthly rent to be paid by the lessee during the second year of his lease will be increased 10 percent or $25.00. His new rent will be $275 a month.

Writing a lease tied to the Consumer Price Index sounds good, but in actual practice, the resulting rental increases may have to be tempered with good business judgement and your knowledge of the rental market.

The above example calls for a $25 a month rent increase. But your competitors may only raise their rents on comparable apartments $10 a month. You may have to take a little less than $25 in order to keep from losing a good tenant. A few pages back, we discussed the need of keeping up with inflation through rental increases. It was mentioned that this was a must, "when market conditions permit it."

CAUTION: DON'T BECOME TOO FRIENDLY

It was already mentioned briefly, but bears repeating. Do not become good friends with your tenants. That will be the downfall of your rental income.

I've seen apartment buildings come on the market at prices that should be reasonable for the market, but the low rental income does not come close to justifying the price being asked. I already mentioned the many times a seller has told me, "My rents are low for the area, but they can be raised. You see, dear old Martha lives in Apartment 104. I haven't raised her rent for five years because she is living on a small pension and really cannot afford it. And the Smiths in 105, well, they've had some hard luck and really cannot afford to pay more rent."

It may sound cruel, but it's the seller who will be having the "hard luck" if he continues with this present rental policy. Expenses and inflation will continue taking their ever increasing toll on his profits. *They* have no compassion. As it stands, if the seller of this property is still collecting the same amount of rents that he was five years ago, his building is probably going to be worth the same or less than he paid for it five years ago.

Never forget that you own a "money making machine" operating at full capacity, which means keeping your rents up with the market. You have now heard this repeated two or three times. I hope by now you believe it.

Compassion for your tenants is important. No one wants a landlord who reminds them of the old time rent-collecting villains of silent movie days. But your own investment goals are important also. You did not buy the *Always Full Apartments* to operate as a charity home.

AVOID RENEWAL OPTIONS

A renewal option, giving the tenant the right to renew the lease for an additional term, like the lease itself is a one sided agreement for the benefit of the tenant. It is, in fact, even more one sided than the original lease. As long as the tenant complies with all the terms and conditions of the original lease period, *he* has the right to decide if he wants to exercise his option and stay for an additional term. You have no say in the matter. You may have another, more desirable tenant, wanting that apartment at a higher rent. You are out of luck unless the present tenant decides not to exercise his option. Once he finds out someone else is willing to pay more rent for his apartment than he has to pay if he stays, he'll stay!

TYPES OF LEASES AND HOW THEY WORK

Net Leases

You have probably heard the terms: Net Lease, Double Net Lease and Triple Net Lease. This type of lease is usually used in the leasing of stores, offices or industrial buildings.

There has been some discussion that there is no such thing as double and triple net leases. A lease is either a "net" lease or it isn't a net lease. Since most investors still use the first concept, we will discuss what each type of "net" means.

Net Lease infers that the tenant (lessee) pays all real estate taxes and the landlord (lessor) pays all other expenses.

Double Net Leases infer that the lessee pays all taxes and property insurance and the lessor pays all other expenses.

Triple Net Leases state that the tenant pays everything, taxes, insurance, repairs and maintenance, etc. The lessor pays only the mortgage payments on the property.

Obviously, a property with a Triple A tenant leasing on a Triple Net Lease basis makes an excellent management free investment. They are also difficult to find.

There are a limitless variety of clauses that can be written into a lease to clarify the responsibilities of both the lessee and the lessor. Some business leases may have 40 to 50 clauses written into them.

Percentage Leases

It is common practice to write commercial leases, especially in shopping centers where major tenants are involved, on a percentage basis. The tenant pays a base rent, usually less than the current market rent. He also agrees to pay a percentage of his gross income, over a pre-determined minimum, as additional rent. Here is how a percentage lease might work.

ABC Chain Store leases 25,000 square feet of store space at a base rent of $2.00 a square foot. This amounts to $50,000 a year base rent. They also agree to pay two percent of their gross sales over $2,500,000 as additional rent. (Two percent of the first $2,500,000 is $50,000 which represents their base rent.)

Assume ABC Chain Store has a gross volume of $3,000,000 for the year. The owe an added rent of two percent of the $500,000 over the $2,500,000, or $10,000. Their total rent for the year will be $60,000. There will often be a maximum limit written into the lease.

Percentage leases can also assist a new tenant in the center. By offering him a percentage lease, he will be able to pay a lower initial rent, giving him time to build up the dollar volume of his business before being faced with major rent costs. The landlord, in effect, is gambling along with the tenant that the business will be successful. If the tenant does become successful, the landlord could end up with an even higher rent than if he had been locked into a base rent only. It also helps him get vacant space leased up and at least bring in some income to help offset operating expenses.

Sub-Leasing

Leases will often allow the tenant to sub-lease all or part of his rental space. In the case of an apartment, it would restrict the tenant to leasing the entire apartment, not taking in a boarder. Sub-leasing is done with the consent of the owner or lessor. Most leases spell out that this consent cannot be unreasonably withheld.

Commercial lessee's often sub-lease a portion of their space in order to help offset their rent costs. Perhaps they had to take more space then they needed or they wanted extra space available for planned expansion. The sub-lease should not be for a term in excess of the primary lease, without the consent of the lessor.

A simple rental apartment lease requires only a pre-printed form lease. This type of lease is very adequate for most rental situations. Once you have established your rental standards and are prepared with a lease, you are ready to locate a tenant.

HOW TO LOCATE AND QUALIFY PROSPECTIVE TENANTS

Ways to Locate Prospective Tenants

There are numerous ways of letting prospective tenants know you have an apartment for rent. The two most common are vacancy signs on the property itself and rental ads in the local papers.

Your leases should be written with a clause requiring the present tenant to give you at least 30 days notice, prior to the expiration of his lease, if he intends to move. This gives you 30 days to locate another tenant. Ideally, you want to have a tenant ready to move in the day after the present tenant moves out. You'll need just enough time to clean up the apartment for the new tenant.

Many landlords keep a permanent rental sign on their building. When they know an apartment is going to become available in a month or two, they can start qualifying prospects who are willing to wait.

Newspaper ads should spell out terms, rent and at least the general location of the building. This will save you a lot of unnecessary calls from rentees who do not qualify because of price, etc.

Should You Use Rental Agencies? There are agencies in most areas who specialize in finding apartments for tenants. They are paid in one of two ways. They may charge the lessee or prospective tenant a fee to find them an apartment. They can also charge the lessor for "listing" their apartment for lease and offering it to apartment hunters. This fee is generally payable only if they find a tenant who accepts the apartment.

Caution: In order to perform the above functions and collect a rental fee, most states require the agencies to be registered real estate brokers, and the agents must also be licensed sales people. In many areas, where rental apartments are in demand and the rental market is a lucrative one, there has been a surge of non-licensed rental agencies appear. They skirt the law by offering to sell a "list" of available apartments to a prospective tenant. Since the agents are not licensed by the state real estate commission, they cannot physically show the apartment. They merely sell you the list for a fee of $10 to $25. It is up to you to check out the leads. Unfortunately, most of these lists are compiled by listing the apartment rentals that are listed in the paper. At times the agency will call on an ad or sign to get additional information. Persons buying the list are often disappointed to find that many of the apartments offered are already leased or have different terms than as represented on the list.

In Southeast Florida, many of these agencies were closed down after many customer complaints reached the authorities. If you intend to use one of these agencies, check them out carefully. Your best bet is to employ a registered and licensed real estate company.

How to Find Tenants for Stores and Offices? Newspaper advertising and signs on the property are the most common methods of locating tenants for commercial buildings and stores. If you have a sizable rental space available, try trade magazines and also contacting major chain stores in your area. Determine who would be a likely tenant for your building. Is the store space suitable for a drug store, discount store, food store? Is the office space suitable for an insurance company, attorneys, or an accounting firm?

Who would desire your industrial space? Is there a manufacturing company moving into your area. Contact your local industrial board. What about the tenants in the area? Could any of them be considering expansion? You may have to divide a large space if you cannot find a single tenant to lease all of it.

Use your imagination. Don't be afraid to contact many prospective tenants. But research the market first. Chances are a major store will not be interested in your space if they have another store close by.

Qualifying Tenants

This brings us to the area of qualifying a tenant. Of utmost importance: Be certain that none of your qualifyng can be interpreted as discriminatory as far as race, color or creed. It is against the law. There has even been a legal battle won by a young couple who took as invasion of privacy, a potential employer who asked the woman if she intended to have children in the near future. Although this was a job application situation, the same could apply to a landlord who is trying to make sure he will have no children in his building.

You can, however, restrict your tenants to mature adults, no children or pets, retired age people, etc. it is important to try to maintain a compatable balance of tenants in your building. When seven of your apartments are rented to retired couples, avoid leasing the eighth to a young couple with a small child, or a young bachelor who throws late night parties. Satisfied tenants **are** less apt to move when their lease expires.

As part of your tenant qualification procedure, you should have a personal application form to be filled out by a potential tenant. You should at least obtain answers to these questions:

1. Name and present address;
2. Present landlord's name and phone number;
3. Age and marital status;
4. Credit references;
5. Previous landlords;
6. Financial situation; and
7. Occupation.

These questions allow you the opportunity to qualify the tenant and determine his financial ability to pay the rent, his stability, employment-wise, and whether or not he has had rental problems in his previous locations. Don't be afraid to call prior landlords and ask if they had any problems with your prospect.

SHOWING THE APARTMENT

Once you decide you would like these people as tenants in your building, you will want to "sell" them on your apartment. And you *are* in the selling business. Point out the features your apartment has over the competition. Perhaps its location, a self-cleaning oven, a dishwasher, laundry room, abundant closet and storage space, etc. Know what appeals to the type of tenant you are seeking. An elderly couple may be happy to know that they will be one half block from the shopping center, or that there are other tenants in your building in the same age range and situation that they are. Use these features in promoting the apartment. Never send a prospective tenant to an apartment, accompany him. You can be certain that a present tenant will point out only the things he doesn't like about living there.

WHAT TO DO IF YOU ARE FACED WITH CONTINUAL VACANCIES

It is not likely the time could come when you must re-evaluate the type of tenants you have in your building. Chances are you will not own the property long enough to have rental problems due to economic changes in the area but you should be aware of what actions you can take if you are suddenly faced with continual vacancies.

First, analyze why you are having vacancies. Is your competition having the same problem? A general market slowdown is not as easy to cure. When, on the other hand, most of the buildings around you are staying full, take a look at your building. Does it need sprucing up? Do competitive apartments offer more than you do in terms of better or newer facilities for the same rent? Ask potential tenants why they are not interested in your apartment.

Decorating problems can be cured. Updating of appliances can also be accomplished although the capital expenditure is greater and requires careful study. You do not want to spend thousands of dollars on capital expenditures if it will not solve your vacancy problems.

Problems such as competitive apartments have swimming pools or more floor space, cannot be corrected in your building. A small building cannot justify the cost of a swimming pool. Your only solution to a major problem, such as these, may be to consider the "highest and best use" for your building, without major alterations. What can you do to improve your rental picture?

Consider a change in the type of tenants you have. You may want to rent to couples with a child or pet. Perhaps, you can appeal to singles. Two working girls or men can often afford more rent than a young married couple. Maybe you will go for a "swinging singles" building. If all else fails, you can always reduce rents until the rental market improves again.

Chances are, you'll never be faced with a major rental problem, but if the market does become "tight" and you end up with a couple of vacancies at the same time, do not panic. The worst thing you can do is to rent to an undesirable tenant just to keep the rent coming in. He may cause other tenants to vacate and your problems will be multiplied.

The longer you are involved with the rental market, the better you will become at keeping your units leased, even in a slow market. It is not as difficult as it appears.

KEEP ABREAST OF THE MARKET

The most important thing you can do is keep abreast of the market. You should know at all times what your competition is, what they are offering to potential tenants, and what rents they are charging.

Many areas have "hotel/motel" or "apartment owner's associations." Consider joining such an association if it is available in your area. It is the easiest way to keep up with current rental market trends. Apartment owners will also help each other with tenant leads when their buildings are filled and another member has a vacancy.

Local newspapers and lending institutions often make comprehensive market situations. These studies can be obtained by you and will include such things as population trends, rent levels and area occupancies.

Check with your local county appraiser. His office may have an area rental market survey available, which is kept current.

In Broward County (Fort Lauderdale, Florida), for example, the appraiser's office publishes a comprehensive annual report of current market conditions including area vacancies, rent levels, and average operating costs of apartments, shopping centers, office buildings, etc. The report is updated monthly and is available, without charge, to residents in the county. To sum up, you have invested a sizable amount of money in your real estate investment.

You are now pretty much in control of your investment. It is up to you to know what is going on in the market place so that your property will produce to its maximum.

It is only through following the procedures outlined in this chapter that you will be able to offer your property for sale at the appreciated price that you will expect. If you have kept your rent level current, if you have maintained your property well, if you have enjoyed an ever increasing profit picture over five or so years, you are ready to consider moving up into a larger property.

15

When You Should Sell
And Why

After five years of ownership of the *Always Full Apartments*, you are convinced that no other investment vehicle offers as much as your real estate investment in terms of overall, after tax returns, and appreciation. And, that statement can be made as a blanket, positive statement no matter where you are located, unless you really goofed in your investment selection. Assuming you did your homework and followed the procedures in the first 14 Chapters of this book, you've no doubt had a profitable and pleasant experience with your own *Always Full Apartments*.

The building has produced as you had projected and is doing well. So why would you want to sell? Not only that, you have probably made the same mistake many investors make and have "fallen in love" with your property. Remember, you were cautioned about that in an earlier Chapter. The investment has performed well, given you excellent profits and you have "lived" with it for five years and know it inside out.

Well, just in case you didn't believe it the first time, I'll repeat it. You purchased the *Always Full Apartments* as a "money making machine," nothing more and nothing less. When it no longer is functioning as it was intended to do, regardless of the reason, it is time to consider changing investment properties. Don't feel too sad. You'll probably fall in love with your next property too.

FIVE COMPELLING REASONS FOR SELLING YOUR PROPERTY

How do you determine when it's time to sell? The average individual has an annual physical examination to check up on his physical condition. Your investment, like you, needs an annual check-up to insure it is still functioning well and is healthy.'

There are five possible motivating factors, any one of which will tell you it's time to get out of your present real estate investment and into another. We'll look at each of them one at a time.

Incurable Problems

If you are experiencing problems that you cannot cure, it is probably time to sell. Hopefully, this will not happen because your chance for realizing appreciation on the sale will also be affected by the problems your building is experiencing. These problems include such things as a deteriorating neighborhood, major expenditures needed to update the building, or continual vacancies due to an abundance of more desirable rentals in your area. Each of those problems could have been avoided by carefully following the guidelines in Chapter 7 on locating an investment.

Changes in Goals or Situation

An investor may decide it is time to sell because his investment criteria have changed. He may be ready to retire and take life easy. He wants to make one last change in properties and structure it to give him a lifetime steady income. Tax shelters and equity buildup are no longer important to him. His heirs will have that concern.

Perhaps something has happened in his life that has made a change in his investment goals and his present property does not fit his long range investment program. He may be tired of rental apartments and wants to try a small office building or shopping center. Perhaps he inherited a sizable sum of cash or has suddenly changed jobs and has a large tax burden. He may need to invest in a tax shelter rather than a property producing a high income.

Whatever the reason, investors from time to time have logical reasons for an investment change, and I stress *logical*.

Profit

Assuming you have been giving your investment an annual check-up, you have probably noticed that your property is worth considerably more than you paid for it. This fact really hits you when the building next to yours sells for almost twice what you paid for the *Always Full Apartments* and you "know" that yours is a better building.

Before you rush out and sell, don't overlook the effects of capital gains tax on your big profit. We'll cover that subject in more detail in the next Chapter.

Loss of Depreciation Benefits

The first full year you owned the *Always Full Apartments*, it gave you all of your income, tax free, plus a $3756 tax write-off against other income (Figure 12-2). By keeping it, the property will have a $6721 taxable income in the sixth year. Your tax shelter has turned around. Instead of giving you a tax shelter against other income, you now have to pay income tax on part of the income being produced by the building itself.

Figures 15-1 and 15-2 are a computer analysis of the *Always Full Apartments*, analyzing the property over a ten year basis. In order to run this analysis, the exact information that appears on the property analysis form in Figure 12-2 was programmed into the computer.

A minimal four percent growth or appreciation rate was used. This assumes that both the net operating income and the property value will increase four percent each year. It was also assumed that you are in a 32 percent tax bracket. Uncle Sam gets 32 percent of all taxable income produced by your real estate investment.

The first four lines illustrate the market value, loan balances, and your equity at the end of each year.

"Cap Rate" or capitalization rate, is the ratio between the net operating income and the market value of the property. It will not change because both market value and net operating income are assumed to be increasing four percent each year. (CAP rate is discussed further in chapter 17.)

```
MKT VALUE      150000
LOAN 1          72920
LOAN 2          37080
EQUITY          40000
```

END OF YEAR	1	YEAR 2	YEAR 3	YEAR 4	YEAR 5
MKT VALUE	156000	162240	168729	175478	182497
LOAN 1	71180	69305	67284	65107	62760
LOAN 2	36698	36279	35817	35310	34753
EQUITY	48122	56656	65628	75061	84984
CAP RATE	9.99	9.99	9.99	9.99	9.99
NET OP INC	14985	15584	16207	16855	17529
INT PMNT	8918	8742	8557	8354	8135
DEPREC	9750	9487	9238	9001	8776
TAXABLE IN	3683-	2645-	1588-	500-	618
INCOME TAX	1179-	846-	508-	160-	198
CASH FLOWS:					
BEFORE TAX	3945	4547	5168	5816	6490
AFTER TAX	5124	5393	5676	5976	6292
ADJ COST B	140250	130763	121525	112524	103748

CUMULATIVE TOTALS

TAXABLE IN	3683-	6328-	7916-	8416-	7798-
CASH FLOWS:					
BEFORE TAX	3945	8492	13660	19476	25966
AFTER TAX	5124	10517	16193	22169	28461
PROCEEDS	44234	52275	59130	66490	74376
IRR	23.40	26.64	25.84	25.13	24.50

Figure 15-1

END OF	YEAR 6	YEAR 7	YEAR 8	YEAR 9	YEAR 10
MKT VALUE	189796	197387	205282	213493	222032
LOAN 1	60232	57507	54570	51406	47996
LOAN 2	34140	33467	32726	31913	31018
EQUITY	95424	106413	117986	130174	143018
CAP RATE	9.99	9.99	9.99	9.99	9.99
NET OP INC	18230	18959	19717	20505	21325
INT PMNT	7897	7639	7361	7059	6734
DEPREC	4062	3859	3666	3482	3308
TAXABLE IN	6271	7461	8690	9964	11283
INCOME TAX	2007	2388	2781	3188	3611
CASH FLOWS:					
BEFORE TAX	7191	7921	8679	9467	10286
AFTER TAX	5184	5533	5898	6279	6675
ADJ COST B	99686	95827	92161	88679	85371

CUMULATIVE TOTALS

TAXABLE IN	1527-	5934	14624	24588	35871
CASH FLOWS:					
BEFORE TAX	33157	41078	49757	59224	69510
AFTER TAX	33645	39178	45076	51355	58030
PROCEEDS	83388	92977	103173	114002	125501
IRR	23.78	23.15	22.60	22.11	21.67

Figure 15-2

Starting with the net operating income line, we see that the investment is producing $14,985 by the end of the first year. The mortgage interest payments and $9750 depreciation allowance is then removed, leaving us with a taxable income of *minus* $3683 or a $3683 tax loss. Our property analysis form in Figure 12-2 showed a bottom line loss of $3756. Our simplified analysis varies slightly from the computer because we used the short cut method of separating the principal and interest payments on the mortgage. The computer figured it down to the exact dollar.

Assuming you are in a 32 percent tax bracket, you have income tax consequences of minus $1179, or an $1179 tax savings on your other income. This, added to your before tax return of $3945, gives you an after tax return of $5124 the first year.

The "Adj. Cost B" or adjusted cost basis will be discussed in the next chapter. The remaining items are cumulative totals. The first year's after-tax cash flow was $5124, the second year was $5393. Add the two together and the cumulative after-tax cash flow for the first two years was $10,517, as shown in the second column.

After five years ownership of the *Always Full Apartments*, you will have received a cumulative, or total net spendable income of $28,461. And that's after taxes.

If you sell the building at the end of any of the ten years shown on the complete ten year analysis, your proceeds, after capital gains tax, will be shown on the "Proceeds" line. This amount does not include the cost of sale, such as legal fees, etc. In other words, if you sell the *Always Full Apartments* at the end of the fifth year, your proceeds after capital gains tax, will be $74,376. From this amount, any closing costs, real estate professional fees, etc., must be deducted.

The bottom line, "IRR" is internal rate of return. It tells you the overall percentage of return you realized during each year that you owned the property. Assuming you sell at the end of the fifth year, the IRR shows that you realized a 24.5 percent return on your investment for each of the five years you owned the property, and that's *after* capital gains tax has been paid.

Now that you have a better understanding of the computer analysis, let's get back to the fourth reason for selling, loss of depreciation benefits.

Follow the "taxable income" line across for the first five years and then to the sixth. The first year you had a negative taxable income or tax shelter of $3683. Each year this shelter decreased until in the fifth year it is no longer a tax shelter at all. In fact, $618 income produced by the building is also subject to taxation.

Now look at the sixth year. The taxable income jumps to $6271. Six thousand, two hundred and seventy-one dollars of the income the building produced is subject to income tax. You will recall that you depreciated the personal property over a five-year period and were able to take $4500 depreciation allowance each year. Now, after five years, you have used it up, which explains the sizable jump in taxable income in the sixth year. This also explains the reason for selling after five years ownership. You no longer own a tax shelter.

Increased Equity

The remaining reason for selling your property is the result of a large increase in equity brought about by a combination of appreciation and mortgage principal reduction. This is where many investors made a drastic error in analyzing their present position in their property.

Looking at the "before tax cash flow" line on the computer analysis, the average investor would say, "My income the first year was $3945, now five years later, it's up to $6490. I only invested $40,000 so I am now making 16 percent on my investment ($6490 divided by $40,000). His first error, and a very common one, is talking in terms of pre-tax income. When you look at "net spendable" amounts you see that the first year *after-tax income* was $5124. Due to loss of tax shelter benefits, it is only $6292 in the fifth year. But, he made a much larger error in his calculation. His present equity is no longer $40,000 at the end of the fifth year.

Look at the top four items under Year 5. At the beginning of the sixth year (or end of the fifth year), your building, based on a four percent per year appreciation rate, is now worth $182,497. At the same time, you have paid the first mortgage down to $62,760. It was $72,920 when you purchased the building. The second loan has been reduced from $37,080 to $34,752. Your equity is now $84,984 or more than double the $40,000 you invested five years earlier.

When you divide the net spendable income of $6292 by your actual current investment of $84,984, your return is only 7.4 percent. And with $84,984, or twice the capital you started with, you could own two *Always Full Apartment* buildings with no additional outlay of cash.

Formula for Computing Your Actual Present Return: Figure 15-3 is a simple formula for estimating your *actual* present return based on current market value of your property.

Income

1. Cash flow (after expenses and mort-
    gage payments) $ _____
2. Less: Income Tax Paid on this property   _____
3. Net Spendable Income $ _____
4. Plus: Mortgage Principal Reduction   _____
5. Total Equity Income $ _____

Equity

6. Today's Market Value of the Property $ _____
7. Less: Remaining Mortgage Balances   _____
8. Your Present Equity or Investment in
    the Property $ _____

$$\frac{\text{Total Equity Income (Line 5)}}{\text{Equity (Line 8)}} = \underline{\qquad}\%$$

Figure 15-3

Income

1. Cash flow (after expense and mortgage payments) $ 7,191
2. Less: Income Tax Paid on this property   2,007
3. Net Spendable Income $ 5,184
4. Plus: Mortgage Principal Reduction   3,140
5. Total Equity Income $ 8,324

Equity

6. Today's Market Value of the Property $182,300
7. Less: Remaining Mortgage Balances   94,371
8. Your Present Equity or Investment in the Property $ 87,929

$$\frac{\text{(Line 5) \$ 8,324}}{\text{(Line 8) \$87,929}} = 9.5\%$$

Figure 15-4

Here's how it works. Refer to Figure 15-4. On Line 1, fill in your gross spendable income (cash flow). You surely know what that is by now. Well, just in case . . . it's the income produced by your property after all expenses and mortgage payments have been made, but before tax consequences.

On Line 2, you must subtract any income tax you had to pay as a result of owning the property. If you are still in a "tax shelter" position, that figure will be a negative number and can be added to the gross spendable income. The result is entered on Line 3 as "Net Spendable Income."

Next, add in the amount you paid down on the mortgage(s) during the year. This is entered on Line 4. The total appears on Line 5 as "Total Equity Income."

That takes care of the total income produced by the property. Now you need to determine what your actual equity is in the investment. Not what you invested one, two, five, or ten years ago, but how much you have invested today.

You start on Line 6 with the current market value. How do you determine that? The easiest way is to capitalize your current net operating income (N.O.I.) at the same percentage rate as when you purchased the building. The original N.O.I. on the *Always Full Apartments*, the day you purchased it, was $14,985. Capitalized at 10 percent gave you a market value of $149,850 ($14,985 divided by .10 = $149,850). Since we used a $150,000 value, the computer came up with a 9.99 percent CAP rate. We'll use 10 percent for simplicity which will give us a slightly different answer than our computer analysis.

Now look at year 6 on the computer analysis. Line 6 shows an N.O.I. at the end of year 6 of $18,230.00. Capitalized at 10 percent, your building is worth $182,300 at the beginning of the 6th year. This appears as market value, end of year 5 on Figure 15-1. (Again, the computer analysis used a 9.99 percent CAP rate so it shows a market value of $182,497). Using *our* figure of $182,300, enter that on Line 6 as the fair market value.

Your remaining mortgage balances at the end of the sixth year are $94,371. This is entered on Line 7 of Figure 15.4. The difference is $87,929. This is your current, actual equity in the property. It is entered on Line 8.

Now, divide Line 5, total equity income, by Line 8, your present equity and you can see what you are really making on your investment.

The end result shows that your total after-tax return is 9.5 percent, including equity buildup or mortgage reduction. Your first year's return, after taxes, was 18.1 percent, almost double your present return. This is an excellent indication that it's time to sell. From this point on, your *return will continue to diminish each year*.

It is only through making the most of this increased equity that you will be able to pyramid your initial investment into a larger investment and that one into a property that is still larger. We'll discuss ''pyramiding'' in Chapter 19.

You should consider selling or exchanging your property when any of the five previous reasons are affecting the return you are making on your invested capital. And keep in mind, the *current property equity* is your invested capital. After the first year, your initial investment is no longer your equity.

HOW A LARGER PROPERTY CAN OFFER YOU DEPRECIATION BENEFITS AND A HIGHER RETURN

As a rule of thumb, if you can transfer your current equity into a much larger property, say twice the size, with no additional outlay of capital, it makes sense to do so. And, you also start your depreciation benefits over again in the new property. Here's how it works.

Let's assume that, with your $84,984 equity in the Always Full Apartments, at the end of five years, you exchange your building for the *Suite Sixteen Apartments*. It is 16 units instead of your 8. The price is $300,000 and requires $80,000 cash. Everything, for the sake of illustration, is exactly double the *Always Full Apartments* as it was when you purchased it. You may never find an exact double size property, but the basic concept is the same regardless of the exactness. The important thing is to find an investment requiring $80,000. We'll reserve the balance for closing costs.

Figure 15-5 analyzes the *Suite Sixteen Apartments*. Now, let's compare your present position in the *Always Full Apartments* after six years of ownership with the $80,000 equity being transferred into the *Suite Sixteen Apartments*. Figure 15-6 shows this comparison.

The results are quite obvious. You now own a $300,000 real estate investment instead of $182,496 value of the *Always Full Apartments* (Line 1). You also have a tax shelter again (Line 7) which results in a $2404 tax savings on other income the first year (line 9). This means that your after tax spendable income has increased from $6292 to $10,298 (Line 10).

Line 11 shows a larger principal reduction because the mortgages are larger. You are also realizing a four percent appreciation rate on a $300,000 property which increases your appreciation from $7018 on your present building to $12,000 on the new one (Line 12).

Name: *SUITE SIXTEEN APTS.*

Location: *777 SUNSET DR*

Type of Property: *16 UNIT APT. BLDG*   Area _____

Folio:	Ex — S.O.O	File:
Date:	Units: *16*	Lister:
Zoning *R-3*	Pool *NO*	Parking *20*
Size *200 x 250*	Rec. Rm. *NO*	A-C *YES*
Sq. Ft.	Util. Rm *YES*	Heat *YES*
Age *8 YRS*	Office *NO*	TV *NO*
Stories *2*	Lobby *NO*	Furniture *YES*
Sewers *YES*	Elevators *NO*	Waterfront *NO*
Constr. *CONCRETE & FRAME*		

LIST PRICE *300,000*

CASH REQ'D. *80,000*

EXISTING ASSUMABLE FINANCING:

	Amount	Ann. Pmt.	Int.	Years To Go
1st $	*145,840*	*14,300*	*7½* %	*19+*
2nd			%	
3rd			%	

POTENTIAL FINANCING:

				Years
1st $			%	
2nd	*74,160*	*7,776*	*9½* %	*25*
3rd			%	

Description —	# Units	Rent Sch

SCHEDULE GROSS INCOME		45 120
Less: Vacancy & Credit Loss *5%*		2 256
GROSS OPERATING INCOME		42 864
Less: Operating Expenses		
Taxes	4 700	
Insurance	1 160	
Utilities *ELECTRIC*	280	
Advertising		
Licenses & Permits	50	
Management		
Payroll & Payroll Taxes	2 400	
Supplies		
Services *WATER / SEWER*	2 144	
Maintenance		
Reserve for Replacement		
Ground Lease		
LAWN	1 440	
TOTAL EXPENSES %	12 894	
OPERATING INCOME	29 970	
Plus Other Income	0	
NET OPERATING INCOME	29 970	

COMMENTS   CODE _____

INFORMATION HEREIN IS BELIEVED TO BE
ACCURATE BUT IS NOT WARRANTED

INCOME ADJUSTED TO FINANCING:	Actual ☐	Potential ☐	Equity $ *80,000*			
NET OPERATING INCOME	Cap. Rate - List Price		%			29 970
Less: Loan Payment	3rd Loan	2nd Loan	1st Loan	TOTAL		
Interest		7 044	10 938	17 982		
Principal		732	3 362	4 094		
Total Loan Payment		7 776	14 300	22 076	22 076	
GROSS SPENDABLE INCOME	Rate: *9.9* %		(GSI ÷ EQUITY)		7 894	
Plus: Principal Payment					4 094	
GROSS EQUITY INCOME	Rate: *14.9* %		(GEI ÷ EQUITY)		11 988	
Less: Depreciation	Personal Property		Improvements		19 500	
REAL ESTATE TAXABLE INCOME			*TAX LOSS*		(7 512)	

Figure 15-5

	Always Full Apts.	Suite Sixteen Apts.
1. Market Value	$182,497	$300,000
2. Less: Total Loans	97,513	220,000
3. EQUITY	$ 84,984	$ 80,000
4. Net Operating Income	$ 17,529	$ 29,970
5. Less: Interest Payments	8,135	17,982
6. Less: Depreciation	8,776	19,500
7. Taxable Income (Loss)	$ 618	($ 7,512)
8. Gross Spendable	$ 6,490	$ 7,894
9. Less: 32% of Line 7	198	(2,404) Tax
		Savings
10. Net Spendable	$ 6,292	$ 10,298
11. Plus: Principal Payments	2,904	4,094
12. Plus: 4% Appreciation	7,018	12,000
13. Total Return	$ 16,214 (end of 5th Year)	$ 26,392 (End of 1st Year)
14. % on Equity	19.1%	31.1%*

*NOTE: In order to make a fair comparison, the equity used to compute the 31.1 percent was $84,984 or the same equity as in the *Always Full Apartments*. It is assumed that, although there is only $80,000 equity in the *Suite Sixteen Apartments*, the remaining $4984 balance was used to cover closing costs in the title transfer.

Figure 15-6

By merely transferring your equity into a larger property, you have increased your after tax returns on Line 13 from $16,214 to $26,392. That's a $10,000 increase with NO additional cash investment. The bottom line percentage tells the story. The return on your invested capital has increased from 19.1 percent to 31.1 percent.

When you get to the Chapter on pyramiding, you will see how, by repeating this same process, every few years you can end up with a sizable estate and never have to add one additional dollar in investment capital.

The important thing is to give your property an "annual physical" the same as you get. The end of each year is a good time to review your investment, when you are preparing for income tax returns anyway. The year's operation will be fresh in your mind and right in front of you. All you have to add is an estimate of current fair market value and determine your present mortgage balances.

If, after all of this discussion, you are still too much in love with the *Always Full Apartments* to part with them, even though you realize that it makes economic sense to do so, you may have an alternative.

REFINANCING FOR TAX-FREE CASH

Depending on the availability of mortgage money, you may be able to free up some of your excess cash by refinancing your building. Although it is not the best solution, it's better than leaving $84,000 in equity in the property. You won't have to part with the *Always Full Apartments*, and the loan proceeds are tax-free income to you.

Take the current pro-forma on the *Always Full Apartments* to a savings and loan and see what you can do. Usually, the best place to start is with the lender, who currently holds the mortgage. You have a current first loan balance of $62,760. Because it bears an interest rate of only 7½ percent, most lenders will be happy for the opportunity to upgrade it to current interest levels. Your pro-forma now shows a market value after five years of $182,497. (Market value, beginning at sixth year on Figure 15-1.) Assume the lender agrees to a $136,700 loan at 9½ percent interest for a 25-year term. Your new annual mortgage payments will be $14,259.00.

How to Determine Whether Refinancing Makes Sense

Figure 15-7 illustrates the method of analyzing these proceeds to determine if it makes sense to borrow the added funds. The procedure consists of three easy steps. First, determine how much cash you will have to invest after existing mortgages are paid off and mortgage refinancing costs are paid. You have $33,047 in the example.

In the second step, you determine what your added mortgage payments will be on the *Always Full Apartments*. You have increased them by $3221 a year.

The final step is to determine how much return you have to make on your $33,047 proceeds just to break even. In other words, unless the new investment earns in excess of 9.7 percent cash flow, it may not make sense to refinance.

This is just the "cash out of pocket" portion of the overall return. You may be willing to sacrifice some of the cash flow in order to increase your tax shelter, equity buildup and the dollar value of your total real estate assets.

Refinancing to Obtain Cash

STEP I   Determine Net Proceeds Available from Financing:

New First Mortgage	$136,000
Less: Pay Off of Existing Mortgages	97,513
Gross Proceeds	$ 38,487
Less: 4% Refinancing Costs	5,440
Net Proceeds for Reinvestment	$33,047

STEP II   Determine Added Mortgage Payments That Must Be Made on *Always Full Apartments*:

New Mortgage Payments	$ 14,259
Less: Present Mortgage Payments	11,038
Added Mortgage Payment	$ 3,221

STEP III What Return Must Be Made on Net Cash Proceeds to Affect the Added Mortgage Payments on the Always Full Apartments:

$$\frac{\$\ 3,221 \quad \text{Added Payments}}{\$33,047 \quad \text{Net Loan Proceeds}} = 9.7\%$$

Figure 15-7

Whether you are convinced that you should transfer your equity into a larger property whenever you can or just refinance your existing property, you must do something. Letting excessive equity build up in your real estate investment can be a costly mistake.

Never lose sight of the fact that you own a "money making machine."

When it no longer makes as much as it could or should be making, it's time to get a new machine.

Assuming that you are convinced, it is time to sell, or exchange the *Always Full Apartments* for a larger complex, you next need to know how to do it.

16

How to Sell Your Property

A word of caution: The details that are illustrated in this Chapter are for general information purposes only. The subjects of capital gains tax, recapture of excess depreciation, and installment sale tax consequences are complicated and should be prepared by your tax counsel.

This Chapter is intended for basic information only and is not a complete tax guide for the investor. Before entering into a sales contract, you should consult with your tax specialist and have him advise you as to the best way for you to sell.

The tax laws change regularly and need to be referred to prior to sale. Once you enter into a binding contract to sell, it may be too late to think about tax consequences.

Once a determination has been made to "sell" the *Always Full Apartments* the next consideration is how to go about it in such a way as to minimize capital gains tax on the profit. The word sell is in quotes because you may not sell at all. You may want to consider a tax deferred exchange.

Remember when you purchased the complex? You were convinced that the seller was trying to make a killing and had the property priced well above its fair market value. Well, now the shoe is on the other foot. Now *you* are the seller and any potential purchaser will feel that you are the one trying to make a killing. He can also go to the courthouse, as you did, and find out exactly how much you paid for the property.

Perhaps I should clarify something at this point. It was suggested that you check the records at the courthouse and find out how much the present owner paid for a property. You discovered Mr. Seller would make a $70,000 profit at his price. Likewise, the potential buyer you have can find out that you expect to make a $40,000 profit in just five years.

The point is, do not judge a property's value by how much profit you are willing to allow a seller to make. Remember, the value of an investment property is in direct proportion to the income it is producing. I might add, that is the income it is producing today, not what it is capable of producing a year after you buy it provided you can increase all the rents.

Knowing how much the present owner paid for the property may be some help in your negotiations, but has little or no value in determining what the property is worth today.

ESTABLISHING THE SELLING PRICE

You are the seller now. The *Always Full Apartments* have been you pride and joy for the past five years. You have lived with them, leased them and kept them well maintained. Assuming you are a typical seller, pride of ownership will enter into your selling price decision.

We have already determined that based on the income being produced by the building, it has a current market value of about $182,000. In Chapter 17 we will look at the three methods used by appraisers in determining the market value of an investment property, namely: Income Approach, Market Data Approach and Cost Approach.

Pitfalls of the "Pride of Ownership" Method

Like most sellers, you will probably be tempted to use a fourth, non-recognized method of establishing price—"The Pride of Ownership" method. This value is established by combining two factors that do not correlate to the actual value of the property at all. The first, of course, is ownership pride that makes selling difficult for you in the first place. The second is the possibility of "making a killing."

Let's assume that you decide you want to make a larger than normal profit on the sale of the *Always Full Apartments*. Instead of selling it at the current market value of $182,000 you hold out for the $195,000 asking price, and it takes you a year to sell it. Finally, after 12 months, you find a buyer who will pay $195,000 so you made an extra $13,000 profit. What has it cost you to do it?

You have now kept the *Always Full Apartments* six full years instead of five. Looking at Figure 16-1, you will see that your total equity income at the end of the sixth year, after taxes, is $8325. This is a combination of your sixth year after-tax flow shown in Figure 16-1 plus the amount you paid down on the mortgages during year six.

Had you purchased the *Suite Sixteen Apartments* a year earlier, your total equity income would have been $26,392 or $18,067 more. This is $18,067 more than the *Always Full Apartments* earned. One more fact enters into the comparison at this point. The *Always Full Apartments*, by the end of the sixth or beginning of the seventh year has a market value of $189,796. (See Figure 16-1.) This is within $5204 of your $195,000 selling price. What it comes down to, is you lost $10,768 in income in order to gain $5204 in profit by selling at the higher price a year later.

Holding out for the extra large profit did not pay in this case. You would have lost. Had you sold, rather than exchanged, you would have had an increased capital gains of $13,000. Paying capital gains tax would have eaten up another estimated 28% or $3640 of that profit.

So how did you do?

Your Selling Price	$195,000
Market Value	182,000
Extra Profit	$ 13,000
28% Capital Gains Tax	3,640

Your Selling Price	$195,000
Actual Market Value—12 months later	189,796
Actual Pre-Tax Profit	$ 5,204
Less: Capital Gains Tax Above	3,640
Actual After-Tax Profit	$ 1,564

1st Year Equity Income on Suite Sixteen	$ 26,392
6th Year Equity Income on Always Full	8,325
Income Lost by Keeping Always Full	$ 18,067
Less: Actual After-Tax Profit (above)	1,564
Actual Loss	$ 16,503

END OF	YEAR 6	YEAR 7	YEAR 8	YEAR 9	YEAR 10
MKT VALUE	189796	197387	205282	213493	222032
LOAN 1	60232	57507	54570	51406	47996
LOAN 2	34140	33467	32726	31913	31018
EQUITY	95424	106413	117986	130174	143018
CAP RATE	9.99	9.99	9.99	9.99	9.99
NET OP INC	18230	18959	19717	20505	21325
INT PMNT	7897	7639	7361	7059	6734
DEPREC	4062	3859	3666	3482	3308
TAXABLE IN	6271	7461	8690	9964	11283
INCOME TAX	2007	2388	2781	3188	3611
CASH FLOWS:					
BEFORE TAX	7191	7921	8679	9467	10286
AFTER TAX	5184	5533	5898	6279	6675
ADJ COST B	99686	95827	92161	88679	85371
CUMULATIVE TOTALS					
TAXABLE IN	1527-	5934	14624	24588	35871
CASH FLOWS:					
BEFORE TAX	33157	41078	49757	59224	69510
AFTER TAX	33645	39178	45076	51355	58030
PROCEEDS	83388	92977	103173	114002	125501
IRR	23.78	23.15	22.60	22.11	21.67

Figure 16-1

You actually *lost* $16,503 by keeping the *Always Full Apartments* one extra year in order to obtain a $195,000 selling price.

But you are not like the average seller. You are convinced that the time is right to move up into a larger property and that the longer you hold on to the *Always Full Apartments*, the more it will cost you in terms of income tax and lost appreciation. You will sell at a price close to fair market value, not a giveaway, but a "fair market" price to insure a reasonably quick sale.

You offer the property at a price of $195,000, which gives you a little negotiating room. Remember, just because your property analysis form shows your property is worth $182,000, that doesn't mean someone will rush right in and buy it.

HOW TO FIND A BUYER FOR YOUR PROPERTY

You can try advertising your property yourself, but you may consider listing it exclusively with a knowledgeable investment Realtor in order to obtain best results. He has the leads and contacts that you may never be able to locate on your own.

Exclusive Listing With a Realtor

Notice that I said "exclusive" listing. It seems to be common practice in most areas for sellers to give only an "open" listing when he (the seller) is still free to offer it to other Realtors or sell it himself without paying a real estate professional fee. Most investment Realtors will shy away from this type of listing, or at least give it very little attention.

Why? Because they have virtually no protection. They may locate a buyer and show him the property, complete with all the detailed information on the investment, which they have spent considerable time preparing. The next thing the Realtor knows is that the buyer has contacted the seller directly and made a private deal, cutting the Realtor out altogether.

If you decide to employ a Realtor, be honest with him. A good one is well worth the fee he is paid. I apologize for another "plug" for the investment Realtor, but you would be surprised at the number of beginning investors who make costly mistakes due to lack of knowledge of investment real estate.

But this book is intended for the "do it yourself" investor. By learning and using the techniques presented in this book, you *can* do it yourself, successfully, and not make costly mistakes.

Getting back to finding a buyer for your building.

Selling It Yourself: Tips on Preparing an "FSBO" Advertisement for Your Property

You will no doubt receive many calls on your "FSBO" (that's For Sale By Owner) ad. Chances are 90 percent of them will be from Realtors looking for a listing. (If you decide to cooperate with a Realtor on an "open listing" basis, do not spread your property all over among several Realtors. Pick one or two that are qualified to represent you in a professional and ethical manner. Do not be attracted by the usual come-on, "I have a buyer for your property." We all have "buyers" for well-priced investment real estate. You do not want a lot of brokers running around your building, so any broker cooperation should be on a confidential basis.)

Let's talk about the ad that you run on your property. There are several things you need to know.

1. *Never* put the property address in your ad. You will have a parade of cars past your building and may never hear from one prospect. Once he knows the price and location, he can make a judgment as to the property's value without your help. In most cases, his judgment will tell him that the property is overpriced. You also want to keep your offering reasonably confidential from your tenants as well.
2. *Do* put the price in your ad. This will eliminate many calls from unqualified buyers.
3. The Federal Truth In Lending Law also comes into the advertising picture. Suppose you want to advertise "$50,000 down payment." The law also requires that you spell out the complete financing details as well. This includes mortgage balances, interest rates, remaining term of the mortgage, and monthly payment.
4. You *can* advertise, "low down payment," "low interest mortgage," "excellent terms available," etc., as long as the price is the only number that appears in the ad.

5. Make sure your headline attracts the reader and compels him to read the remainder of the ad. If he skips the headline, he'll never call you.

   The mere heading, "For Sale By Owner" always attracts attention. The average buyer automatically figures he can buy at a bargain price because there is no real estate fee involved.
6. Do not try to save a couple of dollars by cutting an ad short. Paint a mental picture that will attract an interested investor.

Below are two typical ads for the *Always Full Apartments*. Which one would prompt your response?

FOR SALE BY OWNER
8 UNITS—GOOD AREA
PRICED AT $195,000
CALL: 987-1234

OWNER MUST SELL!
HIGH INCOME PRODUCING 8-UNIT APT.
BLDG. IN PRIME RENTAL AREA.
BEAUTIFULLY LANDSCAPED. LARGE,
"HOMEY" APARTMENTS, CLOSE TO SHOP-
PING YET IN A QUIET NEIGHBORHOOD.
PRICED AT ONLY $195,000
CALL OWNER AT: 987-1234

Both ads are short, but the second should have more emotional appeal, and hopefully, attract some serious callers. No doubt the first question you will be asked is "Why must you sell?" You can honestly tell the caller that you are purchasing a larger property.

Try several different types of ads until you find one that attracts callers.

Cultivating Your Sales Approach

When a buyer calls, remember, you cannot sell him your property over the phone. Now is when you must do a selling job, the purpose of which is to obtain an appointment with him and *personally* show the property.

You will need to give enough information over the phone to get him interested. Once again, *do not* give him the address of the property. You can spell out the income, financing, breakdown of units, general area, and return he can expect on his investment. At the same time, you have two primary objectives:

1. Qualify him. Can he afford the down payment? Is this the type of investment he is seeking, etc.?
2. Get his name and phone number as soon after the phone rings as you can. A caller who is unwilling to give a name is probably not sincere in the first place. Don't feel badly if you lose him. Chances are you never really had him anyway. He may even be one of your tenants who saw the ad and thought the property sounded familiar.

Once you set up an appointment with a "suspect," and that is all he is at this point, arrange to meet him. It is advisable to pick someplace other than the actual property. If he reviews your analysis and has further interest, take him to the building for a personal inspection.

Now, for the first time, you must become a salesman. You have to sell your "suspect" on the advantages of purchasing the *Always Full Apartments*. You should have at least prepared a property analysis form, showing the potential buyer what he can expect from the investment. You know how you sold yourself on the property. Use the same techniques. Make a list of the outstanding features and financial benefits he can expect.

Selling Points to Use: Listed below are some of the typical selling points you may be able to use:

1. Outstanding Location—close to schools, shopping, beach, public transportation, etc.
2. Excellent neighborhood, quiet, secluded, nice homes in the area, etc.

3. Attractive, well built, well maintained building. Quality construction in cabinets, etc. Top quality appliances.

4. Extra features—large closets, garbage disposals, laundry room, dishwashers, etc.

5. Financing terms available (if they are a selling point).

6. Quality tenants, excellent rental history.

7. Return on cash invested (not just "spendable" return but total equity return).

8. Tax Shelter possibilities.

You will be able to come up with others that apply to your particular property.

Again, you are in a selling position. From the moment you meet your "suspect" start giving your property a buildup. BUT, BE CAREFUL, DO NOT OVERSELL. You can immediately turn a prospect off if he thinks you are "pushing" too hard to sell him your building. His first thought is that there is something wrong with it and you want out. I prefer a "soft sell" approach.

Be honest with him. Answer his questions truthfully. (Remember, he may have read this book, too!)

If there is a more desirable street on the way into your property, take your prospect that way, even if it is longer. If the neighborhood "turns him off" before he ever sees your property, your selling job will be that much more difficult.

All of your "selling" is leading you to one point, *Obtaining a Contract To Purchase*. You should be prepared to draw up a purchase contract and obtain a deposit. But, we are getting ahead of ourselves.

SHOULD YOU CARRY A MORTGAGE

You have another problem facing you when you sell. You do not want to carry any additional financing because you want all your cash to reinvest in another property.

The exception to the rule will be an investor who wants to put his estate in a more "liquid" condition. Perhaps he is 65-years old and feels it is time to get out of real estate. When selling the *Always Full Apartments*, he may consider carrying a second mortgage with $55,000 cash down, at 10 percent interest for 15 years. The mortgage would be in the amount of $42,487, or the difference between the $195,000 price less the first mortgage balance at the beginning of the sixth year—$62,760; second mortgage balance at the beginning of the sixth year and $55,000 cash down.

Mortgage payments would give him $456.47 a month added income for 15 years.

You will be asking a seller to pay $195,000 and be able to assume only the existing $97,513 in mortgages. He must have a 50 percent down payment. There are investors who do not worry about a low leveraged investment, but they are not easy to locate. Review Chapter 9 where methods of getting around carrying second mortgages were discussed.

A 50 percent down payment also creates problems for you. You will have to pay capital gains tax on your entire profit in the year of sale. This will greatly reduce the net proceeds that you have available for re-investing.

Just how much profit will you make if you receive your full $195,000 asking price? Several factors affect this amount.

This brings us to a discussion of Adjusted Cost Basis (A.C.B.).

HOW TO FIGURE THE ADJUSTED COST BASIS IN YOUR PROPERTY

Before you can determine how much profit you will make on the sale of the *Always Full Apartments*, you must first determine your present "basis" in the property. The original $150,000 purchase price has been altered by three factors. The amount of depreciation you have taken, any capital improvements you may have made on the property and the capitalized transaction costs you incurred at the time of sale.

Depreciation Taken

During the five-year period that you owned the property, you received tax shelter benefits because you were able to take a depreciation allowance each year, even though the property was appreciating. During the five years of ownership, you took a total of $46,252 in depreciation. See Figure 16-2.

Now comes the day of reckoning—the IRS wants it back. They get it by having you reduce your basis or cost in the property by the amount of depreciation you have taken. In Step I of Figure 16-2, you will see that this has reduced your basis to $103,748.

On the brighter side, they allow you to increase your basis by adding back in any capital improvements you made while you owned the property, and the capitalized transaction costs you incurred when you sold it, such as real estate professional fees. The second part of Step I shows no capital improvements but does show seven percent of the $195,000 selling price as transaction costs. This increased your A.C.B. to $117,368.

In Step II, the $117,368 A.C.B. is deducted from the $195,000 selling price, giving you a taxable profit of $77,602.

Adjusted Cost Basis

STEP I	Purchase Price		$150,000
	Less: Total Depreciation Taken		46,252
			$103,748
	Plus: Capital Improvements Made		—0—
	Capitalized Transaction Costs of $13,650 (based on seven percent of $195,000 Selling Price)		
		Total	$ 13,650
	Adjusted Cost Basis (A.C.B.)		$117,398
STEP II	Selling Price		$195,000
	Less: A.C.B.		117,398
	Profit Subject to Capital Gains Tax		$ 77,602*

---

*NOTE: Part of this profit will be treated on a capital gains tax basis and part is ordinary income. (See text.)

Figure 16-2

Part of this profit, the portion that is attributed to the depreciation taken in excess of straight-line depreciation, will be taxed as ordinary income. The balance will be taxed on a capital gains basis. This can vary depending upon how long you owned the property, the year you acquired it, etc. The tax laws have changed several times.

How Does IRS Recapture Your Excess Depreciation?

You held the *Always Full Apartments* for five years. Let's look at a typical example of how your profit on the sale will be taxed.

Your total taxable gain on the sale is $77,602 as shown in Figure 16-2. Part of this gain will be taxed at capital gains rates and part as ordinary income. Here is how it works:

Step I	Total depreciation taken in five years		$46,252
	Less: Depreciation taken on Personal Property $22,500		
	Less: Depreciation taken on improvements,		
	Straight-line depreciation only	21,000	
	Total straight-line depreciation taken		$43,500
	Balance of depreciation taken in excess of Straight Line		$ 2,752
Step II	Total Taxable Profit		$77,602
	Less: Excess Depreciation taken (Step I)		2,752
	Profit subject to capital gains tax		$74,850
	Profit subject to tax as ordinary income		$ 2,752
Step III	Probable Tax Consequences		
	$74,850 at capital gains rates (28 percent)		$20,958
	$ 2,752 at ordinary income rates (32 percent)		881
	Total tax consequences		$21,839

This example assumes that adding the $2752 to your other taxable income does put you in the next higher tax bracket. Again, consult with your tax specialist to determine your tax consequences.

AN OUTRIGHT SALE

Assuming you sell your property for $195,000 with all cash ($97,487) your entire profit ($77,632) will be subject to capital gains, with part of it as ordinary taxable income, in the year of sale. A portion of Chapter 10 was devoted to the time value of money.

It is this "use" of what would have been tax dollars, over the past five years that makes the recapture of depreciation upon a sale worth while. Although you have to pay it back when you sell, you've had the use of the depreciation dollars for five years. This is what allowed you to show a tax loss on your property even though it actually offered you a healthy profit. Add to that the fact that you were able to save another $2693 that the IRS would have collected from your outside income as tax.

TAX BREAKS YOU CAN GET WHEN YOU SELL

It's Not Like Selling a House

Almost everyone is familiar with the tax law that allows a home owner to sell his principal residence and avoid paying capital gains tax on the sale, provided he purchases another principal residence of equal or higher value within 24 months. Recent changes in tax laws also allow a home owner a one-time-only profit of up to $100,000 without it being subject to capital gains tax. This is ideal when he reaches the stage in life where he wants to sell his large home and purchase a smaller, more practical home or apartment. This law applies only to individuals over 55 years of age.

This is *not* true of real estate held for investment purposes. You cannot sell an investment property and purchase another, more expensive one within 24 months, and avoid paying capital gains tax. Tax rules are different for real estate held for investment purposes. If you sell investment property, it does not matter whether or not you buy something else, you are still liable for payment of capital gains tax in the year of the sale. IRS does allow the investor a couple of alternatives that will give him a tax break.

Installment Sales and the 30 Percent Rule

You can sell your property on an "installment sale" basis and spread your capital gains tax liability over a few years rather than paying it all in the year of sale. Assuming you elect to report your sale on the installment basis, some technical rules must be met.

The 30 percent rule simply states that, in order to qualify for install-ment reporting of your gain, you cannot receive more than 30 percent of the total selling price in the year that you sell the property. The seller, therefore, will *want* to carry a second mortgage when he sells in order to avoid collect-ing over 30 percent at closing.

You'll recall back in Chapter 8 when Mr. Seller first offered you the *Always Full Apartments*, he said he only wanted $45,000 down payment.

Dividing that by his original $155,000 price, will come out 29 percent. You have probably heard sellers say they want 29 percent down. This is done to insure that they stay well within the 30 percent rule.

You may also recall that when you negotiated his price down to $150,000 he also reduced the down payment to $40,000 or 27 percent down. Had he left the down payment at $45,000 he would have received 30 percent down, which put him right on the line. This brings us to the next rule.

Second Mortgage Principal Payments

The IRS says that if you take back a purchase money mortgage in lieu of cash, all principal payments (not the interest portion) you receive in the year of sale, will be added to your down payment and figured in your 30 per-cent maximum rule. Mr. Seller received almost six months of principal payments or about $200.00. It may not be much but it would have been just enough to put him over 30 percent in the year of sale (30.1 percent to be exact). He would have had to pay capital gains tax on the entire profit he made on the sale, all due in the year he sold the property. The interest por-tion he collects on the second mortgage is treated as ordinary income, the same as savings account interest. This portion would be added to his or-dinary income at the end of the year.

Using the installment sale method of selling your property in reporting your capital gain gives you somewhat of a tax break. The largest portion of your capital gains tax will still be due in the year of sale because that is when you are receiving the largest sum of cash from the buyer. You may schedule the second mortgage in such a way that the buyer makes periodic lump-sum payments. If, for example, you carry a $20,000 second mortgage, you will first of all, not allow any prepayment of the mortgage in the first year. A lump-sum payment would immediately disqualify you for the installment method of reporting your gain. There is nothing wrong with requiring a $5000 or $10,000 mortgage reduction payment in the second year, provided, of course, the buyer agrees.

This method still qualifies you for installment sale reporting but also allows you to recapture the funds that you have tied up in the second mortgage more rapidly. This technique is also helpful when a buyer does not have the entire amount you are requiring as a down payment. He may have access to additional lump sums of cash in 12 or 24 months that he can add to the original down payment.

WATCH THAT DOWN PAYMENT

Whenever a buyer is attempting to purchase your investment property with a small down payment, say less than 20 percent, take a close look at the transaction. Some investors thrive on investing no more than five to ten percent down payment on any real estate purchase. When you are carrying the paper (second mortgage) your security may be inadequate. Take an investor who buys a $100,000 property with only $10,000 or ten percent down. He should be able to recapture his initial investment in just one year. Then he can ''milk'' the investment for everything he can get. Within two or three years, he has tripled his investment. He has also allowed the property to deteriorate, the lawn is dead, major repairs are needed, and, therefore, the quality of the tenants has greatly deteriorated. When his income drops below a level that he can make mortgage payments, he quits making them.

A buyer who makes a practice of purchasing heavily leveraged investments, may be a sound legitimate investor. When you are in a position to sell to him and carry a second mortgage, you will want to protect yourself. Frequently, these buyers set up corporations to purchase. You will want them to execute the mortgage note both *personally* as well as on behalf of the corporation. Since the corporation probably has limited net worth, you want to know that the individual himself is also responsible for the payment of the note. Your attorney will advise you on this.

YOUR LEGAL RIGHTS AS SECOND MORTGAGE HOLDER

The mortgage you are holding, whether a first, second or third, should be written in such a way that you can immediately start foreclosure proceedings when mortgage payments become delinquent. This should also include delinquent first mortgage payments if you hold a second. Since you are in second position, your rights to collect come *after* the first mortgage holder. When the first mortgage holder's payments become delinquent, they will start foreclosure proceedings. Unless you act, you can lose out. Your mortgage, therefore, should give you the right to intervene even if only the first mortgage payments are delinquent.

As a practical matter, it takes months to accomplish a legal foreclosure. During that time, the present owner can literally take everything possible out of the property.

Your mortgage should also contain a clause that allows you to legally step in and take over the operation of the building, the minute problems in making mortgage payments become evident. You are then in a position to protect your interests until final judgments are made.

All of this comes down to the simple fact that the larger the down payment you obtain at closing, the more secure your sale will be. Very few sales, where second mortgages are involved, result in problems. Few buyers venture into a purchase with the idea of walking away from it. But you should be aware that the possibility does exist and that there are courses of action you can take to protect your interests.

HOW EXCHANGING ENABLES YOU TO DEFER
CAPITAL GAINS PAYMENT

There is another option that is available to you that can defer any capital gains payments indefinitely. The IRS will allow you to *exchange* your real estate investment for another property and defer any capital gains tax payment. This must be a ''like for like'' exchange. You must trade for another real estate investment which you are holding for investment purposes. You could not, for example, trade the *Always Full Apartments* for a new home for yourself.

How It Works

You want $195,000 for the *Always Full Apartments* and your equity is $97,487. You must find another property, that you want, that requires at least as much or more equity than your $97,487 and has a larger assumable loan balance.

You have already found the *Suite Sixteen Apartments*. Let's see if they meet the basic requirements:

	Always Full Apts.	*Suite Sixteen Apts.*
Selling Price	$195,000	$300,000
Existing Mortgage Balances	97,513	145,840
Cash Required	$ 97,487	$154,160

An exchange here looks as if it should be tax deferred. The mortgages being assumed are larger than the ones being transferred or given. The equity is also larger than that being given.

Solving the Cash Difference Problem

Which brings us to the next problem, how do you come up with the cash difference between the $154,160 and your equity of $97,487 or $56,673? You do not have to. The owner of the *Suite Sixteen Apartments* can still carry a second mortgage in order to "balance the equities." To make an exchange work, you must balance the equities, either by use of secondary financing or by one party adding cash to the transaction.

In its simplest terms, an exchange will work if the equities of each property are equal. Total price difference between the two is not important, only the equity that each owner has in *his* investment. But it is not quite as simple as adding a second mortgage to the property with the excess equity.

Where to Obtain Cash

Where does the necessary cash come from to pay closing costs, real estate and legal professional fees, etc.? One or both parties can add cash to the transaction or one or more of the properties can be refinanced to create cash.

Refinancing to Create Cash: Let's assume that owner of the *Suite Sixteen Apartments* places a new first mortgage on the property. He is able to obtain a 65 percent mortgage. That is 65 percent of his $300,000 price or $195,000. The interest rate is 9.75 percent for a 25-year term. Refinancing also cost him four points or four percent. Since he refinanced the property through the same lender who already had his first mortgage, he was able to negotiate the four percent charge on only the "new" money or the difference between the $195,000 and the existing $145,840. Four percent of the $49,610 difference is $1,966.00. The lender was happy to agree to this because they were able to upgrade a $145,840 mortgage from a 7.5 percent interest rate to a 9.75 percent rate. The $1966 that it cost to refinance can be absorbed by the seller, passed on to you or split between you.

It becomes obvious at this point that you and your tax counsel and the seller and his tax counsel must all sit down together and work out the consequences of this proposed exchange prior to the owner of the *Suite Sixteen Apartments* going out and obtaining a new mortgage.

You will want to prepare a revised property analysis form on the *Suite Sixteen Apartments* to determine your financial position with the new mortgage. You will be giving up a $145,840, 7.5 percent mortgage for a $195,000, 9.75 percent mortgage. First year interest payments on the original $145,840 will be increased approximately $3,280.00. Your cash flow will be reduced but part of that will be absorbed by a reduction in the principal payment portion of the mortgage because of the new, longer term of the 9.75 percent mortgage.

Results of Refinancing the Suite Sixteen Apartments

	Present Position	Refinanced Position
1. Net Operating Income	$29,970	$29,970
2. Less: Interest Payments	17,982	21,022*
3. Less: Depreciation	19,500	19,500
4. Taxable Income (Loss)	($ 7,512)	($10,552)
5. Gross Spendable	$ 7,894	$ 6,896
6. Less: 32% of Line 4 (Tax Savings)	(2,404)	(3,377)
7. Net Spendable	$10,298	$10,273
8. Plus: Principal Payment	4,094	2,052*
9. Plus: 4% Appreciation	12,000	12,000
10. Total Return	$26,392	$24,325
11. Percentage on Equity	31.1%	26.6%

*NOTE: This amount includes the payments on the new first mortgage *plus* the payments on second mortgage that the seller will still have to carry in order to balance the equities in the exchange.

Figure 16-3

A comparison between the present and proposed position is shown in Figure 16-3. It follows the same format that was used in Figure 15-6 to compare the *Always Full Apartments* with the *Suite Sixteen Apartments*.

You'll notice that Line 4 shows an increase in the tax shelter benefits after refinancing. This is because you will actually be paying out *more* interest to the lender. Your *after-tax* cash return remains, therefore, about the same (Line 7—Net Spendable), because of the added tax savings on tax shelter. The new loan, however, reduces the amount of principal payments you will have during the year (Line 8) from $4094 to $2052.

Although your total after-tax return will drop from $26,392 to $24,325 (Line 10) the amount is not enough to make the exchange undesirable. Line 11 shows your overall return will drop from 31.1 percent before refinancing to 26.6 percent after refinancing.

But, without refinancing the *Suite Sixteen Apartments*, you would not be able to purchase it. The equity was too large for you to handle, using only the equity in the *Always Full Apartments* for the exchange. And, let's face it, even 26.6 percent return is pretty good. What is your money earning now?

Before you read this book, did you ever think someone could convince you to get rid of a 7.5 percent mortgage in order to obtain a larger one at 9.75 percent interest rate? It was mentioned before that investors in real estate need to forget their previous ''hangups'' of paying off mortgages or turning down possible investments because the interest rate is ''too high.''

By now you should be conditioned to realize how properly structured financing can give you a sound, profitable investment regardless of what the interest rate on the mortgage might be.

The exchange looks good for you, so he refinances the *Suite Sixteen Apartments*. Here is where the owner of the refinanced property now stands:

New First Mortgage	$195,000
Less: Pay Off on Existing First Mortgage	145,840
Balance	$ 49,160
Less: Closing Costs	1,966
Net Proceeds	$ 47,194

There is now $47,194 *tax-free* cash in the ''pot'' to work with.

What does that do to the tax deferred exchange? It now looks like this:

	Always Full	Suite Sixteen
Selling Price	$195,000	$300,000
Mortgage Balances	97,513	195,000
Cash Required	$ 97,487	$105,000

The cash spread between the two is now reduced. The seller of *Suite Sixteen Apartments* will not have to carry as large a second mortgage to balance the equities except: How do *you* pay *your* closing costs? *He* has all the cash. We'll assume the total closing costs for each transaction will be seven percent of the selling (or exchanged) price.

Your costs are $13,650 and his $21,000. The easiest way to solve your cash problem is to have him pay your $13,650 closing costs out of his $47,194 proceeds from refinancing. He will then increase the size of the second mortgage on his property by $13,650 to cover this cost Let's now see if your exchange will work.

Balancing Equities in an Exchange

Step I

You Get Suite Sixteen Apt.—Equity	$105,000 (with new mortgage)
You Give Always Full Apt.—Equity	97,487
Balance	$ 7,513 that you owe
Plus: Your Closing Costs Paid by Suite Sixteen Owner	$ 13,650
You Owe Suite Sixteen Owner	$ 21,163*

Step II

Suite Sixteen Owner Had Equity of	$154,160 (prior to refinancing)
He Receives Always Full Equity	97,487
	$ 56,673

---

*Owner to take back a second mortgage to cover the $7,513 balance you owe plus the $13,650 closing costs he paid for you.

Step III

Proceeds from Refinancing		$ 49,160
Less: His closing costs including		
Refinancing	$22,966	
Your Closing Costs paid		
by him	13,650	
		$ 36,616
Net Cash Proceeds		$ 12,544

Step IV

You Get		$300,000 (Suite Sixteen)
Less: First Mortgage	$195,000	
Second Mortgage		
(from Step I)	21,163	
		$216,163
		$ 83,837

Balancing Equities

Step V

A—Your Market Value in Always Full	$195,000
Less: First Mortgage	97,513
	$ 97,487
Your Closing Costs	13,650
Your Equity Before Exchange	$ 83,837

This balances with your equity after the exchange (Step IV)

Step VI

He Gets	$195,000 (Always Full)
Less: First Mortgage	97,513
Equity	$ 97,487
Plus: Second Mortgage from you (Step I)	21,163
Excess Cash after Closing Costs	
are Paid (Step III)	12,544
	$131,194

Step VII
_____

    B—Owner of Suite Sixteen's Market Value $300,000

    Less: First Mortgage (original)   145,840

                                              $154,160

    His Closing Costs   22,966

    His Equity before Exchange $131,194

This balances with his equity after the exchange (Step VI)

Figure 16-4

How This Process Works: Figure 16-4 illustrates the seven step process. It works like this:

Step I: You find that the equity you will assume on *Suite Sixteen Apartments*, after it is refinanced, is $7513 larger than what you are giving on the *Always Full Apartments*.

Step II: His equity is $56,673 larger than the equity you are giving him.

Step III: After paying his new mortgage closing costs, his transaction closing costs and *your* closing costs, he is left with $12,544 from the refinancing of his building.

Step IV: After deducting the new first mortgage and the second mortgage carried by the Suite Sixteen owner, you will have $83,837 equity going into the new property.

Step V: The equity you had in the *Always Full Apartments* was $97,487 less your $13,650 closing costs or $83,837. This balances with the equity you are acquiring in Step IV.

Step VI: The owner of *Suite Sixteen Apartments* receives your $97,487 equity plus the second mortgage of $21,163 he is carrying on *Suite Sixteen* plus the excess cash of $12,544 from Step III, totaling $131,194.00

Step VII: The equity he had in *Suite Sixteen* was $154,160 less the $22,966 total closing costs or $131,194. This balances with the equity he is acquiring in Step VI.

    Although the process seems involved, all we did was make sure both parties in the exchange ended up with the same equity after the exchange that they had prior to it.

In the case of *Suite Sixteen's* owner, his proceeds were part in the equity of the *Always Full Apartments*, part in cash and the balance in the form of a second mortgage against the *Suite Sixteen* which you will owe to him.

Three Tests to Make Sure That You Qualify

Now that we have determined that an exchange between the two properties is feasible, you want to be certain that you really do qualify for a tax deferred exchange. Comparing your original position you will see that the basic tax deferred exchange tests have been met.

1. The property you are acquiring is larger than the one you are giving.
2. You will receive no "net loan relief." You are actually acquiring additional indebtedness.
3. You received no cash or "boot" in the transaction. "Boot" would be something of value in lieu of cash, such as a car or boat.

The exchange should be tax deferred.

Two Way Exchange and Cash Out

What happens if the owner of the property you want does not want yours? In most cases, that is most likely what will happen. The probability of finding two people who want each other's properties is rare. The answer to this problem is known as "A Two Way Exchange with a Cash Out."

Stated in simple terms, you find someone who wants to buy your property, Mr. Smith. Instead of buying your property directly, Mr. Smith enters into a Contract to Purchase the *Suite Sixteen Apartments*.

At the real estate closing, by means of paper transactions, he closes on *Suite Sixteen* and simultaneously trades *Suite Sixteen* for the *Always Full Apartments*.

The end results: the owner of *Suite Sixteen* gets his money out (put in by Mr. Smith in the form of the cash it takes to buy the *Always Full Apartments*).

Mr. Smith takes title to the *Always Full Apartments*. You take title to *Suite Sixteen* and have qualified for a tax deferred exchange.

Multiple Exchanges

An exchange does not have to be confined to just two properties. Therefore, even 15 and 20 way exchanges are possible. The more "legs" to the exchange, or the more properties that are involved, the more complicated the exchange. Now you can understand why you need to have your attorney and CPA involved. Working together, they can save you a lot of money in capital gains tax. It is worth the effort that it involves.

How Long Can You Defer Capital Gains Tax

As long as you enter into a tax deferred exchange every time you trade properties, you can defer capital gains tax for the rest of your life. When you die, your heirs inherit the property at current market value and not at your original adjusted cost basis in the first investment you owned. You may never have to pay capital gains tax.

There are other rules that must be considered to insure a "no tax" situation. Prior to entering into any transaction of this type, your CPA should be consulted.

The purpose of this discussion, as mentioned earlier, is to familiarize you with the possible ways of selling or exchanging your property and being able to retain the maximum proceeds possible for re-investment. This requires a knowledge of how the tax laws work and how to make the most out of the tax breaks allowed by the IRS, and these laws change on a regular basis.

For the knowledgeable investor, minimizing taxes or deferring them altogether, can greatly increase his profits and increase his estate building potential.

17

Rules of Thumb:
Facts, Myths and Guidelines
for Establishing the Value
of Investment Property

This Chapter is devoted to some of the rules of thumb and other methods that are used to establish the value of investment real estate. Some are good, some are bad. Most investors have their own favorite rule of thumb that they use to determine whether an investment is priced within reason or not worth considering at all.

Although I personally do not believe in rules of thumb, I catch myself occasionally using one or two when talking to a potential seller. The most I expect from using this guideline is a quick estimate as to how marketable a property may be at the seller's price.

Even this estimate is often proven wrong because of external features of the property or its financial structure that will never show up in a rule of thumb estimate of value. This chapter will also cover estimates of property value used by appraisers; use or mortgage amortization tables, and capitalization or "CAP" rate and how it works.

THE PRICE PER UNIT RULE

You are showing the *Always Full Apartments* to a potential buyer. Your asking price is $195,000. He tells you that he will never pay more than $20,000 per unit for a property. Yours is priced at $24,375 a unit, so, therefore, it is over priced.

He is using one of the least meaningful rules of thumb there is—the price per unit rule. Yet, it is one that you will find many so called "knowledgeable investors" applying on a regular basis.

Let's see what this rule tells us. "It does not matter how large the apartments are, where the property is located, or how much rent they demand, the building has a maximum value (to this investor) of $20,000 an apartment or $160,000 for the eight-unit *Always Full Apartments*."

What is wrong with this rule? Starting with the size of the apartments, our investor feels that a three bedroom, two bath, 1500 square foot apartment has the same maximum value as a 500 square foot studio or efficiency apartment.

The next item is probably the most important area of poor judgment using this rule of thumb. The value of an investment property is directly proportioned to the amount of income it is capable of producing. What you can afford to pay for it is based on the money it can earn or the return you will realize on your investment. What Mr. Investor is saying is that how much or how little income the building is capable of producing is irrelevant.

A building having apartments all rented at $300 a month is worth a maximum of $20,000 per apartment. A building having all its apartments rented at $600 a month is still worth a maximum of $20,000 per unit. This obviously does not make much sense.

Stating that location also has no bearing on the value of the property is also incorrect. A building located in a prestige, high rent area certainly has more value than the same building located in an area where no one wants to rent an apartment.

Generally, you'll find that the cost per unit rule of thumb is being used by investors who are looking only at the finest quality properties in the best areas and producing the highest income. They are bargain hunting. Their rule of thumb does have a lower limit as far as minimum income, location and size to qualify for the $20,000 maximum unit price. Anything they can buy better than that minimum standard at the same $20,000 maximum per unit price, is a bargain.

THE GROSS MULTIPLIER

The investor who uses a gross multiplier is saying that if a property is priced in excess of six times gross, for example, it is overpriced. When a building is producing an annual gross income of $30,000, the maximum value of the property is six times $30,000 or $180,000.00.

Unfortunately, this rule of thumb does not take operating expenses or mortgage payments into consideration.

A property experiencing excessive operating expenses of say 60 or 70 percent of the gross income may not be worth six times gross, unless the excess operating expenses can quickly be brought into line by a new owner. Looking at the other side of the picture, an efficiently run property, where the tenants pay most of the utilities, is probably worth more than six times the gross income.

This rule, as with the one before it, are at best very inaccurate methods of determining a property value.

NET OPERATING INCOME MULTIPLIER

This rule has some basis for being valid. An investor will say, "I will not pay more than 10 times the net income." Like the gross multiplier, it uses a formula based on the income produced by the property. Unlike the gross multiplier, it uses the Net Operating Income as the base number. You *do* know what N.O.I. is by now, don't you? Well, just in case, it is the income produced by the property after all operating expenses and allowances for vacancies have been removed, but before mortgage payments. This definition has been repeated several times throughout this book because of all the common terms used in the field of investment real estate, "net operating income'' is the one you will hear most often. You will want to know what it is and how it relates to an investment property.

When the property has an N.O.I. of $20,000 this investor is saying its value is 10 times that or he will pay up to $200,0000 for the property. The accuracy of this formula lies in the fact that all the variables in the building operation have been eliminated, namely rental income, vacancies and operating expenses.

The only variable that can alter the accuracy of this rule of thumb is the financing. As you know, financing can completely change the bottom line income. What looks like a good investment, based on the N.O.I. can turn out to be a poor one if mortgage payments are excessively high. Conversely, you learned that creative financing can improve the financial outlook of an investment.

CAPITALIZATION (CAP) RATE

Determining a fair market value of investment real estate by using a multiplier on the net operating income is also known as capitalization or ''cap'' rate. We said that the primary area for error in judging a property value by the Net Operating Income multiplier was the effects of the financing on the investment.

Savings and loan associations and other commercial mortgage lenders generally use the Net Multiplier in establishing property value for loan purposes. They are, of course, looking at the investment *prior* to the effects of financing.

Their formula is based on a CAP rate. The net operating income is ''capitalized'' at a certain percent, say 10 percent, to establish a value for loan purposes. A building producing an N.O.I. of $20,000, capitalized at 10 percent, has a fair market value of $200,000.00. The lender will probably lend a percentage of that amount, such as 65 percent or $130,000.00. You can now see why an understanding of N.O.I. is important to you.

The formula used here is a common and useful one that every investor should understand.

It is known as the ''IRV'' formula, where ''I'' represents ''income'' or net operating income; ''R'' represents ''rate'' or CAP rate; and ''V'' represents ''value'' or fair market value.

The formula is set up like this:

$$\frac{I}{R \times V}$$

or "I" divided by "R" times "V"

If you know any two of the three items in the formula, you can solve for the third by merely eliminating it from the formula and working out the remaining portion.

Example 1: A property producing $18,000 a year in net operating income is priced at $190,000. What is the CAP rate on the investment?

Solution: Remove the unknown factor, "R" and substitute the other two letters with the known figures.

$$R = \frac{I}{V} = \frac{\$18,000}{\$190,000} = 9.47\%$$

The CAP rate is 9.47 percent. An investor purchasing this property as shown, on a free and clear or all cash basis, would earn 9.47 percent return on his $190,000 investment. You probably didn't realize you were basically using the IRV formula back when you were determining the return you expected to receive on your cash investment. The only difference was that you used the income produced by the property *after* mortgage payments were made and divided by your actual cash investment rather than the total property value.

Example 2: A property is to be capitalized at 10.5 percent. It has a net operating income of $12,000. How much can you afford to pay for it in order to realize a 10.5 percent return on your investment?

Solution:

$$V = \frac{I}{R} = \frac{\$12,000}{.105 \quad (10.5\%)} = \$114,286$$

If you want a 10.5 percent return on your investment when the net operating income produced by the building is $12,000, the most you can pay for the property is $114,286. Again, this is based on an all cash basis.

Example 3: You expect a nine percent return on your cash investment of $110,000. Since again, we are talking about a building that has no financing, that means the properties market value is your $110,000. What must the N.O.I. be to give you your nine percent return.

Solution: I = R × .09 × $110,000 = $9,900

An investment property producing an N.O.I. of $9,900 will give you a nine percent return on a $110,000 investment.

As you can see, the IRV formula is very useful. Bear in mind that it does not take financing or mortgages into consideration. All results are based on the property being free and clear of all financing.

What CAP Rate Should You Use?

Savings and loan associations rely on a CAP rate to determine value for loan purposes. Chances are you will not be concerned with establishing a CAP rate for your investments. Your primary concern is the results that you establish when you prepare a property analysis form.

It is a good idea to find out what CAP rate your local savings and loan associations use in determining value. This will give you a quick check as to how close the investment you are considering fits their guidelines. It is especially important when you are seeking a new mortgage.

APARTMENT SQUARE FOOTAGE

The discussion of shopping centers and office buildings pointed out that, in most cases, rent is established on a dollar per square foot per year basis. A 500 square foot office renting for $7.00 per square foot per year will bring $7.00 × 500 or $3,500 a year income.

How important is the square footage of a rental apartment? Most rents are based on "x" number of dollars per month. An apartment that has two bedrooms will rent for more than a one bedroom unit, etc. But, can you expect a 1000 square foot one bedroom apartment to rent for more than a comparable one bedroom apartment with only 900 square feet of living space?

Unless you are in a highly competitive market with many available apartments, probably not. When a tenant has a choice of the two, at the same rent, all else being equal, he will obviously take the larger unit. Conversely, he will pay as much or more for the smaller one if it is in a better neighborhood, better maintained, or offers additional amenities, such as a dishwasher, or swimming pool.

Market conditions are the primary determining factor.

Builders and developers, on the other hand, know how much an apartment complex cost them to build based on a dollar amount per leasable square foot of apartment. In their initial establishing of rents, a developer may determine that he must rent his apartments at $5.25 per square foot in order to cover his cost in the project, spread out over the number of years he considers reasonable to re-coup his investment, plus make a profit. An 800 square foot apartment will then lease for 800 × $5.25 or $4200 a year. This equals $350 per month.

I have heard investors say, "those apartments are too small." They chose to ignore the fact that the units were comparable in size to others in the area. More importantly, the building stayed rented at a good, competitive rent, and that is the prime requisite in purchasing in the first place.

When the building income is suffering because of the size of the apartments or lack of closet space, the square footage consideration then becomes important.

LOCATION: IS IT REALLY CRUCIAL?

Earlier in the book it was pointed out that although location is always an important consideration in buying a real estate investment, it is *not* always the most critical consideration. A lower priced investment property in a working class neighborhood may be as good or better investment than a high priced property in a "Park Avenue" neighborhood. If you are an individual who concerns yourself with the next recession, you may wish you owned a building where you can make a profit without having to demand top rents.

Looking at the other side of the coin, a building located in the middle of the Florida Everglades would probably be overpriced at any price. No one would want to live in it.

When searching for your investment, look at all possibilities. Do not let pride of ownership stand in the way of your real investment goals.

LARGEST NUMBER OF UNITS

A good rule of thumb to keep in mind is: Purchase as many rental units as possible with the cash that you have to invest. This means making the maximum use of leverage or financing. You should leverage your property up to the maximum that you feel comfortable in carrying.

The reason is easily understandable. A four-unit building with one vacant apartment is 25 percent vacant. A 20-unit building with one vacancy has only a five percent vacancy factor. There are additional advantages in acquiring the largest property possible.

Services, such as lawn maintenance, do not increase in proportion to the number of units. It may cost $50 a month for lawn care on a four-unit building but only $150 a month for a 20-unit building. This breaks down to $12.50 per unit per month on the four units but only $7.50 per unit on the 20-unit building. The larger the complex, the easier it is to justify the cost of property management. Most management companies cannot afford to manage small properties.

Finally, the larger the complex, the more dollar appreciation you will realize with your investment and the greater the effects of pyramiding into larger properties.

PERCENTAGE OF OPERATING EXPENSES

As you start looking and comparing investment, you will see a pattern start to develop in the proportion the various operating expenses have to the gross income. Real estate taxes in your area may average eight percent of the gross income, for example, insurance six percent, etc. When you recognize this percentage pattern over and over, you will detect a possible problem where a seller's insurance is only three percent of the gross when most of the others you have examined average six percent. Chances are his building is inadequately insured. If you buy the property, you will have to allow for this increase in your operating expenses.

You will also discover an average overall percentage figure on operating expenses for certain types of properties in your area. In the Fort Lauderdale, Florida area, for example, apartment building operating expenses will usually run 25 to 30 percent of the gross income. When an owner says his expenses are only 15 to 20 percent, I know he left something out somewhere.

Northern cities, where taxes are higher and heating is required, at the owner's expense, operating expenses may be 50 percent or more of the gross income.

IRR OR INTERNAL RATE OF RETURN

You will no doubt hear investors talk about internal rate of return on an investment. You learned from your property analysis what to expect as a return on your cash investment. But what happens when you decide to sell? You would like to know how much you made on your investment for each year you had your money invested. There are, however, several factors that will affect this answer. Our computer analysis in Figure 15-1 tells us what to expect in the way of property appreciation, mortgage principal reduction, and after-tax cash flows over a several year period, but what about:

Any interest that can be earned on those cash flows during the years of the investment.

How about the effects of capital gains tax on the sale of the property. Taxes will reduce your profit. It will also cost you something to sell: closing costs, real estate fees, etc.

IRR answers these questions. The computer analysis gives the investor an IRR line at the bottom of the printout. That percentage figure represents the annual return you can expect from the investment after all of the above factors have been taken into consideration. Looking at the IRR line in Figure 15-1 for the end of year five, it shows 24.50 percent. If you were to sell the property at the end of the fifth year, and it had performed as you had projected, you would have realized an annual return of 24.50 percent on your invested capital for each of the five years you had it invested in the *Always Full Apartments*. And that is after paying all capital gains tax on the sales profit.

What is FMRR or Financial Management Rate of Return?

The IRR concept was a breakthrough in giving an investor a reasonably accurate estimate of expected return on his invested capital. It has one drawback, however. IRR assumes that all of the after-tax cash flows are reinvested at the same rate of return as the primary real estate invest-ment. As a practical matter this is not possible. The first year's after-tax cash flow on the *Always Full Apartments* is $5124 as shown in Figure 15-1. This is not enough capital to re-invest in real estate. FMRR overcomes this inac-curacy by assuming all cash flows will be invested at a "safe rate," such as five percent in a savings account, until sufficient capital has been ac-cumulated to re-invest in real estate. It then earns the same rate as the primary, real estate investment. As you can see, FMRR gives a more "real world" estimate of return on invested capital. Both formulas are complex to figure without the aid of a computer.

A "POOR" INVESTMENT MAY BE GOOD

In the first Chapter we discussed the four types of return you can expect from a real estate investment. Just in case your memory has failed you, they are:

1. Spendable Income (Cash Flow)
2. Equity Income (Principal Reduction)
3. Tax Shelter (Write-off against other taxable income)
4. Appreciation (Annual increase in property value)

Now, let's go back to the *Always Full Apartments* and assume the gross spendable income is reduced from its present $4159 to $500 a year or almost a break-even level. Dividing that by your $40,000 investment, you'll see that your spendable return on your cash investment is only 1.3 percent. Your first impulse is to discard the *Always Full Apartments* as a possible investment. But, let's carry it through all four of the returns you can expect.

Adding the $500 cash flow to the $2047 principal payment, your total equity income is $2547 or 5.7 percent return on your $40,000.00. Still not too good.

Your first year's depreciation allowance is $9750, far in excess of the $2547 equity income produced by the building. Deducting the $2547 from the $9750 depreciation, you have a tax loss or tax shelter of $7302. Assuming your tax bracket is 32 percent, this results in a tax savings on your other in-come of $2305.

Adding the $2305 to the $2547 equity income gives you an *after-tax* return of $4852 or 10.8 percent on your $45,000.

Finally, we'll assume the *Always Full Apartments* will appreciate four percent during the year. Four percent of the $150,000 purchase price is $6000. Adding that to the $4852 after-tax return will give you an overall return of $10,852 or 24 percent on your $45,000 cash investment. Not bad for what initially looked like a poor investment.

Here is how the "poor" investment looks figuring in all four returns:

Source of Income	Amount	Cumulative Total	% Return on $40,000
Gross Spendable Income (Cash Flow)	$ 500	$ 500	1.3%
Plus: Principal Payment	2,047	2,547	5.7%
Plus: Tax Savings on Other Income	2,305	4,852	10.8%
Plus: 4% Appreciation on $150,000	6,000	10,852	24%

The point is, keep all of the possible investment returns in mind when you analyze a potential investment. This does not mean that you should use this to justify an overpriced property. Any investment still offers all four returns, although tax shelter benefits will diminish as the actual income produced by the property increases.

Remember, a greatly overpriced property will be slow in appreciating until present income catches up, market value wise, with the purchase price.

You may, however, find investment opportunities that have great potential even though the present "cash flow" is low. You can examine the overall expected performance of the property to determine if it makes investment sense, and meets your investment goals, even if the price is higher than you would like to pay. Market condition and the limited availability of properties may dictate making some sacrifices in your desire to purchase at "bargain" prices.

HOW TO USE MORTGAGE AMORTIZATION SCHEDULES

As you start working with the financing of various properties, you will need to make use of mortgage amortization schedules. You can pick up a complete amortization book at most savings and loan associations. (Amortization schedules are also included in the Appendix.)

Most schedules are easy to use. You select the table that corresponds to the interest rate and the term or length of the mortgage.

Figure 17-1 illustrates a typical mortgage amortization table for a 15 percent mortgage. Assume you want to know the monthly principal and interest payments for a $25,000, 15 percent, 25-year mortgage.

Using the 15 percent interest table, you merely locate the $25,000 row in the left column and where it intersects the 25-year column, read the amount. In this case, the table shows $320.21. That is the monthly principal and interest payment necessary to pay off a $25,000 mortgage over a 25-year period at 15 percent interest.

Suppose the mortgage balance was $25,200. You would have to combine the $25,000 figure of $320.21 with the $200 amount at the top of the column. Under the 25-year term, the payment on $200 is $2.57, making a total payment of $322.78.

APPRAISAL METHODS: THE INCOME, MARKET DATA, AND COST APPROACHES TO VALUE

There are three basic methods used by appraisers to determine the fair market value of income producing real estate. Here is how each one works:

Income Approach

The income approach to market value is the method you have basically been using throughout this book. It makes use of the IRV formula. You determine the return you expect from your cash investment, and capitalize that percentage by the Net Operating Income being produced by the property.

For example, let's say you expect a 10 percent return on your investment. The N.O.I. produced by the *Always Full Apartments* is $14,985. Remember the formula—$\frac{I}{R \times V}$

$$\text{V or Market Value} = \frac{\$14,985 \quad \text{(NOI)}}{.10 \quad \text{(CAP rate)}} = \$149,850$$

You would be willing to pay $149,850 for the complex.

15% — MONTHLY PAYMENT
Necessary to amortize a loan

TERM AMOUNT	19 YEARS	20 YEARS	21 YEARS	22 YEARS	23 YEARS	24 YEARS	25 YEARS
$ 25	.34	.33	.33	.33	.33	.33	.33
50	.67	.66	.66	.65	.65	.65	.65
75	1.00	.99	.99	.98	.97	.97	.97
100	1.33	1.32	1.31	1.30	1.30	1.29	1.29
200	2.66	2.64	2.62	2.60	2.59	2.58	2.57
300	3.99	3.96	3.93	3.90	3.88	3.86	3.85
400	5.32	5.27	5.23	5.20	5.17	5.15	5.13
500	6.65	6.59	6.54	6.50	6.46	6.43	6.41
600	7.97	7.91	7.85	7.80	7.76	7.72	7.69
700	9.30	9.22	9.15	9.10	9.05	9.01	8.97
800	10.63	10.54	10.46	10.40	10.34	10.29	10.25
900	11.96	11.86	11.77	11.70	11.63	11.58	11.53
1000	13.29	13.17	13.08	12.99	12.92	12.86	12.81
2000	26.57	26.34	26.15	25.98	25.84	25.72	25.62
3000	39.85	39.51	39.22	38.97	38.76	38.58	38.43
4000	53.13	52.68	52.29	51.96	51.68	51.44	51.24
5000	66.41	65.84	65.36	64.95	64.60	64.30	64.05
6000	79.70	79.01	78.43	77.94	77.52	77.16	76.85
7000	92.98	92.18	91.50	90.93	90.44	90.02	89.66
8000	106.26	105.35	104.57	103.92	103.36	102.88	102.47
9000	119.54	118.52	117.64	116.91	116.28	115.74	115.28
10000	132.82	131.68	130.72	129.89	129.19	128.60	128.09
11000	146.11	144.85	143.79	142.88	142.11	141.46	140.90
12000	159.39	158.02	156.86	155.87	155.03	154.32	153.71
13000	172.67	171.19	169.93	168.86	167.95	167.18	166.51
14000	185.95	184.36	183.00	181.85	180.87	180.04	179.32
15000	199.23	197.52	196.07	194.84	193.79	192.89	192.13
16000	212.52	210.69	209.14	207.83	206.71	205.75	204.94
17000	225.80	223.86	222.21	220.82	219.63	218.61	217.75
18000	239.08	237.03	235.29	233.81	232.55	231.47	230.55
19000	252.36	250.20	248.36	246.80	245.47	244.33	243.36
20000	265.64	263.36	261.43	259.78	258.38	257.19	256.17
21000	278.93	276.53	274.50	272.77	271.30	270.05	268.98
22000	292.21	289.70	287.57	285.76	284.22	282.91	281.79
23000	305.49	302.87	300.64	298.75	297.14	295.77	294.60
24000	318.77	316.03	313.71	311.74	310.06	308.63	307.41
25000	332.05	329.20	326.78	324.73	322.98	321.49	320.21
26000	345.34	342.37	339.86	337.72	335.90	334.35	333.02
27000	358.62	355.54	352.93	350.71	348.82	347.21	345.83
28000	371.90	368.71	366.00	363.70	361.74	360.06	358.64
29000	385.18	381.87	379.07	376.69	374.66	372.92	371.45
30000	398.46	395.04	392.14	389.67	387.57	385.78	384.25
31000	411.75	408.21	405.21	402.66	400.49	398.64	397.06
32000	425.03	421.38	418.28	415.65	413.41	411.50	409.87
33000	438.31	434.55	431.35	428.64	426.33	424.36	422.68
34000	451.59	447.61	444.42	441.63	439.25	437.22	435.49
35000	464.87	460.88	457.50	454.62	452.17	450.08	448.30
40000	531.28	526.72	522.85	519.56	516.76	514.38	512.34
45000	597.69	592.56	588.21	584.51	581.36	578.67	576.38
50000	664.10	658.40	653.56	649.45	645.95	642.97	640.42
55000	730.51	724.24	718.92	714.40	710.55	707.27	704.46
60000	796.92	790.08	784.28	779.34	775.14	771.56	768.50
65000	863.33	855.92	849.63	844.29	839.74	835.86	832.54
70000	929.74	921.76	914.99	909.23	904.33	900.16	896.59
75000	996.15	987.60	980.34	974.18	968.93	964.45	960.63
80000	1062.56	1053.44	1045.70	1039.12	1033.52	1028.75	1024.67
100000	1328.20	1316.79	1307.12	1298.90	1291.90	1285.93	1280.84

140

15% — MONTHLY PAYMENT
Necessary to amortize a loan

TERM AMOUNT	26 YEARS	27 YEARS	28 YEARS	29 YEARS	30 YEARS	35 YEARS	40 YEARS
$ 25	.32	.32	.32	.32	.32	.32	.32
50	.64	.64	.64	.64	.64	.64	.63
75	.96	.96	.96	.96	.96	.95	.94
100	1.28	1.28	1.27	1.27	1.27	1.26	1.26
200	2.56	2.55	2.54	2.54	2.53	2.51	2.51
300	3.83	3.82	3.81	3.80	3.80	3.78	3.76
400	5.11	5.10	5.08	5.07	5.06	5.03	5.02
500	6.39	6.37	6.35	6.34	6.33	6.29	6.27
600	7.66	7.64	7.62	7.61	7.59	7.55	7.52
700	8.94	8.91	8.89	8.87	8.86	8.80	8.78
800	10.22	10.19	10.16	10.14	10.12	10.06	10.03
900	11.49	11.46	11.43	11.41	11.38	11.32	11.28
1000	12.77	12.73	12.70	12.67	12.65	12.57	12.54
2000	25.53	25.46	25.40	25.34	25.29	25.14	25.07
3000	38.30	38.19	38.09	38.01	37.94	37.71	37.60
4000	51.06	50.91	50.79	50.68	50.58	50.28	50.13
5000	63.83	63.64	63.48	63.34	63.23	62.85	62.67
6000	76.59	76.37	76.18	76.01	75.87	75.41	75.20
7000	89.36	89.10	88.87	88.68	88.52	87.98	87.73
8000	102.12	101.82	101.57	101.35	101.16	100.55	100.26
9000	114.89	114.55	114.26	114.02	113.80	113.12	112.80
10000	127.65	127.28	126.96	126.68	126.48	125.69	125.33
11000	140.42	140.01	139.65	139.35	139.09	138.25	137.86
12000	153.18	152.73	152.35	152.02	151.74	150.82	150.39
13000	165.95	165.46	165.05	164.69	164.39	163.39	162.92
14000	178.71	178.19	177.74	177.36	177.03	175.96	175.46
15000	191.48	190.92	190.44	190.02	189.67	188.53	187.99
16000	204.24	203.64	203.13	202.69	202.32	201.10	200.52
17000	217.00	216.37	215.83	215.36	214.96	213.66	213.05
18000	229.77	229.10	228.52	228.03	227.60	226.23	225.59
19000	242.53	241.83	241.22	240.70	240.25	238.80	238.12
20000	255.30	254.55	253.91	253.36	252.89	251.37	250.65
21000	268.06	267.28	266.61	266.03	265.54	263.94	263.18
22000	280.83	280.01	279.30	278.70	278.18	276.50	275.71
23000	293.59	292.74	292.00	291.37	290.82	289.07	288.25
24000	306.36	305.47	304.69	304.04	303.47	301.64	300.78
25000	319.12	318.19	317.39	316.70	316.12	314.21	313.31
26000	331.89	330.92	330.09	329.37	328.76	326.78	325.84
27000	344.65	343.64	342.78	342.04	341.40	339.34	338.38
28000	357.42	356.38	355.48	354.71	354.05	351.91	350.91
29000	370.18	369.10	368.17	367.38	366.69	364.48	363.44
30000	382.95	381.83	380.87	380.04	379.34	377.05	375.97
31000	395.71	394.55	393.56	392.71	391.98	389.62	388.50
32000	408.48	407.28	406.26	405.38	404.63	402.19	401.04
33000	421.24	420.01	418.95	418.05	417.27	414.75	413.57
34000	434.00	432.74	431.65	430.72	429.92	427.32	426.10
35000	446.77	445.46	444.34	443.38	442.56	439.89	438.63
40000	510.59	509.10	507.82	506.72	505.78	502.73	501.29
45000	574.42	572.74	571.30	570.06	569.00	565.57	563.96
50000	638.24	636.37	634.77	633.40	632.25	628.41	626.62
55000	702.06	700.01	698.25	696.74	695.45	691.25	689.28
60000	765.89	763.65	761.73	760.08	758.67	754.09	751.94
65000	829.71	827.28	825.21	823.42	821.89	816.93	814.60
70000	893.53	890.92	888.68	886.76	885.12	879.77	877.26
75000	957.36	954.56	952.16	950.10	948.34	942.61	939.92
80000	1021.18	1018.20	1015.64	1013.44	1011.56	1005.46	1002.58
100000	1276.48	1272.74	1269.54	1266.80	1264.45	1256.82	1253.23

141

Figure 17-1

Market Data Approach

As we discussed, this method, in my estimation, makes use of one of the *least* accurate "rules of thumb" in determining a property value—price per unit. The appraiser researches the area and prepares a list of properties comparable to the *Always Full Apartments*. These comparables should be in similar areas, with similar apartment sizes, amenities, appearance and rent structures. These are all buildings that have sold recently. Chances are, they are few and far between and a building that sold a year or two ago can no longer be considered a comparable because of property appreciation that has taken place since it sold.

He then divides the prices at which each building sold by the number of units in the complex. This gives him an average price per apartment to use as a multiplier. This is done for each building in his survey. The average price per unit of each is then correlated or "averaged" to determine a price per unit. Assume he came up with $19,380 per apartment. Multiplying the $19,380 average unit price times the eight units in the *Always Full Apartments*, you arrive at market value of $155,040, based on the market value approach.

Cost Approach

The cost approach method of appraisal estimates what it would cost to replace the entire complex. In other words, if the lot next door to the *Always Full Apartments* was the same size and for sale, what would it cost to buy the land and build a twin building to the *Always Full Apartments*?

First, determine the land value. A study indicates comparable land is selling for $1.50 a square foot. The *Always Full Apartments* is on a 100 × 150 foot lot or 15,000 square feet × $1.50 = $22,500. The lot, therefore, is worth $22,500.

Secondly, what site improvements are on the *Always Full* property? Parking area, lawn, shrubs, trees, etc. You determine it would cost about $9000 to replace them.

Thirdly, what will it cost to duplicate the building?

You determine that the six one bedroom apartments have 550 square feet each or a total of 3300 square feet. It will cost $31.50 a square foot to build or $103,950.

The two two bedroom apartments have 700 square feet each or a total of 1400 square feet. Since you are able to spread cost of plumbing, appliances, etc. over more square footage, your square foot cost for the two bedroom drops to $30.00 or $42,000 for the two units.

Total cost of the structure is $103,950 + $42,000 or $145,950. That would be the cost of a new building. Since the furniture in the apartments is already seven years old, no value was established on it. As a practical matter, if you were to sell that furniture, it would be practically valueless.

The *Always Full Apartments* are seven years old. In order to establish a comparable, you must figure a depreciated value on the $145,950. Assume the *Always Full Apartments* have depreciated 20 percent or $29,190. This leaves a depreciated value of the improvements of $116,760. To this amount, add the $9000 in site improvements and the $22,500 land value, giving a total market value, using the cost approach, of $148,260. Figure 17-2 illustrates all three methods of appraisal in simplified form.

Estimate of Market Value

1. Income Approach:
   N.O.I.—$14,985 Capitalized @ 10% $149,850

2. Market Data Approach:
   8 Units @$19,380/Unit $155,040

3. Coat Approach:
   Land—15,000 Square Feet @ $1.50
           Square Foot $ 22,500
   Site Improvements   9,000
   Building:
      6 Units × 550 Square feet = 3300
      Square Foot × $31.50 = $103,950
      2 Units × 700 Square Feet = 1400
      Square Foot × $30.00 =   42,000
                          $145,950
   Less: 20% Depreciated Value   29,190
   Cost of Improvements (building) $116,760
           TOTAL VALUE $148,260

4. Final Estimate of Market Value   = $150,000

Figure 17-2

Notice that a final line on the analysis is labeled "Final Estimate of Market Value." This is an estimate determined by correlating all three of the appraisal methods. I prefer to give the primary emphasis of the "income approach" since the income being produced by the property is your primary interest. In this particular case, the final fair market value for the *Always Full Apartments* was determined to be $150,000.

The more exposed you become to other investors and investment properties, the more rules of thumb you will hear!

HOW "LIQUID" IS A REAL ESTATE INVESTMENT?

Back in Chapter 16, mention was made of a retired age investor who may sell the *Always Full Apartments* and carry a second or third mortgage because, at his age, he was interested in an investment offering more "liquidity."

Perhaps we should discuss how "liquid" a real estate investment is (or isn't). A "liquid" investment is one in which your cash investment is immediately available to you in the event you need it in a hurry. The money in your savings account is extremely "liquid." It is as close as your bank and a "savings withdrawal" slip.

There is no question that a real estate investment is just not that liquid. This is why you were advised *not* to invest all of your funds in real estate. Keep some in a savings account for emergencies.

But does real estate really "lock up" your capital the way some investors insist it does? There are many "would-be" real estate investors who choose to ignore the many benefits of real estate because they do not want to be locked into a "long-term" investment position. Instead they invest their funds in six or twelve month Certificates of Deposit or the stock market. Where does this leave them?

They can get their investment out of the CD's at any time, but the lender makes it very clear, "early withdrawal will result in a substantial interest penalty." But they entice the would-be investor by assuring him, "But your initial investment is *always* available."

What about the stock investor. Sure, you can call your stock broker and offer your shares for sale . . . at whatever price they will bring on the market at that time. And, the way the market has been, that will probably be at a substantial *loss*.

Well, the same holds true with real estate, considered a *non*-liquid investment. If the investor wants out quickly and is willing to sell at a loss, as he probably will his stock, he should be able to locate an immediate buyer.

If you are like most investors, however, you have been programmed to believe that making a sizable profit on the sale of your real estate investment is not only desirable, it's expected. You *will* make a profit but, the more you expect to make, the longer it may take to locate a buyer.

So, in my estimation, a real estate investment is more liquid than many investors realize. Depending upon how badly and quickly you want to sell, you can always find a buyer "at a price."

As alternatives to finding a "quick" buyer, you can also refinance the property or find someone to give you a second mortgage on your building. Either of these alternatives will give you immediate, tax-free cash, if this is what you suddenly need.

In any event, *do not* shy away from investing in real estate because you cannot get your money back out as easily as you can in your savings account.

CAUTION: DO NOT BECOME A DEALER

Throughout this book, you have been advised to buy a property or properties, hold them for a period of time and then sell or exchange them.

The end result if you sell, is payment of capital gains tax, which may take 28 percent or less of your profit.

In previous chapters we discussed that an investor who converts a rental apartment or office complex to condo and sells off individual units will be classified as a dealer and lose the capital gains treatment of his profit. Likewise an investor who subdivided his acreage and sells off individual lots will be classified as a dealer and his profit will be taxed as ordinary income.

The IRS, however, takes a close look at an investor who is continually turning over properties. Although there are no specifics in the IRS manual, such an investor may be classified as a "dealer" rather than an investor.

As a "dealer," his profit from each sale then gets taxed as ordinary income rather than at capital gains rates. You can see what will happen to the profits of an investor in a 50 percent tax bracket if the IRS classifies him as a dealer.

This law should not affect you, unless you get into a position where you are buying and selling several properties in a one year period . . . and this is *not* what this book is recommending you do. Your accountant can advise you of your status, when you reach that point.

BUYER'S MARKET VS. SELLER'S MARKET

Our final discussion concerning rules of thumb should recognize that at any given time, you can expect to be either in a buyer's market or seller's market. This is no different from the stock market.

You always hope that when you are looking for an investment, you'll be in a buyer's market. In other words, there are more properties available than there are immediate buyers for them. This market condition offers you the best opportunity of easily locating a prime investment. You also have the best chance of negotiating favorable price and terms.

Conversely, when you get ready to sell, you hope to find yourself in a seller's market, where yours is one of the few properties for sale but buyers are abundant. You are then in the driver's seat as far as obtaining a top price and the most desirable terms *for you*.

So, what do you do if you're in a seller's market when you're ready to buy and vice-versa? Suppose you finish this book and go out to find an investment property, but you're in a seller's market and the selection is limited, with potential buyers all around you, and competing with you for the few available properties. You may want to re-read Chapter 7. It was deliberately written to guide you through a seller's market situation. It was assumed you would have to search extensively to find an investment that was right for you.

If you find yourself in a buyer's market, your choice of investment properties should be plentiful and your selection an easy one. Now you want to sell, but find you are in a buyer's market. What do you do?

First of all, keep one thought in mind, "there are always buyers for investment real estate." It is a buyer's market only because there are more seller's than there are buyers. This means that the sellers who have the most salable properties will be the ones who can find a buyer.

Again, review what you learned about selecting your investment in the first place. Location, quality, rental stability, quality of tenants, and appearance of your property, all lead to making it more salable when the buyers are scarce. Now you can better understand the emphasis that was placed on selecting, maintaining and leasing of your building.

When selling during a buyer's market, you may have to be more flexible in your price and terms or you may have to delay selling until the market turns around again. And believe me, it will.

This brings us to the final point in this discussion—the balance between accepting a little less than you hoped for or waiting for an additional one, six or twelve months to buy or sell.

Whether buying or selling, you should know, from the previous Chapters in this book, how much it is costing you to "wait" for ideal market conditions that may or *may not* even occur. You will, no doubt, find that it will pay you to sacrifice a little in order to buy or sell now, rather than to maintain your present investment position. Scratch paper is cheap. Use what you have learned to compare your two alternatives, staying in your present position or making the change, even under less than perfect conditions. You'll see at a glance what is best for you and your investment program.

Rules of thumb and estimates of market value are useful in giving you a quick method of evaluating an investment property, but they are *not* a substitute for taking the time to prepare a complete property analysis, projecting yourself into the ownership. Only by doing so, can you accurately determine how much you can afford to pay for a property and still have it conform to your overall investment goals.

18

How a Professional Can Benefit By Leasing Space to Himself

Perhaps this Chapter does not really belong in this book, but the subject is one that should be of significant importance to a business professional who is looking for a way to "save" tax dollars.

Most professional people, by nature, are so wrapped up in their business that they rarely take the time to either sit down and analyze their financial situation or have it done for them by a tax counsel. Every year, they pay Uncle Sam more and more and end up working harder yet have less after tax income.

The purpose of this Chapter is to open the eyes of the professional who has fallen into the tax trap and hasn't taken the time to look for at least a partial escape, and there is a simple, sound way he can improve "after-tax" income.

A TAX SHELTER SECOND TO NONE

There is an excellent tax shelter available to professional people. It consists of renting their own real estate to their professional corporation. It's workable for doctors, dentists, attorneys, Realtors, and any professional who is incorporated.

Let's use Dr. Smith as an example. He operates his private practice as a professional corporation. At the present time, Dr. Smith is leasing 1600 square feet of office space at a cost of $7.00 per square foot per year, or an annual rent of $11,200. Of course, he can deduct this rent expense from his corporate profit, as an operating expense, but he still has nothing to show for it at the end of the year.

What if he, as a private investor, purchased a small medical building and leased space to his professional corporation. The tax consequences of his corporation remain unchanged. According to IRS, he is still paying rent. The important difference is that he is paying it to himself, as private real estate investor, Dr. Smith, rather than to some stranger.

Now, let's see how private investor, Dr. Smith, fairs on his real estate investment with Dr. Smith, Incorporated, as the tenant. He purchased a small 1600 square foot office building for $75,000 with $20,000 down payment and a $55,000, nine percent mortgage. His annual expenses consist of: mortgage payments—$5500, real estate taxes—$1500, insurance and operating expenses—$2000, for a total of $9000 a year. But, he's paying himself $11,200 in rent, so he made a $2200 profit.

Next, he must consider the income tax consequences. Dr. Smith had a cash profit of $2200 plus, he paid down the mortgage $550 the first year (and that's like money in the bank). His total pre-tax profit then was $2750. (See Figure 18-1, Line 1. His proposed position is compared with his present position.) It was assumed that the $20,000 he invested in the medical building was previously earning six percent in a savings account.

His real estate investment counselor determined that 85 percent of his $75,000 investment was depreciable improvements (the building). He further determined that this could be written-off or depreciated, over a 20-year useful life or five percent per year. Five percent of $63,750 (85 percent of $75,000) is $3187 (Line 2). The property only produced $2750, however, so Dr. Smith has a paper loss of $437 for the year (Line 3).

He next determines what his total return is on his $20,000 investment. Line 4 compares his present pre-tax gross income with the proposed position. He is already $1000 ahead at the end of the year.

On Line 5, you'll see the tax shelter advantages take affect. Assuming Dr. Smith is in a 50 percent tax bracket, one half of his savings account interest will be paid to Uncle Sam. This leaves him with an after-tax income of only $600 or three percent on his savings account.

Since his medical building shows a tax loss, he can reduce his other taxable income by $437. Instead of paying Uncle Sam 50 percent, he saves 50 percent of Line 3. He ends up paying $218 less income tax on his occupational income (Line 5). Since this is a negative number, it is added to rather than subtracted from Line 4. But, his real estate investment offers still more. He reduced his mortgage by $500 during the year. His property also appreciated four percent. Four percent of $75,000 is $3000. This is also added to his total return on Line 7.

How did he do? He ended up with a total sum of $5918, after taxes or 29.6 percent return on his $20,000 investment. That's considered better than the three percent after tax return he made on the savings account. I might add, he no longer minds paying rent each month.

He also owns a $75,000 building which is appreciating at the rate of eight to ten percent per year. If we conservatively figure only four percent appreciation per year, his building will be worth $111,000 in ten years and his mortgage will be paid down to just over $46,000. In ten years, he has increased his equity from $20,000 to $65,000.

CAUTIONS TO CONSIDER

There are several cautions that must be considered by Dr. Smith. First of all, he must be certain that the rent he is paying to himself is reasonable and comparable with others in the area. A formal lease must be executed between the lessor (Dr. Smith, the private investor) and the lessee (Dr. Smith, Incorporated), spelling out all the terms and conditions of a normal lease.

One lease clause that should be included, spells out that in the event IRS disallows a portion of the rent paid by the lessee as being excessive, the lessor (Dr. Smith, private investor) must refund that portion to the lessee. When it is refunded, it is a deduction for Dr. Smith.

It is advisable for a potential investor in this type of situation to consult with a Realtor who is knowledgeable in real estate investments and tax shelters. Together, then, they would obtain the assistance of tax counsel to insure the Doctor's position in his venture.

STILL ANOTHER BENEFIT: YOU CAN REDUCE YOUR CORPORATE TAX LIABILITY

There is another benefit Dr. Smith will gain in leasing his own business. If he makes major improvements to his building, the costs of the improvements can be expensed off over the useful life of the improvements. If Dr. Smith, Incorporated pays for the improvements, he can reduce his corporate tax liability accordingly. If Dr. Smith, private investor, makes the improvements for his "tenant" he can deduct the cost from the operational profit of his building. Since the building is already showing a tax loss, it will now show an even greater one, which can be used to reduce his personal taxable income that he pays himself out of his corporation.

As you can see, professional people, through the leasing of their own building, can realize a tax shelter that is second to none. There is no other investment that will allow him to shift his income as effectively as in leasing his own real estate.

With Uncle Sam taking an increasingly larger bite out of your income each year, wouldn't it be great to put $2000 to $3000 more in your pocket each year, after taxes, and realize the outstanding growth potential of real estate ownership at the same time? And there's a certain security about being your own landlord, as well.

Dr. Smith, Private Investor

	Present Position	Proposed Position
1. Pre-Tax Return on Investment	$1,200*	$2,750**
2. Less: Depreciation Allowance**	-0-	3,287
3. Taxable Income	$1,200	($ 437) Tax Loss
4. Gross Spendable Income	$1,200	$2,200
5. Income Tax – 50% of Line 3	600	(218)
6. Plus: Mortgage Principal Reduction	-0-	500
7. Plus: Appreciation @ 4%	-0-	3,000
8. Total Return, After Taxes	$ 600	$5,918
9. % of Return on $20,000 Investment	3%	29.6%

*Based on 6% Savings Certificate.
**Includes cash flow plus Principal Reduction.

Figure 18-1

19

How to Pyramid
Your Investments

There is one final principle or technique that you need to understand to round out your knowledge of real estate investing—the practice of "pyramiding." Every investment technique you have learned so far has been leading you to this final stage. It is the systematic process of pyramiding your initial investment in real estate into a sizable retirement estate.

I know, you haven't purchased the first building yet and I'm already talking about moving you up into another. But your investment program should be built based on this philosophy.

You'll recall that in the first chapter you thought about your mental attitude of real estate investing and how the bulk of your retirement savings must be placed in a "non-fixed" investment, real estate being the best. If you have not already programmed your thinking to recognize this need, you probably would not have read this far. As a matter of fact, almost every chapter in this book has probably caused most of you to revise your thinking regarding your investment program. And that is exactly what was intended.

We would all like to become wealthy without doing anything, but that possibility is remote. You have already decided how active you are willing to become in the management of your investment and in its operation. Your willingness to handle all or part of it yourself has a direct bearing on your profits.

Hopefully, you have also made another mental commitment . . . "not to fall in love with your property." As a rule of thumb, you learned that when your initial equity in a property has doubled, it's time to trade up.

THE PREMISE BEHIND PYRAMIDING

That is what pyramiding is all about. It is based on the premise that each year, through appreciation (caused by our never ending inflation), mortgage principal reduction, and tax-free cash flows produced by the investment, your equity in the property is increasing. In fact, on a conservative basis, it should *double* every five to seven years. When it does, you could own a building twice the size as your present one, *with no additional outlay of cash*.

One final mental attitude you must have is don't become discouraged. You may have a tendency to look at your $10,000 or $25,000 investment and say to yourself, "There is no way that small amount can be pyramided into a million dollar estate." Believe me . . . *it can*! And you'll see how by just taking it one step at a time.

Have you ever painted the inside of your home? Before you started, you determined how many gallons of paint you needed to do the job. If you like painting as much as I do, the thought was a depressing one—seven rooms, four walls and a ceiling in each room, window frames, doors and door frames, and shutters (Oh, how I hate painting shutters). Just sitting back and looking at the immensity of the overall project was enough to keep me from starting. But, you do not paint a whole house in one afternoon. You take it one wall at a time, one room at a time, and before you know it, you have accomplished your goal.

When I started thinking about writing this book, I knew I wanted to give an investor the benefit of the ideas and techniques that I had accumulated over several years, through several investment schools and from practical applications with many investors, including myself. The thought of trying to combine all this information in one twenty chapter book was overwhelming. But, just like painting a house, it had to be taken one step at a time, one chapter at a time.

Which gets us back to the theory of pyramiding. Don't worry about reaching a dollar goal or level in 10, 15, or 20 years at this point . . . it will happen. Concentrate on today . . . this year.

Remember the young boy in chapter two. He agreed to work as a handyman for a wealthy gentleman. His pay was to be one cent the first day, two cents the second, and so forth for thirty days. Each day his pay would be double that of the previous day. If you haven't already figured out how much he made, here it is:

Day	Amount	Day	Amount	Day	Amount
1	1¢	11	$ 10.24	21	$ 10,485.76
2	2¢	12	20.48	22	20,971.52
3	4¢	13	40.96	23	41,942.04
4	8¢	14	81.92	24	83,886.08
5	16¢	15	163.84	25	167,772.16
6	32¢	16	327.68	26	335,544.32
7	64¢	17	655.36	27	671,088.64
8	$1.28	18	1,310.72	28	1,342,177.28
9	2.56	19	2,261.44	29	2,684,354.56
10	5.12	20	5,242.88	30	5,368,709.12

I think you'll agree that his last few days were quite profitable. It all started with the theory of pyramiding—and just one penny.

Think in Terms of Doubling Your Investment

This example is offered to illustrate that sizable fortunes can be made by merely doubling your initial investment every so often—and you will be doing exactly the same thing in your real estate investments. You will not be able to double your equity on a daily basis, but you will also start quite a ways into the above chart with your initial investment. Rather than look at the dollars you intend to accumulate, look at the number of times you must double your initial investment in order to end up with the desired amount in the future.

For example, if you start out with an initial investment of $25,000 and want to end up with an equity of $200,000 in twenty years, don't look at the difference in the two numbers and become discouraged. Instead, determine **how** many times you have to double that $25,000 in the next twenty years in order to end up with $200,000. This was pointed out in a earlier chapter. In this case, you must double your initial equity three times: 25 to 50, 50 to 100, and 100 to 200. Now, doesn't that sound a lot easier goal to attain than trying to comprehend how you could possible build $25,000 into $200,000? So, you have 20 years to double your investment three times. That's once every six to seven years. You should have no problem doing this in sound, well located real estate investments.

Advantages That Work for You

Getting back to the advantages you have over starting with just one penny, you have another, even more outstanding advantage in real estate— the use of leverage, other people's money for your estate building program.

You may begin with only $25,000 but you can use it to purchase a property valued at $100,000 or more. As your initial investment doubles to $50,000, your total property value is greatly increasing as well. Still another advantage is in the annual reduction you are making in the principal balance on the mortgage.

Finally, if you are able to add the after-tax cash flows produced by the property, to the equity you have accumulated, you will find your initial investment doubling much faster than you imagine. It's just a matter of numbers, but it really works, thanks to our ever increasing inflation and our continuing demand for more housing, shopping, office, and manufacturing facilities.

The introduction to this book stated that this was not a "get rich quick" publication. Perhaps, you can now see that by following the guidelines of exchanging and pyramiding, you may end up rich in spite of yourself.

HOW PYRAMIDING WORKS IN PRACTICE

Here is an example of how pyramiding really works in real estate. Prior to discussing the practice (and not just theory) of pyramiding real estate investments, some ground rules must be established.

We are going to follow Tom and Barbara Mills through their estate building program. They start out with $10,000 to invest. Their purpose is to pyramid that initial $10,000 into a lifetime estate over a twenty-year period. They intend to add *no* additional cash, but will, at the end of five years, add the cumulative after-tax cash flows produced by their building, to their current equity going into the new property. In other words, at the end of each five-year period, they would determine the current market value equity of their property, and add the income the property had generated over the five-year period. This total amount would be used to exchange their present property for a larger one. An exchange would take place four different times, at the beginning of years 6, 11, and 16, and a final exchange in the twenty-first year.

Because no actual properties were used in this analysis, some basic, conservative ground rules were established:

a) All numbers were rounded to the next lower $1000.

b) No estimate was made as to how much interest they could earn on the cash flows produced by the property, if they were invested until needed when the next exchange took place. It is assumed that this cumulative interest would cover the closing costs on each transaction.

c) It was assumed that the Mills were in a 30 percent tax bracket.

d) All properties were depreciated based on 85 percent of the value being depreciable improvements, a 25-year useful life using the 125 percent declining balance method of depreciation.

e) Net Operating Income was estimated at 10 percent of the market value of the property.

f) A minimal 4 percent growth or appreciation rate was used on all properties.

g) It was assumed that the Mills would be able to get 75 percent leverage on each property they bought after the first one. The first property they purchased required 20 percent down payment.

THE PROFITABLE RESULTS OF PYRAMIDING

Figure 19-1 illustrates the Mills' financial position in the first year of each new investment. Their first property was purchased with 20 percent down on a $50,000 investment. Their cash investment was $10,000.

Pyramiding

		1	2	3	4	5
1.	Property No.	1	2	3	4	5
2.	Beginning Year	1	6	11	16	21
3.	Market Value	$ 50,000	$120,000	$320,000	$860,000	$2,300,000
4.	Mortgage	40,000	90,000	240,000	645,000	1,721,000
5.	Equity	$ 10,000	$ 30,000	$ 80,000	$215,000	$ 579,000
6.	End of 5th Year Equity	$ 23,000	$ 61,000	$164,000	$442,000	
7.	Plus Cumulative After Tax Cash Flow for Reinvestment	7,000	19,000	51,000	137,000	
8.	Total Equity for Reinvestment in next Property	$ 30,000	$ 80,000	$215,000	$579,000	
9.	Market Value —Next Year	$120,000	$320,000	$860,000	$2,300,000	
10.	NET Spend-Income in 1st Year of Each Period	$ 1,000	$ 3,000	$ 8,000	$ 21,000	$ 57,000

Figure 19-1

By the end of the fifth year, their equity, through a combination of four percent appreciation and mortgage principal reduction, had grown to $23,000. They also had accumulated an additional $7000 in after-tax cash flows, giving them a total of $30,000 to invest in the next property.

Starting year six, they exchanged their equity into a $120,000 property.

Five years later, this equity had grown to $61,000 plus accumulated after-tax cash flows of $19,000 for a total of $80,000 (line 8) which was exchanged into a $320,000 property at the beginning of the eleventh year.

After an additional five years (15 years after they started the program) they had accumulated $215,000 in equity, including $51,000 after-tax cash flows, which enabled them to acquire an $860,000 property.

At the end of twenty years, they would make one last exchange. They had $579,000 equity to use in acquiring a $2,300,000 investment property. This property would give them a $57,000 cash flow the first year and, through continuing appreciation, build from there.

In twenty short years, Tom and Barbara Mills had built an initial $10,000 cash investment into a sizable estate capable of supporting them for the remainder of their lives. Through annual rent increases, they will be able to stay ahead of inflation.

You now know how fortunes are made in real estate. The results shown here are not just an "impossible dream." They, if anything, are ultra-conservative.

The concepts are based on the down to earth realities of real estate that have been discussed from page one of this book. They are:

a) Our population is increasing.

b) No more land is being created.

c) Each year, because of inflation, existing land becomes more valuable . . . and inflation has been with us, on an ever increasing level, since the Second World War.

d) Inflation causes rents to increase.

e) As rents increase, property values increase.

f) Real estate is appreciating at least eight to ten percent per year in most areas. (We have been using only four percent in our examples.)

g) No other form of investing offers as high a leverage use as real estate.

h) No other form of investing offers as high a potential return on invested capital as real estate.

i) No other form of investing offers the tax shelter benefits of real estate. (And remember, it does not matter how much you make, but how much you get to keep after taxes that is important.)

The results shown in Figure 19-1 are possible for all real estate investors to achieve, including YOU. Do not become complacent with your first real estate investment. Use it as a stepping stone toward a second, a third, until you know your future is secure. It is easy to do . . . people just like you are doing it every day.

20

A 19-Point Master Checklist
for Getting Started
in Real Estate Investing

We have covered a lot of ground together, discussing everything from finding and analyzing an investment property to acquiring, managing, and selling it. If you are already a real estate investor, you may have picked up some useful ideas that will make your future investments even more profitable. Perhaps some new avenues have been opened up in the type of property or financing that is available to you.

If, on the other hand, you are a would-be investor who is venturing into real estate investing for the first time, your first question may very well be "How do I get started?"

The 19-point checklist in this chapter is designed to answer that question. This checklist covers the logical sequence of events that an investor must follow to get started in real estate investing, and it can be used by beginning and experienced investors alike to make sure that every detail is covered and nothing is overlooked. Keep it handy as a reference tool, and use it in conjunction with the previous 19 chapters in this book. Remember —this book is not a novel that you read once and put away forever. It is a reference manual designed to guide you through all phases of real estate investing. Refer to it often, particularly when you are uncertain of any of the investment phases covered in this checklist.

If you never read another book on real estate investing, you will have learned enough here to make sound investment decisions. Even so, it's never possible to cover every subject in complete detail in one book. If you want to review a specific subject, such as real estate financing, in greater detail, visit your public library to find a good reference book. And if you are unsure of yourself at any step in the investment process, seek out a Realtor who has taken the time to become educated in real estate investing. Ask him to explain N.O.I. (and *you'd* better know what this is by now). Ask him what your tax consequences will be if your purchase the property he is offering. This book will help you come up with the right questions to ask. If he's the Realtor you want, he'll know the answers. If not, find another Realtor.

On the other hand, if he's your brother-in-law and you're stuck with him, *you* may be able to train *him*. You are now an expert on the subject.

Keep in mind that you are considering investing the largest sum of money that you ever have in your life. You owe it to yourself and to your financial security to know enough to make the right investment decisions. The smarter, more informed you are when you face other investors in the marketplace, the more successful your real estate investment program will be. Use this 19-point checklist to get started.

1. Know Why You Need to Invest in Real Estate

☐ Establish in your own mind the need for investing in real estate in order to stay ahead of taxes and inflation. Remember, 95 percent of the retired-age people in this country end up practically broke because they failed to realize the importance of investing the bulk of their retirement funds in real estate and other non-fixed investments. This investment vehicle *increases* in value because of it.

☐ Never forget that your primary purpose of investing is to create a life-long estate for yourself and your loved ones. You may not always want to work for a living. Someday, you'll want to get off that treadmill and relax and enjoy life. The time may come when you are no longer able to work—but your money, your investments never retire. Twenty-four hours a day, seven days a week, 365 days a year, they continue earning money for you. You are the only one who can determine just how much money they earn and how hard they work.

☐ Keep in mind that your future financial security depends on *where* you invest your funds. If they are not producing enough to more than offset the effects of taxes and inflation, you can plan on getting caught in the same financial "trap" as has 95 percent of our population. Unless, of course, you were wealthy from the beginning.

☐ Program yourself right now to at least give real estate investing a try. Once you do, you will never be without it again.

2. Establish Your Investment Goals

☐ Prepare a current financial statement so you know exactly where you stand today.

☐ Prepare a long-range financial statement estimating major expenditures you know you will face in the future.

☐ Determine how much money you think you will need to maintain your present standard of living after you retire.

☐ Allow for inflation. When estimating how much you will need in 10, 15, or 20 years, do not make the mistake made by 95 percent of the retired age people in this country. Allow for at least 10 percent inflation per year. This means that in 10 years it will cost $20,000 to do what you can do this year for $10,000. Suppose you allow for 10 percent and inflation only averages eight or nine percent over the next several years? You're ahead of the game. It's better to have more than you need than not quite enough.

Remember, in a real estate investment, inflation works *for* you instead of *against* you. But you must still determine how many of today's dollars you will need to maintain your present standard of living on tomorrow's economy.

3. Locate Sources of Investment Capital

☐ Consider such sources of start-up capital as savings accounts, cash value life insurance, borrowing against stocks and refinancing of other real estate.

☐ Consider the possibility of borrowing from people you know who would like to earn a higher interest than on their present investment and still have security.

☐ Save one salary. When both husband and wife are working, save one salary if possible to accumulate for investment purposes.

☐ Don't over-leverage. Don't kid yourself. Real estate investing is not like a savings account where $500 or $1000 is a large investment. Although there are ways of buying some properties with little or no cash down, be careful not to over-leverage. You do not want to be in a position where you have to "feed" your investment to keep it running unless you are prepared to take that risk.

☐ Consider a group investment when you cannot come up with enough cash to at least make a down payment on a small rental house.

☐ Buy with no money down. If you decide on owning your own property, without partners, several avenues are open to you if you have little or no investment capital:

a) A property can be *optioned*, if you know you will have enough investment capital available to you in a short period of time to exercise the option and purchase the building.

b) An owner who is very motivated to sell may be willing to consider a *lease/purchase* or an *outright sale* with no cash down payment required. Look at both of these alternatives very cautiously. Can it be purchased at a *below market* price to make the risk worth taking?

c) Purchasing a *distressed* property can be very profitable to you if you are willing to work at it and get it turned around into a profitable investment. Again, these properties must be purchased at *below* market value to be worth considering.

Do not let the lack of investment capital stop you. Once you get that first property and make a profit, you're on your way.

☐ Enlarge your investment holdings as your capital increases. Keep in mind that real estate is not a one-time investment. Just because you own one building does not mean you cannot own more. If you're in the stock market, you probably don't own stock in just one corporation—you diversify. The same holds true with real estate. As your equity builds up, you may want to spread your investments out over several properties. You will be surprised how fast your equity will build in real estate.

4. How Involved Will You Become in Managing Your Property?

☐ Decide how involved you want to become in its operation before venturing into your real estate investment. Consider your options:

   a) You can handle everything yourself.
   b) You can hire a resident manager who lives in the building and takes care of all the minor, day-to-day problems that may arise. You are still in charge of renting apartments, collecting rents and paying bills.
   c) You can employ a professional property management company to handle the renting, bookkeeping, and management end of the property operation. You are then left with a management-free investment. This, of course, costs money and reduces your overall return but, depending on your individual situation, you can be as active or inactive in the day-to-day operation of your investment as you wish.

☐ Do not pass up real estate investing because you are too busy to take care of it yourself. Even after paying the cost of a full management team, your rewards from your real estate investment will still far exceed any of your other investments.

5. Select the Type of Investment Right for You

☐ Consider the various types of real estate investments that may be available to you and right for your particular situation. Single family homes are perhaps the least expensive way to start. On the other hand, an office or store building may offer particular advantages that make such an investment the best one possible for you.

☐ Consider vacant land if you are strictly a speculator. Vacant land offers the greatest appreciation potential.

☐ Consider a small rental apartment building if you are a beginning investor and this is your first real estate investment. This type of investment is the easiest to understand, and you will generally have a large selection from which to choose.

☐ Consider some of the other types of real estate properties available in your area as your investments grow.

6. Determine the Form of Ownership

☐ Consider some form of group ownership if your investment capital on your first venture is limited.

☐ Try to buy controlling interest (more than 50 percent) of the investment if you form a partnership with another investor(s). This can help to alleviate some of the problems that partnership arrangements often create.

☐ Avoid corporate ownership of real estate investments. Under this form of ownership, you are subject to double taxation and will not realize depreciation and tax shelter benefits.

☐ Consider a limited partnership arrangement if you become involved in group ownership. Limited partnerships are excellent forms of group investing—but you must find a knowledgeable general partner. He is the one who will be responsible for the group and the success of the investment.

☐ Make every effort to go it on your own. Individual ownership will generally bring you greater financial rewards and personal satisfaction.

7. Locate Your Investment Property

☐ Give serious consideration to working with a knowledgeable investment Realtor if this is your first venture. The advantages you gain will make it well worth your while. He probably has properties available that you would never locate on your own. While working with him, learn as much as you can. He should be well experienced in what you are learning for the first time, and he will guide you through the analysis and selection of the right investment. He will also get you started on the right foot in the operation and management of your investment.

☐ Do not rush into the purchase of a property that you are not convinced is a good one. Take your time.

☐ Do not, however, delay purchasing until the "perfect" investment comes along—one that meets all of your investment dreams. You will never find it and may never get started in real estate investing. Even if the best you have found falls shorts of your ideal property, compare your expected returns with what you are currently earning on that money. Your thinking will probably become more flexible.

☐ Give yourself a choice of investment properties. Even when there is a small selection of properties for sale, keep researching the market until you can give yourself a choice of at least two. By researching the market, you will also give yourself a valuable education in what the area competition will be when you buy. You will also be able to assure yourself that, even though you could not find an investment that meets all of your investment ideals, it is still the best one you can locate in the present market and it will still give you a sound, profitable start on your real estate investment program.

8. Analyze Your Prospective Investment

☐ Analyze your investment carefully and thoroughly after locating it. Verify all details, especially the income and expenses the seller shows.

☐ Develop a property analysis form you feel comfortable using. It will also serve as a reminder for items you want to know, such as type of units, age of the property, rent breakdown per unit, expense items, lot size, etc.

☐ Use the following list of the various phases of the property to analyze different positions of the potential investment. If the property does not seem to make financial sense after your initial analysis has been made, perhaps altering one or more of these will improve the financial picture and make the property a good investment for you.

    a) *Income:* Can rents be increased, and can they be increased soon after you purchase the property? Is better management needed? Maybe income is suffering because of poor or non-existant management. Would a change in the type of tenant in the building allow for higher rents? Could the building be used in some other way to increase income, such as a motel, small offices, etc. Be certain local zoning allows for any proposed changes.

    b) *Expenses:* Take a close look at operating expenses. Are any of them excessive? If they are, will you be able to lower them? You may not have control over some. If you intend doing your own lawn maintenance and repairs, you may save some money.

c) *Financing:* In Chapter 9, you saw how to adjust the return on an investment by merely applying various financing techniques. Perhaps one will turn your prospective property into a sound, profitable investment. Try various alternatives in financing.

d) *Your overall benefits:* Don't look just at "pre-tax cash flow." Consider all *four* returns you can expect. Determine what your property will give you in the way of a return after taxes. That is the most important result.

e) *Price:* Some properties simply will not make sense unless you can get the seller to accept a lower price.

☐ Never make a decision to purchase based on the "esthetic beauty" of the building or by using a simple rule of thumb to determine its value. Take the time to prepare a property analysis. This is the only reasonably certain way of making the right investment decision. If your property analysis shows that the property does not make financial sense, forget how "pretty" it may be. Don't buy it!

9. Use the Financing Technique That Gives You the Best Results

☐ Use various financing techniques to alter the terms under which you may want to purchase the property. Try various alternatives to see which one gives the best results from your investment viewpoint. Many real estate transactions can be made or broken by the use of creative financing or the lack of it. Use financing to your advantage.

☐ Determine which of these financing alternatives not only serves your needs but will also be acceptable to the seller when he is involved in carrying all or part of the financing. Remember, you will have to "sell" it to him when you make your offer.

☐ Determine just how much financing you feel comfortable carrying. You may be able to purchase a property with only five to ten percent down payment, but if you are going to lie awake nights worrying about your large mortgage payments, don't buy on those terms. You'll be better off settling for a smaller property with smaller mortgages.

☐ Keep the benefits of leverage in mind. Once you decide what you will accept, make the most of it. No other form of investing offers the high use of leverage (other peoples' money) that is available in real estate investing.

10. Consider the Tax Consequences

☐ Analyze your investment from a tax viewpoint. Remember that it does not matter how much you make but how much you get to keep after taxes that is important.

☐ Make maximum use of depreciation and tax shelters. Use the method that offers you the greatest after-tax return on your investment, unless your tax counsel gives you a logical reason *not* to. Remember, if you are a 30 percent taxpayer and your property shows a $10,000 tax loss at the end of the year, it's like putting an extra $3000 cash in your pocket after taxes. That is a "real" part of your investment returns.

☐ Do not try to do it alone. Use a knowledgeable real estate tax accountant to make recommendations.

11. Negotiate the Purchase

☐ Prepare a formal offer to purchase contract to be accompanied by a deposit check prior to making an offer to purchase on the building you have selected. That is the only way a seller will listen and be willing to negotiate on price and terms.

☐ Insert the clauses in the contract that you want for your protection, such as verification of income and expenses by your accountant.

☐ Be reasonable on your offer. You know what the property is worth, at least to you. Do not try to steal it. You'll probably succeed in insulting the seller and having him refuse to sell you the property at any price. But *do* offer five to ten percent less than he is asking.

☐ Go into the meeting knowing what price and terms you will be willing to accept. If his final offer falls short of these terms, do not agree to anything until you have had time to re-analyze the investment based on his final offer. Once you and the seller both execute a contract, it's binding. You cannot change your mind.

☐ "Lock up" the property with a fully executed contract by both parties, including initials next to any changes that were written in later, when the price and terms negotiated are acceptable to both you and the seller. You have reached the point of finding the property you want at a price you can justify. You don't want to lose it now.

12. Take Necessary Steps Before and After Closing

☐ Prepare an estimated closing statement prior to closing so you have an idea of how much cash you will need to close.

☐ Employ a title company or attorney to handle the closing for you. They know how to verify that you are getting clear title to the property. *Never* close your own real estate transaction.

☐ Make a list of the items you expect to receive from the seller at the closing. This includes: keys, insurance policy, original leases, list of service people, any service contracts, and plans and surveys of the property.

☐ Have the "house" utilities changed over to your name. You'll be starting off on the wrong foot if all of the tenant's water is turned off by the water department the day after closing. I've seen it happen.

☐ Visit your property after closing. It will give you a good feeling to know that you now own it.

☐ Meet your tenants. Take a close look at your investment. Walk around the building, taking any complaints you hear with a grain of salt—and you can plan on hearing a few. You should leave your new investment with a feeling of excitement that you have not had since you purchased your first home.

13. Set Up a Record Keeping System

☐ Establish two separate bank accounts immediately after closing: one, a savings account to hold the tenants' security deposits and advance rents; the second, a building checking account to handle all income and expenses for the building. Keeping it separate from your regular checking account will greatly simplify your bookkeeping.

☐ Set up a simple, single entry bookkeeping system for your property. Posting can be done from your building's checking account. At the end of each year, your book serves as a convenient record for tax reporting purposes.

14. Develop Leases That Serve Your Purpose

☐ Develop a lease form that best serves your purpose. Start with a simple form printed lease available at most stationery stores.

☐ Determine who is responsible for what—water, electric, repairs, etc.

☐ Require security deposits and, if possible, advance rents.

☐ Have your leases come due at the best time of year for you. Also, make all rents due on the first of each month.

☐ Try to have tenants lined up prior to a lease expiration. Know what will attract tenants to your building and promote it.

☐ Qualify your tenants before leasing. The best way to have trouble-free tenants is to properly screen them *prior* to leasing them an apartment.

☐ Write cost of living increases into any extensions. Remember, a lease protects a tenant more than it does you. When you enter into a lease for more than one year, be sure to have cost of living increases written into any extensions.

☐ Maintain your building. Remember, a large portion of the expected increase in value of your property while you own it is dependent on maintaining your building, keeping it leased to "quality" tenants and keeping your rents in line with others in the area.

☐ Raise your rents when necessary. Failure to raise rents to combat increased expenses and inflation will result in a lower selling price when you decide to move up into another property. "Reasonable" rent increases are not only a necessity to you but are also expected by your tenants.

☐ Do not become close friends with your tenants. If you do, they will end up sharing in *your* investment profits—and don't forget *who's* money purchased the property.

15. Monitor Your Investment With Return in Mind

☐ Don't fall in love with your property. That could be the start of failing to realize your investment goals. Unlike your home, your real estate investment is nothing more than a "money-making machine." When it no longer does what it is expected to do, get rid of it and buy another.

☐ Monitor your investment. Like you, your investment needs an annual checkup to be certain it is still performing well. Use the simple form in Chapter 15 to determine your actual present return.

When the time comes that you should be in another, larger property, *do it*.

16. Structure the Sale to Suit Your Needs

☐ Establish a reasonable selling price for your property based on actual market value. Do not let "pride of ownership" influence your decision.

☐ Consider listing your property exclusively with an investment Realtor.

☐ If you are selling yourself, prepare attractive ads for your property and cultivate a "soft sell" sales approach to prospective buyers.

☐ When structuring the sale, remember that taking back secondary financing reduces your cash available for reinvestment.

☐ Consider an installment sale to spread your capital gains tax liability over a few years rather than paying it all in the year of sale.

☐ Consider all after-tax alternatives and the time value of money before selling. Consult your tax advisor.

☐ Consider exchanging your property. You may want to consider a tax deferred exchange where you have the opportunity of completely deferring any capital gains tax.

17. Get to Know the Rules of Thumb

☐ Become familiar with the various rules of thumb. They will help you quickly analyze a property that is of interest to determine if it is worth pursuing. Know which rules of thumb are poor methods of determining a property's value.

☐ *Never* rely on a rule of thumb to make a determination to buy or sell. Always work from a complete property analysis.

☐ Become familiar with the various techniques that will be helpful to you in selecting and analyzing investments. Understand the ways in which an appraiser determines the market value of an investment property. Learn how capitalization or CAP rate works and what it means. Obtain a mortgage amortization book. You will need it.

☐ Recognize the difference between a "buyer's" and a "seller's" market. If you buy during a buyer's market and sell during a seller's market, it will be much easier for you. On the other hand, you cannot afford to wait until the "perfect" market opportunity for you arises. It may never happen.

18. Consider Leasing Space to Yourself

☐ Consider purchasing your own office building and leasing it back to your professional corporation if you are a professional businessman, attorney, physician, dentist, Realtor, etc. Tremendous tax advantages may be available to you as a result.

☐ Take care that you are paying yourself reasonable rent, comparable to other rents in the area.

☐ Execute a formal lease between yourself, a private investor, and your corporation.

☐ Expense the cost of any major improvements you make to your building over the useful life of the improvements. If your corporation pays for the improvements, you can reduce your corporate tax liability accordingly.

19. Secure Your Financial Future

☐ Plan on pyramiding your real estate investments to build your estate.

☐ Do not go into real estate investing expecting to become a millionaire in twelve months. Your goal is to acquire *sound* investments and let appreciation take over. Your primary purpose of investing is to secure your financial future.

So now we are back to "taking that first step." Don't be afraid to take the plunge. If you invest using the knowledge you have gained from this book and purchase a well-located, sound, income producing property, your investment should be secure.

You have a distinct advantage in a real estate investment. You have the opportunity of personally examining your investment and verifying its income and expenses and more importantly, controlling its operation. From this point of view, you have more control over a real estate investment than you do your shares of stock. Investing in real estate has long been recognized as the best way to build an estate. No other form of investing offers you the combination of leverage, tax shelter, high return on cash invested and appreciation that can be realized in real estate. "Under all is the land." Each year it is becoming more and more valuable.

You probably will end up quite wealthy. It is hard *not* to do through a prudent real estate investment program. Your possible financial rewards in real estate investing are second to none. But sound investment techniques rather than high risk, get rich quick schemes are the more practical appraoch to real estate investing.

You now *have* these sound investment techniques. You now have the knowledge you need to make *your* fortune in real estate. You are now ready to join the ranks of successful real estate investors, that top five percent whose investments have made them financially independent.

21

Questions and Answers
About Real Estate Investing

The following pages contain a series of questions and answers on some of the basic subjects that were covered in this book. Take time to answer them. They will serve as a review and tell you how much you learned. After each answer is a number(s) indicating the chapter(s) in which that particular subject was covered.

Q. What are the four types of returns available from investment real estate?
   A. Spendable income, principal reduction or equtiy buildup, appreciation, and tax shelter of other income. (1)   (17)

Q. How do you determine if it makes sense to refinance your home to obtain investment capital?
   A. Use the formula in Chapter 3 which tells you how much you must earn on the borrowed cash in order to offset the added mortgage payments on your home. (3)

Q. Why must you consider the effects of inflation when establishing your investment goals?

> A. Ninety-five percent of this country's population over the age of 65 are practically broke because they failed to consider the effects of inflation on their retirement funds. You can plan on needing twice as much in ten years to do what you can today on your present spendable income. (2)

Q. Why is it extremely important to carefully analyze a property that can be purchased with no money down?

> A. Any property that is 100 percent leveraged will probably be at a break even basis or below. It is important to realize that one extra vacancy will no doubt require taking money out of your pocket to keep the investment going.

Q. Why is zoning important when considering the purchase of vacant land?

> A. The future value of vacant land depends upon the use that can be made of it. (5)

Q. How do hallways and wall thickness enter into consideration when leasing office space?

> A. This space is non-usable. It is usually charged to the tenant when figuring his gross leasable space. He pays for that space instead of you.

Q. What is the purpose of a "tax stop" in a shopping center lease?

> A. A tax stop requires the tenant to pay any increases in real estate taxes over the base year. (5)

Q. What is CAM?

> A. Common Area Maintenance, the charge to commercial tenants to pay for maintaining common areas such as hallways and parking lots. (5)

Q. What are the advantages of a sale/leaseback?

> A. Sale/leasebacks offer the investor a management-free investment. The tenant generally pays for everything except mortgage payments. (5)

Q. What are the advantages of vacant land over improved property for investment purposes?

> A. Vacant land is usually held for resale profit in the future. Profits will usually be higher than on improved properties. There is no management requirements with vacant land. (5)

Q. What is the primary problem that occurs when property is held by a partnership.

A. Partners tend to have disagreements. (6)

Q. What is the difference between the "general" partner and the "limited" partner in a limited partnership?

A. The general partner oversees the operation of the investment, makes all of the decisions in its operation, and is liable for the financial success of the investment. Limited partners have no say in the operation and are limited only financially to the extent of their initial investment. (6)

Q. How important is location when selecting investment real estate?

A. Location is always important, but not as much as in selecting a home. Some of the best real estate investments may not be in the prime locations. (7)

Q. How do you determine what the present owner paid for the property?

A. The recorded deed at the county courthouse has documentary stamps attached. The purchase price can be determined from the value of the stamps. (7)

Q. What is the difference between capital improvements and repairs and maintenance?

A. Capital improvements are major improvements, such as a new roof or a swimming pool, and are written-off over a period of years. Maintenance items are repairs that are paid for and written-off as an expense item that year. (8)

Q. What is Net Operating Income (N.O.I.).

A. N.O.I. is the income produced by the property after an allowance for vacancies and operating expenses, but before mortgage payments are made. (8)

Q. How can you verify the income produced by the property?

A. Check with the tenants. Leases can be altered by unethical sellers. (8)

Q. How much leverage should you use when purchasing investment real estate?

A. As a rule of thumb, buy the largest property you can with the cash you have available. This must be tempered with how much leverage you are comfortable in having. Some investors could not sleep nights knowing they owned a property that was 90 percent financed. (9)

Q. When might it be advantageous to refinance, even at a higher rate of interest, than to assume existing mortgages?

    A. When existing mortgages have short terms remaining so payments for principal greatly reduce cash flow. When one or more of the mortgages has a balloon payment due in the near future. (9)

Q. Under what circumstances might it pay a buyer to offer a price *greater* than the listed price?

    A. To obtain better terms for the sale, such as a lower down payment? (9)

Q. How can you convince an owner to accept a lower down payment?

    A. Offer him more for the property, increase the interest rate on his mortgage. (9)

Q. What four factors enter into determining depreciation?

    A. Land/Improvement/Personal Property ratio, Useful life, Component vs. composite depreciation, and type of depreciation used (S/L, 125 percent DB, etc.). (10)

Q. How does a "tax shelter" work?

    A. The depreciation benefits on the investment property give the investment a paper "loss" that can be carried over to your ordinary income, thereby reducing your tax liability. (10)

Q. What is meant by the "time value" of money?

    A. Are you better off taking a smaller sum of money today than a larger sum in the future? What can you earn of that money if you have it today? (10)   (16)

Q. Why do you separate personal property from improvements when figuring depreciation?

    A. Personal property can be depreciated more quickly to give a greater tax shelter. (10)

Q. What is the difference between title insurance and an abstract?

    A. Title insurance is an owner's insurance policy protecting his title to the property from any unforeseen flaw. The abstract is a written, recorded history of the property from the time it was acquired by the United States.

Q. What is a "tenant estopple letter" and why is it used?

    A. A letter sent to the tenants asking them to verify their lease term, amount of security deposit, and the rent they are paying. (12)

Q. Why should security deposits be placed in an account separate from your property operating account?
  A. Security deposits belong to the tenant until they are disbursed at the termination of the lease. (13)

Q. When "posting" your mortgage payments to your ledger, why do you separate the principal portion of the payment from the interest portion?
  A. Interest payments are deducted from your income for tax purposes. Principal payments are not. (13)

Q. How do you determine how much rent to charge?
  A. Make an area survey to determine what your competition is charging. (14)

Q. Should you offer renewal options?
  A. Renewal options should be offered only if cost of living increases are written in to protect the lessor from the effects of inflation. (14)

Q. What factors enter into determining when to sell?
  A. Such factors as: change of goals, problems with the property, excess equity in the property, loss of tax shelter benefits, and reduced return of your current invested capital all point to a decision to sell. (15)

Q. Can you avoid capital gains tax by selling your investment property and purchasing another, more expensive one within 24 months?
  A. No. It's not like selling your home.

Q. What are the advantages of exchanging rather than selling to acquire a new property?
  A. The primary advantage to exchanging is to defer payment of capital gains tax. (16)

Q. What is CAP or capitalization rate?
  A. Capitalization rate is the ratio between the net operating income and the market value of the property. (17)

Q. What is the IRV formula and how does it work?
  A. The IRV formula is $\dfrac{I}{R \times V}$ where I = N.O.I., R = Rate, and V = Market Value. When any of the two factors are known, you can use this formula to find the third. Use it to determine a market value when you know the net operating income and rate you want to earn; the rate when you know the market value and the N.O.I. being produced by the investment; and the

N.O.I. a building must produce to give you a certain return based on the market value of the property. (17)

Q. Why should you buy the largest number of units you can with the investment capital you have available?

A. Operating expenses tend to be less, on a per unit basis, in a larger building. Vacancies are also less critical in larger buildings. (17)

Q. Which of the three appraisal methods is the most reliable for you to use?

A. The income approach establishes value based on the income actually being produced by the investment. (17)

Q. What is meant by "pyramiding" and how can it work for you?

A. The practice of pyramiding transfers your equity every so many years into a much larger investment. This is repeated several times whenever you can own a property twice the size of your present one, with no additional outlay of capital, until your final investment is capable of supporting you for the remainder of your life. (19)

Since the heart of this book is built around the use of a property analysis form, the following question is a practical example of analyzing a typical investment property. See how close you can come to the answer page.

Q. You are considering the purchase of the Quiet Arms Apartments owned by Mr. Otto Owner. The building consists of twelve units. Eight, one bedroom/one bath apartments renting for $225 a month; and four, two bedroom/two bath apartments renting for $250 a month. Here are the other facts yhou need to know to prepare the analysis statement:

Purchase price is $250,000

First mortgage is $135,000 at nine percent interest, with monthly payments of $1,537.50 including principal, interest, taxes, and insurance. (Don't forget, you must remove the taxes and insurance from that payment.)

The owner will carry a second mortgage with 29 percent down payment ($72,000).

He will carry the mortgage for 20 years at 12 percent interest.

Area vacancies run five percent of scheduled gross income.

Real estate taxes are $2900 a year.

Insurance is $1050 a year.

House electric runs $20 a *month*.

Licenses are $25 a year.

You want to hire a resident manager, which will cost you $100 a month.

Water and sewer charge averages $50 a month.

You plan on five percent of the gross operating income for maintenance.

Trash removal is $20 a month.

The coin laundry brings in $100 a month in additional income.

You intend to use the following depreciation schedule:

    Land value—15 percent

    Improvements—75 percent, 25 year life, 125 percent DB depreciation

    Personal Property—10 percent, 5 year, straight-line depreciation

Prepare a property analysis form using this information. Work it all the way down to Real Estate Taxable Income, after depreciation. Look at Figure 10-5 in Chapter 10 if you need help.

• PROPERTY ANALYSIS •

Name: _Quiet Arms Apts._

Location: _____

Type of Property: _12 Unit Apt._ Area. _____

LIST PRICE _$250,000_

CASH REQ'D. _72,000 (29%)_

EXISTING ASSUMABLE FINANCING:

	Amount	Ann. Pmt.	Int.	Years To Go
1st $	135,000	14,113	9 %	
2nd			%	
3rd			%	

POTENTIAL FINANCING:

	$			Years
1st $			%	
2nd	43,000	5,682	12 %	20
3rd			%	

Folio:	Ex — S.O.O	File:
Date:	Units: 12	Lister:
Zoning	Pool	Parking
Size	Rec. Rm.	A-C
Sq. Ft.	Util. Rm.	Heat
Age 8 YEARS	Office	T V
Stories	Lobby	Furniture
Sewers	Elevators	Waterfront
Constr.		

Description —	# Units	Rent Sch.
1 BEDROOM, 1 BATH	8	$225/mo.
2 BEDROOM, 2 BATH	4	$250/mo.

SCHEDULE GROSS INCOME		33	600
Less: Vacancy & Credit Loss 5%		1	680
GROSS OPERATING INCOME		31	920
Less: Operating Expenses			
Taxes	2 900		
Insurance	1 050		
Utilities - ELECTRIC	240		
Advertising			
Licenses & Permits	25		
Management			
Payroll & Payroll Taxes	1 200		
Supplies			
Services - WATER/SEWER	600		
Maintenance 5%	1 596		
Reserve for Replacement			
Ground Lease			
TRASH REMOVAL	240		
TOTAL EXPENSES 25 %		7	851
OPERATING INCOME		24	069
Plus Other Income - LAUNDRY		1	200
NET OPERATING INCOME		25	269

COMMENTS: _____ CODE: _____

DEPRECIATION SCHEDULE:
LAND - 15%
IMPROVEMENTS - 75%, 25 YR.
LIFE, 125% D.B.
PERS. PROP. - 10% - 5 YR - S/L

INFORMATION HEREIN IS BELIEVED TO BE
ACCURATE BUT IS NOT WARRANTED

INCOME ADJUSTED TO FINANCING:	Actual ☐		Potential ☒	Equity $ 72,000			
NET OPERATING INCOME	Cap Rate - List Price:		%				25 269
Less: Loan Payment	3rd Loan	2nd Loan	1st Loan	TOTAL			
Interest		5 160	12 150	17 310			
Principal		522	1 963	2 485			
Total Loan Payment		5 682	14 113	19 795	19 795		
GROSS SPENDABLE INCOME	Rate: 7.6 %		(GSI ÷ EQUITY)		5 474		
Plus: Principal Payment					2 485		
GROSS EQUITY INCOME	Rate: 10.6 %		(GEI ÷ EQUITY)		7 959		
Less: Depreciation	Personal Property = $5000		Improvements = $9,375		14 375		
REAL ESTATE TAXABLE INCOME				TAX LOSS	(6 416)		

---

* Based on Form "B," copyrighted by REALTORS NATIONAL MARKETING INSTITUTE
OF NATIONAL ASSOCIATION OF REALTORS. Copyright 1974. All rights reserved.
Used with permission of copyright owner.
** Reprinted with permission of L.C. Judd & Co., Inc.

Answer

Appendixes

COMPARATIVE DEPRECIATION TABLES

The following tables show the annual and cumulative depreciation for various useful lives under the straight-line, 200 percent-declining-balance, 150 percent-declining-balance, 125 percent-declining-balance, and sum-of-the-years-digits methods. All amounts are expressed as percentages of the basis of the property at the time the useful life begins.

How It Works: Assume you have $100,000 in depreciable improvements, *after* the land value has been removed. You intend to use the 125 percent declining balance method of depreciation and a 25-year useful life. Looking at the 25-year useful life table, under the 125 percent declining balance columns, we see that the first year's annual depreciation allowance is five percent of the $100,000 improvement we are depreciation, or $5000. Now look at the fifth year. We can only take 4.07 percent of the $100,000 in the fifth year. Hence the term "declining balance." Under the fifth year cumulative column we see that we have taken a total of 22.62 percent or $22,620 total depreciation during the five-year period.

Year	Straight-Line		200%-Declining-Balance		150%-Declining-Balance		Sum-of-Digits	
	Annual %	Cum. %	Annual %	Cum. %	Annual %	Cum. %	Annual %	Cum. %
3-YEAR LIFE								
1	33.33	33.33	66.66	66.66	50.00	50.00	50.00	50.00
2	33.33	66.66	22.22	88.88	25.00	75.00	33.33	83.33
3	33.34	100.00	7.41	96.29	12.50	87.50	16.67	100.00
4-YEAR LIFE								
1	25.00	25.00	50.00	50.00	37.50	37.50	40.00	40.00
2	25.00	50.00	25.00	75.00	23.44	60.94	30.00	70.00
3	25.00	75.00	12.50	87.50	14.65	75.59	20.00	90.00
4	25.00	100.00	6.25	93.75	9.15	84.74	10.00	100.00
5-YEAR LIFE								
1	20.00	20.00	40.00	40.00	30.00	30.00	33.33	33.33
2	20.00	40.00	24.00	64.00	21.00	51.00	26.67	60.00
3	20.00	60.00	14.40	78.40	14.70	65.70	20.00	80.00
4	20.00	80.00	8.64	87.04	10.29	75.99	13.33	93.33
5	20.00	100.00	5.18	92.22	7.20	83.19	6.67	100.00
6-YEAR LIFE								
1	16.67	16.67	33.34	33.34	25.00	25.00	28.57	28.57
2	16.67	33.34	22.22	55.56	18.75	43.75	23.81	52.38
3	16.66	50.00	14.81	70.37	14.06	57.81	19.05	71.43
4	16.67	66.67	9.87	80.24	10.55	68.36	14.29	85.72
5	16.67	83.34	6.58	86.82	7.91	76.27	9.52	95.24
6	16.66	100.00	4.39	91.21	5.93	82.20	4.76	100.00
7-YEAR LIFE								
1	14.28	14.28	28.57	28.57	21.43	21.43	25.00	25.00
2	14.28	28.56	20.41	48.98	16.83	38.26	21.43	46.43
3	14.29	42.85	14.58	63.56	13.23	51.49	17.86	64.29
4	14.29	57.14	10.41	73.97	10.40	61.89	14.29	78.58
5	14.29	71.43	7.44	81.41	8.17	70.06	10.71	89.29
6	14.29	85.72	5.31	86.72	6.42	76.48	7.14	96.43
7	14.28	100.00	3.79	90.51	5.04	81.52	3.57	100.00
8-YEAR LIFE								
1	12.50	12.50	25.00	25.00	18.75	18.75	22.22	22.22
2	12.50	25.00	18.75	43.75	15.23	33.98	19.44	41.66
3	12.50	37.50	14.06	57.81	12.38	46.36	16.67	58.33
4	12.50	50.00	10.55	68.36	10.06	56.42	13.89	72.22
5	12.50	62.50	7.91	76.27	8.17	64.59	11.11	83.33
6	12.50	75.00	5.93	82.20	6.64	71.23	8.33	91.66
7	12.50	87.50	4.45	86.65	5.39	76.62	5.56	97.22
8	12.50	100.00	3.34	89.99	4.38	81.00	2.78	100.00
9-YEAR LIFE								
1	11.11	11.11	22.22	22.22	16.67	16.67	20.00	20.00
2	11.11	22.22	17.28	39.50	13.89	30.56	17.78	37.78
3	11.11	33.33	13.44	52.94	11.57	42.13	15.56	53.34
4	11.11	44.44	10.45	63.39	9.65	51.78	13.33	66.67
5	11.11	55.55	8.13	71.52	8.04	59.82	11.11	77.78
6	11.11	66.66	6.32	77.84	6.70	66.52	8.89	86.67
7	11.11	77.77	4.92	82.76	5.58	72.10	6.67	93.34
8	11.11	88.88	3.83	86.59	4.65	76.75	4.44	97.78
9	11.12	100.00	2.98	89.57	3.88	80.63	2.22	100.00

Comparative Depreciation Tables (continued)

Year	Straight-Line Annual %	Cum. %	200%-Declining-Balance Annual %	Cum. %	150%-Declining-Balance Annual %	Cum. %	Sum-of-Digits Annual %	Cum. %
				10-YEAR LIFE				
1	10.00	10.00	20.00	20.00	15.00	15.00	18.18	18.18
2	10.00	20.00	16.00	36.00	12.75	27.75	16.37	34.55
3	10.00	30.00	12.80	48.80	10.84	38.59	14.56	49.09
4	10.00	40.00	10.24	59.04	9.21	47.80	12.73	61.82
5	10.00	50.00	8.19	67.23	7.83	55.63	10.91	72.73
6	10.00	60.00	6.56	73.79	6.66	62.29	9.09	81.82
7	10.00	70.00	5.24	79.03	5.66	67.95	7.27	89.09
8	10.00	80.00	4.19	83.22	4.81	72.76	5.46	94.55
9	10.00	90.00	3.36	86.58	4.09	76.85	3.63	98.18
10	10.00	100.00	2.68	89.26	3.47	80.32	1.82	100.00
				15-YEAR LIFE				
1	6.67	6.67	13.33	13.33	10.00	10.00	12.50	12.50
2	6.66	13.33	11.56	24.89	9.00	19.00	11.67	24.17
3	6.67	20.00	10.01	34.90	8.10	27.10	10.83	35.00
4	6.67	26.67	8.68	43.58	7.29	34.39	10.00	45.00
5	6.66	33.33	7.53	51.11	6.56	40.95	9.17	54.17
6	6.67	40.00	6.51	57.62	5.90	46.85	8.33	62.50
7	6.67	46.67	5.65	63.27	5.32	52.17	7.50	70.00
8	6.66	53.33	4.90	68.17	4.78	56.95	6.67	76.67
9	6.67	60.00	4.25	72.42	4.30	61.25	5.83	82.50
10	6.67	66.67	3.67	76.09	3.88	65.13	5.00	87.50
11	6.66	73.33	3.19	79.28	3.49	68.62	4.17	91.67
12	6.67	80.00	2.76	82.04	3.14	71.76	3.33	95.00
13	6.67	86.67	2.40	84.44	2.82	74.58	2.50	97.50
14	6.66	93.33	2.07	86.51	2.54	77.12	1.67	99.17
15	6.67	100.00	1.80	88.31	2.29	79.41	.83	100.00

Year	Straight-Line Annual %	Cum. %	200%-Declining-Balance Annual %	Cum. %	150%-Declining-Balance Annual %	Cum. %	125%-Declining-Balance Annual %	Cum. %	Sum-of-Digits Annual %	Cum. %
						20-YEAR LIFE					
1	5.00	5.00	10.00	10.00	7.50	7.50	6.25	6.25	9.52	9.52
2	5.00	10.00	9.00	19.00	6.94	14.44	5.86	12.11	9.05	18.57
3	5.00	15.00	8.10	27.10	6.42	20.86	5.49	17.60	8.57	27.14
4	5.00	20.00	7.29	34.39	5.94	26.80	5.15	22.75	8.10	35.24
5	5.00	25.00	6.56	40.95	5.49	32.29	4.83	27.58	7.62	42.86
6	5.00	30.00	5.91	46.86	5.08	37.37	4.53	32.11	7.14	50.00
7	5.00	35.00	5.31	52.17	4.70	42.07	4.24	36.35	6.67	56.67
8	5.00	40.00	4.78	56.95	4.35	46.42	3.98	40.33	6.19	62.86
9	5.00	45.00	4.31	61.26	4.02	50.44	3.73	44.06	5.71	68.57
10	5.00	50.00	3.87	65.13	3.71	54.15	3.50	47.55	5.24	73.81
11	5.00	55.00	3.49	68.62	3.44	57.59	3.28	50.83	4.76	78.57
12	5.00	60.00	3.14	71.76	3.18	60.77	3.07	53.90	4.29	82.86
13	5.00	65.00	2.82	74.58	2.94	63.71	2.88	56.79	3.81	86.67
14	5.00	70.00	2.54	77.12	2.72	66.43	2.70	59.49	3.33	90.00
15	5.00	75.00	2.29	79.41	2.52	68.95	2.53	62.02	2.86	92.86
16	5.00	80.00	2.06	81.47	2.33	71.28	2.37	64.39	2.38	95.24
17	5.00	85.00	1.85	83.32	2.15	73.43	2.23	66.62	1.90	97.14
18	5.00	90.00	1.67	84.99	1.99	75.42	2.09	68.70	1.43	98.57
19	5.00	95.00	1.50	86.49	1.84	77.26	1.96	70.66	.95	99.52
20	5.00	100.00	1.35	87.84	1.70	78.96	1.83	72.49	.48	100.00

Comparative Depreciation Tables (continued)

Year	Straight-Line		200%-Declining-Balance		150%-Declining-Balance		125%-Declining-Balance		Sum-of-Digits	
	Annual %	Cum. %	Annual %	Cum. %	Annual %	Cum. %	Annual %	Cum. %	Annual %	Cum. %
					25-YEAR LIFE					
1	4.00	4.00	8.00	8.00	6.00	6.00	5.00	5.00	7.69	7.69
2	4.00	8.00	7.36	15.36	5.64	11.64	4.75	9.75	7.39	15.08
3	4.00	12.00	6.77	22.13	5.30	16.94	4.51	14.26	7.07	22.15
4	4.00	16.00	6.23	28.36	4.98	21.92	4.29	18.55	6.77	28.92
5	4.00	20.00	5.73	34.09	4.68	26.60	4.07	22.62	6.47	35.39
6	4.00	24.00	5.27	39.36	4.40	31.00	3.87	26.49	6.15	41.54
7	4.00	28.00	4.86	44.22	4.14	35.14	3.68	30.17	5.85	47.39
8	4.00	32.00	4.46	48.68	3.89	39.03	3.49	33.66	5.53	52.92
9	4.00	36.00	4.10	52.78	3.66	42.69	3.32	36.98	5.23	58.15
10	4.00	40.00	3.78	56.56	3.43	46.12	3.15	40.13	4.93	63.08
11	4.00	44.00	3.48	60.04	3.23	49.35	2.99	43.12	4.61	67.69
12	4.00	48.00	3.19	63.23	3.03	52.38	2.84	45.96	4.31	72.00
13	4.00	52.00	2.94	66.17	2.86	55.24	2.70	48.67	4.00	76.00
14	4.00	56.00	2.71	68.88	2.68	57.92	2.57	51.23	3.69	79.69
15	4.00	60.00	2.49	71.37	2.52	60.44	2.44	53.67	3.39	83.08
16	4.00	64.00	2.29	73.66	2.37	62.31	2.32	55.99	3.07	86.15
17	4.00	68.00	2.11	75.77	2.23	65.04	2.20	58.19	2.77	88.92
18	4.00	72.00	1.94	77.71	2.10	67.14	2.09	60.28	2.47	91.39
19	4.00	76.00	1.78	79.49	1.97	69.11	1.99	62.26	2.15	93.54
20	4.00	80.00	1.64	81.13	1.85	70.96	1.89	64.15	1.85	95.39
21	4.00	84.00	1.51	82.64	1.74	72.70	1.79	65.94	1.53	96.92
22	4.00	88.00	1.39	84.03	1.64	74.34	1.70	67.65	1.23	98.15
23	4.00	92.00	1.28	85.31	1.54	75.88	1.62	69.26	.93	99.08
24	4.00	96.00	1.17	86.48	1.45	77.33	1.54	70.80	.61	99.69
25	4.00	100.00	1.08	87.56	1.36	78.69	1.46	72.26	.31	100.00
					30-YEAR LIFE					
1	3.33	3.33	6.67	6.67	5.00	5.00	4.16	4.16	6.45	6.45
2	3.34	6.67	6.22	12.89	4.75	9.75	3.99	8.16	6.24	12.69
3	3.33	10.00	5.81	18.70	4.51	14.26	3.83	11.99	6.02	18.71
4	3.33	13.33	5.42	24.12	4.29	18.55	3.67	15.65	5.81	24.52
5	3.34	16.67	5.06	29.18	4.07	22.62	3.51	19.17	5.59	30.11
6	3.33	20.00	4.72	33.90	3.87	26.49	3.37	22.54	5.37	35.48
7	3.33	23.33	4.40	38.30	3.68	30.17	3.23	25.76	5.17	40.65
8	3.34	26.67	4.12	42.42	3.49	33.66	3.09	28.86	4.94	45.59
9	3.33	30.00	3.84	46.26	3.32	36.98	2.96	31.82	4.73	50.32
10	3.33	33.33	3.58	49.84	3.15	40.13	2.84	34.66	4.52	54.84
11	3.34	36.67	3.34	53.18	2.99	43.12	2.72	37.38	4.30	59.14
12	3.33	40.00	3.12	56.30	2.84	45.96	2.61	39.99	4.09	63.23
13	3.33	43.33	2.92	59.22	2.70	48.66	2.50	42.49	3.87	67.10
14	3.34	46.67	2.72	61.94	2.57	51.23	2.40	44.89	3.65	70.75
15	3.33	50.00	2.53	64.47	2.44	53.67	2.30	47.19	3.44	74.19
16	3.33	53.33	2.37	66.84	2.32	55.99	2.20	49.39	3.23	77.42
17	3.34	56.67	2.21	69.05	2.20	58.19	2.11	51.50	3.01	80.43
18	3.33	60.00	2.07	71.12	2.09	60.28	2.02	53.52	2.80	83.23
19	3.33	63.33	1.92	73.04	1.99	62.27	1.94	55.45	2.58	85.81
20	3.34	66.67	1.80	74.84	1.89	64.16	1.86	57.31	2.36	88.17
21	3.33	70.00	1.68	76.52	1.80	65.96	1.78	59.09	2.15	90.32
22	3.33	73.33	1.56	78.08	1.70	67.66	1.70	60.79	1.94	92.26
23	3.34	76.67	1.46	79.54	1.62	69.28	1.63	62.43	1.72	93.98
24	3.33	80.00	1.37	80.91	1.54	70.82	1.57	63.99	1.61	95.49
25	3.33	83.33	1.27	82.18	1.46	72.28	1.50	65.49	1.29	96.78
26	3.34	86.67	1.19	83.37	1.39	73.67	1.44	66.93	1.07	97.85
27	3.33	90.00	1.11	84.48	1.32	74.99	1.38	68.31	.86	98.71
28	3.33	93.33	1.03	85.51	1.25	76.24	1.32	69.63	.65	99.36
29	3.34	96.67	.97	86.48	1.19	77.43	1.27	70.89	.43	99.79
30	3.33	100.00	.90	87.38	1.13	78.56	1.21	72.11	.21	100.00

Comparative Depreciation Tables (continued)

Year	Straight-Line		200%-Declining-Balance		150%-Declining-Balance		125%-Declining-Balance		Sum-of-Digits	
	Annual %	Cum. %	Annual %	Cum. %	Annual %	Cum. %	Annual %	Cum. %	Annual %	Cum. %
					33-1/3-YEAR LIFE					
1	3.00	3.00	6.00	6.00	4.50	4.50	3.75	3.75	5.82	5.82
2	3.00	6.00	5.64	11.64	4.30	8.80	3.61	7.36	5.65	11.47
3	3.00	9.00	5.30	16.94	4.10	12.90	3.47	10.83	5.47	16.95
4	3.00	12.00	4.98	21.93	3.92	16.82	3.34	14.18	5.30	22.25
5	3.00	15.00	4.68	26.61	3.74	20.56	3.22	17.40	5.17	27.37
6	3.00	18.00	4.40	31.00	3.57	24.14	3.10	20.49	4.95	32.32
7	3.00	21.00	4.14	35.15	3.41	27.55	2.98	23.47	4.76	37.10
8	3.00	24.00	3.89	39.03	3.16	30.81	2.87	26.34	4.60	41.70
9	3.00	27.00	3.66	42.70	3.11	33.93	2.76	29.11	4.43	46.13
10	3.00	30.00	3.44	46.14	2.97	36.90	2.66	31.77	4.25	50.38
11	3.00	33.00	3.23	49.37	2.84	39.74	2.56	34.32	4.08	54.46
12	3.00	36.00	3.04	52.41	2.71	42.45	2.46	36.79	3.90	58.36
13	3.00	39.00	2.86	55.26	2.59	45.04	2.37	39.16	3.73	62.10
14	3.00	42.00	2.68	57.95	2.47	47.51	2.28	41.44	3.55	65.64
15	3.00	45.00	2.52	60.47	2.36	49.88	2.20	43.63	3.38	69.02
16	3.00	48.00	2.37	62.84	2.26	52.13	2.11	45.75	3.20	72.22
17	3.00	51.00	2.23	65.07	2.15	54.29	2.03	47.78	3.03	75.25
18	3.00	54.00	2.10	67.17	2.06	56.34	1.95	49.74	2.85	78.10
19	3.00	57.00	1.97	69.14	1.96	58.31	1.88	51.63	2.68	80.78
20	3.00	60.00	1.85	71.00	1.88	60.18	1.81	53.44	2.50	83.28
21	3.00	63.00	1.74	72.73	1.79	61.97	1.75	55.19	2.33	85.61
22	3.00	66.00	1.64	74.37	1.71	63.69	1.68	56.87	2.15	87.77
23	3.00	69.00	1.54	75.90	1.63	65.32	1.62	58.48	1.98	89.75
24	3.00	72.00	1.45	77.35	1.56	66.88	1.56	60.04	1.81	91.56
25	3.00	75.00	1.36	78.71	1.49	68.37	1.50	61.54	1.63	93.19
26	3.00	78.00	1.28	79.99	1.42	69.79	1.44	62.98	1.46	94.64
27	3.00	81.00	1.20	81.19	1.36	71.15	1.39	64.37	1.28	95.92
28	3.00	84.00	1.13	82.32	1.30	72.45	1.34	65.71	1.11	97.03
29	3.00	87.00	1.06	83.38	1.24	73.69	1.29	66.99	.93	97.96
30	3.00	90.00	1.00	84.37	1.18	74.88	1.24	68.23	.76	98.72
31	3.00	93.00	.94	85.31	1.13	76.01	1.19	69.42	.58	99.30
32	3.00	96.00	.88	86.19	1.08	77.09	1.15	70.57	.41	99.71
33	3.00	99.00	.93	87.02	1.03	78.12	1.10	71.67	.23	99.94
33-1/3	1.00	100.00	.26	87.28	.33	78.45	.35	71.95	.06	100.00

Comparative Depreciation Tables (continued)

Year	Straight-Line		200%-Declining-Balance		150%-Declining-Balance		125%-Declining-Balance		Sum-of-Digits	
	Annual %	Cum. %	Annual %	Cum. %	Annual %	Cum. %	Annual %	Cum. %	Annual %	Cum. %
35-YEAR LIFE										
1	2.86	2.86	5.71	5.71	4.29	4.29	3.57	3.57	5.56	5.56
2	2.86	5.72	5.38	11.09	4.10	8.39	3.44	7.02	5.40	10.96
3	2.85	8.57	5.07	16.16	3.93	12.32	3.32	10.34	5.24	16.20
4	2.86	11.43	4.78	20.94	3.76	16.08	3.20	13.54	5.08	21.28
5	2.86	14.29	4.51	25.45	3.60	19.68	3.09	16.63	4.92	26.20
6	2.85	17.14	4.25	29.70	3.44	23.12	2.98	19.60	4.76	30.96
7	2.86	20.00	4.01	33.71	3.29	26.41	2.87	22.48	4.60	35.56
8	2.86	22.86	3.78	37.49	3.15	29.56	2.77	25.24	4.44	40.00
9	2.85	25.71	3.56	41.05	3.02	32.58	2.67	27.91	4.29	44.29
10	2.86	28.57	3.36	44.41	2.89	35.47	2.57	30.49	4.13	48.42
11	2.86	31.43	3.17	47.58	2.77	38.24	2.48	32.97	3.97	52.39
12	2.85	34.28	2.99	50.57	2.65	40.89	2.39	35.36	3.81	56.20
13	2.86	37.14	2.82	53.39	2.53	43.42	2.31	37.67	3.65	59.85
14	2.86	40.00	2.66	56.05	2.42	45.84	2.23	39.90	3.49	63.34
15	2.85	42.85	2.51	58.56	2.32	48.16	2.15	42.05	3.33	66.67
16	2.86	45.71	2.37	60.93	2.22	50.38	2.07	44.12	3.18	69.85
17	2.86	48.57	2.23	63.16	2.13	52.51	2.00	46.11	3.02	72.87
18	2.85	51.42	2.10	65.26	2.03	54.54	1.92	48.04	2.86	75.73
19	2.86	54.28	1.98	67.24	1.95	56.49	1.86	49.89	2.70	78.43
20	2.86	57.14	1.87	69.11	1.86	58.35	1.79	51.68	2.54	80.97
21	2.86	60.00	1.76	70.87	1.79	60.14	1.73	53.41	2.38	83.35
22	2.86	62.86	1.66	72.53	1.71	61.85	1.66	55.07	2.22	85.57
23	2.86	65.72	1.57	74.10	1.64	63.49	1.60	56.68	2.06	87.63
24	2.85	68.57	1.48	75.58	1.56	65.05	1.55	58.22	1.90	89.53
25	2.86	71.43	1.40	76.98	1.50	66.55	1.49	59.72	1.75	91.28
26	2.86	74.29	1.32	78.30	1.43	67.98	1.44	61.15	1.59	92.87
27	2.85	77.14	1.24	79.54	1.37	69.35	1.39	62.54	1.43	94.30
28	2.86	80.00	1.17	80.71	1.31	70.66	1.34	63.88	1.27	95.57
29	2.86	82.86	1.10	81.81	1.26	71.92	1.29	65.17	1.11	96.68
30	2.85	85.71	1.04	82.85	1.20	73.12	1.24	66.41	.95	97.63
31	2.86	88.57	.98	83.83	1.15	74.27	1.20	67.61	.79	98.42
32	2.86	91.43	.92	84.75	1.10	75.37	1.16	68.77	.63	99.05
33	2.85	94.28	.87	85.62	1.06	76.43	1.12	69.88	.47	99.52
34	2.86	97.14	.82	86.44	1.01	77.44	1.08	70.96	.32	99.84
35	2.86	100.00	.77	87.21	.97	78.41	1.04	72.00	.16	100.00

Comparative Depreciation Tables (continued)

Year	Straight-Line		200%-Declining-Balance		150%-Declining-Balance		125%-Declining-Balance		Sum-of-Digits	
	Annual %	Cum. %	Annual %	Cum. %	Annual %	Cum. %	Annual %	Cum. %	Annual %	Cum. %

40-YEAR LIFE

Year	Annual %	Cum. %	Annual %	Cum. %	Annual %	Cum. %	Annual %	Cum. %	Annual %	Cum. %
1	2.50	2.50	5.00	5.00	3.75	3.75	3.13	3.13	4.88	4.88
2	2.50	5.00	4.75	9.75	3.61	7.36	3.03	6.15	4.75	9.63
3	2.50	7.50	4.51	14.26	3.47	10.83	2.93	9.09	4.64	14.27
4	2.50	10.00	4.29	18.55	3.34	14.17	2.84	11.93	4.51	18.78
5	2.50	12.50	4.07	22.62	3.22	17.39	2.75	14.68	4.39	23.17
6	2.50	15.00	3.87	26.49	3.10	20.49	2.67	17.34	4.27	27.44
7	2.50	17.50	3.68	30.17	2.98	23.47	2.58	19.93	4.14	31.58
8	2.50	20.00	3.49	33.66	2.87	26.34	2.50	22.43	4.03	35.61
9	2.50	22.50	3.32	36.98	2.76	29.10	2.42	24.85	3.90	39.51
10	2.50	25.00	3.15	40.13	2.66	31.76	2.35	27.20	3.78	43.29
11	2.50	27.50	2.99	43.12	2.56	34.32	2.27	29.48	3.66	46.95
12	2.50	30.00	2.84	45.96	2.46	36.78	2.20	31.68	3.54	50.49
13	2.50	32.50	2.71	48.67	2.37	39.15	2.13	33.82	3.41	53.90
14	2.50	35.00	2.56	51.23	2.28	41.43	2.07	35.88	3.29	57.19
15	2.50	37.50	2.44	53.67	2.20	43.63	2.00	37.89	3.18	60.37
16	2.50	40.00	2.32	55.99	2.11	45.74	1.94	39.83	3.04	63.41
17	2.50	42.50	2.20	58.19	2.03	47.77	1.88	41.71	2.93	66.34
18	2.50	45.00	2.09	60.28	1.96	49.73	1.82	43.53	2.81	69.15
19	2.50	47.50	1.99	62.27	1.88	51.61	1.76	45.30	2.68	71.83
20	2.50	50.00	1.88	64.15	1.81	53.42	1.71	47.01	2.56	74.39
21	2.50	52.50	1.79	65.94	1.75	55.17	1.66	48.66	2.44	76.83
22	2.50	55.00	1.71	67.65	1.68	56.85	1.60	50.27	2.32	79.15
23	2.50	57.50	1.62	69.27	1.62	58.47	1.55	51.82	2.19	81.34
24	2.50	60.00	1.53	70.80	1.56	60.03	1.51	53.33	2.07	83.41
25	2.50	62.50	1.46	72.26	1.50	61.53	1.46	54.78	1.94	85.37
26	2.50	65.00	1.39	73.65	1.44	62.97	1.41	56.20	1.82	87.19
27	2.50	67.50	1.32	74.97	1.39	64.36	1.37	57.57	1.71	88.90
28	2.50	70.00	1.25	76.22	1.34	65.70	1.33	58.89	1.59	90.49
29	2.50	72.50	1.19	77.41	1.29	66.99	1.28	60.18	1.46	91.95
30	2.50	75.00	1.13	78.54	1.24	68.23	1.24	61.42	1.34	93.29
31	2.50	77.50	1.07	79.61	1.19	69.42	1.21	62.63	1.22	94.51
32	2.50	80.00	1.02	80.63	1.15	70.57	1.17	63.79	1.10	95.61
33	2.50	82.50	.97	81.60	1.10	71.67	1.13	64.93	.98	96.58
34	2.50	85.00	.92	85.52	1.06	72.73	1.10	66.02	.86	97.44
35	2.50	87.50	.87	83.39	1.02	73.75	1.06	67.08	.73	98.17
36	2.50	90.00	.83	84.22	.98	74.73	1.03	68.11	.61	98.78
37	2.50	92.50	.79	85.01	.95	75.68	1.00	69.11	.49	99.27
38	2.50	95.00	.75	85.76	.91	76.59	.97	70.07	.36	99.63
39	2.50	97.50	.71	86.47	.88	77.47	.94	71.01	.25	99.88
40	2.50	100.00	.68	87.15	.85	78.32	.91	71.92	.12	100.00

Comparative Depreciation Tables (continued)

Year	Straight-Line		200%-Declining-Balance		150%-Declining-Balance		125%-Declining-Balance		Sum-of-Digits	
	Annual %	Cum. %	Annual %	Cum. %	Annual %	Cum. %	Annual %	Cum. %	Annual %	Cum. %
					45-YEAR LIFE					
1	2.22	2.22	4.44	4.44	3.33	3.33	2.78	2.78	4.35	4.35
2	2.22	4.44	4.24	8.68	3.22	6.55	2.70	5.48	4.25	8.60
3	2.22	6.66	4.05	12.73	3.12	9.67	2.63	8.10	4.15	12.75
4	2.23	8.89	3.87	16.60	3.01	12.68	2.55	10.66	4.06	16.81
5	2.22	11.11	3.70	20.30	2.91	15.59	2.48	13.14	3.96	20.77
6	2.22	13.33	3.54	23.84	2.81	18.40	2.41	15.55	3.86	24.63
7	2.22	15.55	3.38	27.22	2.72	21.12	2.35	17.90	3.77	28.40
8	2.23	17.78	3.23	30.45	2.63	23.75	2.28	20.18	3.67	32.07
9	2.22	20.00	3.09	33.54	2.54	26.29	2.22	22.40	3.57	35.64
10	2.22	22.22	2.95	36.49	2.46	28.75	2.16	24.55	3.48	39.12
11	2.22	24.44	2.82	39.31	2.38	31.13	2.10	26.65	3.38	42.50
12	2.23	26.67	2.69	42.00	2.30	33.43	2.04	28.68	3.28	45.78
13	2.22	28.89	2.57	44.57	2.22	35.65	1.98	30.67	3.19	48.97
14	2.22	31.11	2.46	47.03	2.15	37.80	1.93	32.59	3.09	52.06
15	2.22	33.33	2.35	49.38	2.07	39.87	1.87	34.46	3.00	55.06
16	2.23	35.56	2.25	51.63	2.00	41.87	1.82	36.28	2.90	57.96
17	2.22	37.78	2.15	53.78	1.94	43.81	1.77	38.05	2.80	60.76
18	2.22	40.00	2.05	55.83	1.87	45.68	1.72	39.77	2.70	63.46
19	2.22	42.22	1.96	57.79	1.81	47.49	1.67	41.45	2.61	66.07
20	2.23	44.45	1.87	59.66	1.75	49.24	1.63	43.07	2.51	68.58
21	2.22	46.67	1.79	61.45	1.69	50.93	1.58	44.66	2.42	71.00
22	2.22	48.89	1.71	63.16	1.64	52.57	1.54	46.19	2.32	73.32
23	2.22	51.11	1.63	64.79	1.58	54.15	1.49	47.69	2.22	75.54
24	2.23	53.34	1.56	66.35	1.53	55.68	1.45	49.14	2.13	77.67
25	2.22	55.56	1.49	67.84	1.48	57.16	1.41	50.55	2.03	79.70
26	2.22	57.78	1.42	69.26	1.43	58.59	1.37	51.93	1.93	81.63
27	2.22	60.00	1.36	70.62	1.38	59.97	1.34	53.26	1.84	83.47
28	2.23	62.23	1.30	71.92	1.33	61.30	1.30	54.56	1.74	85.21
29	2.22	64.45	1.24	73.16	1.29	62.59	1.26	55.82	1.64	86.85
30	2.22	66.67	1.18	74.34	1.25	63.84	1.23	57.05	1.55	88.40
31	2.22	68.89	1.13	75.47	1.21	65.05	1.19	58.24	1.45	89.85
32	2.23	71.12	1.08	76.55	1.17	66.22	1.16	59.40	1.35	91.20
33	2.22	73.34	1.03	77.58	1.13	67.35	1.13	60.53	1.26	92.46
34	2.22	75.56	.98	78.56	1.09	68.44	1.10	61.63	1.16	93.62
35	2.22	77.78	.94	79.50	1.05	69.49	1.07	62.69	1.06	94.68
36	2.22	80.00	.90	80.40	1.02	70.51	1.04	63.73	.97	95.65
37	2.23	82.23	.86	81.26	.98	71.49	1.01	64.74	.87	96.52
38	2.22	84.45	.82	82.08	.95	72.44	.98	65.72	.77	97.29
39	2.22	86.67	.78	82.86	.92	73.36	.95	66.67	.68	97.97
40	2.22	88.89	.75	83.61	.89	74.25	.93	67.59	.58	98.55
41	2.23	91.12	.72	84.33	.86	75.11	.90	68.49	.48	99.03
42	2.22	93.34	.69	85.02	.83	75.94	.88	69.37	.39	99.42
43	2.22	95.56	.66	85.68	.80	76.74	.85	70.22	.29	99.71
44	2.22	97.78	.63	86.31	.78	77.52	.83	71.05	.19	99.90
45	2.22	100.00	.60	86.91	.75	78.27	.80	71.85	.10	100.00

Comparative Depreciation Tables (continued)

Year	Straight-Line		200%-Declining-Balance		150%-Declining-Balance		125%-Declining-Balance		Sum-of-Digits	
	Annual %	Cum. %	Annual %	Cum. %	Annual %	Cum. %	Annual %	Cum. %	Annual %	Cum. %

50-YEAR LIFE

Year	Annual %	Cum. %	Annual %	Cum. %	Annual %	Cum. %	Annual %	Cum. %	Annual %	Cum. %
1	2.00	2.00	4.00	4.00	3.00	3.00	2.50	2.50	3.92	3.92
2	2.00	4.00	3.84	7.84	2.91	5.91	2.44	4.94	3.85	7.77
3	2.00	6.00	3.69	11.53	2.82	8.73	2.38	7.31	3.76	11.53
4	2.00	8.00	3.54	15.07	2.74	11.47	2.32	9.63	3.69	15.22
5	2.00	10.00	3.39	18.46	2.66	14.13	2.26	11.89	3.60	18.82
6	2.00	12.00	3.26	21.72	2.58	16.71	2.20	14.09	3.53	22.35
7	2.00	14.00	3.14	24.86	2.50	19.21	2.15	16.24	3.45	25.80
8	2.00	16.00	3.00	27.86	2.42	21.63	2.09	18.33	3.38	29.18
9	2.00	18.00	2.89	30.75	2.35	23.98	2.04	20.38	3.29	32.47
10	2.00	20.00	2.77	33.52	2.28	26.26	1.99	22.37	3.22	35.69
11	2.00	22.00	2.66	36.18	2.21	28.47	1.94	24.31	3.15	38.82
12	2.00	24.00	2.55	38.73	2.15	30.62	1.89	26.20	3.06	41.88
13	2.00	26.00	2.45	41.18	2.08	32.70	1.84	28.05	2.98	44.86
14	2.00	28.00	2.35	43.53	2.02	34.72	1.80	29.84	2.91	47.77
15	2.00	30.00	2.26	45.79	1.96	36.68	1.75	31.60	2.82	50.59
16	2.00	32.00	2.17	47.96	1.90	38.58	1.71	33.31	2.74	53.33
17	2.00	34.00	2.08	50.04	1.84	40.42	1.67	34.98	2.67	56.00
18	2.00	36.00	2.00	52.04	1.79	42.21	1.63	36.60	2.59	58.59
19	2.00	38.00	1.92	53.96	1.73	43.94	1.58	38.19	2.51	61.10
20	2.00	40.00	1.84	55.80	1.68	45.62	1.55	39.73	2.43	63.53
21	2.00	42.00	1.77	57.57	1.63	47.25	1.51	41.24	2.35	65.88
22	2.00	44.00	1.70	59.27	1.58	48.83	1.47	42.71	2.28	68.16
23	2.00	46.00	1.62	60.89	1.53	50.36	1.43	44.14	2.19	70.35
24	2.00	48.00	1.57	62.46	1.49	51.85	1.40	45.54	2.12	72.47
25	2.00	50.00	1.50	63.96	1.44	53.29	1.36	46.90	2.04	74.51
26	2.00	52.00	1.44	65.40	1.40	54.69	1.33	48.23	1.96	76.47
27	2.00	54.00	1.39	66.79	1.36	56.05	1.29	49.52	1.87	78.35
28	2.00	56.00	1.33	68.12	1.32	57.37	1.26	50.78	1.81	80.16
29	2.00	58.00	1.27	69.39	1.28	58.64	1.23	52.01	1.72	81.88
30	2.00	60.00	1.22	70.61	1.24	59.89	1.20	53.21	1.65	83.53
31	2.00	62.00	1.18	71.79	1.20	61.09	1.17	54.38	1.57	85.10
32	2.00	64.00	1.13	72.92	1.17	62.26	1.14	55.52	1.49	86.59
33	2.00	66.00	1.08	74.00	1.13	63.39	1.11	56.63	1.41	88.00
34	2.00	68.00	1.04	75.04	1.10	64.49	1.08	57.72	1.33	89.33
35	2.00	70.00	1.00	76.04	1.07	65.56	1.06	58.78	1.26	90.59
36	2.00	72.00	.96	77.00	1.03	66.59	1.03	59.81	1.18	91.77
37	2.00	74.00	.92	77.92	1.00	67.59	1.00	60.81	1.09	92.86
38	2.00	76.00	.88	78.80	.97	68.56	.98	61.79	1.02	93.88
39	2.00	78.00	.85	79.65	.94	69.50	.96	62.75	.94	94.82
40	2.00	80.00	.81	80.46	.92	70.42	.93	63.68	.87	95.69
41	2.00	82.00	.78	81.24	.89	71.31	.91	64.58	.78	96.47
42	2.00	84.00	.75	81.99	.86	72.17	.89	65.47	.71	97.18
43	2.00	86.00	.72	82.71	.84	73.01	.86	66.33	.62	97.80
44	2.00	88.00	.69	83.40	.81	73.82	.84	67.18	.55	98.35
45	2.00	90.00	.67	84.07	.79	74.61	.82	68.00	.47	98.82
46	2.00	92.00	.64	84.71	.76	75.37	.80	68.80	.40	99.22
47	2.00	94.00	.61	85.32	.74	76.11	.78	69.58	.31	99.53
48	2.00	96.00	.59	85.90	.72	76.83	.76	70.34	.24	99.77
49	2.00	98.00	.57	86.47	.70	77.53	.74	71.08	.15	99.92
50	2.00	100.00	.54	87.01	.67	78.20	.72	71.80	.08	100.00

MORTGAGE AMORTIZATION TABLES

The following table will give you the amount necessary to pay off a mortgage over a given period of years at a certain percentage interest rate per year. The tables are set up to give you the amount necessary to amortize $1000.

How It Works: Suppose you want to know the monthly payments necessary to amortize $50,000 over 25 years at an annual interest rate of 12 percent. Locate the 25 year, 12 percent table. It shows a monthly principal and interest payment of $10.53 is necessary to pay of $1000 over a 25-year term. Since our loan is $50,000 or 50 times the $1000, multiply $10.53 times 50. The result is $263.25. In other words, we must make monthly principal and interest payments of $263.25 for 25 years (300 months) in order to fully amortize a $50,000 mortgage bearing an annual interest rate of 12 percent. The table also shows the total annual principal paid and the total annual interest paid for each of the 25 years. Notice that as the mortgage is paid down over the years, the principal reduction portion increases and the interest payment portion decreases.

Note: The final payment shown in these tables is usually lower than the regular monthly payments, since, in the monthly payments, fractional sums are stated at the next higher cent.

MORTGAGE AMORTIZATION

10-YEAR TERM

10% interest - $13.22 monthly payment

Year	Interest	Amort.	Balance
1	97.23	61.41	938.59
2	90.81	67.83	870.76
3	83.72	74.92	795.84
4	75.86	82.78	713.06
5	67.19	91.45	621.61
6	57.62	101.02	520.59
7	47.03	111.61	408.98
8	35.35	123.29	285.69
9	22.44	136.20	149.49
10	8.17	149.49	0

10-1/4% interest - $13.35 monthly payment

Year	Interest	Amort.	Balance
1	99.71	60.49	939.51
2	93.21	66.99	872.51
3	86.01	74.19	798.32
4	78.04	82.16	716.16
5	69.21	90.99	625.17
6	59.44	100.76	524.41
7	48.61	111.59	412.82
8	36.62	123.58	289.24
9	23.34	136.86	152.38
10	8.64	151.56	0.82

10-1/2% interest - $13.49 monthly payment

Year	Interest	Amort.	Balance
1	102.18	59.70	940.30
2	95.61	66.27	874.03
3	88.30	73.58	800.45
4	80.19	81.69	718.77
5	71.19	90.69	628.08
6	61.20	100.68	527.40
7	50.10	111.78	415.62
8	37.79	124.09	291.53
9	24.11	137.77	153.76
10	8.93	152.95	0.81

10-3/4% interest - $13.63 monthly payment

Year	Interest	Amort.	Balance
1	104.65	58.91	941.09
2	98.00	65.56	875.53
3	90.59	72.97	802.56
4	82.35	81.21	721.35
5	73.18	90.38	630.96
6	62.79	100.59	530.37
7	51.61	111.95	418.42
8	38.96	124.60	293.82
9	24.89	138.67	155.15
10	9.23	154.33	0.82

11% interest - $13.77 monthly payment

Year	Interest	Amort.	Balance
1	107.12	58.12	941.88
2	100.39	64.85	877.03
3	92.89	72.35	804.68
4	84.52	80.72	723.96
5	75.18	90.06	633.90
6	64.76	100.48	533.42
7	53.13	112.11	421.32
8	40.16	125.08	296.24
9	25.69	139.55	156.69
10	9.54	155.70	1.00

11-1/4% interest - $13.92 monthly payment

Year	Interest	Amort.	Balance
1	109.59	57.45	942.55
2	102.79	64.25	878.30
3	95.18	71.86	806.44
4	86.66	80.38	726.06
5	77.14	89.90	636.16
6	66.49	100.55	535.60
7	54.57	112.47	423.14
8	41.25	125.79	297.35
9	26.34	140.70	156.65
10	9.68	157.36	-0.70

11-1/2% interest - $14.06 monthly payment

Year	Interest	Amort.	Balance
1	112.07	56.65	943.35
2	105.20	63.52	879.83
3	97.50	71.22	808.61
4	88.86	79.86	728.75
5	79.18	89.54	639.21
6	68.33	100.39	538.82
7	56.15	112.57	426.25
8	42.50	126.22	300.03
9	27.20	141.52	158.51
10	10.04	158.68	-0.15

11-3/4% interest - $14.20 monthly payment

Year	Interest	Amort.	Balance
1	114.55	55.85	944.15
2	107.63	62.77	881.38
3	99.84	70.56	810.82
4	91.09	79.31	731.51
5	81.25	89.15	642.37
6	70.20	100.20	542.16
7	57.77	112.63	429.53
8	43.80	126.60	302.93
9	28.10	142.30	160.63
10	10.45	159.95	0.67

12% interest - $14.35 monthly payment

Year	Interest	Amort.	Balance
1	117.03	55.17	944.83
2	110.03	62.17	882.65
3	102.15	70.05	812.60
4	93.26	78.94	733.66
5	83.25	88.95	644.71
6	71.97	100.23	544.49
7	59.26	112.94	431.55
8	44.94	127.26	304.29
9	28.80	143.40	160.90
10	10.62	161.58	-0.67

15-YEAR TERM

	10% interest - $10.75 monthly payment			10-1/4% interest - $10.90 monthly payment			10-1/2% interest - $11.05 monthly payment		
Year	Interest	Amort.	Balance	Interest	Amort.	Balance	Interest	Amort.	Balance
1	98.62	30.38	969.62	101.14	29.67	970.34	103.64	28.97	971.04
2	95.46	33.54	936.08	97.95	32.86	937.48	100.44	32.17	938.88
3	91.95	37.05	899.03	94.42	36.39	901.09	96.90	35.71	903.17
4	88.06	40.94	858.09	90.51	40.30	860.80	92.97	39.64	863.53
5	83.78	45.22	812.87	86.18	44.63	816.17	88.60	44.01	819.53
6	79.04	49.96	762.91	81.38	49.43	766.75	83.75	48.86	770.67
7	73.85	55.19	707.72	76.07	54.74	712.02	78.36	54.25	716.43
8	68.03	60.97	646.75	70.19	60.62	651.40	72.39	60.22	656.21
9	61.64	67.36	579.39	63.68	67.13	584.28	65.75	66.86	589.35
10	54.30	74.40	504.99	56.46	74.35	509.93	58.38	74.23	515.13
11	46.79	82.21	422.78	48.48	82.33	427.61	50.20	82.41	432.73
12	38.18	90.82	331.96	39.63	91.18	336.43	41.12	91.49	341.24
13	28.70	100.30	231.66	29.83	100.98	235.46	31.04	101.57	239.68
14	18.20	110.80	120.86	18.98	111.83	123.64	19.85	112.76	126.92
15	6.57	120.86	0	6.97	123.84	.20	7.42	125.19	1.74

	10-3/4% interest - $11.21 monthly payment			11% interest - $11.37 monthly payment			11-1/4% interest - $11.52 monthly payment		
Year	Interest	Amort.	Balance	Interest	Amort.	Balance	Interest	Amort.	Balance
1	106.13	28.40	971.61	108.63	27.82	972.19	111.14	27.11	972.90
2	102.93	31.60	940.01	105.41	31.04	941.16	107.92	30.33	942.57
3	99.36	35.17	904.85	101.82	34.63	906.53	104.33	33.92	908.66
4	95.38	39.15	865.71	97.81	38.64	867.90	100.31	37.94	870.73
5	90.96	43.57	822.14	93.34	43.11	824.80	95.82	42.43	828.30
6	86.04	48.49	773.66	88.36	48.09	776.71	90.79	47.46	780.85
7	80.57	53.96	719.70	82.79	53.66	723.06	85.17	53.08	727.77
8	74.47	60.06	659.65	76.58	59.87	663.19	78.88	59.37	668.40
9	67.69	66.84	592.81	69.66	66.79	596.40	71.85	66.40	602.00
10	60.14	74.39	518.42	61.93	74.52	521.89	63.98	74.27	527.74
11	51.73	82.80	435.63	53.30	83.15	438.74	55.18	83.07	444.67
12	42.28	92.15	343.49	43.68	92.77	345.98	45.34	92.91	351.76
13	31.97	102.56	240.94	32.95	103.50	242.48	34.33	103.92	247.84
14	20.39	114.14	126.80	20.97	115.48	127.01	22.01	116.24	131.61
15	7.50	127.03	.23	7.61	128.84	1.83	8.24	130.01	1.61

	11-1/2% interest - $11.68 monthly payment			11-3/4% interest - $11.84 monthly payment			12% interest - $12.00 monthly payment		
Year	Interest	Amort.	Balance	Interest	Amort.	Balance	Interest	Amort.	Balance
1	113.64	26.53	973.48	116.14	25.95	974.06	118.64	25.37	974.64
2	110.42	29.75	943.73	112.92	29.17	944.89	115.42	28.59	946.06
3	106.81	33.36	910.38	109.30	32.79	912.11	111.80	32.21	913.85
4	102.77	37.40	872.98	105.23	36.86	875.26	107.71	36.30	877.56
5	98.23	41.94	831.05	100.66	41.43	833.83	103.11	40.90	836.67
6	93.15	47.02	784.03	95.53	46.56	787.27	97.92	46.09	790.59
7	87.45	52.72	731.31	89.75	52.34	734.94	92.08	51.93	738.66
8	81.05	59.12	672.20	83.26	58.83	676.11	85.49	58.52	680.15
9	73.89	66.28	605.92	75.96	66.13	609.99	78.07	65.94	614.22
10	65.85	74.32	531.60	67.76	74.33	535.67	69.71	74.30	539.93
11	56.84	83.33	448.28	58.54	83.55	452.12	60.29	83.72	456.21
12	46.73	93.44	354.84	48.18	93.91	358.21	49.67	94.34	361.88
13	35.40	104.77	250.08	36.53	105.56	252.66	37.71	106.30	255.59
14	22.70	117.47	132.62	23.44	118.65	134.01	24.23	119.78	135.81
15	8.46	131.71	0.91	8.72	133.37	0.65	9.04	134.97	0.84

20-YEAR TERM

10% interest - $9.66 monthly payment

Year	Interest	Amort.	Balance
1	99.25	16.67	983.33
2	97.49	18.43	964.90
3	95.59	20.33	944.57
4	93.44	22.48	922.09
5	91.09	24.83	897.26
6	88.51	27.41	869.85
7	85.62	30.30	839.55
8	82.45	33.47	806.08
9	78.94	36.98	769.10
10	75.08	40.84	728.26
11	70.81	45.11	683.15
12	66.07	49.85	633.30
13	60.86	55.06	578.24
14	55.11	60.81	517.43
15	48.71	67.21	450.22
16	41.68	74.24	375.98
17	33.90	82.02	293.96
18	25.32	90.60	203.36
19	15.83	100.09	103.27
20	5.35	103.27	0

10-1/4% interest - $9.82 monthly payment

Year	Interest	Amort.	Balance
1	101.76	16.09	983.92
2	100.04	17.81	966.11
3	98.12	19.73	946.39
4	96.00	21.85	924.55
5	93.66	24.19	900.36
6	91.06	26.79	873.57
7	88.18	29.67	843.90
8	84.99	32.86	811.05
9	81.46	36.39	774.66
10	77.55	40.30	734.36
11	73.22	44.63	689.74
12	68.42	49.43	640.31
13	63.11	54.74	585.58
14	57.23	60.62	524.97
15	50.72	67.13	457.84
16	43.51	74.34	383.50
17	35.52	82.33	301.18
18	26.67	91.18	210.00
19	16.87	100.98	109.03
20	6.02	111.83	2.79

10-1/2% interest - $9.98 monthly payment

Year	Interest	Amort.	Balance
1	104.27	15.50	984.51
2	102.57	17.20	967.31
3	100.67	19.10	948.22
4	98.57	21.20	927.02
5	96.23	23.54	903.49
6	93.64	26.13	877.36
7	90.76	29.01	848.35
8	87.56	32.21	816.15
9	84.01	35.76	780.40
10	80.07	39.70	740.70
11	75.70	44.07	696.64
12	70.84	48.93	647.71
13	65.45	54.32	593.40
14	59.46	60.31	533.09
15	52.82	66.95	466.15
16	45.44	74.33	391.82
17	37.25	82.52	309.31
18	28.16	91.61	217.70
19	18.06	101.71	116.00
20	6.85	112.92	3.08

10-3/4% interest - $10.15 monthly payment

Year	Interest	Amort.	Balance
1	106.78	15.03	984.98
2	105.08	16.73	968.26
3	103.19	18.62	949.64
4	101.09	20.72	928.93
5	98.75	23.06	905.87
6	96.15	25.66	880.21
7	93.25	28.56	851.66
8	90.02	31.79	819.87
9	86.43	35.38	784.50
10	82.44	39.37	745.13
11	77.99	43.82	701.32
12	73.04	48.77	652.55
13	67.53	54.28	598.28
14	61.40	60.41	537.87
15	54.58	67.23	470.65
16	46.98	74.83	395.82
17	38.53	83.28	312.55
18	29.13	92.68	219.87
19	18.66	103.15	116.72
20	7.01	114.80	1.92

11% interest - $10.32 monthly payment

Year	Interest	Amort.	Balance
1	109.29	14.56	985.45
2	107.60	16.25	969.20
3	105.72	18.13	951.08
4	103.62	20.23	930.86
5	101.28	22.57	908.29
6	98.67	25.18	883.12
7	95.76	28.09	855.04
8	92.51	31.34	823.70
9	88.88	34.97	788.74
10	84.84	39.01	749.73
11	80.32	43.53	706.21
12	75.29	48.56	657.66
13	69.67	54.18	603.48
14	63.40	60.45	543.04
15	56.41	67.44	475.60
16	48.60	75.25	400.35
17	39.89	83.96	316.40
18	30.18	93.67	222.74
19	19.34	104.51	118.23
20	7.25	116.60	1.64

11-1/4% interest - $10.49 monthly payment

Year	Interest	Amort.	Balance
1	111.79	14.10	985.91
2	110.12	15.77	970.15
3	108.26	17.63	952.52
4	106.17	19.72	932.80
5	103.83	22.06	910.75
6	101.22	24.67	886.08
7	98.29	27.60	858.49
8	95.03	30.86	827.63
9	91.37	34.52	793.12
10	87.28	38.61	754.51
11	82.71	43.18	711.33
12	77.59	48.30	663.04
13	71.87	54.02	609.02
14	65.47	60.42	548.60
15	58.31	67.58	481.03
16	50.30	75.59	405.44
17	41.35	84.54	320.90
18	31.33	94.56	226.35
19	20.13	105.76	120.59
20	7.59	118.30	2.30

20-YEAR TERM (Continued)

	11-1/2% interest - $10.66 monthly payment			11-3/4% interest - $10.84 monthly payment			12% interest - $11.01 monthly payment		
Year	Interest	Amort.	Balance	Interest	Amort.	Balance	Interest	Amort.	Balance
1	114.30	13.63	986.38	116.80	13.29	986.72	119.32	12.81	987.20
2	112.65	15.28	971.11	115.16	14.93	971.80	117.69	14.44	972.76
3	110.80	17.13	953.98	113.31	16.78	955.02	115.86	16.27	956.50
4	108.72	19.21	934.77	111.22	18.87	936.16	113.80	18.33	938.17
5	106.39	21.54	913.24	108.89	21.20	914.96	111.47	20.66	917.52
6	103.78	24.15	889.10	106.26	23.83	891.13	1C8.85	23.28	894.25
7	100.85	27.08	862.03	103.30	26.79	864.34	105.90	26.23	868.03
8	97.57	30.36	831.67	99.98	30.11	834.24	102.58	29.55	838.48
9	93.89	34.04	797.64	96.24	33.85	800.40	98.83	33.30	805.18
10	89.76	38.17	759.47	92.05	38.04	762.36	94.61	37.52	767.67
11	85.14	42.79	716.68	87.33	42.76	719.60	89.85	42.28	725.39
12	79.95	47.98	668.71	82.02	48.07	671.54	84.49	47.64	677.75
13	74.13	53.80	614.91	76.06	54.03	617.51	78.45	53.68	624.07
14	67.61	60.32	554.59	69.36	60.73	556.79	71.64	60.49	563.59
15	60.29	67.64	486.96	61.83	68.26	488.53	63.97	68.16	495.43
16	52.09	75.84	411.12	53.36	76.73	411.81	55.32	76.81	418.63
17	42.89	85.04	326.09	43.85	86.24	325.57	45.58	86.55	332.08
18	32.58	95.35	230.75	33.15	96.94	228.64	34.61	97.52	234.57
19	21.02	106.91	123.85	21.13	108.96	119.68	22.24	109.89	124.68
20	8.06	119.87	3.98	7.61	122.48	2.80	8.30	123.83	.86

25-YEAR TERM

	10% interest - $9.09 monthly payment			10-1/4% interest - $9.26 monthly payment			10-1/2% interest - $9.44 monthly payment		
Year	Interest	Amort.	Balance	Interest	Amort.	Balance	Interest	Amort.	Balance
1	99.56	9.52	990.48	102.09	9.04	990.97	104.59	8.70	991.31
2	98.57	10.51	979.97	101.12	10.01	980.96	103.64	9.65	981.67
3	97.48	11.60	968.37	100.04	11.09	969.88	102.57	10.72	970.96
4	96.25	12.83	955.54	98.85	12.28	957.60	101.39	11.90	959.06
5	94.93	14.15	941.39	97.53	13.60	944.01	100.08	13.21	945.86
6	93.44	15.64	925.75	96.07	15.06	928.96	98.63	14.66	931.20
7	91.78	17.30	908.45	94.45	16.68	912.29	97.01	16.28	914.93
8	90.01	19.07	889.38	92.66	18.47	893.82	95.22	18.07	896.87
9	87.99	21.09	868.29	90.68	20.45	873.38	93.23	20.06	876.81
10	85.78	23.30	844.99	88.48	22.65	850.73	91.02	22.27	854.54
11	83.33	25.75	819.24	86.05	25.08	825.66	88.56	24.73	829.82
12	80.63	28.45	790.79	83.35	27.78	797.88	85.84	27.45	802.38
13	77.68	31.40	759.39	80.37	30.76	767.13	82.82	30.47	771.91
14	74.39	34.69	724.70	77.06	34.07	733.07	79.46	33.83	738.08
15	70.74	38.34	686.36	73.40	37.73	695.35	75.73	37.56	700.52
16	66.74	42.34	644.02	69.35	41.78	653.57	71.59	41.70	658.83
17	62.29	46.79	597.23	64.86	46.27	607.31	67.00	46.29	612.54
18	57.39	51.69	545.54	59.89	51.24	556.08	61.89	51.40	561.15
19	51.96	57.12	488.42	54.39	56.74	499.34	56.23	57.06	504.10
20	46.01	63.07	425.35	48.29	62.84	436.50	49.94	63.35	440.76
21	39.37	69.71	355.64	41.54	69.59	366.92	42.96	70.33	370.44
22	32.09	76.99	278.65	34.06	77.07	289.85	35.21	78.08	292.36
23	24.06	85.02	193.63	25.78	85.35	204.50	26.61	86.68	205.69
24	15.13	93.95	99.68	16.61	94.52	109.99	17.06	96.23	109.46
25	5.29	99.68	0	6.45	104.68	5.31	6.45	106.84	2.63

25-YEAR TERM (Continued)

	10-3/4% interest - $9.62 monthly payment			11% interest - $9.80 monthly payment			11-1/4% interest - $9.98 monthly payment		
Year	Interest	Amort.	Balance	Interest	Amort.	Balance	Interest	Amort.	Balance
1	107.10	8.35	991.66	109.61	8.00	992.01	112.12	7.65	992.36
2	106.16	9.29	982.38	108.68	8.93	983.09	111.21	8.56	983.81
3	105.11	10.34	972.04	107.65	9.96	973.14	110.20	9.57	974.24
4	103.94	11.51	960.54	106.50	11.11	962.03	109.07	10.70	963.54
5	102.64	12.81	947.74	105.22	12.39	949.64	107.80	11.97	951.58
6	101.20	14.25	933.49	103.78	13.83	935.82	106.38	13.39	938.19
7	99.59	15.86	917.64	102.18	15.43	920.40	104.79	14.98	923.22
8	97.80	17.65	899.99	100.40	17.21	903.19	103.02	16.75	906.48
9	95.80	19.65	880.35	98.41	19.20	883.99	101.04	18.73	887.75
10	93.59	21.86	858.49	96.19	21.42	862.57	98.82	20.95	866.80
11	91.12	24.33	834.16	93.71	23.90	838.67	96.34	23.43	843.37
12	88.37	27.08	807.08	90.94	26.67	812.01	93.56	26.21	817.17
13	85.31	30.14	776.95	87.86	29.75	782.26	90.45	29.32	787.86
14	81.91	33.54	743.41	84.41	33.20	749.07	86.98	32.79	755.07
15	78.12	37.33	706.08	80.57	37.04	712.03	83.10	36.67	718.41
16	73.90	41.55	664.54	76.29	41.32	670.72	78.75	41.02	677.39
17	69.21	46.24	618.30	71.50	46.11	624.62	73.89	45.88	631.52
18	63.99	51.46	566.84	66.17	51.44	573.18	68.46	51.31	580.22
19	58.17	57.28	509.57	60.22	57.39	515.79	62.38	57.39	522.83
20	51.70	63.75	445.82	53.58	64.03	451.77	55.58	64.19	458.65
21	44.50	70.95	374.88	46.17	71.44	380.33	47.98	71.79	386.86
22	36.49	78.96	295.93	37.90	79.71	300.63	39.47	80.30	306.56
23	27.57	87.88	208.05	28.68	88.93	211.70	29.96	89.81	216.75
24	17.64	97.81	110.25	18.39	99.22	112.49	19.31	100.46	116.30
25	6.60	108.85	1.40	6.91	110.70	1.79	7.41	112.36	3.95

	11-1/2% interest - $10.16 monthly payment			11-3/4% interest - $10.35 monthly payment			12% interest - $10.55 monthly payment		
Year	Interest	Amort.	Balance	Interest	Amort.	Balance	Interest	Amort.	Balance
1	114.63	7.30	992.71	117.13	7.08	992.93	119.64	6.73	993.28
2	113.74	8.19	984.53	116.25	7.96	984.98	118.79	7.58	985.71
3	112.75	9.18	975.35	115.27	8.94	976.05	117.83	8.54	977.17
4	111.64	10.29	965.07	114.16	10.05	966.00	116.75	9.62	967.56
5	110.39	11.54	953.53	112.91	11.30	954.71	115.53	10.84	956.72
6	108.99	12.94	940.60	111.51	12.70	942.02	114.15	12.22	944.51
7	107.43	14.50	926.10	109.94	14.27	927.75	112.60	13.77	930.75
8	105.67	16.26	909.85	108.17	16.04	911.72	110.86	15.51	915.24
9	103.70	18.23	891.62	106.18	18.03	893.69	108.89	17.48	897.77
10	101.49	20.44	871.18	103.95	20.26	873.44	106.68	19.69	878.08
11	99.01	22.92	848.26	101.43	22.78	850.66	104.18	22.19	855.90
12	96.23	25.70	822.56	98.61	25.60	825.07	101.37	25.00	830.90
13	93.11	28.82	793.75	95.43	28.78	796.29	98.20	28.17	802.73
14	89.62	32.31	761.44	91.86	32.35	763.95	94.62	31.75	770.99
15	85.70	36.23	725.21	87.85	36.36	727.60	90.60	35.77	735.23
16	81.31	40.62	684.60	83.34	40.87	686.74	86.06	40.31	694.93
17	76.38	45.55	639.05	78.27	45.94	640.81	80.95	45.42	649.51
18	70.86	51.07	587.99	72.58	51.63	589.18	75.19	51.18	598.34
19	64.67	57.26	530.73	66.17	58.04	531.15	68.70	57.67	540.68
20	57.72	64.21	466.53	58.98	65.23	465.92	61.39	64.98	475.70
21	49.94	71.99	394.54	50.88	73.33	392.60	53.15	73.22	402.48
22	41.21	80.72	313.83	41.79	82.42	310.19	43.86	82.51	319.98
23	31.42	90.51	223.33	31.57	92.64	217.55	33.40	92.97	227.01
24	20.45	101.48	121.85	20.08	104.13	113.42	21.61	104.76	122.26
25	8.14	113.79	8.07	7.16	117.05	3.62	8.32	118.05	4.22

30-YEAR TERM

	10% interest - $8.78 monthly payment			10-1/4% interest - $8.96 monthly payment			10-1/2% interest - $9.15 monthly payment		
Year	Interest	Amort.	Balance	Interest	Amort.	Balance	Interest	Amort.	Balance
1	99.75	5.62	994.39	102.26	5.27	994.74	104.77	5.04	994.97
2	99.16	6.21	988.19	101.70	5.83	988.91	104.21	5.60	989.37
3	98.52	6.85	981.34	101.07	6.46	982.46	103.60	6.21	983.16
4	97.80	7.57	973.78	100.38	7.15	975.31	102.91	6.90	976.27
5	97.01	8.36	965.42	99.61	7.92	967.40	102.15	7.66	968.62
6	96.13	9.24	956.18	98.76	8.77	958.63	101.31	8.50	960.12
7	95.16	10.21	945.98	97.82	9.71	948.92	100.37	9.44	950.69
8	94.10	11.27	934.71	96.77	10.76	938.17	99.33	10.48	940.21
9	92.92	12.45	922.26	95.62	11.91	926.26	98.18	11.63	928.59
10	91.61	13.76	908.51	94.34	13.19	913.07	96.90	12.91	915.68
11	90.17	15.20	893.31	92.92	14.61	898.47	95.47	14.34	901.35
12	88.58	16.79	876.53	91.35	16.18	882.30	93.89	15.92	885.44
13	86.82	18.55	857.99	89.61	17.92	864.39	92.14	17.67	867.77
14	84.88	20.49	837.50	87.69	19.84	844.55	90.19	19.62	848.16
15	82.74	22.63	814.87	85.56	21.97	822.58	88.03	21.78	826.39
16	80.37	25.00	789.88	83.20	24.33	798.26	85.63	24.18	802.22
17	77.75	27.62	762.26	80.58	26.95	771.31	82.97	26.84	775.39
18	74.86	30.51	731.75	77.69	29.84	741.48	80.01	29.80	745.60
19	71.66	33.71	698.05	74.48	33.05	708.43	76.73	33.08	712.52
20	68.13	37.24	660.82	70.93	36.60	671.84	73.09	36.72	675.80
21	64.24	41.13	619.69	67.00	40.53	631.31	69.04	40.77	635.04
22	59.93	45.44	574.25	62.64	44.89	586.43	64.55	45.26	589.78
23	55.17	50.20	524.06	57.82	49.71	536.73	59.56	50.25	539.53
24	49.91	55.46	468.61	52.48	55.05	481.69	54.02	55.79	483.75
25	44.11	61.26	407.35	46.57	60.96	420.73	47.87	61.94	421.82
26	37.69	67.68	339.68	40.02	67.51	353.22	41.05	68.76	353.06
27	30.61	74.76	264.92	32.76	74.77	278.46	33.47	76.34	276.73
28	22.78	82.59	182.34	24.73	82.80	195.66	25.06	84.75	191.98
29	14.13	91.24	91.11	15.83	91.70	103.97	15.72	94.09	97.90
30	4.58	100.79	9.68	5.98	101.55	2.42	5.35	104.46	6.56

	10-3/4% interest - $9.33 monthly payment			11% interest - $9.52 monthly payment			11-1/4% interest - $9.71 monthly payment		
Year	Interest	Amort.	Balance	Interest	Amort.	Balance	Interest	Amort.	Balance
1	107.28	4.69	995.32	109.78	4.47	995.54	112.29	4.24	995.77
2	106.75	5.22	990.10	109.27	4.98	990.57	111.79	4.74	991.04
3	106.16	5.81	984.30	108.69	5.56	985.02	111.23	5.30	985.74
4	105.50	6.47	977.84	108.05	6.20	978.82	110.60	5.93	979.81
5	104.77	7.20	970.65	107.33	6.92	971.91	109.90	6.63	973.19
6	103.96	8.01	962.64	106.53	7.72	964.20	109.11	7.42	965.78
7	103.06	8.91	953.74	105.64	8.61	955.59	108.24	8.29	957.49
8	102.05	9.92	943.82	104.65	9.60	945.99	107.25	9.28	948.22
9	100.93	11.04	932.79	103.53	10.72	935.28	106.15	10.38	937.85
10	99.69	12.28	920.51	102.29	11.96	923.33	104.93	11.60	926.25
11	98.30	13.67	906.85	100.91	13.34	910.00	103.55	12.98	913.27
12	96.76	15.21	891.64	99.37	14.88	895.12	102.01	14.52	898.76
13	95.04	16.93	874.71	97.65	16.60	878.53	100.30	16.23	882.53
14	93.13	18.84	855.87	95.73	18.52	860.01	98.37	18.16	864.38
15	91.00	20.97	834.90	93.58	20.67	839.35	96.22	20.31	844.08
16	88.63	23.34	811.57	91.19	23.06	816.30	93.82	22.71	821.37
17	85.99	25.98	785.60	88.53	25.72	790.58	91.13	25.40	795.97
18	83.06	28.91	756.69	85.55	28.70	761.88	88.12	28.41	767.56
19	79.79	32.18	724.52	82.23	32.02	729.87	84.75	31.78	735.79
20	76.16	35.81	688.71	78.52	35.73	694.15	80.98	35.55	700.24
21	72.12	39.85	648.87	74.39	39.86	654.29	76.77	39.76	660.49
22	67.61	44.36	604.52	69.78	44.47	609.83	72.06	44.47	616.03
23	62.60	49.37	555.16	64.63	49.62	560.21	66.80	49.73	566.30
24	57.03	54.94	500.22	58.89	55.36	504.86	60.90	55.63	510.68
25	50.82	61.15	439.08	52.49	61.76	443.10	54.31	62.22	448.47
26	43.92	68.05	371.03	45.34	68.91	374.20	46.94	69.59	378.89
27	36.23	75.74	295.30	37.37	76.88	297.32	38.70	77.83	301.06
28	27.68	84.29	211.01	28.47	85.78	211.55	29.48	87.05	214.01
29	18.15	93.82	117.20	18.55	95.70	115.85	19.16	97.37	116.65
30	7.56	104.41	12.79	7.47	106.78	9.07	7.63	108.90	7.75

30-YEAR TERM (Continued)

	11-1/2% interest - $9.90 monthly payment			11-3/4% interest - $10.09 monthly payment			12% interest - $10.29 monthly payment		
Year	Interest	Amort.	Balance	Interest	Amort.	Balance	Interest	Amort.	Balance
1	114.80	4.01	996.00	117.31	3.78	996.23	119.81	3.68	996.33
2	114.31	4.50	991.51	116.84	4.25	991.98	119.34	4.15	992.18
3	113.77	5.04	986.47	116.31	4.78	987.20	118.82	4.67	987.51
4	113.16	5.65	980.82	115.72	5.37	981.84	118.22	5.27	982.25
5	112.47	6.34	974.49	115.05	6.04	975.80	117.56	5.93	976.32
6	111.70	7.11	967.39	114.30	6.79	969.02	116.80	6.69	969.64
7	110.84	7.97	959.42	113.46	7.63	961.40	115.96	7.53	962.11
8	109.88	8.93	950.50	112.52	8.57	952.83	115.00	8.49	953.63
9	108.79	10.02	940.48	111.45	9.64	943.20	113.93	9.56	944.07
10	107.58	11.23	929.26	110.26	10.83	932.38	112.71	10.78	933.29
11	106.22	12.59	916.68	108.92	12.17	920.21	111.35	12.14	921.16
12	104.69	14.12	902.56	107.41	13.68	906.53	109.81	13.68	907.48
13	102.98	15.83	886.74	105.71	15.38	891.16	108.07	15.42	892.06
14	101.06	17.75	869.00	103.80	17.29	873.88	106.12	17.37	874.70
15	98.91	19.90	849.11	101.66	19.43	854.45	103.91	19.58	855.13
16	96.50	22.31	826.80	99.25	21.84	832.62	101.43	22.06	833.07
17	93.80	25.01	801.79	96.54	24.55	808.08	98.64	24.85	808.23
18	90.76	28.05	773.75	93.50	27.59	780.49	95.48	28.01	780.23
19	87.36	31.45	742.31	90.08	31.01	749.48	91.93	31.56	748.67
20	83.55	35.26	707.06	86.23	34.86	714.63	87.93	35.56	713.12
21	79.28	39.53	667.53	81.91	39.18	675.45	83.42	40.07	673.06
22	74.48	44.33	623.20	77.05	44.04	631.42	78.34	45.15	627.92
23	69.11	49.70	573.51	71.59	49.50	581.92	72.62	50.87	577.05
24	63.08	55.73	517.78	65.45	55.64	526.28	66.17	57.32	519.73
25	56.32	62.49	455.30	58.55	62.54	463.74	58.90	64.59	455.14
26	48.75	70.06	385.24	50.79	70.30	393.44	50.70	72.79	382.36
27	40.25	78.56	306.69	42.07	79.02	314.42	41.17	82.02	300.35
28	30.73	88.08	218.61	32.27	88.82	225.61	31.07	92.42	207.94
29	20.05	98.76	119.86	21.25	99.84	125.77	19.35	104.14	103.80
30	8.07	110.74	9.12	8.87	112.22	13.55	6.15	117.34	-13.53

APPENDIX – PROPERTY ANALYSIS FORM

This property analysis form, or one similar to it, should be prepared for every property you are considering as an investment. Fill it out completely. Try different financing methods. Use it to compare with others you have prepared on other investment properties. This type of analysis is the most accurate method of determining the value of investment real estate.

LC Judd & CO., INC. REALTORS FOUNDED IN 1838

_____ Office
_____ Address
_____ Telephone

LIST PRICE _____

CASH REQ'D. _____

EXISTING ASSUMABLE FINANCING:

	Amount	Ann. Pmt.	Int.	Years To Go
1st	$ _____	_____	____%	_____
2nd	_____	_____	____%	_____
3rd	_____	_____	____%	_____

POTENTIAL FINANCING

				Years
1st	$ _____	_____	____%	_____
2nd	_____	_____	____%	_____
3rd	_____	_____	____%	_____

• PROPERTY ANALYSIS •

Name: _____
Location: _____
Type of Property: _____ Area: _____

Folio:	Ex — S.O. O	File:
Date:	Units:	Lister:
Zoning	Pool	Parking
Size	Rec. Rm.	A-C
Sq. Ft.	Util. Rm.	Heat
Age	Office	T.V.
Stories	Lobby	Furniture
Sewers	Elevators	Waterfront
Constr.		

Description —	# Units	Rent Sch.

SPECIMEN FORM

SCHEDULE GROSS INCOME	
Less: Vacancy & Credit Loss	
GROSS OPERATING INCOME	
Less: Operating Expenses	
Taxes	
Insurance	
Utilities	
Advertising	
Licenses & Permits	
Management	
Payroll & Payroll Taxes	
Supplies	
Services	
Maintenance	
Reserve for Replacement	
Ground Lease	
TOTAL EXPENSES	%
OPERATING INCOME	
Plus Other Income	
NET OPERATING INCOME	

COMMENTS: CODE: _____

INFORMATION HEREIN IS BELIEVED TO BE ACCURATE BUT IS NOT WARRANTED.

INCOME ADJUSTED TO FINANCING: Actual ☐ Potential ☐ Equity: $

NET OPERATING INCOME	Cap. Rate - List Price:		%			
Less: Loan Payment	3rd Loan	2nd Loan	1st Loan	TOTAL		
Interest						
Principal						
Total Loan Payment						
GROSS SPENDABLE INCOME	Rate:	%	(GSI + EQUITY)			
Plus: Principal Payment						
GROSS EQUITY INCOME	Rate:	%	(GEI + EQUITY)			
Less: Depreciation	Personal Property	Improvements				
REAL ESTATE TAXABLE INCOME						

Glossary of Real Estate Terms

Acceleration Clause—Usually written into a mortgage allowing the lender to accelerate or call the entire principal balance of the mortgage when the payments become delinquent.

Amortization—The reduction of a loan through periodic payments in which interest is charged only on the unpaid balance.

Analysis of Property—The systematic method of determining the performance of investment real estate using a property analysis form.

Appraisal of Property—The evaluation of fair market value of a specific property, usually performed by an appraiser.

Base Rent—The fixed rent paid by a tenant as opposed to any rent he may pay as a result of extra charges or percentage rents.

Basis Adjusted Cost (ACB)—The value of the real property established for tax purposes. It is the original cost plus any allowable capital improvements, plus certain acquisition costs, and less any depreciation taken.

Boot—Something of value received other than cash, such as a car or boat.

Capital Gain—That profit on the sale of an asset that is subject to taxation.

Capitalization Rate (CAP)—The percentage of return on an investment when purchased on a free and clear or all cash basis.

Common Area—The area in commercial buildings that are shared by all of the tenants, such as elevators, hallways, and parking lots.

Common Area Maintenance (CAM)—The charge to tenants to maintain the common areas.

Contracts, Option—A contract, with consideration, given to a purchaser of a property, giving him the right to purchase at a future date. If he chooses not to purchase, he forfeits his deposit to the seller.

Contracts, Purchase and Sale—The standard contract drawn between two or more parties in which one agrees to sell and the other agrees to purchase a given property at a pre-determined price and terms.

Debt Service—The payment of mortgage payments.

Deductions—The expenses which the IRS allows you to deduct from your gross income.

Deed of Trust—Used in some states instead of a mortgage.

Depreciation—The amount by which you write-off the value of your real estate investment over the useful life of the investment.

Depreciation, Allowable—The amount that the IRS will allow for tax purposes.

Depreciation, Component—The separating of the various components or parts of a property so that various useful life periods can be applied.

Depreciation, Composite—The improvements are not broken down into components for depreciation purposes.

Depreciation, Declining Balance method—Use of accelerated depreciation where the allowable depreciation becomes less each year.

Depreciation, Straight-Line method—The improvements are depreciated in equal installments each year.

Depreciation, Sum-of-the-Year's-Digits method—A formula by which an improvement can be depreciated rapidly in the early years. (See text.)

Economic Life—The expected useful life of a property based on economic conditions and not on the building structure's life.

Equity—The amount of invested capital you have in a property.

Equity Build-up—The amount you pay down on the mortgage principal balance each year, which increases your equity in the property.

Equity Return—The percentage ratio between your equity in the property and the total of cash flow plus mortgage principal reduction.

Escrow—Funds held in trust, either to pay taxes and insurance, or held as a deposit of the purchase of real property.

Exchange, tax deferred—The trading of one investment property for another in such a manner to defer payment of capital gains tax on the transaction.

Exemptions—The allowance given by the IRS for each individual in a household, who is a dependent, and the allowance for being over 65 years of age or blind.

Fair Market Value (FMV)—The value established on real property that is determined to be one which a buyer is willing to pay and a seller is willing to sell.

First User—The first owner of an income producing property.

Highest and Best Use—That use which allows an investment property to earn the maximum market rent.

Improvements, Capital—Major improvements made to a property that are written off over several years rather than expensed off in the year in which they are made.

Income, Gross Equity—The combination of cash flow and mortgage principal reduction, before taxes.

Income, Gross Spendable—Pre-tax cash flow.

Income, Net Spendable—Income or cash flow after taxes.

Income, Scheduled Gross—The total income a property is capable of producing if 100 percent leased.

Indicated Gain—That gain on the sale of an asset that may be subject to capital gains tax.

Installment Sale—The 30 percent rule, which allows you to pay capital gains tax on an installment basis, provided certain tests are met. (See text.)

Interest Averaging—The method of determining the overall average interest rate being paid where more than one mortgage is involved.

Interim Financing—The temporary financing by a lender during the construction or other preparation of real property for resale.

Leases, Cost of living increases—Periodic increases written into a lease to protect the lessor from the effects of inflation.

Leases, Land or Ground—The land under real property is sold and leased back, usually on a long-term basis.

Leases, Percentage—Rent is tied to the gross sales volume of the tenant.

Leases, Sub—The Lessee leases part of his premises to another user.

Legal Description—Identification of a property which is recognized by law, which identifies that property from all others.

Lessee—The tenant in rental space.

Lessor—The owner of the rental space.

Letter of intent—Used in place of a formal written contract with a deposit. The prospective purchaser informs the seller, in writing, that he is willing to enter into a formal purchase contract upon certain terms and conditions, if they are acceptable to the seller.

Leverage—The use of financing or other people's money to control large pieces of real property with a small amount of invested capital.

Limited Partnership—An investment group in which one partner serves as the general partner and the others as limited partners. The general partner bears all of the financial responsibility and management of the investment. The limited partners are obligated only to the extent of their original investment.

Listings, Exclusive Agency—A signed agreement by a seller in which he agrees to cooperate with one broker. All other brokers must go through the listing broker. The seller, however, reserves the right to sell the property, himself, to any buyer he finds on his own and not owe a fee.

Listings, Exclusive right of sale—A signed agreement between the seller and a broker giving him the exclusive right to sell. All other brokers and the seller are obligated to work through him.

Listings, Open—A listing given to one or more brokers, none of which have any exclusive rights or control over the sale by other brokers or the owner of the property.

Merchant's Association—Usually found in shopping centers. An association which pays for such things as security guards and sales promotions of the center. Each tenant pays toward the association.

Mortgages, Balloon—A mortgage amortized over a number of years, but requires the entire principal balance to be paid at a certain time, short of the full amortization period.

Mortgages, Constant—The interest rate charged on a mortgage consisting of both the rate being charged by the lender and the rate that represents the amount of principal reduction each period.

Mortgage, Deed—The document that pledges real property as collateral for an indebtedness.

Mortgage, Deferred Payment—A mortgage allowing for payments to be made on a deferred or delayed basis. Usually used where present income is not sufficient to make the payments.

Mortgage, Discounted—The selling of a mortgage to another party at a discount or an amount less than the face value of the mortgage.

Mortgage, Interest only—Payments to interest only are made. There is no principal reduction in the payment.

Mortgage, Note—That form of indebtedness that, when executed by the borrower, shows his intent to pay back the loan.

Mortgage, Points—The charges made by the lender when creating a new mortgage.

Mortgage, Second—A mortgage placed on a property in second position to an already existing first mortgage.

Mortgage Wraparound—Sometimes called an all inclusive deed of trust. A mortgage that includes any existing mortgages on the property. The buyer makes one large payment on the wraparound and the seller continues making the existing mortgage payments out of that payment.

New Basis—The adjusted cost basis you have when transfering into a new property through an exchange. It takes into consideration the basis of your old property.

Operating Costs—Those expenses required to operate an investment property, excluding mortgage payments.

Ordinary Income—Income produced that must be added to your regular taxable income for tax purposes.

Paper—Mortgages carried by individuals, usually the seller of the property.

Personal Property—Property in an investment property, such as carpeting, draperies, refrigerators, etc., that can be depreciated over a shorter useful life than the structure itself.

Pre-payment Penalty—A penalty charge written into many mortgages that must be paid if the mortgage is paid off ahead of schedule.

Property Manager—A manager or management company hired to run an investment property for the owner.

Pyramiding—The process of building an estate by allowing appreciation and mortgage principal reduction to increase the investors equity in a series of ever larger properties.

Recapture—The portion of accelerated depreciation taken that is subject to ordinary income tax when an investment property is sold.

Recognized Gain—That gain on which income tax is due.

Recognized Net Loan Relief—In an exchange, that amount by which the loans acquired are less than the loans given up.

Resident Manager—A individual, usually living in the building, who handles all of the day-to-day problems in the building.

Sale/Leaseback—The tenant in a building, sells it to an investor and leases it back for a period of years.

Tax Bracket—Also referred to a marginal tax rate. That percentage figure at which any additional income, above the investor's ordinary income, will be taxed.

Tax Shelter—The tax write-off possible through the depreciation benefits available on investment real estate ownership. This write-off can serve to reduce the taxpayer's other taxable income.

Tax Stop—Written into leases to protect the lessor from tax increases by passing any increases on to the tenants.

Time Value of Money—The value of a future sum of money if it is paid today.

Trust Account—The separate account in which an attorney or real estate broker hold funds until the real estate closing takes place or other legal disbursement is made.

Useful Life—That term during which an asset is expected to have useful value.

Vacancy Allowance—A projected deduction from the scheduled gross income of a building to allow for loss of income due to vacant apartments or other rental units.

Value, Assessed—The property value as determined by the county appraiser.

Index